Center for Basque Studies
Basque Classics Series, No. 7

The Selected Essays of Julio Caro Baroja

Edited and with an introduction by
Jesús Azcona

Translated by
Robert Forstag

Basque Classics Series
No. 7

Center for Basque Studies
University of Nevada, Reno
Reno, Nevada

This book was published with generous financial support obtained by the Association of Friends of the Center for Basque Studies from the Provincial Government of Bizkaia.

Basque Classics Series, No. 7
Series Editors: William A. Douglass, Gregorio Monreal, and Pello Salaburu

Center for Basque Studies
University of Nevada, Reno
Reno, Nevada 89557
http://basque.unr.edu

Copyright © 2011 by the Center for Basque Studies
All rights reserved. Printed in the United States of America

Cover and series design © 2011 by Jose Luis Agote
Cover illustration: Self-portrait by Julio Caro Baroja

Library of Congress Cataloging-in-Publication Data

Caro Baroja, Julio.
 [Essays. English. Selections]
 The selected essays of Julio Caro Baroja / edited and with an introduction by Jesús Azcona ; translated by Robert Forstag.
     p. cm. -- (Basque classics series ; no. 7)
 Includes bibliographical references and index.
 Summary: "Collection of essays by leading historian and ethnographer on Basque history, culture, anthropology, and language"--Provided by publisher.
 ISBN 978-1-935709-15-2 (pbk.) -- ISBN 978-1-935709-16-9 (cloth)
 1. País Vasco (Spain) 2. Basques. I. Azcona, Jesús. II. Forstag, Robert. III. Title.

DP302.B46C37213 2011
946'.6--dc23

                              2011044018

Contents

Note on Basque Orthography.. 7
Introduction: The Life and Work of Julio Caro Baroja 9

Part 1
Basque Times and Spaces

1. Neighboring Peoples and the Historical-Cultural Context......... 41
2. The Basque Country, 1500–1800.............................. 65
3. Cultural Cycles and Basque Identity 79

Part 2
The Basques, Their Origins, and Their Language

4. Origins: Basque-Iberianism 99
5. Historical-Cultural Problems of the Basque Language............ 115
6. On the Basque Lexicon... 131
7. The Basque Country and Dialectology........................... 145

Part 3
Economy and Society in the Basque Mountains

8. The Historical Basis of a "Traditional" Economy................. 163
9. The Structure and Functions of the House...................... 179
10. Agriculture and Cattle Raising.................................. 207

Part 4
The Basques, Other Peoples, and Other Worlds

11. Regarding the Basque Shipbuilding and Iron Industries.......... 221

12. The Basques and the Sea 239
13. The Feeling of Belonging in the Basque Diaspora 253

Part 5
The Basques Yesterday and Today

14. The Basques Yesterday and Today............................... 267

Endnotes 285
List of Sources 325
Suggestions for Further Reading 327
Index 331

Note on Basque Orthography

The standard form to refer to the Basque language today is Euskara. Most English-language texts on the Basque Country have traditionally employed only the French and Spanish orthographic renderings of Basque place names. Here, in light of the standard Basque orthographic renderings of these same place names by the Basque Language Academy (Euskaltzaindia), we will endeavor to use these Basque versions, with an addition in parentheses of the French or Spanish equivalents on first mention in each chapter.

Some exceptions to this rule include the use of Navarre (Nafarroa in Basque, Navarra in Spanish) and Lower Navarre (Nafarroa Beherea in Basque, Basse Navarre in French); the hyphenated bilingual cases of Donostia-San Sebastián, Vitoria-Gasteiz, and Iruñea-Pamplona; and occasions where French or Spanish place name variants are used to make a linguistic point. In the latter case, the Basque equivalents appear in parentheses after the French or Spanish place name. While we have preserved the original renderings of surnames, on occasion—where the surname clearly corresponds to a town or village—a Basque equivalent of these is provided in parentheses.

Additionally, on occasion we anglicize certain Basque terms, rather than use the original Basque, French, or Spanish terms themselves. Thus, for example, inhabitants of Zuberoa (Soule), instead of being rendered here as *zuberotarrak* or *xiberotarrak* (from the Basque alternative Xiberoa), or *Souletines* (in French), are described here as Zuberoans. Baiones and Baioneses is our anglicization of the "people of Baiona" (Bayonne) instead of *Baionesak* (Basque) or *Bayonnais* (French).

Occasionally, Caro Baroja cites words and phrases in Basque to make a point. We have preserved his original renderings, but where applicable added the standard modern Basque variants of these words and phrases in parentheses. For longer phrases—proverbs and sayings for example—we have maintained the original orthography.

It should be noted that, for much of the period under study here, there was little consistency in the rendering of either place names or personal names in any of these languages (in fact, Caro Baroja himself renders some place names in a mixture of languages, although we have standardized the toponyms here); a fact of life that is apparent in a region of Europe where multiple cultures and identities overlap. We see such lack of consistency as a more flexible way of appreciating this diversity.

Introduction:
The Life and Work of Julio Caro Baroja

> "Garibay is representative of a particular era in the
> Basque Country and he is also a figure who reflects the common
> phenomenon of Basques assuming an increasing importance in the
> wider affairs of Spain."
>
> — Julio Caro Baroja, *Los vascos y la historia a través de Garibay*

I

From his birth in Madrid on November 13, 1914 to his death in Bera (Vera de Bidasoa) on August 18, 1995, the life and work of Julio Caro Baroja were inextricably woven into the context of his family, the politics of his time, and a distinct academic and social milieu. Bridging a period between the end of the nineteenth century (which in Spain effectively lingered well into the twentieth) and an era that, in the last decades of his life, augured a future that was constructed on the ruins of a forgotten past, and that was characterized by an ongoing and seemingly endless conflict in the Basque Country, his life and work are, in large part, a reflection and product of his sociopolitical milieu.

Caro Baroja's work during the first phase of his career—a period that spanned more than two decades—is only comprehensible within the context of a postwar Spain in which Franco's dictatorship attempted to employ folklore and tradition for the purpose of creating a unifying Catholic and nationalist myth. The period from 1940 until the mid-1960s was thus something of a golden age for the study of folklore and traditional practices and customs. This same period also marked a high point for the kind of research of specific folkways that Caro Baroja conducted. His research tends to support the thesis that, beneath the apparent diversity of the different regions of Spain, there is an underlying common legacy rooted in the distant past. This legacy values the "natural" authority of ecclesiastical and civil leaders and family patriarchs, the "heads of families." The modernity of the decades preceding the military rebellion was erased from history, forgotten in the service of the new regime's political and ideological objectives. The object of this intentional forgetfulness was to prevent an acknowledgment of the achievements of the Second Republic and to "unite" all Spaniards in the preservation of traditional Catholicism, seen as the root of the ancient and imperishable glories of Imperial Spain. The roots of Spanish Catholicism, and especially the peninsula's medieval history, were explored in depth. The self-proclaimed National Uprising thus not only unearthed the long-buried past, but also became its self-appointed curator.

This state of affairs began to change in the mid-1960s. These changes were introduced by the technocratic ministers affiliated with Opus Dei who assumed posts at that time. Although it might seem paradoxical at first glance, those who consolidated themselves as a religious force under the auspices of Franco's regime also became catalysts of economic change.

For Caro Baroja, this was also a time of personal disorientation and uncertainty. The technocrats were intent on transforming the historical image of Spain. This resulted in "the paradox of those who most radically contravened tradition being considered the most conservative—most 'orderly' elements." What order? one might ask. The answer: the order imposed by the construction of a country, which had been "poor but beautiful" now "appeared superficially rich, but in fact had grown alarmingly ugly."[1] The Spain that Caro Baroja had imagined and experienced was disappearing before his eyes. "I am nothing more than a mirror that continues to reflect a world that has past," he wrote.[2]

Some years after he wrote this, the democratic transition and the establishment of the autonomous provinces seemed to confirm this perception. The different peoples of Spain were reduced to "contemplating their own navel." The "image of Spain needed to once again become transparent and pristine. No one can restore such an image to men of my age. Let's at least hope that it can be renewed for the younger generation as something pure and perhaps even holy."[3] Although he saw himself as different from those who collaborated with and supported Franco's regime, he in fact was not all that different. The "likeness" of the self-description that he provided in *Semblanzas ideales* did not reflect either the statement just cited or similar statements that appeared elsewhere in his writings. As Caro Baroja would have it, he had distanced himself from the Franco regime from the very beginning, had represented "true liberalism," and had even been "a leftist." He even regretted not having gone into exile. His actions during Franco's dictatorship, however, spoke louder than such words.[4]

Having been introduced at fifteen to the study of the traditional life of Basques and other peoples of Spain in the library of his uncle Pío in Bera, and then, during the Civil War, studying ancient history and eventually earning a doctorate in that subject as soon as the war was over, Caro Baroja proceeded to serve as an assistant in the Department of Ancient Spanish History and the Department of Dialectology and Popular Traditions at the University of Madrid (1943–1948). These were the only two new departments created by Franco's regime in the social sciences. In 1944, he was named director of the Museum of the Spanish People, a position he held until 1955. He was also commissioned by the army to conduct studies in the Spanish Sahara, which at that time was a Spanish colony. The relationships he established at that time with George M. Foster and Julian Pitt-Rivers introduced him to the study of Andalusian folklore. These three men, through their mutual interaction, were able to transcend the regime's own political agenda for these kinds of studies. The "agenda" here refers to what fell within the acceptable limits of anthropological study by "foreign" and "native" anthropologists. And while their research did not have an immediate influence, it was felt after the political climate changed in the 1970s.

Given this intellectual climate and career path, it should come as no surprise that the disappearance of something to which Caro Baroja had dedicated so many years of his life was something that he experienced as a personal crisis. This crisis was aggravated by the deaths of his uncle Pío as well as of other family members and close friends. These losses resulted in a severe and prolonged depression.

After he recovered from this crisis, Caro Baroja began a new stage in his life, both in personal and academic terms. He resigned his administrative and academic positions in order to devote himself exclusively to reading, study, and the development of his thought. It was at this time that a theoretical change could also be discerned in his writings. He began to see culture in general and Basque culture in particular in a different light. The turning point in this transformation can be dated to the end of the 1960s and the beginning of the 1970s. It was at this time that he seemed to realize on an intellectual and emotional level that he needed to redefine the purpose of his life and work. Specifically, he came to the conclusion that the theory and methodology of the *Kulturkreislehre,* a German anthropological school of thought on the diffusion of cultures that was a legacy of Barandiarán's early influence on Caro Baroja, was fundamentally defective because it did not sufficiently appreciate historical events and the transformative effects of those events, both on culture and on individual lives—including his own life. His writings during this period reflect not only the effects of history on these realities, but also how history becomes an inextricable part of both of these phenomena and thus contributes to determining what one does and who one becomes.

We do not know how Caro Baroja experienced this transition. We also do not know how he came to access the writings that became the sources of his new thinking. Yet we can deduce on the basis of what he has left behind that the process must not have been easy. His new ideas directly contradicted those of Barandiarán, the old master whom he had always looked up to. In addition, this new thinking distanced Caro Baroja from all of his own previous work. On top of all of this, this change coincided with both the eruption of "the Basque question" into public consciousness. During this period he published several books containing his older research—which had previously been published in academic journals for scholarly audiences—an opportunity he used to fuel this transformation.

This was a rather murky stage in Caro Baroja's life. On the one hand, he discovered what would become some of the key elements of his theory and methodology in the mid 1980s. On the other hand, in certain cases, he continued to function within the framework of the criteria of the *Kulturkreislehre*. This resulted in ambiguities and contradictions in his writings. Clear examples of this can be seen in the revised editions of *Los pueblos del norte* (The peoples of the north), *Los Pueblos de España* (The peoples of Spain), and *La vida rural vasca* (Basque rural life). In the first of these works, he declared that "the historical-cultural method . . . has resulted in a certain tendency to mental schema and ontological metaphysics." Yet, at the same time, he marveled at the fact that Strabo specified "a kind of 'cultural area' that coincided with one of the 'cycles' established by Gräbner, and utilized by ethnologists of the Vienna."[5] In *Los pueblos de España,* he said, referring to *Los pueblos del norte*, that "the historical-cultural and anthropo-geographical framework constituted the most solid foundation."[6] Finally, in *La vida rural vasca,* which reflected the highest degree of reworking for the new edition, he explicitly distanced himself from the *Kulturkreislehre*. And yet he did so in a single lapidary statement without providing any further explanation. Yet it is possible to infer the reasons from a close reading of the work. For example, he writes that what had been studied and analyzed in 1944 represented "pure archeology." In addition, he pointed out a number of the mistakes that he had made. One such mistake, in his view, was not having given sufficient weight to history, instead focusing on psychological factors. Another error was the underestimating of technological and economic factors. Caro Baroja left no doubt in this work that he considered technology and economy to be not only the primary engines of change, but also the factors responsible for transmuting and metamorphosing psychological and social factors. The rectification of this error led him to "a comprehensive rejection of the premises—which were even accepted by some philosophers—regarding the supposed ahistoricism of the lives of rural folk, of the immobility and isolation of small rural communities and societies, of their 'illiteracy,' etc." Instead, Caro Baroja stressed "the need to describe the characteristics of rural life in time and space, just as is done for large, urban, and better known societies."[7] Despite these kinds of statements, found elsewhere in the book as well, Caro Baroja also declared in the prologue that part of his goal was to "discover something hidden and enigmatic,"[8] a focus that was consistent with Barandiarán's approach.

These contradictions and ambiguities are all the more jarring when one takes into account that it was at this same time, as Caro Baroja himself declares in a footnote, that he published the articles based on the work of the biologists Jakob von Üexküll and Georg Kriszat.[9]

The influence of these German biologists on his work during the 1970s was limited to providing the theoretical frame of reference of "cultural cycles," something he did in the *Etnografía histórica de Navarra* (Historical Ethnography of Navarre).[10] Specific references to concrete historical circumstances and individual lives within defined milieus are at most merely suggested in certain cases.

Caro Baroja spent the majority of the 1970s and the beginning of the 1980s reediting his previously published work while conducting new research, and in writing a steady stream of articles containing his reflections on a wide variety of subjects for nationally distributed newspapers. He also published new books dealing with history, ethnography, and folklore. *Las formas complejas de la vida religiosa: Religión, sociedad y carácter en la España de los siglos XVI y XVII* (Religion, society, and character in sixteenth and seventeenth century Spain)[11] and *La casa en Navarra* (The house in Navarre)[12] were works of history. *La estación de amor, fiestas populares de mayo a San Juan* (The love season, popular May festivals for Saint John)[13] and *El estío festivo (Fiestas populares de verano)* (The festive summertime [popular summer festivals])[14] were books that explored popular folklore.

It was during these years that Caro Baroja took his place as one of the most distinguished Spanish intellectuals. This was reflected in frequent interviews, regular participation in conferences, his writing prologues of books written by other authors, tributes, and television appearances. He became widely recognized as a "learned man" and a "humanist" who combined in his person the kind of accomplishments and characteristics that are typically not found in a single individual: "historian, anthropologist, amateur painter, occasional flute player, and great conversationalist all in one." "A cultural treasure to be enjoyed by all of the people of Spain," because "thanks to people like Julio Caro, future generations will be able to continue to believe in the individual human being as the most worthy object of study." This was the view stated by Ángel Sánchez Harguinday in his prologue to Caro Baroja's *Comentarios sin fe* (Commentaries without faith), which comprised a selection of his newspaper columns.[15]

Whether or not one agrees with these and similar statements regarding his life and work, it seems to me that, in the mid-1980s, Caro Baroja reinvented himself and placed everything that he had written up to that time in proper perspective. The ambiguities, contradictions, and doubts of his past work disappeared, and his anthropo-historical research at last possessed a clear theory and methodology. More importantly still, he was now able to properly appreciate his own life and accomplishments.

It was during that time that, among the many books that he had written, he chose to return to his work on Garibay,[16] attempting to fully realize the promise of the subtitle that he had chosen for that volume: "essay for an anthropological biography." Garibay's life and work became a singular obsession for him and constituted an essential framework of his view of the importance of lives and works of single individuals within a society. Caro Baroja also made strenuous efforts to present his own memoirs (written with an "anthropological intent") in a way that reflected his conceptualization of the importance of the individual.[17]

Many years had passed since he had compared himself to Garibay. Yet when his "Género biográfico y conocimiento antropológico" was published in 1986, this comparison was transformed into a fusion of their lives. Caro Baroja applied his view of Garibay to himself, and thus his contention that the enduring impact that an individual can have on the society in which he lives became a central element of his thought. Both Garibay and Caro Baroja made their influence felt in two important ways, and thus displayed a similarity to one another despite the distinct sociocultural contexts in which they lived. "Garibay's first influence resulted from his intense interest in the language and customs of a single closed society, while his second influence, harking back to a title of a work of history of his time, could well be called 'imperial' or 'Caesarean,'"[18] as he had indicated some fourteen years previously. Caro Baroja's influence was similarly twofold. "I have lived half of my life in the Basque Country and the other half in Madrid. I have devoted myself to the study of linguistics, folklore, ethnography, and the history of ancient Spain. In doing this, I have needed to consider the interests of the existing state and of neighboring countries and, in the face of the violence of actions taken in their defense, I have often had my doubts about the legitimacy and grandeur of certain institutions. Nearly four hundred years before I was born, a man from the same stock as my maternal ancestors confronted a similar constellation of interests and conflicts, *mutatis mutandis*. How, in his life and work, did he resolve the problem of living history? This is the key question, for while history cannot tell us how to live, our existence does not in itself allow us to understand history. Both history and life are separate and irreducible entities. Tragically, we must decide to serve both of these masters."[19] Both Garibay and Caro Baroja served life and history, and resolved that contradiction as best they could.

Life and work, for both Garibay and Caro Baroja, constitute two aspects of the same reality, a single entity that reflects the "problem of living history" which every person is obliged to confront. The achievements of men are only clear in the light of the interdependence of their own lives and of history. "Man and life constitute a closed cycle. The life of man, within the context of the history of the time in which he lives, constitutes another cycle. In and of itself, most of the content of human life is incomprehensible. Such is not the case when human life is considered within the context of history."[20]

Life and work develop in parallel fashion and mutually clarify one another. Life is lived within the context of history, and history clarifies life. Yet, at the same time, history is clarified *by* life, given that life determines the central axes that define societies throughout the course of their histories. It is through individual lives that history is made.

Here, as in other instances, Caro Baroja is deliberately concealing what he really thinks and feels. Modesty thus trumps thought, and in effect relegates it to dark and impenetrable shadows. He could have clarified things if he wanted to, and yet he chose not to. Perhaps this was because he was more a man of action than of words. In what follows, I will attempt to express what I assume Caro Baroja would have said if he had followed to their logical conclusion his own ideas regarding time, space, and the different perceptions of people throughout history in accordance with their respective "surrounding worlds." As part of this undertaking, I will cite some suggestive examples that appear in the revised edition of his work *La vida rural vasca*.[21]

II

> "Any kind of anthropology that divorces itself from the individual human being may have merit as sociology, as a theory of culture, or as a particular methodology. Yet it cannot be called anthropology in the strictest sense of the word."
>
> — Julio Caro Baroja, "Género biográfico y conocimiento antropológico"

As regards the various schools of anthropology, Caro Baroja was of the opinion that the search for causal laws and universal principles had led to the systematic ignoring of individual persons. For Caro Baroja, classifying and comparing the past and the present, and seeing their relation to one another within the framework of some schema, function, structure, or model led inevitably to a relegation of individuals to a secondary order of importance.

For Caro Baroja, individual human beings, or *man-in-himself*, are the worthy objects of anthropological research— in preference to abstract or even partially mythical entities such as "society" or "culture." The focus on such abstraction resulted in not being able to see the trees that collectively comprised the forest. In other words, in Caro Baroja's view, an excessive concentration on society and culture blinded one to the individuals comprising those abstract entities. Yet, at the same time, it seems fair to suggest that he may himself have had the opposite problem of "not being able to see the forest for the trees."

If the proper object of study of anthropology is man-in-himself, then the problem of the anthropologist consists in searching for, verifying, and describing "the impact of a man or woman within a given group, and of determining how this impact manifests itself, leaving supposed 'laws' or 'rules' aside."[22] Caro Baroja believed that sociologists and anthropologists placed too much faith in the importance of institutions, beliefs, and rites as regulators of society and individual human lives in a way that bears a resemblance to "certain physical and mathematical laws." Not only is such an analogy to social life inapposite, but in effect it suggests the exact opposite of what is really happening. Individuals "adopt, as they can, their own attitudes before what society pretends to impose and does impose on many." Even in cases in which it appears that a strong and coercive system imposes itself on individuals, not everyone acts in the same way. Such circumstances can result in "distinct and even contradictory cases."²³ Man-in-himself with "irreducible characteristics," is still both coherent and self-contradictory. This contradiction manifests itself early in the family's core. "The contradiction begins within the most important social circle—that of the family. It is then again manifested elsewhere. Thus, the individual (myself in the present case) is subject to a self that is inherently mutable."²⁴ It is for this reason that Caro Baroja does not favor the exact and coherent descriptions of "sociological and anthropological recipes." What is of primary explanatory importance for him is "lived experience," and not deduced truths that relegate such experience to a secondary order of importance.

From all this, one can deduce that Caro Baroja conceives of people as possessing a unique point of reference and security serving as a compass. This is nothing more or less than his life itself. And, as Baruch Spinoza said, life fundamentally tends to preserve itself. Everything beyond one's own life is uncertain, insecure, without bearings, and unintelligible. Events occur without any apparent purpose, and without any defined reference points. The anchor of a person is life. It is life that requires the person to choose one course of action over another, or to move in one direction rather than another. People are always at a crossroads that imposes the need to make a decision that has as its purpose the preservation of life.

In the lives of human beings, it is impossible to specify in advance the decisions that particular individuals will make. Unpredictability is thus the order of the day, and behavior among individuals may indeed be so variable that it is difficult to identify a common denominator. The task of the anthropologist is to "study with a greater degree of subtlety the nexus between the individual and his surrounding world." This is the case whether the objects of study are "representative individuals" or "ordinary people." Behavioral options may in either case be quite varied and different. "The similarity among people who superficially resemble one another is not as great as one might think."²⁵

The variety of options that people have, and the different ways that they impact their respective surrounding worlds, is best shown by using the biographical method. This was the recommendation of Immanuel Kant in the prologue to his last book, *Anthropology from a Pragmatic Point of View* (1798). The biography not only provides "individual portraits and profiles . . . but also tells us a great deal regarding the society or societies in which the person being wrote about lived."[26] This allows us to appreciate the importance of collective life on particular individuals, and to reflect on how, in situations that are apparently similar in nature, individuals "make, as best they can, their own choices.[27] Caro Baroja maintained—citing Franz Boas and Elsie Clews Parsons in support of his thesis—that this was the best way of learning about "cultures and societies from the inside."[28]

The obstacles that stand in the way of understanding man-in-himself through biographies are considerable. It also is not easy to attain such knowledge directly. This is the case even as regards the exploration of one's own life. According to Kant, disguise, dissimulation, selfishness, and other tricks one uses to project a false image of oneself are many and varied. The preservation of the "ego"—of one's own intimate conception of self, is typically a very high priority, one in the service of which an individual is capable of employing the greatest degree of deception in order to prevent its revelation.[29] Kant cites biography and literature—in the absence of anthropological research during his time—as the best means of attaining practical knowledge of "the human species." Kant made pointed and precise observations of both himself and those he directly observed. He was—it seems needless to say—thoroughly Kantian in applying to human actions the same analytic precision that characterized his philosophical writings. In Kant's opinion, temporality—history—was a factor that modified "local" peculiarities. And yet, he maintained, human nature was something that was immutable. Anthropology arose from men such as Shakespeare and Montaigne, men who "possessed knowledge that was worthy of man."

The biographical emphasis of Caro Baroja's approach is not exactly what some anthropologists of the past and present have recommended. It is also different from what Kant himself envisaged. Whether consciously or unconsciously, Caro Baroja constructed the very foundation of the thesis he sought to defend on the basis of his research on those characterized by Davydd Greenwood as "oppressed minorities"[30]—the thesis that, within a society, there is not a single option, but many varied options.

In my opinion, "oppressed minorities" cannot be considered representative of the majority population unless it can be demonstrated that there are those among the population that does not feel itself to be oppressed who exercise various options. Otherwise, one falls into the error of making an overgeneralization without having properly researched the matter in question. It is of course true that, throughout Spanish history, "oppressed minorities"—*moriscos*,[31] witches,[32] Jews,[33] and religious dissidents and critics[34]—peoples that Caro Baroja was one of the first Spaniards to investigate, contradict the stereotypical, monolithic, and homogenized image of the existence of an authority and a religion capable of imposing uniformity upon all. However, the existence of such groups, however numerous, also does not prove that everyone exercised such freedom. Accusations of witchcraft were not leveled exclusively from the Holy Office of the Inquisition. As Caro Baroja himself pointed out, it was at times an accused person's own neighbors who made such charges, and who did so for reasons that had nothing whatsoever to do with religion.[35]

It is likely that academia's "order of discourse" (Michel Foucault), for whatever reasons, did not allow Caro Baroja to enter into a consideration of either the "surrounding world" in which such repressive actions occurred, or of the options that some exercised in response. Such a consideration would have been conducive to a clarification of what actually occurred, given that individual options and surrounding worlds are two sides of the same social reality within which people live. Historical-cultural surroundings and historical biographies are objects of studies that are difficult to conduct with a high degree of precision. The greater the number of historical periods that one seeks to encompass, the more difficult the task becomes. The studies conducted by Caro Baroja are more useful in terms of showing how the periods in question should be studied than in terms of their explanatory value as pure history. Such studies are also useful for understanding both the differences among individuals during those periods and, especially, the interaction among different components and/or spheres of social life.

Such limitations might be ameliorated to a certain extent, however, by what Caro Baroja wrote in the updated version of his monograph on Bera (*La vida rural vasca*). This was the place where he lived for extended periods of his life, and that he knew better than any other. The twenty years that had passed since he wrote the first edition of the work allowed him to determine the primary factors responsible for the changes that occurred during that time. These changes gave the lie to the theoretical principles that had served as his guide back in the 1940s. He also made certain modifications to other earlier works that allow us to see how and why individuals exercised different options. Specifically, he refers to those motives that spur individuals' actions. All "surrounding worlds" contain these same motives, regardless of differences in time and space. I will begin by identifying the elements and the interdependencies that exist among them before establishing the greater or lesser importance of some in relation to the others. Finally, I will identify the motives of individuals' actions. What I am presenting here is an interpretation of what Caro Baroja wrote, in different places and in highly unsystematic fashion, regarding individual factors.

In surrounding worlds, time, tools (Caro Baroja refers to them generically as "things"), and people are in constant motion and collectively constitute a unit. The time of "things" is inseparable from the time of men, and men do not exist separately from those things. In addition, these things not only provide a means of measuring time, but they also—through men's perceptions—provide the cultural meanings and significance that keep human beings together.

In the collective life of people, the "material world" of technology and its applications and the "spiritual world" of social and cultural life are inextricably intertwined. Thus, the notion of any purely technological study or any purely cultural study is nothing more than a "mental aberration."[36] The need to consider both of these phenomena together, just as in the case of the need to consider time and space together, arises from their coexistence and interdependency. Any change in one of these factors necessarily alters the other factors to which it is inextricably related.

All of this is applicable to what transpired in Bera between 1944 and 1974. The disappearance of rural material culture during that time necessarily meant the disappearance of other dimensions of culture. The process of economic change that began in the decade of the 1960s brought everything down like a house of cards. Nothing was like it had been before, including the landscape within which traditional society had previously existed. The change in material culture also created an upheaval in the social world of the town, in the relationships and interrelationships among individuals, as well as in the psychic world of beliefs and ritual practices. The collective world of human beings does not contain stagnant compartments, but rather dynamic and interactive compartments. It is unquestionable that what can occur within such a scenario are "crises of change and transition"[37] that may have disparate effects upon all of the other elements involved. Some such elements may become revitalized and survive within a different context, while others permanently vanish.

The task facing the anthropologist who tries to incorporate these kinds of historical processes into his work is by no means easy, but also not impossible. Although there are many gaps and much barren ground, the anthropologist's mission is to classify tools in their own time and space. Within any given "surrounding world" the particular tools in question may vary considerably. Especially under changing circumstances, "old tools" and "new tools" may coexist, with each being associated with different timeframes within the same physical space. Later, account must be taken of the diversity of perceptions that exist among different individuals, perceptions that reflect their different social positions and their different occupations within the economic system. Finally, and on the basis of these considerations, the meanings and significance that the diverse persons within the society derive must be shown, as well as the decisions that each of them make. What we have here is a sequence that is both causal and logical, given the importance of material culture. At the same time, we have a demonstration of the nonexistence of any kind of mechanical order, "whether of a physical or social nature."[38] Change occurs as a result of its own internal dynamics and not in accordance with any predetermined plan or order. There is also no moral goal or purpose evident. Things do not happen for the purpose of being judged, "for identifying what is better or worse, or to spur us to search from some general all-encompassing reason that explains what is going on."[39] It is movement itself which changes everything. Irrespective of one's desires, everything is in a state of constant flux, just as in the conception of Heraclitis: "the observer, the process observed, everything. In such a process, there is no point of reference where one can say: 'I am going to plant myself here and see what happens, since I myself am in a state of constant flux...'"[40] The world of men is a world that is constantly in motion, a motion that sometimes is slow and other times fast—at certain times, very fast indeed and characterized by sudden bursts of activity. History is an incessant succession of different surrounding worlds.

One of the salient characteristics of all surrounding worlds is diversity and heterogeneity, not only of the elements that comprise it, but of the actions of individuals that live within them. This diversity and heterogeneity encompasses all aspects of social life: physical spaces, activities, forms of production, beliefs, and ritual practices. A single environment is in effect a kaleidoscope in constant motion, and is characterized by highly differentiated elements. Caro Baroja does not explicitly describe this characteristic, but he does suggest it in some of his writings. In doing so, he goes against the grain of many of the commonplaces in circulation regarding the Basque Country. Homogeneity is one such commonplace. Thus, the Basque Country is often written about as if its people and industries were the same throughout the entire territory. This kind of assumption reflects a false notion of a static reality. In order to clarify the points he attempted to make, Caro Baroja often resorted to photography. "A portrait," he wrote, "cannot presume to have depth. But the person portrayed always has depth." He was referring here to the functional and structural "models," but these words could also be applied to the simplistic assumption of homogenization. He specifically mentions the naval and fishing industries. About the former, he writes that, "it had different characteristics in Navarre, Bizkaia (Vizcaya), and Gipuzkoa (Guipúzcoa). Each of these places had its own unique context."[41] Araba was differentiated from the other areas because of its limited industrial production. In other regions of the Basque Country, distinctive characteristics emerged as a result of attempts to locate "mines of iron and other minerals." Even in what seemed to be the most isolated places, such as the five towns, there is documentation "that reflects the fact that, at that time [i.e., in the Middle Ages], there were miners present—the equivalent at that time to the mining technician, an office of German origin."[42] He makes the same point in reference to those who earn their living from the sea. "The humble riverside fisherman views the sea in one way. The sailor and high-seas mariner sees it in quite a different way. There are as many seas as there are sets of eyes and men who undertake seafaring activities."[43]

In Caro Baroja's opinion, it is the different occupations that determine the different perceptions. "A shepherd will pay close attention to one set of elements, and a farmer to a different set. A warrior moving from the South to the North will have a view of the world that is different from a warrior who moves in the opposite direction."[44] This is one of the determining factors. Other factors are "the diversity of social and economic situations" that exist among individuals and the "economic interests" defended by diverse groups. Yet there is also a collective identity superimposed upon this diversity, one that consists of the superstructure erected by the human collective—in other words, those elements of society considered "myth" or "mythological."[45] Yet this mythical superstructure does not serve as a motive force. Another factor weighing upon society as a whole is race and religion. Yet these, too, do not function as motive forces. "There is no doubt that such elements of the surrounding world make their presence felt," yet "individual members of a society will each have their own economic interests to defend within this 'world.'"[46]

What is noteworthy in this connection is that Caro Baroja did not apply such thinking in his own research. In my view, he was obsessed with the idea of historical-cultural cycles and, beginning in 1971, he attempted to fit his view of the distinctive characteristics of surrounding worlds within such a framework. In doing so, he endowed these characteristics with a new kind of dynamic, and also with a new kind of objectivity and a more specific scientific quality than the concepts of "cultural area" and "cycles" that had been previously used by anthropo-geographers and historians such as Friedrich Ratzel and Eduard Meyer.[47] However, when Caro Baroja writes about the historical-cultural cycles of the Basques, he does so, in contrast to the observations cited above, by attending only to the "new and fundamental idea" that differentiates each cycle from the other cycles.

The historical-cultural cycles of the Basques become progressively shorter over the course of history. The first cycle is obscured in the dim mists of the past, and is characterized by gentilitious entities or blood relationships. Later, "general mobility," the emergence of cities and fortified towns, and the open roads constructed to facilitate travel to pilgrimage sites gave rise to "urban way stations." The "enterprises of discovery, conquest, and colonization; wars and reprisals; internal divisions; the hegemony of 'Spanish nationalism;'" and the "polymorphism of the present situation" are all "fundamental characteristics" that make up each of the cycles of Basque history that Caro Baroja identifies.[48]

Caro Baroja's cycles are not characterized by anything that can be called complex, heterogeneous, or self-contradictory. They also don't reflect a diversity of perceptions, of meanings, or of definitions. What the cycles instead appear to represent is the collective reality shared by all. All elements of individual identity have, however, completely disappeared. Wilhelm Koppers, who adhered to the *Kulturkreislehre,* had suggested the possibility of diversity within the *oldest* cycles but, unsurprisingly, he did not present any evidence to support this claim.[49] Caro Baroja, however, did not even suggest the presence of this kind of diversity in the centuries that he investigated, and therefore he can be accused of the same oversimplification that he claimed other thinkers were guilty of. The fundamental and novel aspects of the cycles Caro Baroja describes refer only to the world of perceptions and meanings that promote dominant beliefs. Within his scheme, time is social and spaces are exclusively political in nature. And time and spaces are, for Caro Baroja, determined by the definitions imposed by collective entities for the purpose of maintaining social order and for ascribing roles to the individuals subject to that order.

Yet history moves inexorably forward and no one can make it stop. At times, history is also explosive and chaotic in nature. The "joy of incessantly moving forward, rejecting all meanings consecrated by past acceptance, and casting aside all notions of order," is, in the words of Georges Balandier,[50] the fate of all cultures. Basque culture is no exception, despite the fact that many historians have seen it (and some continue to see it even today) as stagnant.

III

> "It is clear that the historical-cultural method, just as the evolutionary method before it, has created a certain tendency toward mental schemata and ethnological metaphysics. Some followers of this method thus reject Stendhal's counsel to 'see things as they are' but instead insist on making reality conform to their own preconceptions."
>
> — Julio Caro Baroja, *Los pueblos del norte*

There are events that occur in life that can completely undermine one's existing view of oneself and one's fellow human beings, and that act as a spur to a radical rethinking of fundamental assumptions. Such events need not be either important or dramatic. It is also not necessarily the case that the changed view referred to here results from a brilliant flash of insight, a revelation from on high, the impact of the wise words of a teacher or writer, or as the product of intensive and prolonged rumination. Change can have many different causes, including those that are accidental, random, banal, or entirely unexpected.

We see a good example of this phenomenon in the character of María in Pío Baroja's novel, *La dama errante* (The wandering lady). Within the gloomy depths of the water and shadows of the River Clyde, nothing can be seen from the boat that is taking her to London. Yet, at the same time, everything in her life at that point has radically and irrevocably changed. Even those incidents that had occurred in the previous journey to Portugal that had tested the limits of her endurance, "took on, over the course of a few days, the character of distant and hazy recollections that had been overshadowed by the more startling impact of later events."[51]

What has brought about María's shift in perception, a renewed sense of security and freedom, and a reawakened capacity to dream of and aspire to something beyond her previous monotonous existence was in fact something entirely banal: the mere fact of refraining from the actions that, up until that point, had essentially constituted her existence. "The interruption her normal routine had changed her view of life and of other persons, and she now saw her own life, as well as that of her father and of the rest of her family, in an entirely different light."[52]

Something similar must have occurred to Caro Baroja given that, after dedicating so many years of his life to investigating traditional Spanish and Basque culture from the perspective of traditional historical methodology and the *Kulturkreislehre*, he embraced an entirely different viewpoint. "The old ethnographer has packed his bags and walked off into the sunset, and sociologists, economists, urban planners and others have taken his place." With this sad farewell, Caro Baroja concluded the final paragraph of the epilogue of his work on rural Basque life.[53] And here also, I will attempt to make some sense of certain important issues that Caro Baroja himself did not clarify.

The release of a new edition of a work that had originally been published in 1944 represents a crucial turning point in Caro Baroja's career. The object of the research that he had dedicated so much of his life to, ever since his teenage years, has disappeared. "Pretty much all of that is now archeology," he wrote. The fact that he devoted a considerable proportion of this work to a description of "material things" provides the proper context for his observation of the change that has taken place. He was nothing less than shocked when he realized something that seems to have previously escaped his notice: "a material change that is so radical that it also wrought a fundamental change in every aspect of social life."[54] What has disappeared is not merely material culture (i.e., technology, construction materials, etc.) but also includes the fundamental basis of subsistence: crops and animals. And, with these things, a social and mental world has also vanished. Beginning in the 1960s, a "new cycle" commenced in rural Basque life that was dominated by industry and commerce, a cycle that left in its wake the traditional beliefs and social structure of years gone by.

What was lost was precisely what had been considered quintessentially Basque: the bond between houses and church sepulchres, the *carro chillón*,⁵⁵ the traditional yoke and its oxen, the *laya*, iron foundries, traditional mowing, the commons, and apple orchards. Even ethnic characteristics were disappearing. Only the language remained. However, Caro Baroja did not believe that it was destined to survive for long, and he contended that the demise of *euskera* would mean the end "not of one, but of various historical cycles."⁵⁶

It was also evident that the ineluctable march of history and of change had a decisive impact on the Basque Country's social life. The forces of history leave their imprint everywhere, even in places many believe are left untouched by them—such as rural communities. Human beings are not the only "things" that disappear: Social institutions, along with their structures and functions, also have a life span, and eventually vanish from the scene. Ideal types remain unchanged only in theory. Prosperity and bankruptcy, political change and upheaval, birth and death, and the vagaries of the faraway national and international relationships affect individual beliefs and local social institutions, resulting in their disappearance, adaptation, or transformation. Nothing remains unchanged, either in terms of its "original state" or of the state which obtained over the course of many years in the more recent past.

Any supposed fossilization of a culture or human society in its "original state," or with respect to its "tradition" or "customs" is more moral preaching than it is the statement of an ethnographic truth (or, in Caro Baroja's words, of "ethnological metaphysics"). In general, Caro Baroja's view is that "the morality and the science of customs have been closely tied together ever since the separate social sciences arose as distinct disciplines. Even "research that presumes to be highly objective" has an "intrinsic moral or moralizing slant."⁵⁷

The discovery of the historicity of rural societies is what led Caro Baroja to view Basque culture differently than he had previously. Basque culture is not in the least primitive. In response to those who believe that the Basques have preserved their original primitive state throughout their history, Caro Baroja wrote *Los vascos* (*The Basques*), a work in which he vigorously rejected any such notion. This means that such a hypothetical original state has also not been preserved even in the venerable farmhouses, which Caro Baroja argued "that researchers of a romantic bent have believed that they saw in the farmhouse a faithful reflection of past eras that were both primitive and paradisiacal." Instead, the farmhouse (*caserío*) represents a mixture of "very modern traits and very traditional ones."⁵⁸ Caro Baroja makes the same point in reference to shepherding, the organization of which "has been obliged to change through the centuries until it adopted the features we see today."⁵⁹ He noted that there were still further changes that had taken place in the thirty years between the two editions of the book. "We ethnographers who trod across the Basque territories during the thirty or forty years ago have found that everything we studied back then has suddenly been transformed into archeology."⁶⁰

Succumbing to his vain wish that this past had not vanished, he ends up doing the very thing that he has censured—inserting moral values in ethnographic research. Industrial and technological development "involved a radical change with respect to the institutions and ideas that, until just a short time ago, were considered by those in authority to be essential for both moral development and the wellbeing of a considerable part of the population of Europe as a whole."⁶¹ The legacy of the moralists and philosophers of the late seventeenth century endured until the beginning of the twentieth century, only to subsequently be eviscerated by those who claimed to be defending "traditional institutions, beginning with the family itself." And yet, in spite of this, the disappearance of what could be considered to be quintessentially Basque was everywhere in evidence. Thus, to cite a specific example, to be the heir of a *caserío*, an absolutely vital matter in the Basque Country in days gone by, has lost its previous importance. The world of beliefs, rituals, and relationships among neighbors has disappeared along with the crops and animals that provided food in ages past. The same thing has happened with crops of flax and the textile mills that were the heart of the country's garment industry. "The apple orchards were left to die and were not replaced by other crops, The lime quarries have been abandoned, the highland roads are either no longer maintained in good condition or have been shut down, cooperative work among neighbors has become increasingly rare, and family relationsh have grown progressively more difficult."⁶² What was considered so distinctively characteristic of Basque life in times past is now in the process of disappearing forever. And this means the disappearance of the "romantic" aspects of the Basque life of yesteryear. "I for one can't say whether this is good or bad. What I can say, however, is that it is 'less poetic' for those observing the phenomenon at close quarters."⁶³

Caro Baroja expressed similar reflections, yet in more dramatic fashion, in 1967, when he wrote that, in the evolution of peoples such as the Basques, certain things disappear and are replaced by "others that do not have a distinctive provenance." The forests and the delightful country expanses have shrunk, the rivers have all dried up, and the rural societies of yore have passed into history. . . . In short, everything that flourished so vigorously over the course of centuries is now no more. . . . And with all these things, with the rivers and the groves of chestnut trees, many forms of the old culture have also passed away. Now very little remains of the history and culture of the past, and what does remain has suffered the effects of erosion and wear caused by human activity."[64] The ferneries no longer reflect anything that is "natural, authentic, or original." Instead, they are "the product of deforestation and exploitation."[65]

As for the Basque language, it has "clearly been in retreat since the sixteenth century and, even though it has become "a public language," it has lost its essential and socially cohesive role."[66] "The best conserved part of the past world," that of the people who live in the highlands during most of the year, "has itself not remained untouched by history" and is now on the verge of disappearing. With its disappearance, something else is also irretrievably lost: that "Golden Age" in which "animals spoke and acted as if they were human beings," when pagans constructed dolmens, when crops were assiduously cultivated—that world of long ago, "from the innards of which arose the man of the Basque Country, guided and protected by the saints. Although a few very old men are still left who can speak about all this in great detail, they will, I think, be the last of their kind."[67] It could hardly be more obvious that Caro Baroja mourns the loss of this vanished world.

And with all this, there was yet another loss: the longstanding symbiosis between the mythological past and a "rigid adherence to the precepts of the Church." Rocky precipices, mountains, caves and rivers, populated by "female deities, storm gods and *lamiñaz* or *lamiak*; long stretches of time when the existence of sorcerers and witches was an ever-present reality; a calendar filled with festivals reflecting 'traditional Christian devotion' and 'customs related to family and community life.'" All of these things, which were such distinctive aspects of Basque life over the course of centuries are, with the exception of a few isolated redoubts, a thing of the past. There is also no longer "a fixed social order that is reflected by a cohesive community."[68]

It was around this same time that the anthropologist William Douglass demonstrated that the very fabric of traditional Basque life had completely unraveled. Basque life had by then acquired the characteristics of industrialized societies: individualization, a market economy, and so on. In his accurate and subtle exposition, Douglass showed how this change was experienced by the older generation, who had been left practically alone in their homes or—even worse—confined to city apartments. Older Basques experienced both of these alternatives as equally traumatic, while at the same time recognizing that they would do no differently themselves if they were younger.[69]

Caro Baroja saw this entire enchanted world as being in the process of extinction. The Basques of the past, along with their distinctive world, were being replaced by the new world of "the utilitarian Basques." The latter, according to Caro Baroja, had "laid waste" the homeland and were responsible for the disappearance of the world that their forefathers had inhabited for centuries. "The Basque Country has held its own in comparison to the rest of western Europe in terms of the great men that it has produced." Yet these men of genius were those who had left the country, and not those who stayed at home. The former had "always gained their fame elsewhere."[70] Those who stayed behind, on the other hand, were "provincials" and "those who had no future." These were the men who gathered together to chat over coffee, convened their local meetings and committees, and took communion in their local churches—men of the *batzarre* or *batzoki*."[71]

Caro Baroja thus offered a dark vision of what had transpired. Yet his critical attention focused most strongly on clerical morality and on the fantastic theories of the supposed origin of the Basques. "During the past two centuries, Basque politics" has been characterized by "a kind of democratic-clerical ideal" that represents a quest for "an original social order." Disregarding their history, the Basques of the eighteenth century embraced the mythical figure Tubal and identified with "Cantabrians" and with the "ancient Iberians." After a time, these connections were dispensed with in favor of a search for "a nexus between the Basques of today and the prehistory of the dolmens, etc. . . . There is no doubt that, in terms of the social and even the artistic order, a large proportion of the population of the Basque Country has taken the intellectual and sentimental position that can be summed up in a single word: 'neoprimitivism.' And, like all movements representing a return to the past, this neoprimitivism bore little actual relation to what it sought to connect with."[72]

Beginning in the late 1970s and early 1980s, Caro Baroja's position became much more clearly defined. On the basis of his writings dating from that period, we can infer that he felt that the Basques and their culture were not in the least anomalous in comparison with other peoples of Western Europe. Conjuring an isolated region that never existed, given that "the Basque Country is one of the most complex nerve centers of the continent"[73] and making that territory serve as the locus of the millennial Basque culture and way of life, is a chimera—a false explanation. Such a fabrication represents "nothing more than a rhetorical exercise": the snatching of a single element from the vast constellation of a complex history and inflating the importance of that element in the service of creating a usable past. This is what "the Basques are up to when they identify a nexus between prehistory and contemporary village inhabitants," thus bypassing "all of the intervening history."[74] This is exactly what Barandiarán did. "He gave us some useful ideas regarding the world of Basque rural inhabitants, but he always stressed those characteristics of their lives that struck him as the most primitive and archaizing, while ignoring other possible characteristics."[75]

Such an enterprise is fundamentally "a tiresome and tedious game" of "political-historical" rhetoric. And yet the saddest thing of all is that it is not always merely a game, and at times represents the "danger of fanning the flames of fanaticism" with calamitous consequences.[76] And this was a fanaticism and calamity that both Basques and non-Basques were equally guilty of, the former characterized by "enthusiasm and a certain degree of self-absorption," and the latter "indignant over the existence of a language and of customs that they do not claim as their own." Instead of dedicating themselves to forming "new syntheses" or contributing "new discoveries," these kinds of fanatics devote their time and energy to poring over "texts filled with old information and ideas." "Basques are not some kind of duck-billed platypuses or some isolated branch of the family of nations. Conversely, they are also not everyday farm animals that have been nurtured in incubators or other similar devices in order to fulfill a particular purpose."[77] Contrary to what many presumed was true, Caro Baroja had contended for many years that the real historical past of Basque culture is not remote, but relatively immediate—so "immediate, that it weighs upon our conscience today, just as it weighed upon the conscience of our fathers and grandfathers. It is this past that has endowed us with our specific characteristics within the contemporary world."[78] Among these characteristics are the quests to preserve "their language, their distinctive collective identity, and their enigmatic quality."[79]

These conclusions of Caro Baroja about the Basques and their culture seem understandable in light of his own life experience and surroundings. Following Bernard Lahire, Caro Baroja represented "plural man." His case represents an example of the "individual who has lived within various different scenarios, contexts, force fields, and battlegrounds, etc.," and who, as a result, reflects "what these varied experiences have made of him."⁸⁰ A full appreciation of the life of such an individual necessarily involves "studying the individualized, incorporated, and interiorized expression of a larger social reality."⁸¹

What neither Caro Baroja nor Lahire took into account, however, is the world of individualized emotions that are capable of changing one's worldview, theory, and methodology. This is precisely what occurred in the case of Julio Caro Baroja.

IV

> "At the age of forty-two, I felt that another important stage of my life had come to a conclusion, a stage that had had a powerful impact, that was filled with great sorrows as well as wonderful friendships, and one in which my vision of the world attained greater depth and clarity."
>
> — Julio Caro Baroja, "Una vida en tres actos"

The surroundings (*"Umwelt"*) that J. von Üexküll and G. Kriszat identified refer to what is capable of being perceived by different organisms, can only be defined in terms of each individual, and are vital for the survival of their species. Every perception is thus determined by a vital nexus. Each species makes a selection from among the constellation of factors that account for reality. This selection is what is perceptible and unique to the individual of that species. Everything else is relegated to the shadows, as if it did not even exist.

Of course, the environment of human beings is different from that of animals. Still, one observes certain similarities at the structural, functional, and vital levels. The perceptible worlds of both are determined by their biological needs. Erich Rothacker, citing von Üexküll's *Theoretische biologie*, demonstrates this similarity by showing how a holm oak tree is able to provide different kinds of environments to animals and to men. Foxes, owls, squirrels, ants, and other animals focus on certain parts of the tree that correspond to their needs, ignoring other elements of the tree. Ants make homes in the tree's cracked bark, owls take up sentry on the tree's sturdiest branches, foxes dig and hunt among the roots and litter. These animals see nothing that does not affect their environment. Human responses to the oak are the same: the lumberjack sees a quantity of lumber, a child might see terrible gnomes and frightening fairies. Given that humans are endowed with a sense of magic, perhaps a face can be discerned in the bark. "Each separate environment isolates from the tree a specific aspect of it whose properties correspond to both the perceptible and motivational data of the respective functional radii."[82]

As I have pointed out, Caro Baroja includes within the human environment factors such as occupations, social positions, economic strategies, and interests. For him, as for Rothacker, "all perceptions are determined by a vital nexus."[83] Yet the actions involved are historical-cultural in nature, and "limit" the sensitivity field that Rothacker calls "cultural shadows."[84]

For Rothacker, the character of different perceptions, resulting from the distinct meanings attributed to that which is perceived, arise from one's personal experience. "Both the perceptions and the meanings arise from the same source—the body." Without a significance previously experienced by the "id", and the emotional layer, "there is no objectification (i.e., perception, concept, intellection) carried out by the 'ego' that acts in such a way as to allow the individual to incorporate the perception."[85] Images, feelings, "existential modalities," and occupational activities allow for the production of different perceptible worlds or, what amounts to the same thing, of the different environments in which different human beings live, all of which reflect their specific interests. "Our vision is filtered through many different layers of reality that are like transparent glass, the presence of which we are entirely oblivious of."[86] This represents the specific way in which human beings live. In contrast to all other animals, men experience reality in a highly personalized way.

Rothacker's conceptualization of the "environment" is more vivid and intimate than that of Caro Baroja, given the inclusion of emotional aspects. This is perhaps one of the most important differences between Rothacker and Caro Baroja, in terms of academic discourse. Caro Baroja's "environment," as applied to his own life and the lives of "oppressed minorities," is more external, as is the case of theorists who see the "milieu" as the locus of all influence, as opposed to thinkers such as von Üexküll and Kritszat, who focus on the organisms' perceptions. One finds no mention of feelings, emotions, or images in Caro Baroja's theory, and his environments lack any kind of "motive force" that "fill the space" (in the words of Simmel) or that even represent "life as experienced" (in the words of Rothacker).

The fact that a theorist has not incorporated an emotional element into his conceptualization of the surrounding worlds of others or of himself does not mean that he does not experience (or, perhaps better, suffer) profound emotional upheavals. Practically all of Caro Baroja's life was characterized by physical illnesses and social setbacks, by internal conflicts and disagreements with others, and, more than anything else, by an anguished obsession with death. His fragile health, his "neurasthenic temperament," and his "reflective and rigorous" mental habits, along with the fact that, within a relatively short time, he experienced the death of a number of people with whom he was very close, left him feeling lonely and obsessed with death. His transition "from maturity to old-age" also engendered a brooding tendency on his part, and led him to continually reflect on his own death. A turning point in this regard was reached in 1956. "I was about to turn forty-two, and I was in shockingly bad physical health. My social life also left a lot to be desired. I thought about adopting a different point of view, like a sick person who has grown weary of the same monotonous routine."[87] It was in 1957, when anything to do with "longing, loving, and wishing" was a thing of the past, that he felt at his weakest. "In other words, even though I was not physically dead, I felt like I was almost dead."[88] And yet, paradoxically, this marked the beginning of his embracing a new outlook on the world, on the Basques and their culture, and on his own life and work. I have discussed the fruits of this transformed outlook above.

In the words of the title of the penultimate chapter of his memoirs, his life was "one death after another" from the 1930s until the late 1950s. His maternal grandmother died in 1935. He had always been very close to her, and she had been a real stabilizing force in the family home. In 1943, the same year that Caro Baroja published his first book, his father died, "worn out from the toil and disappointments of his life." In 1950, his mother died "after a painful illness that lasted three years." José Ortega y Gasset, a close friend of his, died in 1955. Then in 1956, his uncles Pío and Ricardo both died. He compared his own experience to what was happening in Spain as a whole. "What happened in my own life is a reflection of what was occurring in public life: appearance predominated over substance. I clung to an ideal past and I lived in the shadow of the last representatives of that past." "I am nothing more than a mirror that continues to reflect a world that has past . . . a world that perhaps never really did exist, except in the minds of a few men."[89]

In the final stage of his life, he once again took up the subject of death. He was acutely aware that all things pass. Charon and Hermes, looking down from the mountain top, had borne witness to the fact that men and cities are destined to meet the same end: destruction and death.

Hermes helped Charon contemplate life from a new perspective that left him "aghast at the stupid things that men get all worked up about." "In sum, one must live as if our own end were imminent."[90] His own work made him somewhat uneasy, both because he did not know how to classify it and because of its internal contradictions. "There are many obvious contradictions" and he also was painfully aware of "constant discrepancies" between what he had written before and what he believed was true during the last period in his life."[91] He came to see his work as not constituting either history or anthropology, but instead as something akin to the "manufacture of belts or the weaving of bobbin lace." Figuratively speaking, it was filigree work that one did to pass the time.

In his final years, Caro Baroja found his life and the world around him unfathomable. He made the following declaration in one of the last interviews he granted: "More than an optimist or a pessimist, what I feel more than anything else is bafflement, surprise, and wonder. Everything surprises me. I tend to think that the world—for good and for ill—is unfathomable, and that we will never be able to fully understand it."[92] A few years previously, he said he could not decide whether it was better to live or to die: "Is it good to live just for the sake of living? Is death an irredeemably bad thing? Is what was wished for yesterday necessarily desirable today?"[93] "For me, death has always concerned the death of others. I don't really think about my own death that much, and at times I think that it is not something that is overly important. I wouldn't say that I think it is something good, but at times I think of it as something that would free me from certain individual and collective grievances."[94]

At the age of sixty, Caro Baroja felt like a fish out of water, a man condemned to conduct a never-ending monologue that nobody else was listening to. He felt that he occupied a place somewhere in between two extremes: that of "our traditional knowledge" and that of "modern—or supposedly modern—knowledge." He poses a question to himself and then quickly answers it: "The solitary man crosses himself and wonders, 'My God! What might I have been able to accomplish in the face of this avalanche if I were only thirty years younger!' But, fortunately, the solitude that has dogged him ever since his youth now protects him."[95]

These were years that saw the inclusion of social anthropology in "the department of a certain university in Madrid" and the demise of subjects "that had until recently enjoyed the greatest academic prestige."[96] Franco's dictatorship has breathed its last, and the new "fanatical" and "ideological" students were, in his view, excessively credulous. He sees himself as one of the lone wolves and he acknowledges that he is a bore. But he rises in his own defense: "So what? The impertinence of a solitary man hardly matters in the face of the collective and polished impertinence that today stands so proudly triumphant."[97]

His death, as he himself had mused in 1981, may in fact have constituted a liberation from "certain individual and collective grievances."[98] At last, he was released from his constant physical complaints and from the "ritualistic" Basques. Caro Baroja had written in 1984 that Basque identity constituted a kind of sign of group solidarity that functioned as an admission ticket allowing one to participate in certain political "rituals," in the same way that mysterious words were a part of certain religious rituals in the ancient world. Basque "ritualism" may end up becoming something like the Arval brethren or of the Salii who were employed by brotherhoods to chant on solemn occasions: "it hardly mattered what the words they chanted meant."[99] The failure to follow the "pious traditions" always constitutes "a tremendous and unpardonable betrayal."[100] In this statement, Caro Baroja showed himself to be a faithful disciple of Epicurus. His statements about life and death in his final years were also thoroughly Epicurean, and reflected the writings of the philosopher Emilio Lledó about that venerable school.[101]

Beyond the phobias and philias—both his own and those of others—his contribution to the study of Basques and of their culture is important because he restored them to their rightful place in history. In general, it can be said that his studies, although sometimes incomplete and in other cases somewhat off the mark, generally do point in the right direction. Those who undertake research in the future will be greatly in his debt, given his categorical rejection of the mental schema and the ontological metaphysics underlying much of the research that has been published on the Basques. The selection of texts in the present volume reflects this important contribution of Julio Caro Baroja to Basque studies.

Selected Bibliography of Julio Caro Baroja

Los Baroja. Madrid: Ediciones Taurus, 1972.

The Basques. Reno: Center for Basque Studies, 2009. Translation of *Los vascos*, see entry below.

Las brujas y su mundo. Madrid: Ediciones de la Revista de Occidente, 1961.

La casa en Navarra. 4 vols. Pamplona: Caja de Ahorros de Navarra, 1982.

"Ciclos culturales e identidad vasca." In *Problemas de ayer y de hoy*, 9–39. San Sebastián: Editorial Txertoa, 1986. Originally published 1981–1983.

Comentarios sin fe. Madrid: Editorial Nuestra Cultura, 1979.

Julio Caro Baroja and F. J. Flores Arroyuelo. *Conversaciones en Itzea*. Madrid: Alianza Editorial, 1991.

"Cosas humanas y tiempos de ellas." In *De la superstición al ateísmo*, 17–29. Madrid: Ediciones Taurus, 1974. Originally published in 1973.

"La crisis del caserío (1964)." In *Baile, familia y trabajo*, 133–141. San Sebastián: Editorial Txertoa, 1976.

Julio Caro Baroja y E. Temprano. *Disquisiciones* antropológicas. Barcelona: Editorial Gedisa, 1985.

La estación de amor (Fiestas populares de mayo a San Juan). Madrid: Ediciones Taurus, 1974.

La estación de amor (Fiestas populares de mayo a San Juan). Madrid: Ediciones Taurus, 1979.

El estío festivo (Fiestas populares de verano). Madrid: Ediciones Taurus, 1984.

Etnografía histórica de Navarra. 3 vols. Pamplona: Editorial Aranzadi, 1971–1972.

Las formas complejas de la vida religiosa: Religión, sociedad y carácter en la España de los siglos XVI y XVII. Madrid: Editorial Akal, 1978.

"Género biográfico y conocimiento antropológico." In *Biografía y vidas humanas*, 7–37. San Sebastián: Editorial Txertoa, 1969.

La hora Navarra del XVIII (Personas, familias, negocios e ideas). Pamplona: Diputación Foral de Navarra/Institución Príncipe de Viana, 1986.

"Una imagen del mundo perdida." In *Reflexiones nuevas sobre viejos temas*, 77–121. Madrid: Ediciones Itsmo, 1990.

Inquisición, brujería y criptojudaísmo. Barcelona: Editorial Ariel, 1970.

Introducción a la historia económica y social del pueblo vasco. San Sebastián: Editorial Txertoa, 1974.

Los judíos en la España moderna y contemporánea. Madrid: Editorial Arión, 1961–1962.

El laberinto vasco. San Sebastián: Editorial Txertoa, 1984.

"El mar en situaciones tópicas." In *De la superstición al ateísmo*, 59–100. Madrid: Ediciones Taurus, 1974.

"Mundos circundantes y contornos histórico-culturales." In *De la superstición al ateísmo*, 31–57. Madrid: Ediciones Taurus, 1974. Originally published in 1973.

Palabra, sombra equívoca. Barcelona: Tusquets Editores, 1989.

"Problemas psicológicos, sociológicos y jurídicos en torno a la brujería en el País Vasco." Homenaje a Julio Caro Baroja. *Príncipe de Viana*, no. 206 (Septiembre–Diciembre 1995): 1,017–1,030. Originally published in 1971.

Los pueblos de España. 3rd ed. Madrid: Ediciones Istmo, 1976. Originally published in 1946.

Los pueblos del norte. 2nd ed. San Sebastián: Editorial Txertoa, 1973. Originally published in 1943.

Semblanzas ideales. Madrid: Ediciones Taurus, 1972.

"Situación actual de la antropología." *Alcoveras*, no. 0 (1980): 16–18.

Sobre la religión antigua y el calendario vasco. 2nd ed. San Sebastián: Editorial Txertoa, 1982.

"Sobre los vascos (Reflexiones de 1967)." In *Sondeos históricos*, 141–162. San Sebastián: Editorial Txertoa, 1978.

"Sofismas en torno a la mitología." In *De la superstición al ateísmo*. Madrid: Ediciones Taurus, 1974.

De la superstición al ateísmo. Madrid: Ediciones Taurus, 1974.

"El último Avrencerrejo." In *Vidas poco paralelas (con perdón de Plutarco)*, 51–68. Madrid: Ediciones Taurus, 1981.

Los vascos. 3rd ed. Madrid: Ediciones Itsmo, 1971.

Los vascos y el mar. San Sebastián: Editorial Txertoa, 1981.

Los vascos y la historia a través de Garibay. 3rd ed. Madrid: Editorial Caro Raggio, 1981. 2002. Originally published in 1972.

La vida rural vasca. 2nd ed. San Sebastián: Editorial Txertoa, 1974. Originally published in 1944.

"Una vida en tres actos." *Homenaje a Julio Caro Baroja.* Príncipe de Viana, no. 206 (Septiembre–Diciembre 1995): 1577–589. Originally published in 1971.

Vidas mágicas e inquisición. Madrid: Ediciones Taurus, 1967.

References Cited

Balandier, Georges. *El desorden*. Barcelona: Editorial Gedisa, 1996.

Baroja, Pío. *La dama* errante. Vol 2. Madrid: Biblioteca Nueva, Obras Completas, 1976.

Douglass, William A. *Oportunidad y éxodo rural en dos aldeas vascas: Echalar y Murélaga*. Donostia-San Sebastián: Editorial Auñamendi, 1977.

Greenwood, Davydd. "Julio Caro Baroja: Sus obras e ideas." In *Semblanzas* ideales, by Julio Caro Baroja, 263–284. Madrid: Ediciones Taurus, 1972.

Kant, Immanuel. *Anthropologie du point de vue pragmatique*. Paris: Librairie Philosophique J.Vrin, 2002. Originally published in 1878.

Koppers, Wilhelm. "Individualforschung unter den Primitiven in besonderen unter den Yamana auf Feuerland." In *Festschrift P. W. Schmidt*, 349–365. Wien: Mechitharisten Congregations-Buchdrukerei, 1928.

Lahire, Bernard. *El hombre plural: Los resortes de la acción*. Barcelona: Ediciones Bellaterra S.L., 2004.

Lledó, Emilio. *El epicureismo: Una fiiosofía del cuerpo, del gozo y de la amistad*. Barcelona: Editorial Montesinos, 1984.

Rothacker, Erich. *Problemas de antropología cultural*. Mëxico: Fondo de Cultura Económica, 1957. Originally published in 1948.

Sánchez Harguindey, Ángel. "Prólogo." In *Comentarios sin* fe, by Julio Caro Baroja, 5–12. Madrid: Editorial Nuestra Cultura, 1979.

Part 1

Basque Times and Spaces

I

Neighboring Peoples and the Historical-Cultural Context

I

There is a general familiarity with the changes that have occurred to the political divisions of the earth as a result of human activity, and which have been recorded for posterity in the successive editions of atlases that have been published. Thus, the *Stieler Handatlas* that was published prior to 1914 bears little similarity with the edition published a mere five years later, and the atlases of 1939 and 1969 portray still different realities. All manner of changes are reflected in historical atlases. All of the venerable European countries have suffered small variations within more or less short periods of time. From ancient to contemporary times, the changes that have occurred on the Iberian Peninsula (*Hispania* or Spain) are highly discernible, and reflect societal transformations occurring within the context of the marked immutability of what is now popularly called the "physical medium." I will be discussing some of these transformations shortly.

There are geographical determinists who are wedded to the notion that it is an understanding of this medium (or "milieu") that is essential for understanding human action. But such a stance, which is uncritically accepted in many quarters, carries with it a potential element of self-deception, especially when it comes to writing history or, in general, to understanding human activity throughout the course of history.

Because the ways that the physical medium can be interpreted by man are highly specific to cultures, societies, and general conceptions of the world. The matter becomes even more complex when we find the same people living in two of these supposed media that, while contiguous, are very different from one another. If history has any useful purpose at all, it is that of destroying the fallacies and methodological generalizations of those who erect rickety structures upon what appear to be solid foundations. I think that it was Napoleon who said that "a man cannot become an atheist merely by wishing it." In a similar vein, it may also be said that one cannot become a geographical determinist merely by wishing it, or that all those professing Marxism are not necessarily Marxists. But enough of this. Let's dispense with the word *medium*. Instead, let us ask what a man sees, feels, suffers, and enjoys in each of his *perceptible worlds*, each of which are so undeniably imposing from a material point of view? If he is a shepherd, then he will perceive first and foremost a number of significant elements. If he is a farmer, then he will perceive different significant elements. If he is a warrior, and if his path of conquest is from south to north, he will see things differently than if he is a warrior who is marching in the opposite direction. Because when we observe people living within what is apparently an immutable space, it is important to always keep in mind that some may have, or do have, shared blood ties and a shared religion that is different from that of other peoples. It is of course undeniable that the specific parcel of the world where people live is a determining factor, and everyone will have economic interests to defend within that specific place. Yet these interests will always be defended against specific important factors, during specific historical periods, and by specific generations of individuals.

Let us show what we are talking about here by providing a number of concise and concrete examples for the purposes of clearing up a number of misunderstandings that are more prevalent in our time than they were previously, precisely because structural and functional models are now continually being propagated within the field of anthropology. And this propagation is occurring without sufficient account being taken of either the temporal dimension of all human activity or of the principles of historical relativism and of a dialectic of the facts themselves. According to such a dialectic, the principle of "change" is fundamentally important for understanding human societies. One frequently sees language in the titles of anthropological studies such as "in a changing society." But we need to ask ourselves: What societies do not change at a more or less accelerated pace? The image of stagnant societies that are tied to a specific physical medium has been highly favored by certain folklorists, anthropologists, and sociologists. The notion of "adaptation to a medium" was also regnant for a certain period of time. A historian cannot accept either the reality of such an image or the truth of such a dogma. What is typically presented as such an image is in fact an individual portrait that was created at a given time by a painter whose depiction has been more or less faithful. One cannot rightly claim that a portrait has any temporal profundity. Yet the individual being portrayed inherently possesses such a quality.

II

In this sense, then, it can be said that things repeat themselves in a way that is downright scary for those who are aware of the repetition that is occurring. Those lacking such awareness perceive all unfolding events as new and extraordinary occurrences that have never before been seen or heard. The greatest paradox of our times is that, while we have more means at our disposal than ever to be aware of what is going on, we in fact remain unaware, and we theorize about our lack of awareness. It is not only young people that tend to scorn historical knowledge, but also a fairly large number of professionals. These people believe that "the here and now"—the events occurring in our society today—are all novel phenomena, including the rural exodus to the cities. Such people also believe that "ancient" societies experience a nearly total immobility, and that they were subject to invariable rules. Any historian, whatever his or her specialty, knows how false this is. But other specialists deny the mendacity of such claims as part of their research—research, it should be noted in passing, that is also oblivious of other knowledge regarding the psychic, essential nature of man, and that flies in the face of the knowledge and experience of ancient moralists. The pages that follow represent a modest essay that applies a criterion of relativity that I have discussed elsewhere[1] and about which I have something more to add. I will base my exposition on various case studies that I have recently carried out, the results of which I will summarize here.

The first of these refer to ethnic variations that occur in specific settings, from ancient through medieval times (specifically, from the second through the twelfth centuries AD) in particular areas of the Iberian Peninsula. I think that my distinctive contribution here lies in the interpretation I offer of data that have long been known. This because we live in an era that veers between the extremes of dogmatic mechanism in both its denial of certain principles and in its admission of others, on the one hand, and various forms of existentialism that are at odds with an idealist stance, on the other. Thus I, as an historian and an ethnologist, find myself obliged to continue researching within the old framework of speculation—a method characteristic of a critical idealist, and one introduced by Kant to his disciples, among whom were both philosophers and scientists—and specifically biologists. I will be referring primarily to Kant's observations in the second part of his *Critique of Pure Reason*, where he analyzes "teleological reasoning" and where he also examines the idea of "purpose" in relation to Nature (especially 42),[2] and will do so in a way that is considerably more pointed than that of previous thinkers and scientists.

It has become increasingly clear to me that, instead of once more entering into a dispute regarding the "theory of the medium" and wrestling with the likes of Bodin, Montesquieu, Taine, Buckle, and all the rest, that I will be served much better in following the disciples of Kant. From one of these disciples, I have derived the notions of the "perceptible world" and the "surrounding world," concepts that differ considerably from what is commonly called "the medium."[3] Many years ago I, like many of my contemporaries, plunged into the deep waters of the writings of Jakob von Üexhüll (1864–1944), which leaving aside their controversial nature,[4] have served as the basis of a great deal of productive research. What I seek to do here is to illustrate the ideas of the "perceptible world" and the "surrounding world" from the historical point of view because, even if it is the case that each animal species appears to have worlds of its own that have special meaning for it (meaning which is gleaned *exclusively* from the outside), for man, apart from that meaning which is biological in nature, there are *other* meanings that are social and historical-cultural in nature. To discover and describe these perceptible and surrounding worlds may involve work that is every bit as novel and problematic as the tasks that biologists took on some years ago.[5] But, perhaps more than discovering these worlds, what is necessary is to rationally account for their existence in ways that also serve to invalidate all of the historical, deterministic, or mechanical logomachies that continue to pass for "scientific discourse," but that really represent nothing more than tired old myths and magic. From a critical point of view, Kant had already taken not only the defenders of a natural purpose who attributed everything to causality or fatalism, but also those, much greater in number, who defended the idea of a purpose derived from an intelligent being or from hylozoism—in other words, realists.

"Medium," "race," and "moment" were the three fundamental forces that Taine attempted to emphasize in his historical analyses.[6] We will see how the clarity of his system turned murky as a result of certain examples, and how these examples take on new meaning from a dynamic point of view (i.e., of the kind found among the moralists) and from the standpoint of nonmechanistic biology.

Other research that I will be summarizing refers to variations in the interpretation of natural phenomena and elements: the countryside or meteorological events.

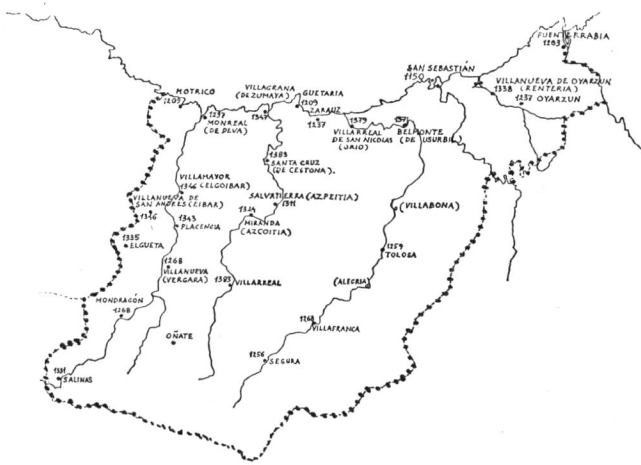

Figure 1.1. Gipuzkoa, with the date of foundation of its principal towns.

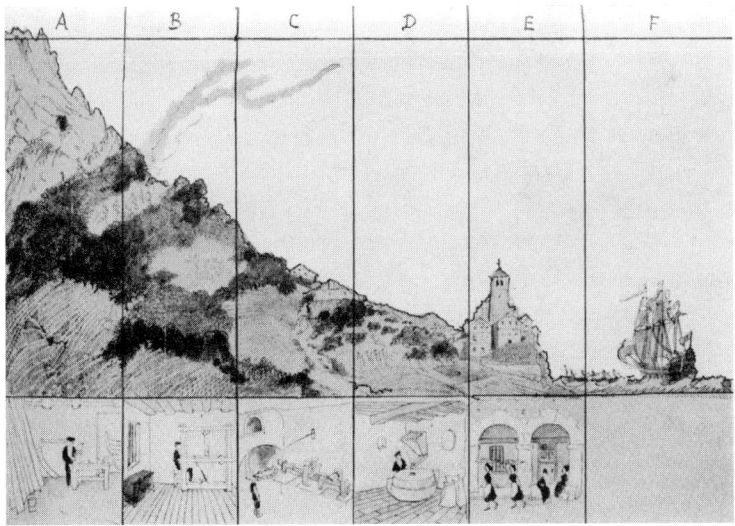

Figure 1.2. Schema of the "Nordic-maritime valley," applied to Gipuzkoa and the other zones of the Basque Country. A and B, high country (firewood, charcoal, pasturage); C and D, low country (agriculture, ironworking); E and F, the coast and sea (fishermen and high seas sailors).

III

If we consider a map of the province of Gipuzkoa with its current boundaries, or even a map from the time of the Renaissance, we will quickly understand that this territory consists of a physical environment that possesses a certain degree of unity, and is clearly bordered on the north by a body of water and on the south by a water divide, and that is defined by various waterways that run through it. The traditional divisions of the province also give us an idea of the value that has been ascribed to these waterways, and to the frequently employed characterizations of *highlands* and *lowlands* in relation to the coast. Depicting the life of the inhabitants of Gipuzkoa on the basis of their geographical location and providing an idea of the arrival and nature of the principal nuclei of the population in relation to the ocean and rivers is an easy task, just like similar endeavors in which "sections of territory" and surroundings can be used as the frame of reference (figures 1.1 and 1.2). If we do a little historical research, we will find that both the territorial unity and the name of Gipuzkoa date back to medieval times. Initial documentation and the first appearance of something that can be called "guipuzcoano" can be identified.[7] It turns out that those who had previously resided in those lands were not called Gipuzkoans. Furthermore they organized the territory in a different way. Gipuzkoa was included, on the one hand, in three different divisions that exceeded its proper boundaries, extending far south of the water divide. To the east and west, there were Vascones in the extreme north and west; Varduli in the majority of the territory, and who also resided south of the present-day boundaries, as previously indicated; and the Caristii, who also had a dominant presence in lands farther to the south. The relationship of these peoples with the three Basque provinces is clear (figure 1.3), even if their distribution is not. It is for this reason that any precise depiction of their geographical distribution is impossible. Ancient peoples lived in surroundings that were very different and more complex than those of the modern world. The Nordic valley schema, which was valid for the Middle Ages and the Renaissance, and perhaps for later periods as well, does not really clarify the situation of the inhabitants in ancient times.

The Varduli lived in the south, which in general terms can be understood as extending to the Ebro River.[8]

In the case of the Vascones, who lived in a highly diverse array of environments (figure 1.3), the complexity is even greater. If we examine a cross section running from east to west along their northern border,

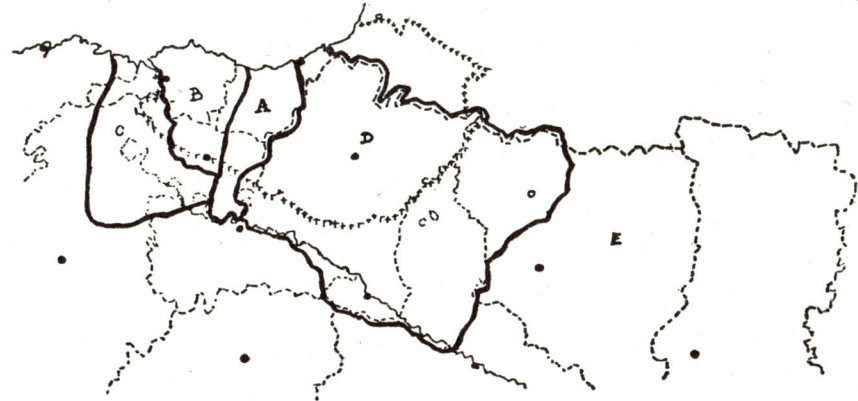

Figure 1.3. Repartition of the ancient Basque-Navarrese territory: (a) Vardulii, (b) Caristii, (c) Autrigones, (d) Vascones, (e) Ilergetes.

we see that they occupied a section of coast in the Pyrenees, settling first in the lowlands and then in the highlands. If one or several cross sections running from north to south are examined, it can be seen that the water divide is surpassed; that they occupied areas of medium altitude; and that they reached as far as the Ebro Valley where, in the foothills of the Iberian System, beneath Moncayo, their borders were to some extent reconfigured by the kingdom of Navarre, after the *Reconquista*. In the case of the Vascones, and in contrast to what occurred to the peoples previously discussed, the fragmentation resulted from a separation of a band or zone in the far east, which in the Middle Ages formed the basis first of the county of Aragon, and later of the kingdom of Aragon. And the river of the Vascones, which was the Aragon, would, as we all know,[9] later give its name to distant lands. In ancient times, peoples did not share their territories with other peoples, as would later occur in medieval and modern times. They considered the territories that they occupied to be their exclusive domains.

If we study another ancient people that was an eastern neighbor of the Vascones, we can see the same condition of "autonomy" as that which would later be established. In reality, the people that I am referring to here, the "Ilergetes," occupied lands extending from the Pyrenees, along the mouth of the Cinca River, to the lower reaches of the Ebro River within what is currently the province of Zaragoza. The Ilergetes, then, occupied the great fluvial plain extending from the Segre and its tributaries to the Cinca River and its tributaries. We thus have a coherent framework for understanding the "Cisiberian" distribution of peoples, which is completely distinct from the state of affairs when the kingdom of Aragon had fully developed, or with Catalonia, whose borders would much later delineate an extensive stretch of the Noguera Ribagorzana. Included in their territory was Lleida (Lérida) on one end and Huesca on the other.[10] Upon close reflection, the aforementioned facts raise a number of important questions. How did the old social organization based on tribal affiliation function within such a widely different array of environments? What were the possible economic bases of these particular physical environments? What were the distinct spiritual and social bases, other than that of common paternal descent or blood relationship, in the broadest sense of the term?

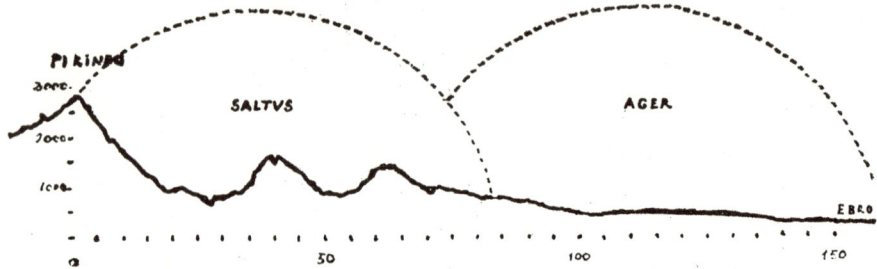

Figure 1.4. Profile of the territory of the Vascones and Ilergetes in ancient times.

Both the Vascones as well as the Ilergetes had an *ager*, or a more fertile cultivated and cultivable land, to the south. They also each had a *saltus*, or a more wooded area, to the north (figure 1.4). The long river that initially gave the peninsula its name, the Ebro, served for them as a fundamental point of reference in their dealings with other peoples, especially with their enemies.[11] But the Romans and the Carthaginians also at some point began using this river as a boundary for the purpose of determining their respective spheres of influence. Greek geographers would later contend that it was in the upper course of the Ebro River that Roman civilization penetrated to the greatest extent, and thus that the populations that settled on its banks were those that already displayed a higher degree of Romanization by the beginning of the first century, AD. Afterward, the tribal image of the surrounding world gradually began to break up in somewhat irregular fashion.

Generally speaking, it is interesting to observe how Strabo's vision of the peninsula is based upon distinct stages of knowledge. His vision is, like the old errors, a cause of grave conflicts, and would come to be a burden on those who later had to correct them. Figure 1.5 is a schematic

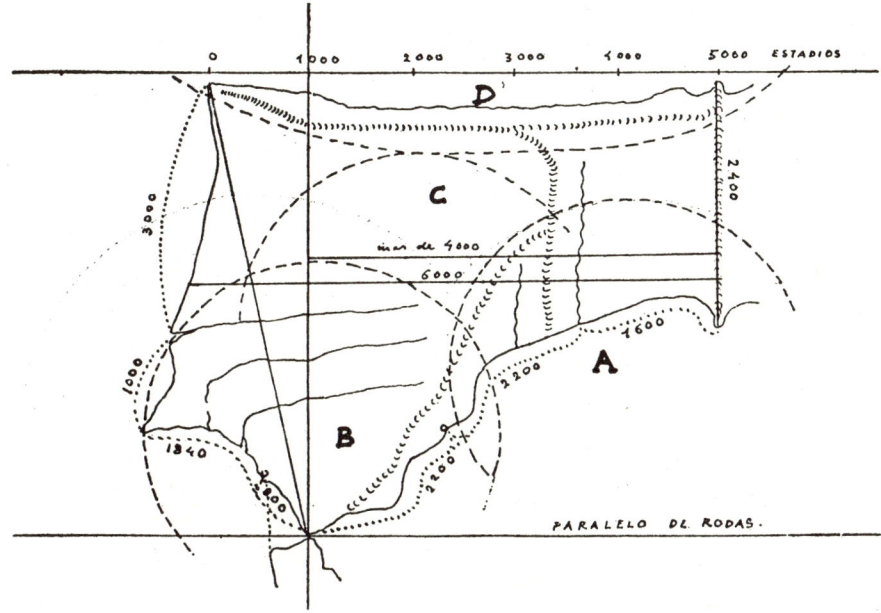

Figure 1.5. The Iberian Peninsula according to Strabo, with the four consecutive visions from the year 218 BCE to 19 CE.

depiction of Iberia according to Strabo, based on data drawn from various parts of his *Geography*, which were extracted from various sources. It is clear that his vision of the Ebro Valley and his conception of the position of the Pyrenees and the ocean in relation to the Mediterranean Sea harks back to the time of the first arrival of the Romans in Spain, and the common thesis of that era that, because the Pyrenees constituted a system that ran from North to south and not from east to west; the fact that the Carthaginians crossed these mountains constituted a threat to Rome and Europe of a somewhat different order than one would conclude on the basis of more comprehensive information. The first vision (A, in figure 1.5) is an awkward fit with the second vision of the south, and with the relative position of the Guadalquivir (Betis), Guadiana (Anas), and Tajo (vision B) in relation to one another. The northern section represents a faulty conception, It was only in Strabo's era that the remainder of the north was explored. Be that as it may, his description of the peoples that dwelled in the peninsula is, from a cultural standpoint, of immense value, since it depicts degrees and variations of the presence of the different populations. It can therefore be said that visions A, B, C, and D could easily be duplicated in time and space.

In the second century, Ptolemy enumerated all of the peoples using names that are more familiar to us than those used by Strabo. Afterward, well into the Middle Ages, there remained a memory of the existence of the Vascones and other peoples, but not of the Ilergetes. This fact is significant, and without a doubt reflects a lesser degree of persistence of tribal categories.[12]

Leaving aside the erroneous conception of orientation that prevailed throughout the Middle Ages, it is evident that other observations of the ancients are only accurate in a highly qualified sense—for example, the assertion that the Pyrenaic mountain range constitutes an ethnic frontier. The separation between Celts and Iberians was not delineated by mountains, which were rather far away. This is because, to the northwest, the ancient Aquitanians were for the most part more closely related to the Iberians than the Celts.[13] On the other hand, the Celtic penetration of Catalonia is such a widely established fact that it hardly needs to be argued.[14] Similarly, it is not difficult to show that, during the early Middle Ages and even later, the peoples of southern Gaul exercised a strong influence on Navarre, the Upper Aragon, and Catalonia.

IV

Although I in no way want to give the impression that I know things of which I am entirely ignorant, I do believe that, with respect to the humanities and history in general, and specifically as regards ethnography, it is possible to greatly advance our understanding by objectively studying the relationships in space and time of distinct societies, and the consequences of a specific relationship that has already been studied.

In this context, how is one to compare the conceptions and relationships of a tribal society with those of an expanding imperial power such as the Roman Empire, or with the Germanic peoples moving inexorably southward—or with the Islamized Arabs and Berbers.

A moralist with a very keen eye would have to once again examine the synthetic images that Seneca passed down to us regarding the movements of men in ancient times,[15] their motives, and the results of their actions. Historians have usually limited themselves to noting these matters for the record in their exposition. It should also be acknowledged that the explanatory remarks that they offered were rather shallow and formulaic.

We will return to an examination of the peoples who dwelled in the Pyrenees Mountains of the Iberian Peninsula.

The Romans to a large extent redefined the meaning of tribal organization by creating new administrative units, provinces, and legal jurisdictions, classifying population centers in accordance with legal categories of their own definition and placing the former reference units in one or another of the new jurisdictions. We can thus see that the world of which the previously reference zones formed a part was, from the time of Augustus to the beginning of the fifth century, different from both what it had been in the third to first centuries before Christ, but also from what it would later become at that defining moment in history when the great invasions took place, and when Hispanic-Roman populations, along with more or less indigenous peoples, fought against the Visigoths and the Franks over the course of several centuries.

Thus, a state of affairs that has come to be referred to as "Völkerwanderung" appears to be very distinctive in nature in reference to the surrounding world of a particular society. In addition, it is noteworthy that it is largely the descendents of German peoples—specifically, the descendents of those whose movements were aggressive and swift, and that covered large areas, who coined that word, and who later introduced the concept of "living space" in order to legitimate a number of undertakings to expand their boundaries. Be that as it may, the people or peoples who were perpetually in motion have their own way of interpreting the routes that they used—one that is in accordance with the notion of the existence of a number of different horizons. At the same time, this understanding is very fluid and is also determined by another notion, which has also been studied from a biological standpoint: that of the "magic path."[16] This term refers to a path that leads in single direction, with men or animals drawn by specifically defined stimuli or impulses. The fact that the movements of groups of animals prefigure those of human societies in certain cases seems to be beyond question. But, as always, the autonomy of the human species is, in this respect, wedded to a vast array of motives and stimuli that are difficult to reduce to simplified schemas.

The route taken by an invading people is unquestionably different from that of the sailor, fisherman, peasant, shepherd, wood merchant, or raft pilot.[17] In sum, it may be said that there are routes that men follow as a result of being guided by impulses that are ephemeral in nature, and that arise as a result of particular situations that may be either hostile or benign. The Way of St. James is an extraordinary example of what a spiritual pilgrimage has come to mean in Europe—a route that man has created at a specific historical moment, and that attained a popularity and attracted a widespread interest that later gradually diminished, yet not before exercising an influence on distinct spheres that, to all appearances, had nothing to do with one another.

Yet, apart from the "residual" character that certain human actions have for future generations, they are nonetheless meaningful in terms of the new ways that spaces become organized. In Spain, one of the most well-known historical phenomena is that of the *Reconquista*. This word inherently contains a schematic, spatial and temporal conceptualization which has come to be applied a posteriori, like that of the "Thirty Years' War" and so many other phenomena.

However, in general terms, the basic conclusions we can draw as a result of breaking down situations in terms of specific and relative times and spaces are as follows:

1. A sweeping movement of peoples with a common religion, from the east to the west and the south to the north.
2. A massive withdrawal of other peoples in the face of this advance, in cases in which they avoided being crushed by the onslaught.
3. A comprehensive constriction of the spheres of action of the peoples facing invasion, and a more immediate presence of the enemy in the context of a territorial constriction that represented a dramatic reduction of living space in comparison with both the tribal units of ancient times and—to an even greater extent—of the Roman administrative divisions.
4. A movement of reaction of these peoples driven into increasingly narrower spaces who once again gradually increased their sphere of activity and created new living spaces.

All of this is very well known in terms of both the political history of the Middle Ages and historical geography.

At the same time, it appears that none of these phenomena have given rise to any ethnographic speculation. We know the general lines of the successive stages of the *Reconquista*. In relation to the old territory of the Vascones as well as ancient Aragon, three different divisions or sections can be established (figure 1.6). Within these sections, certain designations that are meaningful in terms of spatial-temporal relations can be noted. One of these is "Extremadura," which was applied to the portion of the frontier not delineated by either the Duero[18] or the two provinces that retain the name in present times. These and other names, like *Old* Castile and *New* Castile; Old Catalonia and New Catalonia;

and others toponyms of the South such as Arcos and Jerez de la Frontera refer to a particular perception of the presence of the enemy. None of this means anything to the modern layperson.[19] And do they really have specific meaning for specialists? I really don't think so. In the first place, there is a marked difference among peoples in their understanding of any "extreme" expansion.

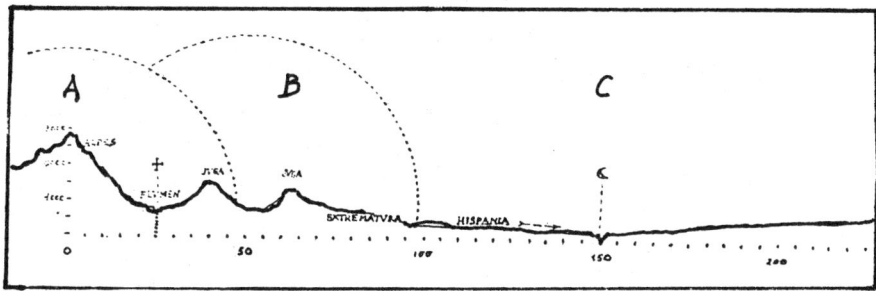

Figure 1.6. Primitive Aragon (circle A): from the peaks of the Pyrenees (called Alps in some texts), with the "flumen" (Aragon) and a pre-Pyrenean range ("iuga"). The first Reconquest (circle B) with the pre-Pyrenean range ("iuga") and *tierras nuevas* ("new lands") and "Extremadura." The Ebro Valley (and "Hispanis" properly speaking) under Island (C).

The will of the former inhabitants of the territory *to return in order to reconquer the lands they formerly possessed* is clear in the case of Navarre. On the southern boundaries, the Navarrese defined their border more or less along the same lines as their predecessors, the Vascones. The territory of Aragon, on the other hand, was separated from that of the Vascones and therefore had a different destiny. In the latter case, expansion did not end at the former boundaries. The initial sense of the enemy presence in the south is rather clear in both instances.[20] The enemy in both cases is beyond Pre-Pyrenees mountains.* But another important question arises: To what extent did the enemies, who arrived in a vigorous and continuous advance from the south to the north, establish their lines in reaction to the resistance they encountered, as opposed to their perception of the most agreeable sectors of the surrounding territory? There was one Arab historian who reported how little impressed the peoples arriving from the South were by Navarre, and how much of Northern Spain they were able to see.[21] For their part, Ambrosio de Morales and some other Spanish historians of southern or central Spain,

---

* The Pre-Pyrenees ranges act as a natural barrier and provide a sharp contrast of geographical zones from north to south. —ed.

who were uninformed regarding the physical environment of the Basque provinces and the north in general, seem to imply (not without what seems to me a certain degree of malice or hostility toward these regions' inhabitants) that, if the Muslims did not advance toward those areas, it was not because of any resistance that they encountered, but because of how uninviting the land was.[22] There is no need to argue about this matter: What is clearly evident is that the significant physical or cultural elements or stimuli are extremely important for understanding the struggle with and constituent elements of the enemy presence, *as long as we place them in proper historical perspective*. For this reason, it is necessary to impose a serious restriction on any theory of geographical determinism that is not structured in accordance with both historical-cultural and biological principles.

Perhaps historical-cultural is a rather vague and inadequate term. It is no less vague to speak of social issues in the abstract. Other words within the habitual lexicon of historians, sociologists, ethnologists, and folklorists may seem more concrete. However, there is a tendency to believe that terms taken from the physical and mathematical sciences are ipso facto "more scientific"—both in theory and in fact—and that they can be applied to the humanities, and most especially to sociology. For a long time, following the positivist era, there was a great deal of talk about things like crystallizations, segments, social pressures, and so on. The time has perhaps arrived to use more precise biological concepts.

V

For example, in accordance with the cases under study, we can affirm that the notion of "enemy presence" exercises an effect upon any social group—sometimes in a very threatening way and sometimes in a manner that is more symbolic in nature.

There are currently many expressions used in Spain for the purpose of expressing the animosity among neighboring peoples that do not obviate collaboration of different kinds among these selfsame peoples. We also know that, among contemporary rural inhabitants, who theoretically ought to be exhibiting a high degree of cooperation with their neighbors, there abides a great deal of enmity. The enemy presence is felt most especially among individual families without causing a great deal of disruption, and is also a reaction against collective thinking and feeling that is felt to be alien to one's own. But if we hark back to a somewhat earlier era, we see that this principle was applied in a different way. It is in this connection that fortified manor house of the fourteenth and fifteenth centuries that makes us wonder where the constructor of such an edifice saw the presence of his enemy. Potential enemies could well appear anywhere and from any direction, even if careful attention had been paid to one's area of geographical settlement—whether near a river, on a bridge, on a hill that overlooked a valley, or at the opening of a narrow mountain pass. The organization of a society of a particular time, and not its natural "medium" or "environment" were the most prominent determining factors for its choice of geographical settlement. And it is these selfsame factors that resulted in the disappearance of the previous form of social organization. Thus, the fortified family manor house became, as best it could, a farmhouse that was at times far from comfortable. We think of even earlier societies than those of the late Middle Ages in particular areas, in which we can observe the nature of the fundamental "enemy presence" and its possible rationale better than in other societies.

And here we once again observe the importance of the two lines of the *Reconquista* of Navarre and Aragon.

If we compare the surrounding world of the ancient peoples of zone under consideration here with that of their medieval counterparts (figures 1.4 and 1.6), we can see that, at the beginning of the *Reconquista*, the latter was severely limited in terms of its economic possibilities, given the immediacy of the *enemy presence*. With respect to ancient societies, a distinction can be made between those that were tribal in nature and those that were dominated by a strong state. In the tribal societies, the enemy presence is not as close as it was at the time of the *Reconquista*. Those earlier societies lived in an environment that can be thought of as varied. The enemy presence, on the other hand, was something subject to change, depending on treaties and alliances.

The most important task facing an ethnographer thus appears to be that of determining the physical surroundings where a given people at a given historical moment confronts its enemies. In other words, in terms of the cycles that the biologists to whom we've previously made reference established for species that struggle against one another, species whose survival strategies are determined by this struggle, the cycle of one's enemies—transferred to the human social sphere, is of fundamental importance, although at the same time subject to a different interpretation, on account of the fact that enmity among species differs from enmity among men. In the latter case, the external surroundings—where they are thought of as beginning and ending—are more fluid and historically variable. In this way, we see that history has a dynamic distinct from that of biology, which on the one hand complements and restricts it, but on the other hand reflects it. This is because the concepts of "struggle" and "enemy" are eminently interchangeable between the two fields, even though relations among historical enemies are fluid, and the varieties of enmity are widely varied. The notion of struggle among men extends to widely varying spheres, and the significant elements that determine ecological exploitation, and the kind of "spoils" that are available, are subject to change—sometimes at a dizzying pace.

VI

In the animal kingdom, it seems to be the case that the primary struggle unfolds in accordance with a kind of fate that pits one species against another. Spiders and flies, carnivorous and herbivorous animals, all live within a framework that, while hardly mechanical, is certainly inexorable. Apart from cases of the highly varied kinds of warriors, it can justly be said that man lives in perpetual struggle with his fellows. One example of this is the enmity frequently observed between shepherds and farmers. The debate over whether Spain should be an agricultural or a livestock-farming country has resulted in a great deal of conflict among Spaniards over the course of previous centuries.

Another thing that should be remembered in this connection is the hostility—both cultural and otherwise—that existed in sixteenth century Aragon between "old Christians" on the one hand (who were dry-land farmers and cultivators of grain) on the one hand and converted Moors (who grew plants and worked irrigated and fertile lands). These two groups of people held distinct economic conceptions of life—conceptions that were as different as their religious ideas. There was a general and pervasive mutual hostility between these two groups.

What can one say, then, of previous eras, when those who dwelled in the Pyrenees and the lands just south of the Pyrenees lived in their cramped and constricted lands across from the plains that were the domain of Islam!

In the previous scenario, the Christians dwelling in the north did not have access to the entire course of their rivers (as had been the case before, and as would once again be the case in the future) and were also not able to drive their flocks and herds southward during the long and harsh winters. It is difficult to imagine life in the Pyrenees, Erronkari (Roncal), Hecho, and other similar valleys with raft pilots who could not reach the Ebro, and with shepherds unable to make use of not only the northern reaches of Extremaduras, but also the pasturage of the Bardenas and of lands farther south. The complexity of the situations in which men found themselves in those times requires us to eschew any mechanical notion of their behavior. And in this connection, it must be said that the label of "mechanical" applies to any interpretation that conforms to rigid laws, whether of a physical or social nature; eliminates any consideration of cultural change; and does not take sufficient account of the depth and temporal significance of the material under investigation. The articulation of the elements in the life of men is rather autonomous. Each human group acts in a different way: colonizing Romans; Carthaginian warriors; Greek merchants and intellectuals; Vascones of the plains; Vascones of the forest; Aragonese of the ancient county or Aragonese living away from their homeland. Each of these groups lives in accordance with different economic, legal, and religious rules. In this connection, it is important not to lose sight of the role of religion in shaping their vision of the world—even in a spatial sense. It is important to remember here that a Roman grammarian, Festo, defined "religious" in terms of the practices of one's own city, and "superstitious" in terms of the practices of those living elsewhere. This is a point that has frequently been made.

In this connection, one would do well to remember that the Cantabrians stoned those who had killed their parents outside of certain designated boundaries within which the essence of the most direct and intimate blood relationship was thought to reside. The weight of many diverse attributes ascribed by pagans to their natural surroundings is perhaps greater than that of Christians. In this regard, however, it is possible to conduct research that can go a long way toward clarifying the nature of the enemy presence within a specifically religious context.

VII

Some social anthropologists claim that one of the characteristics of social life that is clearly revealed by research is the fact that, while individuals perish, structures endure. I find such an assertion difficult to understand in the light of the findings of ethnological and historical research. Individuals perish—well and good. Structures do endure longer, but they also change and they also eventually disappear. In this regard, the mechanistic view of utilitarian functionalists is not in the least helpful, not even the biological analogs with regard to a plan ("Bauplane," in von Üexkull's sense) or evolution (in the sense of Darwin and others). Instead, we must turn to more complex explanations that are inherently less mechanical than those conceived by so many thinkers within the fields of sociology and anthropology. In our country, structures have endured for a fairly long time (longer than individuals) and then have disappeared. The same thing happened with lineages. These changes were accompanied by changes in the notion of the enemy presence. A major problem confronting the ethnologist is the study of the enduring influence of these modes of organization. This is another problem that cannot be resolved by employing a few simplistic criteria such as, for example, "survival" or "change of meaning." No. As always, the matter is much more profound and much less clear. Let's examine some examples that are in part taken from situations that we've discussed above.

We previously indicated that the province of Gipuzkoa attained its current shape at a particular moment in time. This shape encompasses other shapes that are a history of human habitation the effects of which can still be seen, but which was considerably more visible some forty or fifty years ago.[23]

A valley, a river basin, a bridge, a medieval tower attached to a bridge and overlooking it, houses clustered around a church or a hermitage, a windmill or a rural workshop—even a foundry. In the distance, various demarcation lines, houses isolated in the mountains, and small villages with similar characteristics. Such a landscape was "typical" from the fifteenth through the nineteenth centuries (figure 1.7). It took shape during an era in which every lineage tower of these villages either held dominion over a territory or aspired to do so, and in which such towers controlled a bridge, and had the use of a windmill and even a foundry. The owners of these towers were enemies of some of the owners of nearby towers and the friends of other tower owners. The violent circumstances reflected by this distribution of towers no longer obtained by the end of the fifteenth century. Though mutilated, the tower still survives. Some of the former economic privileges also still remain, while others, such as port and bridge tolls, have vanished. The church no longer functions as a patron, and the particular crops that are grown and the minerals that are mined have changed. Be that as it may, the form of the society does still remain, and it exercises a determining influence on those who *live their lives within social organizations that are different from those that gave rise to that particular form.*

Let us examine a different case. During the early Middle Ages, a district was carved out that was called the county of Álava, the shape of which will be familiar to all. This county was transformed into the

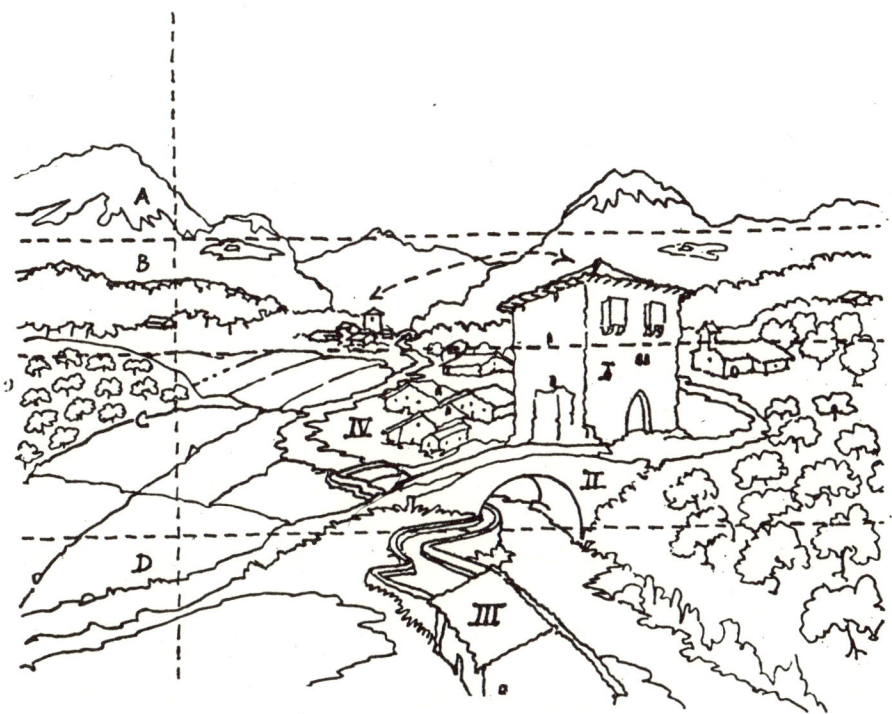

Figure 1.7. Schema of the Gipuzkoan countryside with medieval elements: (a) highland or mountain, (b) intermediate countryside, (c) the main productive lands, and (d) lowlands. The tower (i) dominates the road and bridge over the river (ii). On the banks of this last is found the mill or ironworks (iii) with the urban nucleus alongside (iv).

contemporary province of the same name (Araba) by means of a series of expansions. Scattered throughout this territory are settlements and valleys, a multitude of villages that had perhaps already been established during Roman times, and that *today* have all but disappeared. Upon the ruins of these places, other settlements comprising larger towns have arisen as a result of considerable effort. These newer settlements are the product of comprehensive planning. Now if we consider the old form of rural organization, we can conclude that the county was for a long time organized in accordance with a particular schema consisting of an eastern and a western sector.

Two sectors, an eastern and a western, are depicted. The eastern sector is dominated by one lineage, and the western sector by another. Each of these lineages has an imposing fortification, and each also overlooks demarcation lines and bridges. A market is located on intermediate ground. The new planned population centers diminish all of its economic

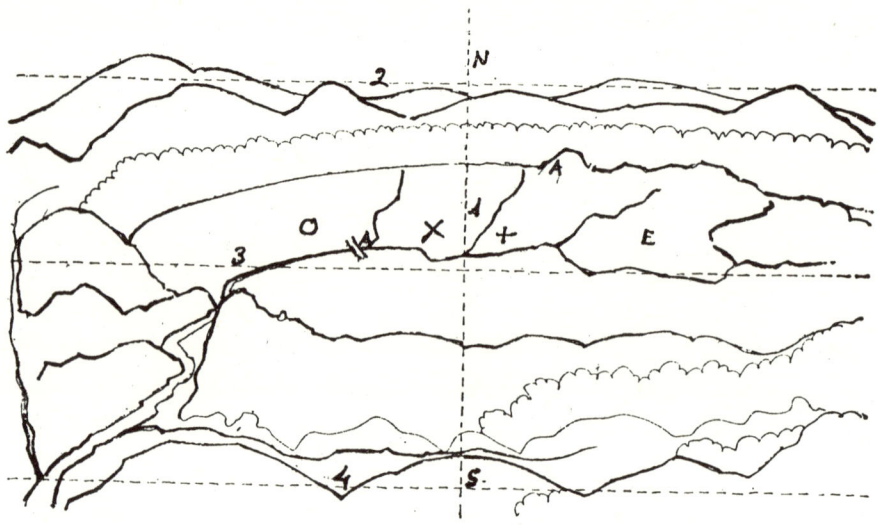

Figure 1.8. Schema of the organization of Araban territory during the last centuries of the Middle Ages with two orientation centers: eastern and western. Numbers 1, 2, and 3 refer to strategically important openings. "A" refers to the seat of the Oñacino band (Mendozas to the west), and Gamboinos (Guebaras to the east). "X" refers to the point of meeting of the bands.

significance, although it continues to have religious importance (figure 1.8). The characteristics can be observed today on the land, the old organization having left its mark in a way that is unmistakably deceptive. The phrase "adaptation to the medium" would be an optimistic characterization. "Submitting oneself to the weight of tradition" is of a similar ilk, though with a different conceptual underpinning.[24]

But let us continue. In many parts of the unirrigated portion of Spain, from Navarre south to Andalusia, there are towns of a particular character that conform to the following schema (figure 1.9). In the bend of a river, or perhaps at the confluence of two rivers, walled urban settlements that have arisen. These settlements were more or less planned, divided into parishes or precincts, and with a rising high above them. These settlements overlook the fertile plain of a river, along with its bridge and one or more "outlying districts," a zone of orchards and another zone of olive groves or small or large areas of unirrigated cultivation. This form is an old one, and well suited to eras in which particular notions of the enemy presence were more prevalent than they are today. This may or may not be on account of the boundary between Christians and Moors, or between different Christian kingdoms and rival lords, and so on. Peoples lived in this way until the twentieth century. Yet by the eighteenth century and in some cases even before, castles began to *fall into ruin*, outlying districts began to *expand*, and new tensions arose.²⁵

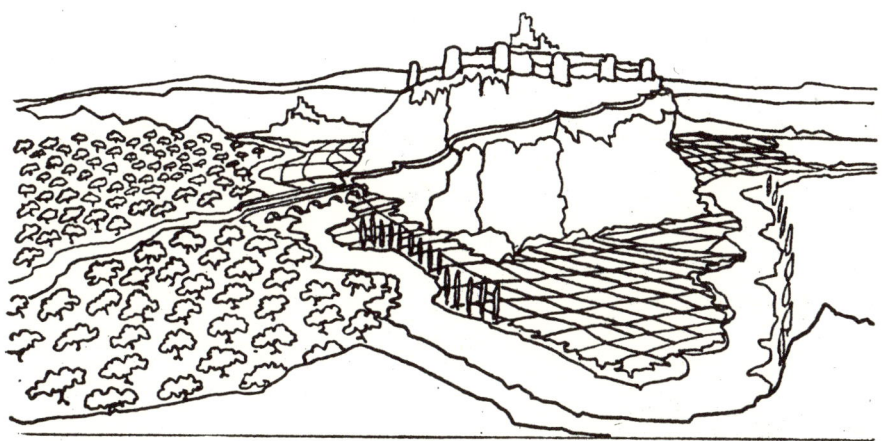

Figure 1.9. Schema of the Mediterranean-style fortified town made of stone, constructed above a river bend, with olive trees, irrigated land (gardens), and cereals production.

It would be overly harsh to tell those who live on high ground that they are "survivors," and any assertion that the meaning of their people had changed would be fraught with ambiguity. The material weight of the past has many other facets, and this can be shown in many different examples. We will now examine a southern coastal people (figure 1.10). On the coast itself, alongside the beach, we find a small port. Then there is a "cavity" with a vast area of planted crops. In one area of this cavity there is a rocky mound where the main settlement area has been established, with its church, castle, and fortifications. Then there is the cavity, which comprises a rather extensive area until the point where the land rises, surrounded by mountains, and with imposing peaks visible in the distance. In this connection, I think of the towns on the coast of Granada and Malaga, which were founded so many centuries ago: Almuñécar, Salobreña, and so forth.

If there is any case in which the significant elements have changed, it is in these instances. It can still be seen how the early town was not only established on high ground but also, as it were, with its back turned to the sea. The "enemy presence" was in the sea itself, mainly because of the threat of pirate incursions. Today, on the contrary, the trend is to face the sea, and what was once the primary source of agricultural wealth—

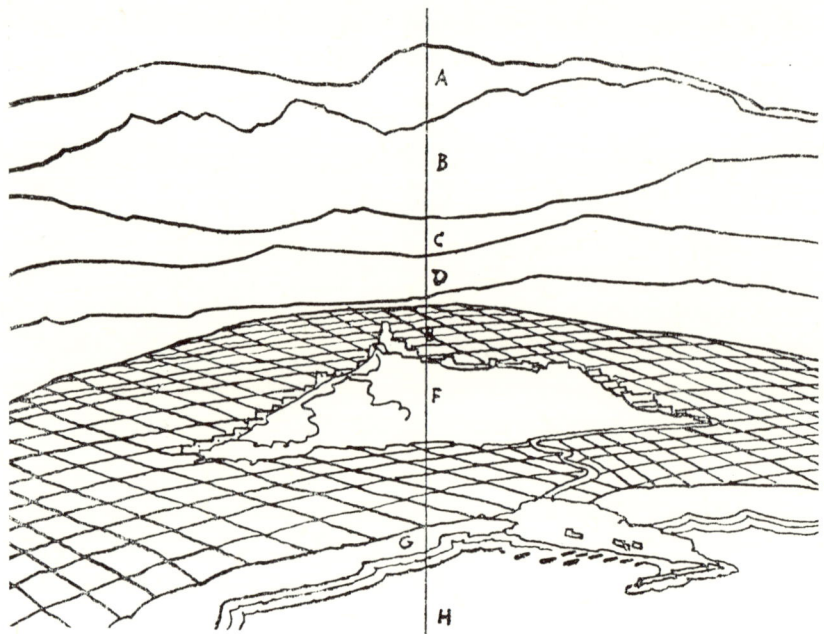

Figure 1.10. Schema of a Mediterranean Andalusian maritime town: (a) Mountains with perpetual snow, (b) lower and nearer mountain zone, (c) transit zone, (d) dry lands, (e) land irrigated for tropical crops (sugarcane, etc.), the *hoya*, (f) urban settlement, (g) beach and port, and (h) Mediterranean sea.

the cavity with its sugar cane and other irrigated crops, has steadily lost importance relative to the tourist industry.[26] Nevertheless, it is also true that people have lived in the "historic center"—not for centuries, but for millennia, just as people have lived in accordance with many past forms of organization. Thus, it is important to study the phenomena in question without being blinkered by simplistic and crude criteria.

And thus, in this same southern region and amid the landscape of giant mountains which we have described above, we find peoples that can be described as "hanging" on very steep slopes and at surprisingly high altitudes where there is very heavy snowfall, and which have terraced houses made of clay instead of the dwellings with sloped roofs that can be found in other mountain settlements.[27] A similar phenomenon can be observed in the Atlas Mountains.[28] Both in Andalusia and Morroco, the distribution of terraces and roofs is along geographical lines that have little to do with "medium" per se. It is even possible to point to the weight of "tribal traditions" to explain it, as is done in so many other instances.

The explanation for the distribution of any given territory according to a genealogy or lineage harks back to biblical times, and the settlement of the twelve sons of Jacob, who were the progenitors of the twelve tribes of Israel. The same pattern was followed in lesser-known instances. It was the "sons of" who appear to have adhered to such a form of organization in the tribal organization of northern "white" Africa beginning in pre-Islamic times. It serves many different purposes.

There are a number of vestiges of such a system of organization in Spain, especially in its toponymy: names of Valencian, Murcian, and Andalucian towns that contain the prefix "Bena-" or "Beni-" followed by a proper noun.[29] There are other cases in which the toponym is more problematic. Let's take a look at a map of the irrigated lands of Murcia,[30] according to the schema of D. F. Botella y Hornos. In it, we can see:

1. A large irrigation ditch leading from the river or another natural channel.
2. A number of secondary ditches.
3. A number of "tertiary" ditches.
4. Ramifications of the tertiary ditches (figure 1.11).

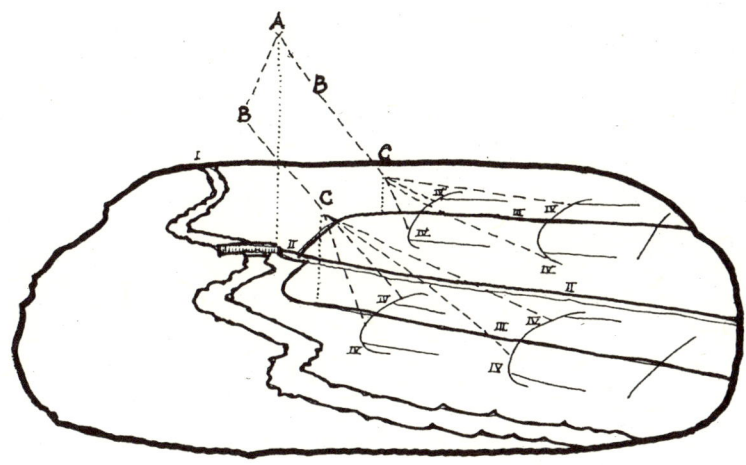

Figure 1.11. Schema of Murcian irrigation: (i) natural channel and flow, (ii) main aqueduct, (iii) secondary aqueducts, (iv) tertiary aqueducts, and (v) first genealogical bases. "B" and "C" show the division into lineages that give rise to aqueducts with family names.

Why are Islamic tribal names used to designate the secondary and tertiary ditches? Can we conjecture that what occurred here is similar to what occurred in the case of the *cabilas*: a process of water distribution according to lineage and paternal blood relations? This is an issue that remains to be resolved by Arabists. If they do resolve it, it can still not be concluded that the Islamic tribal designations continue to be used for the orchard. Instead, it can only be contended that important tangible consequences of such designations can still be seen.

I will now conclude these reflections, which I think are useful for the purpose of ameliorating certain tendencies toward a mechanistic approach to anthropological research and, at the very least, to show that ethnology is a historical discipline that does not simply consist of the preliminary gathering of facts, but that has its own reason for being—something that seems to have unfortunately eluded so many people between 1940 and 1970. Those of us who began our studies earlier were not so complacent with regard to our theoretical approach, and were not so haughty in our adherence to dogma.

VIII

The pride I am referring to here is that which results from feeling that one has arrived at a quintessential theory—that one has attained a kind of "gnosis." Such pride carries with it a mutually dismissive attitude among different theoretical schools. I have at times heard anthropologists and field researchers contemptuously announce that they were not interested in the "material culture" of the region that they studied, and that the most they were willing to do was assign the task of compiling a kind of "inventory" or "catalog" to a subordinate that could be used as an appendix for their speculations of a higher order. This kind of thinking seems to be one of the many aberrations that have resulted from the same teaching methodology, arising from an overrating of the "subject" and a kind of laziness when it comes to classification. In the final analysis, what does "material culture" really mean? How can one speak of functionalism, structuralism, or any other theory without having a clear understanding that the material world and the spiritual world of human beings cannot be separated from one another when it comes to either fieldwork or theoretical speculation? This is because "material," if you will, is what comprises the physical environment where one lives. Other things that are "material" are work tools used by the people under study, as well as the animals and plants of their environments. All of this, of course, in addition to the men and women themselves. A purely "technological" study is nothing less than another mental aberration.

2

The Basque Country, 1500–1800

The subject of this chapter is, in my opinion, most critical, given that it involves a large and varied number of topics that need to be properly dealt with but that, given the limited space at our disposal, will be somewhat difficult to deal with in a clear and coherent manner.

In any case, taking as a point of departure the two aspects of life of both the country and its people, insofar as its "rural," "urban," and "industrial" norms as depicted throughout the Middle Ages and the beginning of the modern era, we need to provide some general ideas regarding the research that ought to be undertaken regarding the specific state of affairs during the sixteenth, seventeenth, and eighteenth centuries.

Each moment, each period of time (even if it has not yet been defined), has particular problems.

The future can never be explained in terms of the present and, at any given moment, one can never be sure of what is going to happen in the future on the basis of the data currently available. However, the present can often be explained in terms of the past. Yet sometimes, while the past sheds an illuminating light on the present, it comes to be distorted by virtue of being seen solely in light of the present.

The interests of modern individuals are tied to those of yesterday. Yet the contemporary individual struggles to truly understand the "present" experienced in the "past."

What was the present for Basques at the beginning of the sixteenth century? What about the seventeenth century? These are technical problems that must be resolved by professional historians.

Today, we explain all of these presents in light of the past: this is to say, in light of what interests us about those presents and in light of the later fruits of the activities conducted during those times that we are aware of. Yet I reiterate that we must always be aware of the fact that everything has its own time and its own "present," and we have no right to infer conclusions or to posit consequences unless we have researched the living space and the living time of each generation and of each group in terms of its own struggles. In the same way, to do full justice to the current experience of each of you as individuals, we would need to examine your own concerns, not in terms of the past of your parents and grandparents, or the future of your children, but by focusing on the here and now.

The difference in circumstances among different eras appears to be quite marked whenever we conduct any sounding or survey of the country in distinct eras.

We have many of the elements we need to understand the situation at the beginning of the sixteenth century. These elements—from the testimony of writers to laws and social and economic documents—give the impression that the writers believed there had been a significant change from to the fifteenth century and before. In the preamble of the *Fuero de Vizcaya* and other legal texts one finds evidence that men at the beginning of the sixteenth century clearly understood their present to have a more highly developed legal culture, which was able to construct more cogent arguments than in the past, when the lack of culture was evident for all to see.

Furthermore, the accounts of the country's historians reveal that the force of lineages and bands had clearly been compromised, and that, even though these entities were still meaningful, they were neither as important nor as efficient as they had been previously.

On the other hand, given the situation of Europe and of the world as a whole, the Basques, who were noted for their mobility and seafaring throughout the Middle Ages—activities that led them to discover waters ranging from the northern seas to the eastern reaches of the Mediterranean—redoubled their efforts in this regard. We thus find (and, here again, one must distinguish between the people and the country) that there are many Basques who conduct much of their activity *outside of the country*.

In speaking of the Basques, or the meaning of Basque history, we must thus first and foremost establish a fundamental distinction between the activities of Basques within their traditional living space and the activities of Basques outside of their homeland, in contexts that are entirely different and singular, even during the Middle Ages. For if we see the Basques repeatedly represented during the Middle Ages as warlike and seafaring, by the end of the fifteenth and the beginning of the sixteenth centuries—and to an even greater extent afterward—another activity must be added to the two previously mentioned because of its inherent potential political and social consequences. Esteban de Garibay would later write in characterizing the people of his race and land that, apart from being warriors, sailors, blacksmiths, and men of action, Basque men also had a natural predilection for "affairs of the quill." What were termed "affairs of the quill" in the sixteenth century are not exactly what we would think of as literary activities. Basques who showed a proclivity for such affairs could therefore not exactly be thought of as poets, dramatists, or writers. Instead, they were men who conducted business using specialized knowledge ranging from calligraphy to accounting. And thus, in a country bereft of universities, secondary schools, and large university-like institutions, what we might call basic instruction was cultivated all the more intensively. Basic instruction in the Basque Country is a subject that has not been adequately studied. It is a level of instruction that depended on sanctuaries and on rural notary and clerk's offices. It involved plucking boys from the towns and even from villages and training them not only to write in Spanish, but to also draft public documents in proper calligraphic style: beautifully, elegantly, and intelligibly. Moreover, the accountants and others who did the training also taught their charges how to keep books, make entries, and provide that type of specialized knowledge.

Garibay himself writes of his early training, and writes of the scribes who first taught him the alphabet. He also explained what the sanctuary of Santa Catalina de Badaya in Araba (Álava) meant to the Gipuzkoans who resided on the border with Araba—and to the Bizkaians who resided in the south of Bizkaia—as regards such activities. Garibay informs us that, in this urbanized world of small towns that are considerably smaller than those of other parts of Western Europe, there is a high priority ascribed to the teaching of boys born into completely Basque families who know their own language quite well, but who also learn Spanish as an academic discipline, and with a higher degree of rigor than students in Castile itself. This notion of the Basque people, who bear the burden of their own distinct language and who supposedly express themselves poorly in their second language of Spanish, is one of the many commonplaces that one hears bandied about. It is also a characterization that doesn't really make a great deal of sense if one has a proper appreciation for the bourgeoisie of the Basque provinces from the sixteenth through the nineteenth centuries. The best evidence of the equivocal nature of this stereotype is the fact that, in disproportionate numbers, the most prominent authors of treatises and teachers of Spanish calligraphy are Basque. The activities of such men transcended the boundaries of Basque country: Juan de Iciar, Madariaga, and other great calligraphers—all the way up to Iturzaeta—did not live in the Basque Country. Yet these men continued to steadfastly uphold the notion—which can be characterized to some extent as democratic—of the irrelevance of class and social status to the importance of acquiring a basic education. Such an attitude constitutes a pointed defense of the individual, because the boys in training accompanied the functionary, with his calligraphy and knowledge of mathematics, to the court or to foreign cities. The boy apprentices also assumed the role of pages and, with their specialized knowledge, were able to attain positions that encompassed a body or system of knowledge. It was thus that, as can be seen in a famous passage of *Don Quixote*, there was a time when people inevitably thought of a *"vascongado"* or *"vizcaíno"* (Basque, according to the usage of the times) when they thought of those who served in the role of secretary, accountant, or men to whom were entrusted important business matters. In this way, as I have said, a discrete group of persons constituting a highly important component of the bureaucracy of the sixteenth, seventeenth, and eighteenth centuries came to be formed by Basques in far-flung areas: from the Americas to the Habsburg Empire and Flanders. They could be found everywhere. They were thus enabled to assume important roles not only in business, but also those of a private, delicate nature.

This state of affairs gave rise to all manner of encomiums singing the praises of the efficiency, loyalty, and honesty of these men of the quill. Garibay himself, and later many others, proposed something similar to Lope Martínez de Isasti in the *Compendio historial de Guipúzcoa* (Historical compendium of Gipuzkoa), which includes a long list of functionaries and persons of all classes who are dedicated to the secretarial tasks and the economic management of the vast interests of the crown during the fifteenth, sixteenth, and seventeenth centuries.

The new lists can be used as a compass for anyone seeking to conduct research on families, groups of shipbuilding contractors, and businessmen of various social classes who had ties to the state in those times.

This scenario has also given rise to malicious notions of the historical role of Basques. For example, the canon of Llorente, in a collection of documents on the Basque provinces that was published in five volumes during the reign of Charles IV of Spain, which interpreted the *fueros* as institutions reflecting the grace of the crown rather than popular freedoms, privileges, or exemptions, added to this important collection of papers a list of the notable Basque figures who held high office during those centuries. Thus the questionable hypothesis is introduced that it was the importance of these gentlemen in the royal court, in the most important tribunals of the state, in government offices, and in secretariats that bolstered these concessions and resulted in the granting of these favors.*

This is not true, but in the end, whether or not it is true, the role of this restless Basque on the *outside* is also important for understanding part of what has been termed the country's *wealth*, since the wealth of a comfortable family and the physical wealth of its land are two different things. In order to thoroughly appreciate the breadth of this distinction between outside and inside, much more thorough research is needed. We must go beyond the rather naïve viewpoint of the Gipuzkoan historians such as Isasti and others who have listed admirals, secretaries of state, bishops, generals, and so forth. What we need to know is what the entry of Basques onto the world stage during the great enterprises of the fifteenth to the eighteenth centuries actually means, in social and economic terms, for good and for ill.

The concern of some influential men of that time regarding the internal political and economic situation of the Basque provinces is evident. Furthermore, it is important to note that their *interests* and their *theories* often clashed with those of insiders. There is discord in the interpretation of what should be going on in the country between the views of Basques living abroad—whether Idiáquez, the royal chronicler Esteban de Garibay himself, or some other high-ranking functionary of Philip II—and what is answered in the country regarding the Directives of the Seignoir, or those of Gipuzkoa or Araba. This is because, at times, Basques living abroad tended to exalt the dignity and majesty of the land, and this was something that Basques living within the homeland found rather scary. For example, not very long ago, there was talk of how much honor it meant for Gipuzkoa to have had the title of a kingdom. And, in fact, some Gipuzkoans who were at court in Madrid during the reign of Philip II wanted to restore the designation that had been applied ever so briefly and sporadically. In Garibay's memoirs, there is a very interesting chapter in which he describes how he was involved in these negotiations

---

* Referring to the Basque fueros, or special charters. —ed.

and how he came to find—much to his surprise—that the Gipuzkoans rejected the title of kingdom. They contended that they had never been a kingdom and that they had no desire to be a kingdom. It is clear that such a circumstance gave rise to the evaluation of titles in social and economic terms, because many cautious and clear-sighted people came to the conclusion that, if a province were to become a kingdom, then it would be obliged to abide by all of the obligations incumbent upon a kingdom. And so they prudently reasoned as followed: Given that our province is small, and given that our internal economy gives us nothing but grief, it is better to remain a province—better to continue living in accordance with the dictates of a few canons and financial patrons who are already well established, rather than to harbor higher aspirations as a result of being lured by the bait of an honorary designation that might be nothing more than a dangerous trap.

Thus, in many instances, the interpretation of events in the sixteenth century differs according to one's point of view. The Basque Country clearly had some strong supporters on the outside within the social class that we are concerned with here and yet, at the same time, it found itself in the position of needing to defend itself from the points of view of Basques who lived abroad. On the other hand, this was a time of great prosperity and notable expansion that would continue for some one hundred years. During this time, no dire problems reared their head. On the contrary, there were a series of opportunities for progressive improvement. But even as early as the reign of Philip II, and later during the seventeenth century, during the era of the Habsburgs, the scenario began to change. The time of the great Basque courtiers had by then become a thing of the past—as had the prosperity of yesteryear. Instead, there was now a time of crisis in the Basque Country. The major crises that began during the reign of Philip III (even though one could see the approaching bankruptcy in the final years of Philip II) was closely watched and accurately predicted by a number of Basque observers.

I will not be discussing the particular observers in question in great detail. Yet it is important to remember that they included men who prophesied both the bankruptcy and the decline of naval power of the Spanish monarchy vis-à-vis the English monarchy and other powers. Many of these observers (some of whom were very important figures, most notably General Zubiaur) are Basques who lived not only outside the Basque Country, but outside Spain, who were prisoners in England, and who were able to witness first-hand the actual conditions in the competing states.

This kind of man, who takes account of the actual situation on the ground, is very typical of Basques, as we will see when we discuss naval matters.

But within the country there were signs of unrest even in the seventeenth century, specifically during the time of the Count Duke of Olivares. This unrest was caused by a phenomenon that would be observed with increasing frequency: the opposition and antipathy of many elements of the monarchy to the autonomy of the Basque Country, the fact it could draw up its own legislation, to the special nature of the Basque provinces in contrast to other lands within the monarchy.

Around the time of the Bilbao uprisings in 1634, there was a great deal of uneasiness in Madrid regarding the future of Bizkaia, and many Basques (or persons of Basque origin) who were close to the court analyzed, and gave their opinion of, the situation that was unfolding. For example, Antonio de Mendoza, a secretary working in the time of Philip IV, was asked to draft a report on the situation, and he gave several speeches reflecting an idiosyncratic and highly debatable view of what was going on that are, nevertheless, an unmistakable indication that something was indeed taking place.

This courtier, a descendent of the distinguished Mendoza family, who lived in Madrid, and who can best be thought of as being disaffected from the Basque Country rather than as being exiled from it, is an illustration of the declining importance in the land of the old lineages of factions. This helps explain the decreasing numbers of those loyal to the monarchy. Viewing the factions as the most loyal elements of the monarchy is somewhat debatable and, in the end, beside the point. Be that as it may, in Mendoza's view, the old families were, for example, closely connected to past history, to the relationship between the kings and the Bizkaian nobility. Mendoza considers the general decline of these families, and their concomitant loss of social and economic influence, to be critically important, and he provides a number of examples of members of such families who live isolated and forgotten in their homes. He concludes that this state of affairs has resulted in the country losing a direct connection with the monarchical institutions.

On the other hand, there is another matter worthy of detailed analysis and historical research, and that is Mendoza's assertion that Bilbao held a place of primary importance among the nobility of Bizkaia. In his view, it is not a matter of the nobility itself possessing great political importance, but rather of the most powerful city exercising a very high degree of pressure. This city, he adds, is one that had become a home of many outsiders—both strangers and foreigners. He does not say from where these people arrived. What he does say is that those who controlled the fate of what could be called the "humble" or "inferior" classes were those who held real economic power, and that these persons had ties—including blood ties—with England, Holland, and other lands.

It is evident that this view of Bilbao as a town that enjoyed a certain degree of autonomy within the dominion of Bizkaia, that contained a certain foreign component, and that had ties to important foreign commercial endeavors, was one that was prevalent in the seventeenth century. These generalizations and written observations from the pen of a Madrid courtier would seem to be worthy of research that would evaluate, qualify, and specify the extent of their accuracy.

The criticism of the social and political role of the Basques in affairs outside of Basque territory during the tense period following the time of Olivares has been remarked upon in various books and pamphlets, and in works such as *El buho gallego* (The Galician Owl), which Don Andrés Mañaricua is currently studying with his customary meticulousness and undeniable skill. This supposed influence was also the subject of works authored by Basque apologists in response to the criticism, which Llorente collected from earlier sources and which generally contended that the influence of Basques in Spanish life was excessive. Quevedo even wrote a satire portraying Basque secretaries, accountants, admirals, and others. Such figures were seen by Garibay, Isasti, and other writers as the most honest functionaries of the Austrian crown. Quevedo, on the other hand, saw such individuals as people who took in everything around them, and bitingly refers to what he calls "Cantabrian pen pushers."

I think that this aspect of the struggle, of the tension that prevailed during a time of political decline, must be studied in order to explain many of the events that transpired afterward. But, to return to our main pursuit here, which is that of viewing events within the context of their own times, I also think that there is a far more positive and important task: that of studying the activities and subsequent return to the Basque Country of those who have lived and prospered abroad, and the significance of these people within the internal economy. There are, I believe, two ways of attaining a comprehensive view of this phenomenon—both of which will require many years of careful research. One would be the internal and direct approach, taking as a point of departure lists of personalities, and which might also involve writing biographies of many of these individuals. However, as is the case with all older societies (and even more so with Basque society), the Catholic religion is of primary importance. One might even say that there is no undertaking in such societies that does not have some facet that has to do with religion. In addition, I believe that, in order to understand the place of Basques both within the homeland and abroad, it is important to devote some significant effort to studying the guilds, brotherhoods, and religious groups in general in accordance with ethnic criteria. This might seem to be a rather abstruse and complicated matter, but in fact it is not. I will discuss this issue on the basis of research that I myself have conducted.

Many years ago, a priest from Navarre wrote a book on the brotherhood of San Fermín de los Navarros de Madrid, recording its history from its founding in the time of Charles II until the modern era. This is a brotherhood that is still in existence today.

By examining the lists of the earliest brothers, it is possible to get an idea of the role of Navarrese outside of their homeland since the founding of the brotherhood. In Madrid, one finds listed important merchants, large traders, influential functionaries of secretariats, some doctors, significant numbers of friars, an occasional clergyman. Later, in the viceroyalties of the Americas, there are records of brothers in Lima and Mexico City who in some cases held positions that were more important than those of their [Spanish] metropolitan counterparts.

An examination of the history of the brotherhood of San Fermín de los Navarros throughout the seventeenth and eighteenth centuries reveals the important social and economic role of Navarre in Spain during that time. I have previously authored a book titled *La hora Navarra del XVIII* (The Navarran "Time" in the Eighteenth Century), in which I stress the collective and individual importance of a series of personalities who are precisely those who emerge as figures of primary importance in a study of the religious brotherhood.

At the same time, the brotherhood of St. Ignatius was functioning in Madrid, and this brotherhood was also ethnic in composition. As was the case for the brotherhood of San Fermín (or for those brotherhoods that functioned that were devoted to the worship of San Fermín) the members were Navarrese (for obvious historical reasons) under the patronage of St. Ignatius. This saint was much closer in time to, and much more influential within, the modern world. The brotherhood of St. Ignatius comprised his countrymen—Gipuzkoans, Bizkaians, and Arabans. The documents produced by the brotherhood of St. Ignatius are much more difficult to find today than those of the brotherhood of San Fermín (there is still hope that they haven't been destroyed). To a great extent, they depended on *colegios* of the Society of Jesus in Madrid. When the dissolution and expulsion of the Jesuits was decreed, the papers of the organization ended up in various different institutions. It is therefore feasible to conduct a parallel study of the brotherhood of St. Ignatius, which would perhaps be more important than that of San Fermín, since the members of the former were drawn from three provinces, and those from the latter from only one. According to some of the directors of the brotherhood of San Fermín, the three aforementioned provinces are very closely tied to Navarre. Thus, in the eighteenth century, we can see that there was a kind of Basque-Navarrese solidarity outside of the Basque Country in two religious associations that represented Gipuzkoa, Bizkaia, and Araba, along with Navarre, and that carried out activities not only in Madrid but also in other parts of Spain, such as the large southern ports, as well as in the Americas.

In order to get a clear idea of the economic role of the Basques at this time, I think that the most direct and positive approach is to examine the list of the members of the brotherhood of St. Ignatius and to point out the most prominent personalities on that list: admirals, office secretaries, officials who would later, in the court of Philip V, once again assume an importance in the court of an order that the Basque secretaries of Philip II, and even of Charles I, had enjoyed. During the era of Philip V, Navarrese such as Goyeneche y Ustáriz, Bizkaians such as Quadra, and Gipuzkoans such as Orendáin (the Marquee of Peace) and others held positions of prominence in the court. The influence of these men had an impact on the Basque Country, because their actions directly benefited their homeland.

These findings could profitably be complemented by other indirectly related studies that might provide definitive information regarding the scope of this activity. Such endeavors could look to the work of Padre Tellechea in Gipuzkoa and Navarre as an example, and include studies of churches, convents, hospitals, markets, and charitable foundations established by men who gained their wealth in one way or another from the sixteenth through the eighteenth centuries.

According to general Spanish history texts, the era of Charles II was, from a political standpoint, a miserable and ill-fated period. From the social and economic point of view, however, at least in the Basque provinces and Navarre, it was not so miserable and ill-fated, given the number of monuments that were erected, and the extent of commercial activity carried out at that time—all of which reflects a genuine prosperity.

The completion of a chronological inventory of the aforementioned foundations and other elements that continue to form part of the lives of existing peoples, and the preparation of a chronological research program, would be activities that would shed a great deal of light on the relationship between the Basque Country and foreign lands during the period under consideration. Such matters have not been adequately studied with the needed degree of scholarly rigor.

We know a good deal about the end of the eighteenth century and the period of the Enlightenment. And yet we know very little about the particular character of the era that can be called the "pre-Enlightenment." We know little about the positive aspect of this era—of those people who were prosperous, who amassed great wealth, and who lived fulfilled lives. We know even less about those far greater numbers of people who toiled in obscurity.

Yet just as during the time of the Count Duke of Olivares there were the signs of tension reflected in the letters and speeches of Don Antonio de Mendoza and the correspondence of Jesuits, in the time eighteenth century of Philip V we find growing number of authors and texts that speak of a popular hidden aspect of the Basque psyche. This supposed secret element has always endured in a parallel archaic and primeval world that legitimated it and even privileged it vis-à-vis the more known aristocratic and pseudo-aristocratic world.

In this regard, the most important figure is Father Larramendi, who has gained increasing prominence in recent times. He is a theorist of egalitarianism who has also collected information regarding the opinions of previous eras and has explicated his findings. He has a fresh viewpoint of the Basque Country—one that is profound from the social standpoint. He is not one to trust in simplistic formulas such as "the reconstruction of the past." Rather, any individual must be analyzed in the context of his or her own time. Larramendi attempted to take as his starting point any individual action, an approach that reflects a rather idiosyncratic notion of equality. The usefulness of such an approach is debatable. An older contemporary of his whom he undoubtedly met, Don Juan de Goyeneche, utilized a similar point of departure, and ended up being a diehard capitalist whose progeny held titles and honors. Larramendi's praise for the humble classes of his country is nothing more than an intellectual stance that reflects his ideal. A more realistic approach lies along other lines.

There is another era which began with the outbreak of the War of Spanish Succession, and which was characterized by tensions, popular unrest, and struggles that can largely be explained in terms of the ideological issues that we are addressing here. But the life of the common people in the Basque Country during the eighteenth century has not been widely studied. We know of a number of instances of mutiny and of popular uprisings during the time of Charles II, but we know little of the true bases of the economy of the common people of the country during this time. From the little available information that exclusively refers to the mountains of Navarre and the Atlantic region, it is possible to conclude that there is a chapter of history that has been entirely unexplored: that which concerns the famines that occurred during the War of Spanish Succession. These serious famines have never been thoroughly studied. These famines were unquestionably advantageous in agricultural terms, as reflected in the observations of a certain priest from the mountain of Navarre in reports that have been conserved by the Academy of History, yet this is a matter that awaits further research.

Such documentation could not have referred to a purely local phenomenon, since it includes a general description of a crisis that the country as a whole was enduring at that time.

Whenever the subject of the eighteenth century in the Basque Country arises, we tend to think—sometimes with a certain squeamishness—of the Enlightenment of Charles II, of the *caballeritos* [little gentlemen] of Azkoitia (Azcoitia), of the shipbuilding companies and commercial development of the Real Sociedad Bascongada, and so on. What we don't give much thought to is the contrast or discord between that world, with its relative splendor and elegance, and which was rather well known, and the real life of the common people. It was only with the eruption of the grave crises under Charles IV and Ferdinand VII that the wretchedness that had previously been hidden finally emerged, and the actions of common people began to be properly recognized.

In reality, it was not the revolution or the Napoleonic invasions that dealt the most serious blow to the old regime and the old society, but an event that occurred earlier: the war with England at the end of Charles III's reign. The war with England entailed the collapse of the shipping industry and the ruin of the shipyards. Furthermore it brought about a crisis in the state of industry as a whole, and paved the way for a series of shattering disasters between the years of 1793 and 1876. We tend to think that our history comprises two important elements—a remote past and a more recent past. The reality, however, is this more recent past weighs most heavily upon the psyche of our grandfathers, fathers, and ourselves, and that has most significantly endowed us with the peculiar characteristics that we possess in modern times. The War of the Pyrenees, the Peninsular War, the War of the Hundred Thousand Sons of St. Louis, the Seven Years' War, the Second Carlist War: This series of wars within a relatively short period of time are what have most profoundly embittered the lives of the Basque people. And it is the experience of these wars, more than economic, sociological, or legal problems—or mere controversies, such as those we spoke of previously—that have most profoundly affected the Basque people. What I am referring to here is violence—the horror of war itself—invasion, the destitution of families. Yes, it is these products of war, from the War of the Pyrenees to the much more recent past, that have had the greatest impact on us. These wars entailed terrible technical and economic catastrophes, such as the destruction of the wood-based shipping industry, the ruin of the old foundry systems, and the fall of the American empire—the destruction of societies that had been systematically organized in accordance with the dictates of the ancien regime. It is profoundly moving to read the papers of the Brotherhood of San Fermín from the era following the War of Independence, papers in which it was proclaimed that hardly any reason remained for the Brotherhood's existence, since there were no members able to take on the tasks at hand. Given the lack of lifeblood to sustain the existence of this Navarrese ethnic and religious brotherhood, the situation in the Basque provinces must surely have been infinitely worse.

At what point can we end this drama, and just how important was it? These are not questions that I can summarily deal with here. I think that, in order to have some idea of the scope of the crisis, we must once again undertake a rather specialized study of some of its effects on the physical aspects of the country and the actions of its people. Such features have been modified over the generations, but have never displayed the characteristics of the kind of cataclysm or total revolution that was seen during the War of the Pyrenees and throughout the course of the nineteenth century.

Afterward, there was an era of prosperity and hope, but this occurred during a period much closer to the lifetimes of those who are still alive. What I propose here is that we continue to examine the more remote past, the centuries gone by, with respect to industry, technology, and the lives of all of Basque people who resided in the Basque Country. From such a study, we will be able to draw conclusions to explain modern turbulence—this era that seems to be characterized by industrial and technological progress but that does not follow the kind of identifiable pattern that can be discerned in the history of the people and its land from the fifteenth through the eighteenth centuries.

This study of eras and patterns is a fundamentally important task not only for historians, but also for economists and contemporary politicians. Still, it is important to recognize that the majority of politicians are for the most part ignorant of such matters, and that economists sometimes either overcomplicate or oversimplify the subject—a tendency that is more harmful still. But these are matters to be dealt with elsewhere.

3
Cultural Cycles and Basque Identity

I

For many years now, there has been a good deal of talk in many different circles within the Basque Country and abroad of *ethnic identities* as something that should be studied and practically defended—in short, as phenomena that are essentially political in nature. But it is also common, as far as I can tell, that the same notion of identity is interpreted in highly diverse ways, and that those parties that clash over competing identities either resort to highly diverse concepts, or consider only one aspect of the principle of identity.

"Identical" refers to "that which is the same" throughout its existence. Such a notion makes sense, especially in reference to an individual or being that has a body which is subject to a life cycle. I am identical to myself at ten years old, at thirty years old, and at eighty years old, if I should live to the age of eighty. Yet such a notion of identity also encompasses considerable and inexorable changes.

If we turn from living beings to languages, cities, and societies, we can make the same assertion. The Basque language is identical to itself so long as it exists, and so is the city of Iruñea-Pamplona identical to itself, and so is any community of inhabitants of any valley, as long as that valley has inhabitants. Yet once we accept this, we must also accept that "identity" or "identities" can be approached in two different ways: one *static* and one *dynamic*. Static observation turns transformations into abstractions, while a dynamic point of view acknowledges the movement inherent in any subject that we study.

The word *dynamis* arose prior to the development of the sciences, and therefore existed before any concept of "dynamics" as such. Dynamics is a philosophy that is applied not only to human, moral, intellectual, and physical efforts, but also to all other kinds of activities. If we speak of a *dynamic identity* in reference to a people, we are not inappropriately applying a calque of physics or mechanics, and we are also not following the positivist tendency to look exclusively to the physical and mathematical sciences for models of research in the humanities. Instead, all we are doing is accepting the notion that identity is subject to change.

The question before us, then, is how to study those changes in terms of an entity that is identical to itself—in our case, Basqueness.

For this purpose, we will begin with the reminder that those who have previously dealt with this subject have generally done so in terms of static principles of identity.

The first principle of identity referring to Basques and Basqueness, posited many years ago (and that many posit, or attempt to posit, today), is the Basque language.

It is not easy to write a history of this characterization in terms of language. One might even find antecedents of such a characterization in ancient texts (i.e., of authors such as Strabo and Pomponius Mela), which describe the difficulty of recording the names of the towns in the north of the Iberian Peninsula. References to the language can be found in the accounts of medieval pilgrims, and Scaliger referred to its unintelligibility. Mariana referred to the rustic character of the Basque language, and a saying became common in Spanish characterizing "Basque" as referring to anything so murky and confusing that it was impossible to understand. This saying was recorded in dictionaries published during the time of Philip V, and can be found in contemporary dictionaries as well.

From "the inside," what we find is that Basque speakers have traditionally drawn a radical distinction between their own language (*euskera, euskara, uskara*) and other languages (*erdera*), and between Basque speakers (*euskaldun*) and speakers of *all* other languages. One who speaks a language other than Basque is referred to as an *erdeldun*, a word which has much the same meaning as "barbarian" did for Greeks. The Basques thus defined both "us" and "the other" in linguistic terms.

Apart from these language-based indices of identity, there are others that also represent a collective creation. Such indices are, strictly speaking, what are called "collective representations" regarding the general nature of Basques as a whole. And these representations have served as the foundation for the construction of a plethora of commonplaces that have even become assimilated into the stock of knowledge regarding "the psychology of different nations." Commonplaces of a similar origin have arisen regarding Spaniards, Italians, Frenchmen, Germans, Englishmen, and others. Such commonplaces have been accepted as legitimate even by philosophers of the stature of Kant and Hume, as well as by other thinkers of the nineteenth and twentieth centuries. In reality, the kinds of collective representations being referred to here arise from two classes and sources that are completely different from one another.

The Basques have constructed some of their own collective representations throughout the centuries. Much could be written about these for the purpose of showing that they have notably changed over the course of time. Thus, the kind of Basque identity reflected in texts of the sixteenth and eighteenth centuries are certainly different from one another. Similarly, the representation of Basque identity in the first half of the nineteenth century is different from that of our own times.

On the other hand, the collective representations of Basques by their neighbors in Spain and France, and by travelers from more distant lands, not only differ from one another. In addition, each of these representations—considered separately—varies over the course of time. The Spanish representation of the Golden Age can be reconstructed on the basis of an examination of the writings of Cervantes, Lope de Vega, Tirso de Molina, Quevedo, and other luminaries. Any of these representations can be seen as essentially true and valid, according to the writer's judgment. Those foundational texts have been studied continually over the course of several centuries.

In any case, such representations also reflect a static image and communicate—in effect—that "this is what Basques are like."

A third kind of image is provided by the ethnographic and cultural studies that have been conducted by Basque and non-Basque anthropologists who have investigated the popular culture and social structure of the communities of the Basque Country from the end of the nineteenth century until the present time. As is well known, this kind of research has been conducted by important national figures, who have also studied both Basque archeology (especially prehistoric archeology) as well as the physical characteristics of the Basque people. Aranzadi began research that was later continued by his disciples, especially Barandiarán. Other researchers of diverse ages, some quite young, have continued along the trail originally blazed by Aranzadi. The activity of all these men is based on the premise that "Basque identity" can be determined on the basis of scientific study. Yet, to a large extent, this kind of work consists of the search for invariable characteristics within a single kind of setting—generally a rural environment.

II

Despite the fact that I find interesting all of these efforts to find the essence of "Basque identity" (not only the valuable scientific efforts that I've just referred to, but also efforts of a different sort, and that have a different foundation), I think that it is necessary to approach the subject by applying a method that clarifies certain fundamental aspects of the question itself. This is because I take as my own point of departure the ideas that I have set forth at the beginning of the present essay, and that can be succinctly summarized as follows: Every identity is dynamic—or, in other words, variable.

The problem that confronts us, then, is how to study the variability inherent within the concept of identity. To say that we should apply a historical method is a tautology. On the other hand, alternative kinds of methods (i.e., a strictly evolutionary method, in the orthodox sense of the word, or a historical-cultural method, in its academic form) hardly seem suitable to me.

Nevertheless, from the various concepts related to the historical-cultural method, we can extract a fundamentally important idea that we will utilize in a manner that is a dramatically different from the way it is typically employed. I refer here to the concept of *cycles*. This word was already being used by German historians at the end of the nineteenth century and the beginning of the twentieth. It was also used by ethnologists Leo Frobenius and Fritz Graebner, the former interpreting the concept one way and the latter another. Yet long before, the great Italian historian Giambattista Vico used the term as part of his brilliant conceptualization of history.

We will be using the concept of cycles here in a rather less ambitious manner than the above-mentioned authors. A historical cycle begins when something fundamental and new occurs that subsequently develops and then undergoes a process of decline until a new cycle begins that has certain characteristics that are different—perhaps dramatically different—from its predecessor. Within each specific geographical setting, and in reference to distinct human populations, cycles reflect both very striking dynamics, as well as realities that are not accounted for by familiar concepts such as evolution. Cycles sometimes seem to partially repeat themselves (this has at times occurred in Basque history). Others are very different from one another because the dynamic of each cycle is different, as we will also soon see.

Let us now explore the concept of cycles with specific reference to Basque history.

First Cycle

Let's begin with the first cycle, going back to the remote beginnings of our history, a time that has been reconstructed on the basis of sparse and highly uncertain data. We could well conclude that this first cycle ends with the Roman conquest of the northern lands of the Iberian Peninsula, at the end of the Cantabrian Wars (i.e., during the first decades of the first century AD). During this cycle, what is now Basque territory was shared by a series of ethnic groups (which should never be called tribes, as modern historians are wont to do). Thus, the concept of "ethnic affiliation" or "blood relationship" seems to have been more important to them than "territoriality." In other words, the existence of the Vascones, Varduli, Caristii, and Autrigones preceded in time the territories of Vasconia, Vardulia, and Autrigonia.

These peoples were distributed along an area ranging from the Bay of Biscay to the Ebro River (in some areas extending beyond the river). The Vascones drew a clear distinction between an *ager* with extensive agriculture and a *saltus* or woodland territory, which was their permanent stronghold. It appears that these peoples organized themselves in territorially based divisions and subdivisions (as the Cantabrians and the Asturians did), creating small settlements (on high ground whenever possible) that were fortified to a lesser or greater degree. Such groups must have had a weak economy based on shepherding and agriculture. It appears that they had goats and pigs, and that they fed themselves with acorns and crops that they cultivated using rudimentary implements. There also is evidence that women inherited property to a greater extent than men. In addition, it appears that there was worship of a lunar deity and of male goats. In sum, these societies appear to have lived in primitive and isolated conditions that intensified the farther northeast their geographical location was. In the mountainous subdivisions, pasturage may go all the way back to the time of the proliferation of dolmens.

Second Cycle

This period can be reconstructed with a greater degree of certainty, not only because of surviving Greek and Latin texts, but also because of inscriptions and archeological remains that have come down to us, in addition to linguistic evidence (i.e., based on such phenomena as currently spoken speech and toponymy).

The essential feature that marks the beginning and continuation of this cycle is the creation and use of general system of roads that contained a number of different hubs. The principal roads in this system were: (a) a paved road from Tarragona to the Bay of Biscay that passed through Iruñea-Pamplona and Oiartzun (Oyarzun); (b) Another road that stretched from Bordeaux to Astorga, passing through Orrega (Roncesvalles) as well as Iruñea-Pamplona (these two great highways were connected to other, secondary, roads); and (c) a road that followed the northern bank of the Ebro, and that bordered the Basque Country on the south.

Human settlements of some importance were established along these roads. Other previously existing settlements expanded in size. This seems to be the case in the far south for the towns of Cascante and Calahorra. This system of roads led to the development of towns and cities, immigrant settlements, and the introduction of Latin language and culture that, in the Ebro Valley, quickly replaced previously existing languages and cultures.

But Romanization was also evident in the central region of Navarre, in the plains of Araba (Álava), and on the coast. The Ptolemaic tablets include the names of ports and of discoveries that reveal the development of coastal shipping routes (especially those involving the coast of Gaul), as well as the export of minerals.

At the same time, a change was taking place in the organization of the way people lived. The primary objective of the Romans was to force people living in settlements on high ground to relocate on the plains. There were two reasons for this: to exercise a higher degree of control and to increase agricultural production. The origin of many of the villages of western Europe lies in such settlements, which began as estates or small towns that often bear the names of their former occupants, such as the Araban villages of Antoñana and Krispiña (Crispijana), as well as numerous others of masculine gender. Inscriptions have come down to us that can be compared and combined with these toponyms, some of which are even in Greek.

During the first and second centuries, this process continued. In the third century, there are signs here and elsewhere of a crisis. A crisis of far greater magnitude occurred in the fifth century with the invasion of

Germanic tribes. Mobility within the region was also adversely affected by banditry and peasant uprisings. Urban life grew more confined and impoverished, with some human groups disappearing in the fifth century or, later, in the eighth century, when the Arabs penetrated very far north in the peninsula.

Yet, in the end, the extensive process of Romanization had a profound effect.

Third Cycle

The third cycle may be conceived as beginning in the fifth century and ending in the tenth century. This cycle was characterized by retreat and fragmentation. First in the north, and then later in the south, it appears that both the Visigoths and the Franks were locked in continuous struggle with the Vascones. Mobility within the region, as well as Roman institutions in general, broke down completely. Entire towns disappeared. The south of the region was to a large extent separated from its northern component. The Visigoths briefly occupied Iruñea-Pamplona as well as lower-lying regions. The Arabs then later also occupied Iruñea-Pamplona, where they remained for a far longer period of time. This would have important linguistic and cultural consequences.

During the first half of this cycle, however, Christian culture of Roman origin persisted among certain bishoprics and cathedral towns. The oldest such cities are Calahorra and Cascante, in the south. Iruñea-Pamplona is also highly important in this connection, as is the northern city of Baiona, Lapurdum. Both of these cities were cultural centers, as were a number of very old monasteries in the Pyrenees that flourished for centuries and had great economic resources. Yet life remained essentially rural. Warrior families controlled villages, and churches functioned under lay patronage.

The old pagan names that had been given to the native inhabitants of the region disappeared by the ninth century, and there were no longer references to Vascones, Varduli, and so on. However, as part of the conclusion of this important phase—this backward movement that Vico characterized, in a highly generalized manner, as "a feral state"—a number of dynastic systems emerged, with kings that arose not from peoples or territories but from cities. Once more, Iruñea-Pamplona played an important role in this regard, because the Pyrenean kings were called "kings of Pamplona" much earlier than they were referred to as "kings of

Navarre." An analogous phenomenon occurred farther west, in Oviedo and Leon.

Rural populations seem to have grown exponentially, and many villages that exist today must surely have their origins in this cycle, as witnessed by names such as Barasoa (probably Barasoain —ed.), Beraskoain (Belascoain), Baternain (Paternaín), and so on. During this cycle, the Basque language appears to have become consolidated, and documents contain the first names and words that are in the form of the language that is used today.

Fourth Cycle

In a rather surprising manner that once again brings to mind Vico's notion of "occurrences and recurrences," the period of time beginning in the tenth century and ending at the conclusion of the fifteenth century witnessed a cycle that in some ways duplicated the second cycle described above. What occurred during this period, for reasons completely different than those of the second cycle was, once again, a notable broadening of the horizon. A new system of mobility was created, with the creation of numerous additional roads. In addition, there was an intense process of reurbanization. The new system of mobility was created largely as a result of the need for routes to allow visitors to reach Santiago de Campostela. Thus, the spur to development here was not imperial politics but was instead a religious impulse. The Navarrese kings showed an appreciation of the importance of this religious impulse. Two mountain passes in the Pyrenees brought visitors into Navarre on their way to the holy site. Both Navarrese monarchs and Castilian kings of the Navarrese dynasty of Ferdinand I ordered the construction of roads and urban way stations along those roads. Yet, in addition to the force of faith, there was another important causal factor in this phenomenon, and that was the growing awareness that general communication generated increased wealth for the kingdom by facilitating trade. The economic purpose of many settlements is clearly evident given that, when kings conceded municipal charters, fueros, and municipal privileges, they explicitly mentioned their economic purpose. It should be borne in mind that this extensive process of urbanization encompasses a number of different phases, each characterized by its own objectives and results. The first of these phases saw the creation of entirely new urban settlements along the pilgrimage route. Other settlements were created as extensions of—and yet separate from—small villages that already existed. These settlements were established by outsiders—for the most part, by "Franks" from southwest

France, who introduced new commercial practices and artisan techniques. These outsiders aroused the ire of the native inhabitants, resulting in localized conflicts. In some cases, actual civil war broke out (something that occurred in Iruñea-Pamplona. The Navarrese kings (especially Sancho the Wise) are responsible for the creation of other settlements in both border regions and in their domains outside of Navarre, such as the harbors of Donostia-San Sebastian, Laguardia (on the Ebro River), and Vitoria-Gasteiz, and perhaps also at Agurain (Salvatierra) in Araba. All of these developments were constructed in accordance with a rigorously conceived plan. Yet these places also were settled by foreigners, and thus also at times became sites of ethnic conflict, as was the case in Vitoria-Gasteiz.

It seems a reasonable inference that the separation of the kingdom of Navarre from the lands of Araba and Gipuzkoa and its union with the kingdom of Castile was in large part due to such conflict. Be that as it may, under the Castilian kings, both urbanization and the construction of new roads continued during the second phase. Both of these phenomena also continued to occur in Araba, accelerated in Gipuzkoa during the thirteenth and fourteenth centuries, and began in Bizkaia at a later stage. Thus, Bilbao is a fairly modern city.

The fueros indicate that the native inhabitants often gave their blessing to the foundation of settlements, which involved the concession of privileges such as various monopolies, markets, and so forth. In this way, more planned towns arose, with names that were also used in other parts of the peninsula, as well as in France and Italy: Segura, Mondragón, Salvatierra, Villafranca, Miranda, Belmonte, and so on.

III

The consequences of these distinctive dynamics are evident. Basque ports became increasingly important, especially during the course of the fourteenth century. And one can point to another change that allowed for the development of the naval industry, coastal shipping, and deep-sea fishing. Even the iron industry and the manufacture of weapons and tools owe their development to this change.

This naval development can be traced back to the Norman settlement of Baiona and the subsequent importance that this port assumed in the commercial life of southwest France. Baiona served as a model to emulate. Yet this model, like any other model, became the source of important conflicts and struggles. Whether on the coast or inland, in the settlements along roads or in the border regions, there was an ongoing clash between the old rural population and the modern urban population.

A similar clash occurred later, in both the countryside and the towns, as a result of bloody power struggles among bands and lineages in the lands between the ocean and the Ebro. In sociological and legal terms, we could say that the population of the towns had a conception of life, work, law, and society corresponding to the phase or stage in which (according to Durkheim) "organic solidarity" was of primary importance. On the other hand, the lineages, which were organized in bands, had a more archaic conception that (again according to Durkheimian theory) reflected their prioritization of "mechanical solidarity" and its attendant repressive social systems that are based on blood relationship and force.

The struggle between the royally appointed *corregidores* and the brotherhoods on the one hand, and the lineages on the other, is the most salient expression of this conflict. Be that as it may, in both commercial and industrial terms, the country no longer lived in isolation. Castilian wool was shipped from Basque ports, and herring and bream from Bermeo was sent to other parts of the Peninsula. Artistic styles, first Romanesque and then Gothic, became widespread, and Basque ships reached ports in the far north of Europe and the eastern Mediterranean, in addition to continuing to engage in deep-sea fishing.

Fifth Cycle

Far-reaching political and economic changes in the fifteenth century brought the fifth cycle to an end. First, the Navarrese monarchy experienced crises as a result of civil wars: The old kingdom breathed its last, hemmed in by its Castilian and Aragonese neighbors. Second, in Bizkaia, Gipuzkoa, and Araba, factional wars became even more commonplace, if that is possible. Third, there were pointed disagreements and arguments between representatives of the crown, on the one hand, and shipbuilders and other parties on the other that had major repercussions in the shipping industry. The political crises and economic difficulties were resolved in ways that did not satisfy all parties but their resolution is what marked the beginning of a new era. The union of Aragon and Castile, the completion of the *Reconquista*, the discovery of America, and the annexation of the kingdom of Navarre are all events that occurred in rapid succession. Collectively, they marked the beginning of the fifth cycle of Basque history, which began at the turn of the sixteenth century and concluded at the end of the eighteenth century when a new crisis erupted as a result of the revolution against the ancien regime. Civil wars and clashes between lineages came to an end. Navarrese, Arabans, Gipuzkoans, and Bizkaians all participated in voyages of discovery, conquest, and colonization of the Americas and the Pacific. Wood-based naval architecture underwent a series of technical changes, and commercial shipping increased in volume. The arms industry necessarily experienced notable changes, given that firearms were replacing older weapons. Certain regions continued to suffer from the exhaustion of primary materials (mainly as a result of deforestation in the mountains). Laws were codified or printed, and the cultural level with respect to basic education notably increased. This could be seen in the number of teachers from Gipuzkoa and Bizkaia—the heart of the Basque Country—who worked in other parts of the peninsula. This led to Basques becoming known for their ability in "matters of the quill" (in other words, their reputation as good calligraphers, skilled wordsmiths, and able teachers). This explains the fact that the country's youth, from the time of the Catholic Monarchs until the reign of Charles III, held administrative and secretarial positions in the courts of Charles I, Philip II, Philip III, Philip IV, Charles II, and, most especially, Philip V, some of them achieving positions of high importance. This sometimes gave rise to envy, discontent, and whisper campaigns against them. Yet it was not only such positions for which Basques became known. Basques (or "Bizkaians" in the common parlance of the times) also achieved prominence in commerce, banking, and in the Royal Navy.

It was also during this period when Basque texts were first printed, and in which there was a hitherto unseen proliferation of history writing. From the cultural point of view, it is important to point out a change in religious life due to the influence of the Council of Trent, and the foundation and development of the Society of Jesus (the Jesuits). Despite all of this, the Basque urban settlements had no more than modest numbers, compared to those in other parts of Europe, and even other parts of Spain. The rural element of the Basque population continued to be important, and it was only at the beginning of the eighteenth century that, in southern Navarre and Araba, the Basque language area began to recede, following lines that became increasing more pronounced. This recession from south to north continued during the nineteenth and twentieth centuries.

IV

The political decadence of the Spanish monarchy during the time of Philip IV, along with the attempt to implement certain measures during the time of Philip V, resulted in expressions of discontent and unrest in the Basque Country that later became much more pronounced. This despite what I've previously said regarding the influence of Basques in public life.

Sixth Cycle

The period from 1792 until 1876 may be said to encompass a much shorter cycle in Basque history than those previously described. Yet this sixth cycle cannot be considered to form part of the dynamic of "occurrence and recurrence." Instead, it can best be thought of as a *catastrophic cycle* in terms of its dynamics. In only one respect can it be considered something of a recurrence: humans regressed to a feral state. The war between Spain and France at the end of the eighteenth century ended in a way that was hardly satisfactory for Spain. The central government believed that the Basque provinces had been indifferent and perhaps even disloyal, and it planned a series of reprisals. In addition, the naval industry had already been in crisis for some time. Yet what was mainly responsible for sinking the Basque Country into an abyss of poverty and uncertainty were the Napoleonic Wars (1808–1814), which also led to the loss of the colonies that had so long served as a source of Basque wealth. Afterward, there was a radical ideological division that ended with the First Carlist War, which saw the rural sector and some towns within the Basque Country identifying as Carlists, and the majority of the bourgeoisie identifying as liberals. Political unrest continued afterward, culminating in the Second Carlist War. As a consequence of these two wars, the foral privileges were drastically cut. This led to the idea taking hold among those who had been defeated that two wars had been "lost by the Basques" at the same time. Basque Liberals, however, drew a sharp distinction between "provincial freedoms" (or "collective freedoms"), which accepted the Inquisition, the unity of the faith, and so on, and "individual freedoms," which, as men of their time, were of greater interest to them.

Seventh Cycle

The seventh cycle was also of short duration and highly eventful, yet in a way that differed from the previous cycle. It may be thought of as beginning with the end of the Second Carlist War and ending with the beginning of the Civil War of 1936. It has highly contradictory aspects. On the negative side were large masses of apparently defeated people, as well as a growing awareness that the main pillar of Basque identity—the Basque language—was in sharp decline. It was this situation that had resulted in the two civil wars of the nineteenth century. Another negative aspect of this era was that the masses, who were essentially religious, remained under the influence of a politicized and—frankly—uneducated clergy. The "foral tragedy" was, however, accompanied by an economic prosperity in the urban and industrial regions (especially those of Bizkaia), by a skyrocketing growth of capitalism and banking systems, and by an enormous growth of an urban and suburban population that was mainly of foreign origin. In other words the country, which was conservative in character, decreased in relative importance as a result of these changes. The political conflicts typical of industrial societies inexorably unfolded. The development of Basque capitalism led to the emergence of socialism among workers—both Basques and non-Basques.

Also emerging, in opposition to the dynastic governments, was a nationalist party that partially embraced the program of the defeated Carlists while adding certain ideas of its own. In literature, the arts, and sciences, the prominence of Basques was greater than ever, but not within the Basque Country and not on the part of persons identified with the aforementioned political groups. Instead, the Basque contribution in these fields was from individuals living elsewhere, both in Spain and abroad. Within the Basque Country, there was a growing eagerness for greater knowledge of the language, customs, and anthropological characteristics of the Basques. In sum, the seventh cycle was one of "cultural and social polymorphism," and also of political polymorphism. Yet, as a whole, the era represented halcyon days for a country largely satisfied with itself and with a pronounced sense of its own superiority (like the Catalans) vis-à-vis the rest of Spain.

Eighth Cycle

The eighth cycle can be thought of as beginning in 1936 with a return to a feral state that, while not medieval, represented an enormous regression in all aspects of life. We can also see this cycle as, in many ways, a continuation of the previous cycle, given that "polymorphism" continued apace. Yet, at the same time, there were substantial and dynamic changes. The period from 1940 through 1983 can be divided into a number of phases, the brevity of which in no way detracts from their importance.

The war ended with the total victory of forces that were inimical to any idea of autonomy or nationalist expression. The only nationalism allowed was Spanish nationalism. Any leftist thinking, from liberalism to communism, was prohibited. An attempt was made to impose a unity that extended to religion as well. The prevalent ideas that were projected by the ruling power were those of Spanish "autarchy" and "traditionalism"—and even "imperialism" (a viable prospect in the event of an axis victory in World War II). Yet such ideas were chimerical and evanescent and, in the end, many people quickly grew tired of them. Recovery from the Civil War was slow and life in many areas of Spain was harsh. There was a deeply felt intellectual void as well. The first twenty years of this cycle are very different from those that followed, and traditionalism, autarchy, and imperialism gradually gave way to a politics of "realism," which in practice meant the nation living off the fruits of the fascist victors. This same tendency was seen in the Basque Country, beginning around 1960 and ending at the same time as European prosperity as a whole began to wane. Industry recovered and the population increased at an alarming rate. Thus, while previously there had been talk of urbanization and reurbanization, there was now discussion of an inexorable "suburbanization." Study of the Basque language began to be more or less tacitly permitted. Basques no longer held a prominent place in Spanish literature, although they did retain an important position in the arts (i.e., in terms of the tastes of that era). But the most important events during this time were political in nature. Basques in the "diaspora" that resulted from the Civil War had an image of themselves, their homeland, and of Spain that they projected wherever they went. Basque nationalists within the homeland harbored similar conceptions.

Spain once again became a venue where cryptic phenomena occurred and, in sociological terms, this had a powerful impact. The dynamics of the cryptic have not been studied in general terms, but it is a factor of tremendous importance. Basque and Catalonian crypto-nationalism, crypto-communism, and crypto-socialism were expressed during the dictatorship in various ways. Clandestine solidarity served as an element of cohesion for those who lived within a cryptic world, because it served to bolster individual self-importance and collective identity. And any instances of martyrdom only enhanced such a dynamic. Thus, while the "Spanish miracle" was taking place (an event of short duration but one that had very important material results), discontent was fermenting among a significant mass of people, and especially among young people. Political forces underwent a process of nearly total reconstruction in accordance with prewar models.

Franco's death and the restoration of the monarchy did nothing more than reveal what had previously either been hidden, or simply unrecognized.

V

We have now reached the present time, and we can now distinguish between a "dynamic identity" and "a static identity." A fundamental characterization of Basqueness in terms of the Basque language seems helpful and unhelpful in equal measure, and is itself an issue that has caused not only controversy but even violent disputes. In many areas of the Basque Country, there are signs that seem to suggest that this is a place where one must speak Basque, as if it were some sort of syllogistic truth, the validity of which one dare not question. These signs in the Basque language are sometimes seen in towns where the ancient tongue has not been heard for at least a hundred years. The local language has a unifying purpose, and there is a great deal of stubbornness in this regard. The Basque language is not only employed as a means of normal communication, but also for the purpose of spreading violent political ideas.

In other words, a language can be used for the purpose of differentiation and as a marker of belonging to a particular group. Such a phenomenon creates particular reactions and tensions. This once again leads us to the primitive idea of "us" and "the other." Except that, in this instance the other does not refer to outsiders.

What is the larger social context of the other in the present instance? Given that the majority of the inhabitants of the Basque nation do not speak the Basque language, are not rural, and are of foreign origin, speculating on the possibility of imposing the unifying criterion of language is, for many of the country's inhabitants, not only unimaginable, but also entirely unacceptable.

On the other hand, it also hardly appears viable to reconstruct a traditional, rural and folkloric Basque culture, given the rural land ownership crisis, the breakdown of the nuclear family, and the decline of agriculture and artisanship—and when the practice of traditional customs has been endangered for more than thirty years, and is very nearly extinct altogether. "God and the old laws" is a nationalist slogan. It implies a political program that is unacceptable to leftist nationalists. Language, customs, laws, and beliefs cannot be imposed either by force or by democratic political provisions.

In addition to nationalist extremists, there are those who think along socialist or Marxist lines, as well as those with a conservative orientation. In addition, there are even some independents.

Basque society reflects an absolute polymorphism in which opposing forces clash with one another. Cycles do not repeat themselves. On the other hand, problems not only repeat themselves but grow worse with time. A dire struggle among social and cultural forces is taking place. And it is precisely this reality that reflects the dynamic identity of the Basque people. One need not search for it elsewhere, creating ideal abstractions or reconstructions of what was or ought to be Basqueness. We have to accept that there are people within our nation who are resistant to external influence (as is the usual case), and who defend the ancient language, customs, and laws. At the same time, there are groups of people who aren't interested in any of this, but who instead focus on economic problems: capitalists and workers. In the larger urban areas, these latter groups outnumber the former, and serve as the breeding grounds of a right wing and a left wing that mirrors those seen in the rest of Spain. In smaller towns, and in the countryside, the nationalist tendency is stronger. The clash between rural agriculture and urban factories has been going on for a very long time, and the conflict between nationalism and socialism precedes the outbreak of the Civil War in 1936. Each group has constructed its own collective image of itself, and another image of those who oppose it. These opposing images evoke the memory of similar opposing images of bygone eras of "insiders" and "outsiders." Beyond the borders of the Basque Country, there is yet another collective representation of Basques—an unflattering representation that has resulted from the violence and extortion that Basques have perpetrated on one another.

In the face of the abovementioned forces, we ought to point out that there is also a very recent element that has arisen in Basque society but that already has come to characterize the current cycle in which we are living today: The appearance among youth of radical tendencies. Such tendencies do not resemble those that were seen among the Russian nihilists of the nineteenth century, but are rather more passive in nature (the word "*pasotismo*" ["passivity"] accurately reflects their approach). These tendencies are exacerbated by the commerce in drugs (both soft and hard drugs) and are seen in adolescents of all social classes. Thus, Basque identity is today characterized by conflict that is more intense than ever. Aggravating this situation is the fact that the Basque Country shares a border with two different states whose interests almost always diverge from one another. The point here is not to propose simplistic solutions. Nevertheless, it seems important to point out that problems will continue to present themselves in more mechanical ways that affect entire masses of people, and also in ways that are governed by emotional factors. It is therefore necessary that solutions be commensurately thoroughly analyzed and carefully reasoned, and that easy recourse to rhetorical and formal devices give way to an effort to get to the heart of what is really going on. Yet such an approach does not seem viable. Because the same exercise of reason, when it comes to addressing the kinds of issues presented above, quickly reveals that we do not have all the data at our disposal that would be needed to propose satisfactory solutions.

I would like to make a few final observations regarding this matter. At first glance, it would appear that the durations of the cycles proposed above are rather varied, and that events occur at a more rapid pace in the more recent cycles. Yet it would also appear necessary to dismiss overly rigid concepts such as evolution that assume purely progressive processes. Each cycle involves the disappearance not only of institutions and ways of living, but of techniques that once represented the summit of perfection but that have come to be replaced by others that are superior. This is what happened in the case of the venerable wood-based shipbuilding architecture, which became completely passé during the course of the nineteenth century. It should be pointed out that, within each cycle, it is important to introduce principles of probability in the sense of the definition of this term provided by Cournot in his theory of history. In other words, one must constantly take account of both the individual factors and the chance occurrences that resulted (e.g., the Arab invasion of Spain, monarchs having or not having successors to their crowns whether the successors intelligent or dull, success or failure in war). One must also take account of the fact that principles such as diffusion are also mechanical, because societies respond in one way to processes of technical diffusion and they respond—or may respond—to the diffusion of spiritual or religious ideas in quite another way. Even processes of regression are different from one another. But in our case, as in many other cases, we can see that researchers have studied the data without being able to draw more than very limited and unilateral theoretical conclusions. This applies whether the researchers in question are economists or historians of economy, whether they are historians with a political agenda, or whether they are judges. Within the field of ethnographic and anthropological research, there is also a prevalence nowadays of unacceptable oversimplification and unilateral viewpoints—all this at the cost of ignoring highly important factors.

One problem that sociologists, anthropologists, and historians need to concern themselves with (and that men like Ratzel and Durkheim previously identified) is that of the interpretation of space within societies or among ethnic groups. An issue of which there is even less awareness is that of the interpretation of space within a single ethnic group but in different historical periods. With respect to Basques, this latter kind of research is perhaps the most exhilarating kind that could be conducted at the present time. This is due to the fact that a country that by the end of the Middle Ages appeared to be wedded to the forest, with a very sparse—and in some cases very isolated—population (recall in this connection the testimony of Alonso de Palencia), has come to be one of the countries of highest population density and most irregular distribution in all of Europe. The Basque conception of space is therefore not static (as can be readily seen in a number of literary texts) but rather dynamic. Today, there is a disjuncture between the country and its people that is reflected quite clearly in the contrast between the geographical area of the country and the total population of its people, considered throughout the historical period beginning with the eighteenth century and ending at the present time. But who thinks about such things? And, most importantly: What good can thinking about such things do?

Part 2

The Basques, Their Origins, and Their Language

4

Origins: Basque-Iberianism

A Brief History of Basque-Iberianism

The notion that the Basque language is the sole descendent of the language that is thought to have been spoken in remote times throughout the Iberian Peninsula has always had many proponents. Contrary to what most people believe, this idea was not introduced by Wilhelm von Humboldt, even though it was he who is responsible for presenting the hypothesis to an international audience with the methodological rigor characteristic of his time—a rigor conspicuously lacking in the Spanish authors who had previously advanced the same theory. However, given that the basic data employed by Humboldt stem from Spanish sources, it seems fitting to begin the present exposition by briefly mentioning some of these sources before moving on (and in doing so momentarily wiping the slate clean, perhaps somewhat disrespectfully) to a direct examination of certain classical texts that it seems to me have not been given their due by the wildly speculative Basque-Iberianists of the sixteenth to the eighteenth centuries, by modern authors who are presumably more scientific in their orientation, or by those who have single-mindedly attempted to refute the equation "Basque = Iberian."

The history of the problem has been recounted previously on a number of occasions[1] There is no need to repeat here all of the opinions that have been published on the subject over the centuries. Instead, we will limit ourselves to drawing attention to those theories that are truly important and influential. What I am attempting to do here is to show that the discussion regarding the Basque = Iberian equation has from the beginning been conducted in terms that are rather abstract and that, among scholars, there have been two predominant points of view: one that holds that a single language was at one time spoken throughout the entire peninsula and one that contends that the supposed evidence in defense of such primitive linguistic unity is simply inadequate.

Lucio Marineo Sículo is the author who is generally cited in histories as the first to defend the hypothesis that the first inhabitants of the peninsula spoke a language that was essentially the same as modern Basque. Paulo Merula (inspired by Joseph Justus Scaliger) defended this view. Still, it should be noted that all three of these men believed that the Basques were a more primitive people who chronologically preceded the Iberians.[2]

For our purposes, it is the opinion of the chronicler Esteban de Garibay (1525–1599) that holds considerably more weight.

Garibay also essentially contended that Basque was the first language spoken in Spain, although he also recognized the presence, from earliest times, of other peoples who disrupted linguistic unity on the Peninsula. His reasoning is of no value whatsoever in modern times. However, Garibay was a figure who contributed most prominently to the reduction of ancient Cantabria to the present Basque territory—a reduction that has caused no small amount of confusion. Nevertheless, some of the toponymic parallels that he establishes during his reckless linguistic speculation (specifically as regards etymology—etymological speculation has often been the downfall of historians and philologists) were incorporated into Humboldt's own particular "Basque-Iberianist" hypothesis, which he attempted to defend, and which seems entirely novel in our own time: a linguistic connection with the Mediterranean and Asia Minor.[3] Given Garibay's use of the mythological chronology of Spanish kings, the first of which was named *Ibero* (from whom the name of Iberia is derived), the confused scholar from Arrasate (Mondragón) can justly lay claim to being the first bona fide Basque-Iberianist.*

On the opposite end of the spectrum was Ambrosio de Morales, who made some very astute observations regarding the linguistic configuration of ancient Spain in a work that appeared at about the same time as Garibay's. Morales did not dispute that Basque was "one" of the ancient languages used in the peninsula, but he contended that it was never as widely used as some had insisted. Morales insisted that

---

* Many of the documents mentioned here as well as further background on this chapter can be found in English in Juan Madariaga Orbea, *Anthology of Apologists and Detractors of the Basque Language* (Reno: Center for Basque Studies, 2006). —ed.

it was probable that a number of languages had been used since very early times—languages of which we have very little evidence.[4] Mariana[5] and Bernardo Alderete[6] shared Morales's view. Nevertheless, Garibay's thesis gained considerable popularity. It was, more than anything else, numerous obscure local historians—of the kind who record the most patent absurdities of the most implausible chronicles and legends—who championed Garibay's thesis. Two such apologists were Andrés de Poza and Baltasar de Echave. The former was the author of a very strange treatise printed in Bilbao in 1587 on ancient Spanish—and, especially "Cantabrian"—history, while the latter wrote a pamphlet that was equally strange, printed in Mexico in 1607, on the antiquity and nobility of the Basque language.[7]

Much more influential than the ideas of the previously mentioned authors are those of the French Basque historian Arnaud Oihenart Etchart given that, on the one hand, his practical knowledge of Basque gave him an advantage over the scholars that maintained a skeptical attitude and, on the other hand, his critical acumen was several magnitudes greater than that of Garibay and several later historiographers. Oihenart lived during the seventeenth century (he died around 1675). He was very well versed in classical texts. Thus, on the basis of a text of Strabo that will be cited below, Oihenart established the linguistic unity of the Lusitanians, Galicians, Asturians, Cantabrians, Varduli, and Vascones. But after doing this, he threw textual criticism to the winds, and contended that Basque was the language of the entire peninsula from early on, and that it was one of the sources of the Spanish language. In support of this thesis, he presented a series of Spanish words that he considered to be of Basque origin. In addition, he cited the names of certain ancient towns that contained Basque elements. For example, he insisted that "ilia" meant "city." This hypothesis would be cited constantly by Basque-Iberianists. However, Oihenart's list of Castilian or Spanish words does not withstand close scrutiny. Be that as it may, it is he who should be recognized as the first clear exponent of Basque-Iberianism.[8]

A writer who expressed himself with equal clarity was Father José de Moret (1615–1682). In his *Annales del reyno de Navarra* (Annals of the kingdom of Navarre), one of the strangest works of Spanish historiography of the seventeenth century, Moret declared that ". . . from time immemorial in texts of ancient writers, we see cities, mountains, and rivers with Basque names throughout Spain, serving as evidence that it was the original language of all Spain before the arrival of later invaders, as Dr. Navarro and other serious writers argues."[9] This hypothesis was developed rather extensively in Moret's *Investigaciones históricas de las antigüedades del Reyno de Navarra* (Historical Investigations on the Antiquities of the Kingdom of Navarre), which contains a wealth of material that was used by later writers[10] and that is an indispensable source even today for the geographical history and archeology of Navarre. In the presentation of his arguments, Moret is even better than Oihenart, because he had an uncanny knack for making the most compelling points and for discarding those points that were rather more dubious.

It was in the eighteenth century, when Spanish scholarship reached its zenith, that the Basque-Iberianist thesis was stated and restated. Yet, during this period, the exposition of Basque-Iberianism was either tinged with romanticism or presented in a sterile and hypercritical manner. Thus, the writings of this era do not represent any real progress in comparison to those of Oihenart or Moret. Basque scholars, who presented their ancient tongue as the language spoken by Adam and Eve in the Garden of Eden, became the subject of virulent attacks on the part of scholars from other regions of Spain, whose own pride was wounded. Thus, what ought to have been a strictly scientific and academic discussion instead turned into a raucous dispute. The examination of an interminable stream of apologias and defenses, of triumphalist and insulting pamphlets, of denunciations of errors and literary backslapping, would be necessary in order to fill out the historical background of the present object of discussion. But this would be about as valuable as a painstaking exposition of everything that has ever been said regarding Tartessos. Thus, we will stick with what is most important, dividing authors, as always, into two groups: the defenders of Basque-Iberianism (i.e., the ancient linguistic unity of "primitive Spain) and those who more or less totally rejected such a hypothesis.

The principal defender of the "positive" position was Manuel de Larramendi Garragori (1690–1766), the renowned author of the *Diccionario trilingüe* (Trilingual Dictionary). This important work was preceded by a lengthy introduction, in which various classical texts were cited in order to demonstrate that Basque was the ancient language of all of Spain, and the primary source of Spanish. This introduction includes an extensive inventory of words that attempts to make the case that an enormous proportion of the Spanish lexicon—and even of the Latin lexicon—is derived from Basque. The etymologies that are used in support of this hypothesis are fanciful. Suffice it to say that those Basque words that were clearly derived from Latin or Spanish were used to support the thesis of Latin and Spanish derivation from Basque.[11] Larramendi was, without a doubt, a passionate man and, in spite of his patriotism, I do not believe that there was another man of his time who better represented local, racial, and democratic pride, based on language and blood, than this Jesuit from Gipuzkoa. It would be interesting for someone studying the origin of Larramendi's racist theories to explore some of his works, such as the *Corografía o descripción general de la muy noble y muy leal provincia de Guipúzcoa* (Chorography or Description of the Most Noble and Most Loyal Province of Gipuzkoa). Scholars from other parts of Spain must not have been pleased with Larramendi's views, since they had their own regional brands of patriotism that were linked to the lands of their birth.

Father Enrique Flórez (1702–1773) showed himself to be an implacable adversary of the ancient linguistic unity of Spain in one of his most famous works, a study of Cantabria. He countered the Basque-Iberianist thesis of Larramendi and others with very good arguments.[12] A certain resentment of "Basque arrogance" shines through his polemic.

Taking as his point of departure, based on the Ptolemaic tablets, the fact that the Cantabrians did not occupy the territory corresponding to the Basque provinces, he proceeded to eviscerate each of the remaining arguments of the Basque-Cantabrians—a particularly strident subgroup of Basque-Iberianists. For Flórez, it was the Romans who imposed linguistic unity on the Peninsula. Prior to the Roman Conquest, there was nothing more than a mishmash of warring peoples of distinct languages and cultures, about whom nothing can be said other than what the classical texts reveal to us when they are read with an objective eye.[13] I admire the modesty and rigor of the Augustine monk more than anyone. Nevertheless, even though I am going to use his methodological approach in this article as my point of departure, I also believe that it is possible to reach conclusions different from his own.

Another opponent of the notion of peninsular linguistic unity was Father Joaquín Traggia de Santo Domingo, a Piarist who, in a polemic against the history of Juan Francisco de Masdeu, wrote: "Spain, having been settled gradually by different peoples that arrived by land and by sea, and at the same time lacking the unity and cohesiveness of enduring dynasties, necessarily contained a variety of different languages."[14] It was also Traggia (whose arguments Masdeu did not effectively counter) who showed a higher degree of critical acumen in his commentary on classical texts that we will shortly examine.[15] In this commentary, Traggia defended the notion of peninsular linguistic plurality. He also introduced the absurd idea that Basque consists of a complicated jargon that grew out of a mélange of different languages during the Dark Ages.[16]

"There is nothing new under the sun." This, or something very much like it, was the conclusion reached by the Catalonian philologist Mosén Griera, who of course employed modern social scientific methodology. He does not seem to have been particularly successful in defending this hypothesis.

In response to Traggia's hypothesis, Pedro Pablo de Astarloa (1752–1806) wrote his most famous work. But before discussing it, we should first recall—even if as nothing more than a matter of passing interest—the views of one of our greatest historians. I refer here once again to the previously mentioned Abbot Masdeu (1744–1817), who in his brilliant but opinionated *Historia crítica de España* (Critical History of Spain), declares that he believes that Basque is a "Celtiberian" language. In order to understand the implications of such an eccentric hypothesis, it is important to understand that he did not recognize the foreign origin of the Celts, who in fact entered the peninsula from the north prior to the Iberians (and this is also the consensus view of historians). Instead, Masdeu contended that Iberians and Celts were the two oldest ethnicities of our nation, and that they are connected with the peoples mentioned in the Bible. According to Masdeu, the Basque language originated in the mixture of languages of these two peoples.[17] We can see here that, at least as far as the matter under discussion is concerned, very little of value was offered by this otherwise very interesting writer, who used data supplied by Moret and Larramendi to support his contention that "a great deal of evidence of the ancient tongue has been preserved in Spain."[18]

Astarloa's research offers original findings, and served as an important stimulus for the later ideas of Humboldt. I would go further still, and say that the studies of this priest from Durango with respect to the Basque calendar are every bit as interesting as the most fascinating sections of the book authored by the German philosopher and linguist. Yet, at the same time, Astarloa's work is imbued with a kind of regional mysticism that very much reflects the spirit of the eighteenth century. It is based in reasoning that is very precise and rigid—which is not the same thing as saying that it is correct. The specific ethnological problem of Iberianism was not of particular interest to Astarloa who, unlike Larramendi and others, did not resort to historical arguments, and his research on toponymy has limited value, and displays limited originality.[19]

Juan Bautista Erro y Azpiroz (1773–1854) followed in the footsteps of Astarloa in a book that could justly be called worthless, but that nonetheless merited the honor of being translated. What Erro (who later became a minister of Don Carlos) essentially set out to do was to use Basque to decipher Iberian inscriptions.[20] While Astarloa's writing was imbued with mysticism and piety, mixed together with more or less solid scientific reasoning, Erro's seems to be lacking any investigative methodology whatsoever. Erro's work thus represents a step backward in terms of previous efforts, which at least have the merit of contributing to the identification of some of the characters of the best-known coin alphabet.[21]

For all of the deficiencies of their published works, the views of these authors continue to be of interest because they give the lie to the current claim that the Basques, actuated solely by notions of a regional supremacy which has been attributed to them for centuries—sometimes with justifiably, sometimes not—have always been hostile to the Basque-Iberianist thesis.

The greatest source of pride of Garibay, Moret, Larramendi, Astarloa, Erro, and so on was their sense of belonging to the most Spanish of Spanish groups, and not to a people that was distinct and irredeemably separate from the rest of the inhabitants of the peninsula (as the followers of Arana-Goiri liked to think). But there is no way of deriving any benefit from such sentiments from a scientific point of view. This is because, in discussing Basque-Iberianism in one era among ardent Basque patriots, addressing the merits of the "differential characteristics" proposed by Dr. Robert, or evaluating the legitimacy of equally dubious notions, it must be recognized that all such ideas are bereft of any real scientific grounding and have indeed hardly been subjected to any critical analysis whatsoever. On the other hand, it is also important to recognize that the critiques of Morales, Alderete, Flórez, and so forth were even more sterile: From Garibay to Astarloa we can at least discern a certain progress in the accumulation of evidence, but from the time of the author of *Viaje* (The Travels) to that of the author of *España Sagrada* (Sacred Spain), there was not an equal measure of advancement in knowledge.

At this point, it is important to make mention of the importance of the work of Lorenzo Hervás y Panduro (1735–1809), who can rightly be considered the most scholarly of Humboldt's predecessors.

The most notable aspect of Hervás's work is that he endowed the word *Iberian* with a more concrete ethnological and linguistic meaning—

namely, the same meaning as that attributed to the word by Humboldt. This was something that set these two men apart from previous writers. For Hervás, the Iberians are the first inhabitants of Spain, as he declares in the following proposition that serves as the title for chapter 7 of section 1 of treatise 3 of his famous *Catálogo de las lenguas de las naciones conocidas* (Catalog of the Languages of the Known Nations): "At the time of the dispersion of the peoples, it was the destiny of the progenitors of the Iberians to settle in the westernmost lands of Europe, which are today called Spain. This area was populated by them in its entirety when the first foreign nations arrived."[22]

According to Hervás, the Iberians spoke Basque. At one point, they not only populated the entire peninsula but also settled in the south of France, and on the mainland and islands of Italy.[23] He makes his case on the basis of a comparison of ancient and modern toponymy. Much of the material that he presented was obviously later used as a source by Humboldt.[24]

Hervás conducted his study of wandering peoples or "nations" who arrived following the Iberians on the basis of one of Pliny's Natural History book 3, chapter 8, which reads: "Marcus Varro records that the whole of Spain was penetrated by invasions of Hiberi, Persians, Phoenicians, Celts and Carthaginians." This text is the ethnological key for all ancient Spanish ethnographers. Of special interest is his research on the Celtic invasions.[25] It is to the personal merit of Hervás that he insisted on the importance for the linguistic history of our country of texts referring to a people who have been a frequent topic of recent speculation, most of it fruitless: the Ligurians.[26]

Yet another thing that stands to the credit of Hervás is that he attempted (not always successfully) to identify real linguistic rules, so that the comparison of words would not be capricious. To this end, he systematically set down series of lexical elements, roots, endings, and suffixes. Even in those cases in which he was obviously mistaken (such as his affirmation that place names ending in "-briga" are Iberian), the material that he presented systematically was very useful, as was his critical history of opinions regarding the ancient language of Spain, which I have used as a source for the preceding exposition.[27]

Beginning with Hervás, the history of Basque-Iberianism is no longer mainly Spanish, and the thesis came to be advocated most passionately by German scholars. The name of Wilhelm von Humboldt became so intimately associated with it that "Humboldtism" came to be a synonym of Basque-Iberianism.

This great philosopher and linguist wrote a number of different works dealing with the Basque language and drawing upon his travels in the north of Spain (the subject of many later monographs). The most interesting of these works for our purposes is his evaluation of the research on the ancient inhabitants of Spain by means of the Basque language.[28]

This work begins with criticism of the ideas of Astarloa, Erro, and others whose work Humboldt considers extravagant and somewhat childish. Yet such a position should not have stood in the way of him referring to the work of other, more objective, authors, such as Oihenart, Moret, and Hervás with more frequency, since it can be justly said that he derived the basis of his own methodology from these three men.[29]

Humboldt, like Hervás, concluded that a single language was spoken throughout the Peninsula—Iberian—of which Basque is a descendent. He came to this conclusion by means of a comparative analysis of ancient place names with Basque words, roots, and sounds in use during his own time. The recognition that, in some areas, Celts mixed with Iberians, does not refute his main point in this regard. Yet, according to Humboldt, pure Iberians inhabited only the Pyrenees and the southern coasts, with mixed Celtic and Iberian populations residing in Lusitania and most of the northern coast. There were various dialects of the Iberian language, and the presence of Phoenicians, Greeks, and Romans also exercised a marked influence on the primitive linguistic situation of the peninsula.

Outside of Spain, a people residing in Aquitania spoke a language that was similar to Iberian. In addition, in the three large islands of Corsica, Sardinia, and Sicily, a language related to Iberian was also spoken. This raises the question of whether it might make sense to search for vestiges of the Iberian tongue in Italy and other Mediterranean countries.

Such findings seem to offer surprising confirmation of the observations of Larramendi Hervás and others.

What, then, was the distinctive contribution of Humboldt? He was first and foremost a man who wrote more clearly and analytically than any of the Spanish scholars. He was also more careful in his use of classical sources for referencing place names (yet, this being said, it must also be recognized that he was by no means cautious enough). The ideas that he offered regarding linguistics in general were excellent, and the racial groups and other categories that he postulated seem more scientific than those of his predecessors. At the same time, it is necessary to recognize that he employs the same arguments as previous linguists, utilizing the comparative method in which a given place name that is similar to another place name constitutes proof of a relationship, even if the first reference was found in Stephan of Byzantium and refers to a certain Italian village, while the other refers to a contemporary Basque hamlet. To be entirely honest, these kinds of comparisons don't exactly strike me as compelling, yet time will tell whether or not they are useful. For now, let us continue with our history.

Humboldt had so many disciples and followers among historians and philologists that it is impossible to identify all of them.[30] Here, we will limit ourselves to citing those whose findings were significant, or who established general theories of particular importance.

Employing such criteria, two men stand out: Emilio Hübner and Hugo Schuchardt. In his enormous compilation of so-called Iberian inscriptions, Hübner presents himself as a follower of Humboldt.[31] In the prolegomena of this work, in which he described the problems involved in the reading of inscriptions (as matters stood at the time of publication) as well as their historical background, one notes that he does not directly address the issue of Basque-Iberianism. It is equally jarring that a man who knew better than anyone else all of the ancient texts that referred to Spain did not make any objective criticism of those texts that referred to the languages of the peninsula (which, after all, was supposedly his main purpose in that section of the book, and which Larramendi and others had previously offered their own interpretations of).

Following Humboldt, it was Hugo Schuchardt who was the greatest champion of Basque-Iberianism. Using Hübner's deciphering of epigraphs as a source, Schuchardt produced a famous work on declension in the Iberian language[32] as well as a series of other highly regarded studies. Yet, in my own modest opinion, the body of Schuchardt's work has not been subjected to sustained and sober criticism, perhaps because of the reverence in which this brilliant German researcher is held among linguists.

Schuchardt's constructions fail for the following reasons. First, he made no effort to specify what era he was referring to in his research. Second, he seems to have used inscriptions that other researchers have identified as Celtic for his construction of Iberian declensions. On another point, the phonetic values that he assigns to the alphabetic signs in some instances calls for drastic modification. In addition, his notion—shared by other linguists—of the Basque = Iberian equation, as well as his inclusion of Iberian among the so-called Hamitic languages, seems to have little basis.[33] Yet, contrary to Gómez Moreno's assertion, such deficiencies by no means render Schuchardt's system as completely devoid of value.

We can thus see that Basque-Iberianism continues to be defended with the same old arguments—mainly by reference to place names. Furthermore, it has gained such wide acceptance that it appears in the works of researchers who are as little given to wild excess as Wilhelm Meyer-Lübke,[34] despite the fact that there have always been linguists such as Julio de Urquijo who have constantly warned against "the familiar insouciance with which Basque is identified with Iberian—and even with Japanese." The author whose words I've just quoted has rightly indicated that, in essence, the comparative method more closely resembles the approach of old Spanish philologists such as Larramendi than that of modern investigators. Urquijo has offered a particularly incisive criticism of the comparative method.[35]

Conclusions

In sum, I believe that it can be concluded on the basis of this extended *excursus* that the language that was the progenitor of Basque, and that was supposedly spoken throughout the peninsula, has to be pushed back very far indeed—to the period between 1000 and 800 BC. And this conjecture is in turn based on the entirely unfounded assumption of a previous linguistic unity. By analogy with a criterion employed in the natural sciences, ethnologists and linguists of the era during which Basque-Iberianism was most influential assumed that the simplest and most homogenous social and linguistic structures were ipso facto also the oldest, and that things grew progressively more complicated with the passage of time. Unfortunately for researchers, this hypothesis is incorrect. A more accurate conclusion is that there was a plethora of different cultures and languages three millennia ago, just as there are today. Evolutionary theories of thinkers such as Herbert Spencer are not credible, however seductive they may appear. Even if we concede that languages and cultures evolved over time, the processes involved in such an evolution were not linear and mathematical in nature. Thus, Basque-Iberianism was and is nothing more than a working hypothesis—a logical hypothesis that entails all of the potential pitfalls of those ideas whose extensive development is inversely proportionate to the empirical evidence in their favor. Any conscientious researcher would have to limit his conclusions to the following with respect to the state of affairs in Spain in the first century BC:

1. A Libyan language was spoken in the south of Spain.
2. In the Guadalquivir Valley, Phoenician was also spoken.
3. Latin was the dominant language in extensive areas of Spain.
4. Celtic languages had been spoken in the center, west, and northeast of the peninsula for several centuries.
5. We are ignorant of the origin of the language in which the southern inscriptions were written, but which Strabo indicated was not the same as the language used in the rest of the peninsula.
6. It appears legitimate to conclude that, in the north, a language was spoken that was hard on the ears of those who spoke Greek and Latin, and that language may be an ancestor of Basque.
7. It is in the region of the Pyrenees where the most solid fragmentary evidence was found of a language having been spoken that was similar to Basque.

Thus, those who seek to clarify the linguistic problems of the center and south by means of studying place names need to study the ancient Libyan languages, as well as Phoenician, Celtic, and so on prior to seizing upon modern Basque, the phonetics of which is highly complicated, and the grammar of which is not well understood. Even when it comes to studying the medieval period, researchers need to take into account, when attempting to construct certain general rules, that Basque was spoken in highly varied areas during that time—and that a wide variety of Romance dialects were spoken in these same areas.

Not long ago, I published an article in which I identified a number of the areas where Basque was spoken at various times. At the conclusion of that article, I made a number of general remarks that were resented in certain quarters.[36] What was considered insolent was my statement that I did not see clear evidence in support of the Basque-Iberian hypothesis. Instead, what we have are writers who have attempted to construct sound ideas on the basis of confusing data and writers who have confusing ideas that are based on sound data. I do not consider myself as belonging to either of these groups. I think that clear data should be conducive to clear ideas, and that confusing ideas necessarily lead to confused thinking—at least for anyone who is not exceptionally clever. For me, a datum that is crystal clear is the progressive receding of Basque, a process that began during the Middle Ages. Yet another fact that is clear is the stronger degree of persistence of Basque in the least Romanized areas of Spain. Those who favor the hypothesis of a diffusion of the Basque language from the southeast to the northeast sharply disagree with me on this point. Yet I do not understand how they can uphold their hypothesis in the face of the following facts:

1. The province of Gipuzkoa (i.e., the area where the Basque language has been preserved to the highest degree) contains the fewest Roman ruins in all of Spain.
2. Bizkaia has a somewhat greater—yet still insignificant—quantity of Roman ruins.
3. The province of Araba, where the use of Castilian was widespread at a very early stage, displays a far more intense Romanization, judging from the archeological remains found there.
4. Within the province of Navarre, the region where Basque has been preserved to the highest degree was the least Romanized, and the region where it has been preserved to the least degree was the most Romanized.[37]

In order to support the notion of a spreading of Basque to the provinces during medieval times, we would have to swallow the notion that, from the territory south of Iruñea-Pamplona and the Ebro, which had an abundance of large cities and where the Latin language had been used for centuries, and from the territory of the Vascones (i.e., as understood in classical terms), Romanized peoples swept northward, imposing a non-Latin language on some other unknown peoples. What is more likely is the exact opposite: that, beginning in the fourth century, the inhabitants of the mountains, who had always been relatively less civilized, took advantage of the weakened condition of the Roman Empire and ventured southward.

Yet if we acknowledge the fact that, in the Middle Ages (until the twelfth century and even afterward) Basque was spoken within the entire territory of Navarre and the Basque provinces, in the north of Huesca, in the southernmost valleys of the current province of Zaragoza, and in a considerable area of Logroño,[38] it remains unknown when that language that Pomponius Mela was unable to pronounce (and which there are grounds to think was Basque or some closely related tongue) disappeared from Cantabria proper. It is highly likely, given the parallels between the history of Vasconia and Cantabria during the Visigothic period, that this unpronounceable language became extinct following said period.[39] Be that as it may, we can assume that the Cantabrians and Asturians had been Romanized to a greater extent than the Varduli and Caristii of Gipuzkoa and Bizkaia, and that peoples such as these—though it may be asserted otherwise—did not retain anything approaching the linguistic integrity that they may have earlier possessed. Still, it should be recognized that, throughout the territory occupied by all these tribes, there were, beginning in a very early period, also greater or lesser concentrations of Celtic settlements, as revealed by archeological discoveries. It was these Celtic settlements that always seemed to be most receptive to Latin culture.

Ever since the time of Strabo, Cantabrians had been conscripted into Roman militias "both the Coniacans and the Pentuisans, who live near the source of the Iberus" (book 3, chapter 3) who may have spoken Latin.[40] There were Cantabrian soldiers in Judea,[41] Varduli and Vascones in Britannia,[42] Vascones in Germania,[43] Asturians in Egypt,[44] and so on. Many of these men returned to their homes, where they would have introduced new cultural and linguistic elements. Yet it can also safely be said that, on the whole, the tribes remained less Romanized that those in any other part of Western Europe.

During the Roman era, there was, in the mountains of Santander, as well as in Araba and in the west of Navarre, not only Roman influence but also a considerable number of Celtic settlements (including those such as *Ambatus*, and so on, which Gómez Moreno mistakenly thought were Ligurian.[45] Celts also settled a number of Autrigonian and Cantabrian cities,[46] as well as those that were established on the banks of the Gállego River.[47] It was the Celts, then, who can be credited with disrupting the linguistic and cultural unity of the north of Spain—if indeed any such unity can be said to have existed. And the farther northwestward we look, the more intense this process of "Celtization" was—just as was the case for Romanization.

In sum, we can conclude that, ever since the remotest past, Basque can be thought of as the language that was spoken, and that continues to be spoken by a people located astride the two slopes of the Pyrenees Mountain Range—and most likely astride its extension (i.e., the Cantabrian Mountain Range) as well. We can further conclude that this people, divided into various tribes and peoples bound by blood relationship, had a distinctive culture until the Celts arrived on the scene. This seems abundantly clear to me. I will proceed to demonstrate the truth of this affirmation in another work that will soon be published. The relationship of the Basques with the rest of the peninsula prior to the Celtic invasions, as well as the origin of the Basques, are subjects that I cannot address here, and that will not be clarified until such time as a thorough study has been conducted that produces conclusive findings regarding the nature of the pre-Celtic languages of the south. All I would like to say here is that the relationship posited by Schuchardt between Basque, on the one hand, and the Hamitic languages of Africa, on the other, is not one that is particularly well established.[48] Conversely, the hypothesis of a relationship between Basque and the Caucasian languages, which seems to have excited very little interest in the peninsula, seems to be the most plausible of all, since it is based on strict linguistic and morphological observations. Furthermore, the findings of physical anthropology support the hypothesis of a similarity between Basque types, on the one hand, and Uralic and Caucasian types on the other.

Roland Dixon saw in the Basque racial type a Uralic element that he thought was highly influential in Europe during the late Neolithic period and that, combined with other influences, resulted in the triangular shape of the face that is so distinctive of the Basques.[49] More recently, George Montandon has insisted that, with the triangular shape of their faces and their long, narrow noses, the Basques bear a peculiar resemblance to the Caucasians.[50] Such a similarity is perhaps more compelling when one takes into account the linguistic similarities between the two peoples that have been established by a number of researchers. Still, it needs to be remembered that the degree of resemblance between the language, subrace and types of Caucasians and Basques is not total, and that race, language, and culture are three different things,[51] even if they are at times very closely related to one another.

Linguistic relationships have been studied by Alfredo Trombetti, Hartmut Winkler, Nicholas Marr, and Karel Oštir. Christianus Cornelius Uhlenbeck wrote a positive review of their work, which was later updated by René Lafon[52] (who in turn took into account Aldolf Dirr's careful research on Caucasian languages). These specific relationships, from which any ideas that seem phonetically dubious in the least have been eliminated (it goes without saying here that the purely phonological similarities upon which Basque-Iberianism was founded have been eliminated as well) appear to hold better for some of the Caucasian languages (of which there are many) than for others.[53]

In spite of all this, one should approach with caution the idea echoed by Strabo regarding the similarity of the "Iberians" of the west in general and the Iberians of the Caucasus. This notion assumes that two migrations occurred: one from east to west and another from west to east. In Strabo's words: "For instance: the migration of Western Iberians to the regions beyond the Pontus and Colchis."⁵⁴ When exactly did such movement occur, such that the Greek historians would have had any reliable knowledge of it? A Spanish scholar of the seventeenth century wrote, referring to this text and to others like it, and as part of a general refutation of the commonly held notion that Spain was founded by the biblical Tubal: "But this cannot be affirmed [either]. For these things go beyond the work of human understanding, and no work [book or writing] comments on the antiquities of Hispania in itself enough to be recommended.⁵⁵

Some months after becoming aware of this, I read with great interest a substantial article by the Dutch linguist Uhlenbeck in which he summarizes various ideas regarding the origins of the Basque language in the form of six theses. Four of these theses are interesting for our purposes. In another work that he had hoped to have published in homage to Julio de Urquijo, and that has unfortunately not yet appeared, he posited that one had to seek the origins of Basque in an ancient dialect of the Western Pyrenees that is related to the extinct languages of southern Europe (and, in certain respects, to those of the Caucasus). This dialect, he said, bore some relationship to Iberian, which came from North Africa. This helps explain the similarities that Schuchardt found between Basque declension and the Iberian declension that he reconstructed. It also helps explain the numerous elements of Basque vocabulary that coincide with those of North African languages. The first Indo-Germanic elements that it absorbed were a number of isolated Celtic words, with vast quantities of Latin words being absorbed later, during the Roman era. In the article from which I take these ideas, Uhlenbeck indicated that he now believes that the idea regarding the Celtic elements (and elements of the languages of other Indo-Germanic peoples) that supposedly entered Basque by means of an archaic form of Latin, needs to be revised.

The only point that I would like to add here is my endorsement of the relationships established by Uhlenbeck between Basque and other non-Indo-Germanic ancient languages—even though I don't accept Schuchardt's Iberian declension or Bosch's ethnological disquisitions on the Iberians (which Uhlenbeck finds very convincing). I also would like to express my agreement with his statements regarding Latin elements. Still, it is important to continue to bear in mind that, for a long time, the predecessor of Basque had some intercourse with Celtic languages, and that, within the Basque area, there were numerous Celtic settlements.

5

Historical-Cultural Problems of the Basque Language

The Basque Language as an Instrument of Historical-Cultural Research

In describing the essential characteristics of the Basque language in his seminal work, C. C. Uhlenbeck identified the following key word groups that set Basque apart from Indo-European languages: (1) numbers, (2) pronouns, (3) names indicating family relationships, and (4) verbs.[1] However, he also acknowledged the existence of "delightful analogous elements" between Basque and the Indo-European languages. Yet it is also true that such "analogous elements" could also be made with languages far more distant in both space and time. The question to consider is this: Have these elements arisen as a result of psychological factors (i.e., the identical qualities of the human mind in all areas of human habitation) that are due to relationships that can be analyzed on a historical basis? The problem, then, is parallel to those issues that fire the imagination of ethnologists, who attempt to identify the specific reasons for the curious diffusion of cultural phenomena, beliefs, practices, and customs among widely disparate regions. The particular importance for us of research of this kind can be appreciated when one remembers that, not long ago, the same great Dutch linguist contended that the fundamental origin of Basque could be found in an ancient dialect of the western Pyrenees, which was related to the languages of Southern Europe and the Caucasus in a number of important respects. That dialect was also related to "Iberian," which originated in North Africa. This explains the similarities that Schuchardt emphasized between Basque and certain Hamitic languages, especially the numerous similarities in vocabulary. The first

Indo-Germanic elements incorporated into Basque were a number of isolated words from either Celtic or perhaps (according to Uhlenbeck's latest thinking) from Archaic Latin.[2] The proofs he provides in support of this theory stem from a selective use of sources, as we shall see.

If we examine a linguistic atlas, we find that Basque, which was surrounded on all sides by Indo-European languages, was geographically quite distant from the areas where African languages were spoken. The areas where Basque was spoken were even farther from the Caucasus and more distant still—abysmally so, in historical terms—from the Americas. Yet Basque shows certain similarities with languages in each of these areas as regards fundamental aspects of its structure. At first glance, there would appear to be a complete absence of any relationship between geographical proximity and linguistic similarity. This is shown in the following points, which indicate the elements of Basque that can best be compared with the aspects of other languages:

1. Vocabulary: with certain branches of Indo-European, as well as African and Caucasian languages.
2. Derivation and nominal composition: with Indo-European languages.
3. Declension: with African languages of what was at one time called the Hamitic group, and with Caucasian languages (apparently as a result of borrowings from Indo-European languages).
4. Inflection: with Caucasian and certain North American languages.

Mainly on the basis of the Basque vocabulary found in dictionaries, certain theorists have contended that Basque is a Romance language that was formed at the beginning of the Middle Ages. But the arguments of those holding this view seem forced. We can now determine the extent of the Latin element in the Basque language without making wild generalizations, without introducing fanciful etymologies, and by taking due account of phonetics, semantics, and history.[3]

Speculation based solely on vocabulary proves little. Anyone who takes a Latin grammar and compares it with grammars of Greek, Sanskrit, and on and on discovers the sensational parallelism Bopp first clearly described. Someone looking at a Basque grammar will also come across a number of parallels, but will also undoubtedly identify more differences than similarities. When it comes to the derivation of words, there is no fundamental difference between Basque and Indo-European languages. Uhlenbeck, a frequently cited linguist, demonstrated this in a detailed work in which he identified the Basque suffixes that are used to derive and form new words.[4] Among them are a considerable proportion of words of Latin origin and others that are perhaps of Celtic origin. For this reason, anything that we are capable of researching regarding place names and onomastics in ancient Spain regarding Basque sheds little light on the most important linguistic problem. Leaving aside this kind of derivation, what we find in Basque is a special form of declension, which was very strongly emphasized by Schuchardt, in opposition to Van Eys and other linguists in the second half of the nineteenth century, who made too much of the distinction between monosyllabic, agglutinating, and inflected languages, a distinction that was popularized in textbooks by authors like Hovelacque, in which Basque appeared in the second group.[5] Basque, in contrast to Latin, Greek, and similar languages, has a single declension that is valid for all nouns and pronouns, regardless of gender. In analyzing "casual" suffixes, linguists such as Charencey and Von Arndt[6] found a basis for positing a similarity between Basque, on the one hand, and Ugro-Finnic and Uralic languages on the other. Other linguists, such as Schuchardt,[7] Uhlenbeck,[8] and H. Winckler[9] saw the similarities in casual suffixes and vocabulary[10] as sporadic. Nevertheless, these men did concede a distant relationship, based on loan words, between Basque and the above mentioned language groups. Generally speaking, the activities within this field of scientific speculation can be divided between those who defend the thesis that Basque is essentially related, primarily, to Caucasian languages and, secondarily, the Hamitic languages; and those who invert the importance of the two aforementioned relationships. Yet it appears that, with the passage of time, the Hamitic hypothesis has become less popular and that the Caucasian hypothesis has grown stronger. We will first examine the reasons for the decline of the former in order to better assess the value of the latter, taking as our point of departure the points of comparison indicated above.

Basque and the Languages of North Africa

The idea of an intimate kinship between the ancient inhabitants of the Iberian Peninsula and those of North Africa has been around for some time now, and is based on reasons that can be readily grasped by anyone. It is a relationship that could even be seen as "logical." Nevertheless, the most important evidence of such a relationship was not examined until relatively recently, when it has been adduced with a marked degree of clarity. As regards the linguistic aspect of such a relationship, it is important to keep in mind that the most scientifically rigorous of the linguists who have examined the hypothesis, Schuchardt, who studied it especially carefully at the end of his life, taking the Basque language as his starting point, felt that it was an interesting but unproven hypothesis. We should also remember that one of the first theorists who suggested the possibility that Basque was related to the languages of North Africa was the German philosopher Liebniz.[11] In the nineteenth century, Charencey discovered astonishing parallels between the Basque and Coptic lexicons, and Giacomino[12] in turn found extensive comparisons between Basque and Egyptian. Von der Gabelentz, whose knowledge of Basque left quite a lot to be desired, attempted to demonstrate its affinity with Berber tongues. A missing element in all of this theorizing was a comprehensive linguistic study of North African languages, without which it was impossible to draw truly meaningful conclusions. Nevertheless, Schuchardt, in his study of Iberian declension as well as in other research, had endorsed the idea of such affinity. A definitive presentation of his position can be found in two articles, published in 1912 and 1913 respectively. These articles took their inspiration (as regards the part dealing with Africa) from the earlier work of Reinisch (1832–1919). The first includes a number of studies regarding the possible relationship with Nubian.[13] The second article explores the relationship between Basque, on the one hand, and Berber, Egyptian, Coptic, Nubian (again), Semitic languages, High Cushite, Low Cushite, Nilotic, and Middle Sudanese.[14] On the basis of an analysis of the vocabulary of each language within this vast group, and then comparing each of them with Basque, he identified up to 154 Basque words that might be related to various African and Asiatic words of various origins. In terms of grammatical and phonetic analogies, he pointed out the similarity between Basque and Nubian in the use of "r" and "p" at the beginning of words. He also found a similarity in declension between the two languages, in pluralization (Basque "-k", Nubian "-ku", etc.), the genitive case (Basque "-en", Nubian etc. "-n") and the dative case (Basque "-I", "-ki", Nubian "-ki", "-gi"). As regards syntax, a number of presumed similarities were proposed by Schuchardt. Yet we should remember here, prior to embarking upon a discussion of the possible lexical relationship between Basque and African languages, that the differences in grammatical structure between one group of languages and another is something that has been demonstrated relatively recently by Zyhlars, and it can thus be said that, at the very least, the reputation of Schuchardt's work has suffered as a result.[15] Zyhlars begins by offering his opinion that the classifications proposed by Reinisch are antiquated. Specifically, he vehemently contested Reinisch's assertions that certain languages were Hamitic (e.g., Nubian, Barea, Fula, etc.). Secondly, the lexical comparisons that had been adduced by Schuchardt suffered from phonetic irregularities. As a consequence, Zyhlars maintained that any similarities were coincidental. In support of this contention, he presented a list of German words that bear a clear resemblance to Coptic words. As regards inflection, Schuchardt had maintained that, since it is difficult to know what the earliest form of Hamitic languages was like, there is no way of determining those of its characteristic verb systems that could be compared to Basque. Zyhlars argued that it was indeed possible to reconstruct verb conjugations of ancient Hamitic, and that such a reconstruction showed that it bore no relationship to Basque. Zyhlars also refuted Schuchardt's contention that there were important similarities in syntax. The importance of Zyhlars's polemic is considerable from the general point of view of linguistic "Iberianism." And yet, from another point of view that might be called essentially cultural, many of the parallels indicated by Schuchardt are quite interesting.

If one assumes that all of the comparisons are legitimate, what we see is that there are many more parallels with some languages than with others. The most important source of parallels would thus be Berber, with more than forty linguistic similarities. Second is Coptic, also with around forty parallels. Third would be the languages comprising the Nubian subgroup. In fourth place would be Arabic with which, like Nubian, thirty similarities had been identified. Fifth in importance are Egyptian and Hebrew. Sixth are Blin and Badauje. Seventh are Kunama, Ethiopic, and Assyrian. Eighth are Qwara and Chamir. Ninth on the list are Barea, Saho, Afar, Somalian, Galla, and Hausa. And, finally, tenth in importance, are Qimant and Kafa. The remaining languages for which some measure of similarity was noted are not important for our purposes. If we examine a linguistic map of Africa, what we see is that the greatest similarities are with languages spoken closest to the Mediterranean Sea, a zone of extensive proto-historic and historic cultures. Furthermore, the similarities with such languages sometimes involve concrete historical concepts (although, in other cases, the parallels are very general in nature). Of great interest in this respect is a comparison of the Basque word for "God," first recorded in the twelfth century AD (*Urcia*) and the word for the supreme divinity of the Berbers in the sixth century (*Gurzil*). This was the first similarity listed by Schuchardt. Yet perhaps more interesting are the following parallels: between the Basque words for iron (*burdin, burni*) and their Phoenician and Hebrew counterpart (*barzal*: twenty-sixth on Schuchardt's list); between the Basque and Hausa words for wheat (*gari* and *gero* respectively: twenty-ninth); and between the Basque and Somalian words for "tree bark" (*azal* and *asal*: thirty-fifth). Also noteworthy is the resemblance between the Basque word for "fox" (*asari*) with *bassária* (Ancient Lybian) and *basar* (Coptic), and the Basque and Sudanese words for "dog" (*zakur* and *sagar* respectively: forty-eighth on Schuchardt's list). Then there is the similarity between the Basque *a(h)untz* ("goat") with both the Assyrian (*enzu*) and Arabic (*'anz*) words for that animal (fifty-second); Basque *ak(h)er* ("he-goat") with Berber *ankuar, ikerri, iker* (fifty-third); *marro* ("ram" [animal]) with Afar *mara* (fifty-fourth); *umerri* ("lamb") with the Assyrian *immeru* and the Arabic *immar* (fifty-fifth); *be(h)I* ("cow") with Tuareg *ta-beggiu-t* (fifty-ninth); *nagusi* ("lord") with the Hebrew *nogés* ("sovereign") and the Ethiopian *negus* ("king," eighty-seventh); *(h)iri, uri* ("city") with the Hebrew *'ir* and the Sumerian *uru/eri* (eighty-ninth). Finally, there is the parallel between Basque *berri/barri* with the Coptic *bere, berre,* and *berri* (124th).

If we take into consideration the reservations of Zyhlars, the evidence that was considered decisive for supporting the Basque-Iberian hypothesis does not really amount to much from the linguistic point of view. Yet, as I indicated earlier, it is of considerable historical and cultural interest. Let's take for example the Basque designation *Illiberris* (new city). Given that the word for "city" is *ir* in Hebrew and *uru/eri* in Sumerian, and that the Coptic word for "new" is *berri*, the corresponding Basque words (*iri, uri,* and *berri*) may bear reference to the Mediterranean cultural milieu where states with large cities flourished, without using the parallels mentioned to defend the notion of an ancient linguistic unity. Also interesting are the similarities between the words for "goat," "billy goat," "ram," and "lamb." However, given that similar-sounding words are also found in other language groups, the issue simply becomes more complicated, instead of being clarified. The significance of coincidences, which at times are surprising indeed, between words in Basque and those in African and other languages is in fact limited to the cultural arena. Thus, instead of continuing to theorize about linguistic relationships and believing in a unity that is supposedly revealed by a substratum, it would be much more productive to study the parallels that have been identified from an objective, ethnological standpoint. I have sometimes actually thought that, in cases in which there is a similarity between many different words in two languages, what would be most useful would be the statistical method devised many years ago by the Polish anthropologist Czekanowski for determining the nature of the relationship between the disparate languages in question. This same method is now successfully being used in both the United States and Germany in order to verify a number of historical hypotheses within the field of ethnology.[16] This selfsame method, or one like it, would also shed considerable light on matters having to do with the relationship between the languages of the peninsula and the oldest Indo-European languages of Western Europe, the study of which is currently in the throes of a serious theoretical crisis.

Basque and Caucasian languages

The hypothesis of a connection between Basque and Caucasian languages, which has perhaps been the theory that has aroused the least interest in Spain, has had its proponents outside of the peninsula. These men have contributed anthropological data to the previously published linguistic and morphological observations that could in fact support the notion of a relationship between modern Basque and Uralic and Caucasian languages. Dixon thought that there was a Uralic element that was highly influential in Europe during the Neolithic Era and that, together with other factors, underlay what he considered the characteristic triangular facial shape of Basques.[17] Montandon has more recently posited that Basques and Caucasians[18] share in common that distinctive triangular facial shape, as well as a typically long and narrow nose. Such a similarity is interesting to linguists, although it is important to recognize that linguistic and racial similarities between Basques and Caucasians by no means constitute an exact parallel.

The problem regarding the relationship of Basque with the Caucasian languages interested both Hervás and Humboldt, but neither of these men had sufficient data regarding the Caucasian languages. In 1879, Father Fita indicated that there were some general affinities with Georgian.[19] A. d'Abbadie had previously noted other vague parallels. It was Schuchardt, however, who, employing new research data, demonstrated the most important analogies and affinities.[20] Inspired by these findings (or perhaps acting independently of Schuchardt's influence) Trombetti gathered the most definitive evidence of a relationship, a task that he began at the start of the twentieth century, and that resulted in 1925 in the publication of his extensive monograph *Le origini della lingua basca*.[21] Other, less fortunate, authors embarked upon the same enterprise. These included Winckler[22] (who was harshly criticized by both Uhlenbeck[23] and Gavel[24]) and Marr, a Russian linguist whose general theories were not widely accepted in the West, but who is recognized as a great Caucasologist. Yet it was actually the publication of Uhlenbeck's positive findings (a study that partially endorsed Trombetti's findings) on the possibility of a relationship between Basque and Caucasian languages[25] that spurred many specialists from Italy, France, Germany, and other nations to embrace the idea as a useful working hypothesis. Among these scholars were Dirr[26] and Bouda.[27] Thanks to studies conducted by the Russian scholars, we now have an excellent linguistic map of the Caucasus and an organization of materials that made their work all the more appealing. The Caucasus has been characterized from ancient times as a region with a high degree of linguistic diversity. Strabo wrote that Dioscurias, a port on the Black Sea, was during his time a commercial hub comprising seventy human groups, each speaking its own language, that lived isolated and bereft of intercourse with one another amid fierce and solitary surroundings.[28] Other historians raised the number of peoples resident in the area to three hundred. Referring to Caucasian Albania, a region farther east, on the Caspian Sea, the same geographer identified some twenty-six different languages spoken in that area.[29] Yet it has only been recently that specific knowledge of the Caucasian languages has been attained.

It is possible that many languages described by Strabo are extinct. Basing himself on the most careful research findings, Bleichsteiner has organized contemporary Caucasian languages into three large groups. The first of these is Northwest Caucasian, with four main languages. The second is Northeast Caucasian, with five subgroups and twenty-nine languages. Finally, there is Southern Caucasian, with four languages, including Georgian.[30] There are important differences among these languages, but there are authors such as Dumezil who have even contended that Basque is most closely related to the Northwest Caucasian group.[31] This seems to be an exaggeration. A careful examination of the tables at the end of Trombetti's long monograph, consisting of grammatical parallels between Basque, on the one hand, and "Hamito-Semitic" and "Caucasian" on the other, reveals closer affinities than Uhlenbeck acknowledged in his previously published work.[32] Furthermore, although it seems that the highest number of parallels is with Georgian, there are a variable number of parallels with the other languages, those with North Abkhasian tongues being the most common, according to my account. It is very difficult to provide a detailed analysis of comparative grammar. I would just like to make a few observations here.

Suffixes that are used to derive names, in a nominal inflection, are case suffixes. In addition, in personal pronouns, as well as in the names of numbers, there are analogies (with the vigesimal system employed in both Georgian and Basque). Finally, there are strange coincidences of structure among verbs, with a passivity of transitive verbs present in both Basque and some of the Caucasian tongues, a psychological correlation that Schuchardt had emphasized in 1896.[33] What, then, is the usefulness of all these findings from an ethnological-historical standpoint? Given that Trombetti's sole purpose was to establish his doctrine of linguistic monogenesis, I will not attempt to fit his observations into any historic scheme. Yet we should point out here that, among the lexical comparisons that are listed in the aforementioned work (of which there are a total of 355, and which include comparisons with both African and Indo-European languages), there are a number that are of cultural interest.[34] As Uhlenbeck points out, it is evident that the Basque word *gari* is the same as Armenian word *gari* ("barley," taken from a Caucasian language. In Ingiloy, the word for barley is *kher*, while in Georgian, Mingrelian, and other languages, it is *kheri*. In addition, the concordance between Basque *garagar* ("barley"), Tabassaran *gargar* ("oats"), and Kurinian *gerger* is very surprising indeed.[35] Other surprising findings: that the Basque element *bas(a)* ("desert," "forest") is related to the Churkian *waça* and other similar words; that there is a certain similarity between Basque and Caucasian names of days, and the words for "fire," "walnut," "apple," "birch," "dog," "ass," "cow," "he-goat," "boar," "butter," "measurement," "flour," "chariot" (*gurdi* in Basque, and *warda-n*, *warda*, *vardy-n* in various Caucasian languages), city (*yir* = "town" in Kandyagash; and *ili*, *il*, or *al* in various dialects of Turkish = "people" or "tribe."; and *castillo* = *kala*. All of these parallels have a high degree of historical-cultural importance.[36] If Caucasian and Basque are related, the separation could not have occurred either before or after the Bronze Age. We have already seen that the chariot must have been introduced to Spain, and become widely used, by that time, and that the Basque wheel is similar to the Caucasian wheel. Yet it is not possible to link these facts with archeological findings in any definitive manner. "Bronze Age" is the very outer limit beyond which the ancestors of the modern Basques could not have arisen. Yet within that limit, there are so very many possibilities.

The Quintessential Characteristic of the Basque Language

The quintessential characteristic of the Basque language is the structure of the verb. Although it may seem a bit dry and dull in a book of this nature, I would like to make a number of observations in this regard, employing what could be called a popularizing style. My purpose in doing this has to do with the fact that historians have in the past tended to dismiss any kind of linguistic investigation. For a long time, Basque grammars imperfectly reproduced the theory of grammars of any modern Indo-European language, whether a Romance or Germanic language, and have attempted to fit Basque into such a schema. But during the second half of the nineteenth century, Federico Müller[37] provided the outlines of another theory—the passive theory—that was later defended by Stempf[38] and subsequently adapted, expanded, and refined by Schuchardt.[39] Even though a number of distinguished Bascologists, such as Vinson,[40] never accepted it, and many Basques continue to be unaware of it, it was nevertheless championed by a younger generation of linguists. Leon,[41] Sarohïandy,[42] Gavel,[43] and others have presented new evidence and selected examples that support the passive theory. Its defenders demonstrate that, contrary to Latin and other Romance languages, a transitive verb does not exist in Basque. There are, instead, a number of different intransitive verbs, as well as other verbs that, in terms of their relationship with their subject and complement, behave like the passive or Romance verb. The definition of subject in basic grammars (i.e., "the word designating the person or thing involved in the situation, or carrying out the action expressed by the verb") is not helpful for Basque, since it does not apply to the passive verb. What a subject is in reality, as Gavel points out—is a noun, pronoun, or substantiated locution that, either expressed or understood from context, bears a special relationship with the verb form, exercising upon it a preponderant influence.[44]

Leaving aside for the moment the matter of intransitive verbs, let's look at a few examples in which the passivity that I've referred to can clearly be seen. We take these from Gavel as well, adapting them to Spanish. Thus, one would say in Spanish that "*El herrero ha vendido el caballo*" ("The blacksmith has sold the horse") and "*El herrero ha vendido los caballos*" ("The blacksmith has sold the horses"). In Basque, the translation would be: *Arotzak zaldia saldu du* and *Arotzak zaldiak saldu ditu*. It is clear that, in the Spanish phrases, the subject is neither "horse" or "horses," since neither of these words modify the verbal form *ha vendido* ("has sold"), modifying instead *herrero* ("blacksmith"). Thus the verb in both phrases is in the third-person singular, for the purpose of subject-verb agreement. Furthermore, *vender* ("to sell") in Spanish is a transitive verb, since its subject is a word that indicates the author of the action, rather than the person or thing experiencing the effect of the action. But if we now make a parallel examination of the Basque phrases, what we find is that the words that exercise a preponderant influence on the verbal form are *zaldia* ("horse") or *zaldiak* ("horses"), and not *arotzak* ("blacksmith"), which is the agent. This is the case because, in the second phrase, the verb has taken the form *ditu*, which expresses plurality, in order to agree with *zaldiak*. The actual subjects, then, are *zaldia* and *zaldiak*, which are in the nominative case, while *arotza* has the active "-k" of another declension that, in Spanish, could be interpreted as the equivalent of a complement of the agent preceding the preposition *por* ("by" in this case). Thus, the literal translation in Spanish of *Arotzak zaldiak saldu ditu* would be as follows: *Por el herrero los caballos han sido vendidos* ("By the blacksmith the horses have been sold").

In the face of the confusion created by the rules of grammarians that are unaware of this passive theory, or who do not accept it, those who defend it can formulate the following three very simple rules that define the true properties of the transitive verb:

1. The verb always agrees in number with its subject.
2. The subject of the verb is in the nominative case.
3. The active always refers to the agent that is the complement.[45]

The passive theory has a number of additional implications that need not detain us here. Returning to the general problems which we set forth previously, what is important to point out in the present context is that this passive character of the action verb, which is present in Basque, is something that also exists in the Algonquin family of languages of North America, as well as in a number of other languages (e.g, Athabascan, Haida, Chimesian, Chinook, Kusaal, Kus, and Pomoan). A linguist as familiar with these tongues as he is with Basque has made a detailed study of the passive character of these languages.[46] He has, however, made no attempt to systematically analyze the parallels and explain them in historical terms. Instead, he has simply affirmed that the similarity can be accounted for on the basis of psychological reasons. Within the field of linguistic psychology, there are those who have defended the notion of an internal evolution that allows for the identification of a series of phases and that, within this evolution, passive structure represents an earlier stage than active structure in terms of active verbs. Moller attempted to demonstrate that the primitive Indo-European conjugation was entirely passive prior to becoming active, and Uhlenbeck himself also believed that passivity represented an earlier stage.

If we accept this notion, then Basque would appear to have its roots in the remote European past, and all of the loan words or similarities to Indo-European do not carry enough weight to deny it its originality, even though some have attempted to do this, actuated more by political motives than anything else. When the problem of the historical relationship of Basque with other languages is presented in this way, can one reasonably conclude that the similarities between Basque and the Caucasian languages are a result of the emigration of a people across territories having different cultures and languages, until arriving in the West? Or is it more plausible that, during an era prior to the great Indo-European expansion, there existed from the Caucasus to the Pyrenees a large family or branch of peoples speaking the same or similar languages, of which the Basques in their mountain fastness represent the sole remnant?

Relationships among Languages and Cultural Diffusion

The second of the above theories is currently more popular. We have already seen that Uhlenbeck has championed it. In addition, Father Schmidt, in a very controversial book that he published nearly twenty years ago on the language families and linguistic cycles of the world, established the existence of a family of Japhetic languages that included the following: (a) Carian, Lydian, Misio, Lycean, Pisidio, Licanio, Cilician, and Capadocian in their most primitive states; (b) Etruscan; (c) Caucasian languages; (d) Elamite; (e) Mitanni; (f) Hittite; (g) Basque; and (h) Sumerian.[47] This classification was constructed on the basis of an analysis of the best-known of the aforementioned languages (specifically, Basque and the Caucasian languages) but also includes tongues that are less well known, but that came to be classified within the Indo-European language family. Among those who accept such a scheme—or one that is similar, there is considerable disagreement regarding the interrelationships among the included languages, and it is difficult to associate Father Schmidt's categorization with data from archeology and other disciplines. The problem of relationships among languages, when approached in general terms and in reference to the remote past, is conducive to the same kinds of misunderstandings that are seen in the positing of cultural relationships.[48] This is something that is important to keep in mind.

Archeologists[49] long ago, when studying the proliferation of dolmens, identified a "Pyrenean culture" during the Bronze Age. This culture had two main centers: one in Catalonia and another in the Basque Provinces and Navarre.[50] The link between these two centers has gradually been revealed.[51] The Catalonian center includes more striking examples of dolmens than the Basque center, and it is important to point out that a group of covered galleries in Catalonia includes furnishings that are older than many small dolmens or megalithic cists, which perhaps gives us reason to believe that not all of the Pyrenean cultures are as old as was formerly believed. Leaving aside for the moment the archeological problem, and studying the area of dispersion and the circumstances of the Basque/Navarrese and Catalan dolmens, we can conclude that they could only have been constructed by a shepherding people. The middle sierras, which are abundant in pasturage, and where they are found in abundance, is not suitable for agriculture, and the flatlands of places such as Urbasa and Encia remain, even today places where one can study the ancient pastoral ways of life. Such areas are also found in other northern zones, as we will soon see. Archeologists studying prehistoric settlements, and who conducted research regarding the abovementioned area of the Pyrenees, thought that it was occupied by the descendents of Paleolithic peoples, and that the modern descendents of those peoples are primarily the Basques.

Although it is not especially relevant, it is interesting to note that Basque words have been identified that seem clearly to be the products of life during the Stone Age. Barandiarán, the greatest Basque ethnological researcher, has written: "Some Basque nouns that have the component *aitz* (stone), such as *aizkora* (axe), *aitzur* (spade), *aizto* (knife), *azkon* (arrow), and *zukalaitz* (chisel), date back to the Stone Age and Copper Age—or perhaps to even earlier eras.[52] This assertion seems to be accurate (although there are philologists who have contended that it is vulnerable to a number of objections), as do many others that are based upon an analysis of current Basque vocabulary. We should note here that some Basque words are similar to those of Indo-European origin. For example, the word for silver, *zillar*, bears a striking resemblance to the English *silver*. The Basque language reveals that silver and gold were known before copper and tin, because the words for the latter are derived from the former: *urre* is gold and *urraida* (*aide* = similar) is copper; *zillar* is silver and *zirraida* is tin.[53] In studying these and other nouns, it should be borne in mind that their similarity with words in languages that have a very different structure may be on account of trade. It is also important to remember that, at the end of the Bronze Age, and at the beginning of the following period, the peninsula must have been the site of numerous colonizations and settlements. It was the site not only of settlements of peoples of obscure and complicated origin, but also of peoples who were part of the vast Indo-European family, whose movements are themselves shrouded in the dim mists of time. Until just a few years ago, all of the Indo-European peoples who came to the peninsula were subsumed under the label of "Celts." Yet the view of those people speaking "Aryan" languages has recently grown far more complex. The generally accepted ethnological hypothesis is that of the ancient Greek historian Diodorus, who contended that Celts and Iberians fought over the possession of Iberian territory, made peace with one another, shared the land, and married one another, thus giving rise to the Celtiberian people, whose customs he provides a general description of. His hypothesis and description is inspired by the observations of Posidonius c. 160–130 B.C.[54] But if the term "Celt" seems, from a linguistic point of view, to have a relatively clear referent, this is far from the case for the designation of Iberian, as either a noun or an adjective. We have in fact just seen that the analysis of what has linguistically been conceived as Iberian, which is of African origin, has given rise to a number of misunderstandings that are essentially analogous to those arising from an analysis of what archeologists conceive as "pre-Iberian." It would thus be beneficial, prior to moving on, to summarize the nature of the relationship with Africa that has been described in considerable detail in the preceding pages. In no way did these relationships imply that it was Africa that had the most profound influence on the peninsula.

  a) According to Baumann and other well-regarded Africanists, there was an ancient bushman culture that was related to the culture of some hunter-gatherer peoples that in the very distant past had spread throughout Western Europe and Africa, and that left traces of itself even in the Sahara. To be included in this large complex of hunter-gatherers are those peoples who produced the paintings of the Spanish Levant, paintings which closely resemble those of the bushmen, who absorbed the pictorial techniques, as well as other cultural and linguistic characteristics (and even certain physical characteristics) from those hunter-gatherers, who possessed European types, and who lived during the High Paleolithic and Mesolithic Ages.

  b) Amid and surrounding these bushmen and other peoples of an even more primitive culture, such as the pygmies, were agricultural civilizations of paleonegrid peoples, and of the Bantu language family. The characteristics of these cultures in many respects resemble those of the European Mediterranean during the Neolithic period. An agrarian culture that is very similar to that revealed by empirical research of certain prehistoric areas of Spain has been found, for example, in Angola, part of Rhodesia, Nyassa, and on the east coast of Africa, from the Rovuma to Zambezi rivers, in the Portuguese colony of Mozambique.

c) These cultures were in turn bordered on the north (leaving aside the desert) by shepherds and farmers of a more advanced culture that had been connected since the Neolithic Period with the peninsula.[55]

d) Finally, we find in this relatively more advanced culture a large number of characteristics that, from the time of the Bronze Age, stood completely outside of the general intercontinental relationships of a complex nature, but that instead arose from local centers of colonization activity on the part of either Semitic or Mediterranean peoples of varied origin. Thus, the repetition of certain words in Spain and Africa should not be considered as due to anything more than the reality that has been portrayed in the preceding pages and no one would dare defend a theory by citing these examples. Leaving aside for the time being those problems that arise from the study of the Basque language and the relationship of Iberia with Africa and with the non-Indo-European peoples of the Caucasus, we must turn to those issues which a number of researchers have identified that involve the expansion of peoples of the aforementioned Indo-European linguistic family prior to the arrival of the Celts, which also corresponds with the beginning of the Basque Iron Age.

6

On the Basque Lexicon

I

The idea that old dictionaries give of a language of course reflects when they were compiled, as well as the circumstances of their compilation. Thus, between the Covarrubias's *Tesoro de la lengua castellana o española* (Treasury of the Castilian or Spanish Language) and what is known as the *Diccionario de autoridades* (Dictionary of Authorities), which are separated by a little over a century, there are marked differences in the quantity and quality of the entries.[1] Afterward, the successive editions of the Spanish Royal Academy have continually introduced new entries, while relegating others to the categories of archaisms or localisms. The lexicon of a language is in continual evolution, for good or ill. This seems so obvious as to hardly need stating. Yet perhaps we don't reflect upon the obvious nearly as much as we should in order to avoid errors and confusion. Let's leave aside for the moment "the Castilian language" (as politicians say) or "the Spanish language" (as academics say). Let's instead turn our attention to another language: Basque. It is well known that the Basque language has for centuries been the target of reforms suggested by linguists of varying degrees of ability. At the end of the nineteenth century, there were writers who resisted accepting the orthography proposed by renowned philologists, and who wanted to instead use the spelling employed in popular texts, of their own time and of previous eras. Nevertheless, reform triumphed in the end and is in currently in the process of expansion. The language's vocabulary has also been the subject of successful campaigns advocating the inclusion of particular words. The example of the word *Euskadi* itself will suffice, for it is a word that, at the turn of the century, gave pause to Basquists and Bascologists.[2] The fact of the matter is that there is always a pressing need for neologisms. The invention of new words has most obviously occurred in conjunction with the introduction of new practices, customs, and ideas, with different kinds of coinages being employed at different times. There have been religious, legal, political, and technical neologisms. In terms of the present discussion, the particular field for which a new word is coined is unimportant. Even though a study on old forms of inventing words in Basque would be interesting indeed, such is not the purpose of the present essay. Instead, I will be focusing on a topic that is perhaps more exciting and equally important, since it also deals with changes—changes in the Basque worldview.

It is well known that ethnologists, by combining archeological research with studies in linguistics and folklore, have been able to provide interesting reconstructions of the "primitive world" of the Basques.[3] Certain words, as well as certain religious, magical, and mythic concepts, seem to have their origins in the remote past. Thus, "reconstruction" would seem to be the best approach. Paradoxically, the problem grows murkier when, instead of reconstructing an image of the very distant past in religious, mythical, and magical terms, we attempt to understand something about more modern and particular "worlds" (i.e., cultures and societies). What we are lacking in this regard is systematic research. We have no more than disperse and unconnected data. Moreover, dictionaries and lexicons that are useful for certain "elements" of vocabulary, and that provide interesting definitions of words that have a specific meaning for conducting the needed research that was previously indicated, are of little or no use when it comes to other purposes. There is no shortage of materials for those interested in studying the Basque words for the sky, the sun, the moon, the months of the year, and so on. Yet if one wants to analyze particular aspects of the Basque notion of work, and the medieval and modern practices related to it, one faces the previously mentioned void. "Modern" dictionaries are dreadful, while older dictionaries are simply suspect. Yet there is no choice but to consult the latter as a last resort. At the very least, the older dictionaries give us an idea of what once was used, but has since passed into disuse. We will now conduct a series of tests using two different dictionaries as references. The first of these will be the dictionary complied by Resurrección María de Azkue (1864–1951),[4] and the second that of Father Manuel de Larramendi (1690–1766).[5] Both Azkue's contempt for Larramendi as a lexicographer and his penchant for coining new words are well known.

Neither of these facts poses any real difficulties. However, a problem does arise from the fact that the eighteenth-century dictionary includes a series of concepts that are for the most part nowhere to be found in the early-twentieth-century dictionary, and these concepts are of essential importance not only for understanding the social and economic history of the Basque country, but also for having a clear notion of the *Weltanschauung* underlying a particular language—in this case Basque—during a particular era. Let's have a look at a few examples of what I am referring to here.

II

Anyone familiar with Basque history knows there are certain key concepts. One of these concepts is the seigniory of Vizcaya. If we open Larramendi's dictionary and look at the corresponding entry, what we find are three different meanings: (1) "domain" (*jabaria*); (2) "territory" (*jabadea*); and (3) "majesty" (*jaunderea*). Why did Azkue (who gives the definition of "to control" for *jabaritu*) eliminate the three words that had been included in Larramendi's dictionary? Why does he only include the word *jaurgo* (a native of Zuberoa)? Azkue's choice here seems arbitrary, considering that in other cases, his dictionary includes entries that have no more than a single reference to the author from which they were taken. It is simply implausible that, centuries ago, there was no word in Basque that was equivalent to Spanish *señorío*.

For "kingdom" (*reino*) Larramendi gives us the Basque *ereiñua/ereñua*, accompanied by his comments on the fact that this represents a kind of word that we will later discuss in terms of the characteristics that define it as a word of Basque origin. Neither of these words is found in Azkue's dictionary. Instead, he gives us *eregue*, along with a number of compounds thereof, some of which seem to be either neologisms or to represent literary usage, and others that are unaccompanied by any supporting references whatsoever—this despite the fact that Larramendi's *ereiñua/ereñua* appear to have been commonly used.[6]

This same kind of omission occurs in other cases that are worth noting. For the translation of the Spanish *fuero* ("jurisdiction" or "code of laws"), Larramendi supplies the Basque equivalents of *oitaratua* and *oitaraudea*. Azkue, on the other hand, provides the very general term *oitura* ("custom") without giving any indication of its legal meaning, which is critically important to understanding the term. Be that as it may, it also seems arbitrary that Azkue does not include the word *fueroak* in his dictionary, since it is a word frequently encountered in nineteenth-century texts, or even *foruak*, which is an older variant that was used in the seventeenth century. The word *lége* or *legue* is found in both Larramendi as well as Azkue. As was so typical of his approach, Larramendi provided an etymology of the words that attempted to show their Basque origins (he did the same for the Latin *lex*). This should come as no surprise, given that there are many instances of this obsession in Larramendi's dictionary. It is useful to examine several of these here.

Larramendi categorically stated that the full-blooded Spanish term of *behetría* (which is no longer used) is a Basque word, and proceeded to provide two alternate etymologies. The first, which construes the word as meaning "towns that freely elect a lord," comes (according to Larramendi) from the Basque *beret-iriac* or *beret-eriac*. The other etymology, which sees the word as being derived from *behetiriac* or *beheteriac*, construes the word as meaning "towns that noblemen (*hidalgos*) are not permitted to enter." Both of these etymologies are ludicrous. Yet the more important question for our purposes concerns the extent to which the word was used (in at least some areas) during the eighteenth century. In Larramendi's work, terms referring to particular legal matters or to institutions typically reflect the eras of their usage in a way that is not seen in Azkue's compilation. Thus, for *concejo* Larramendi supplies the Basque equivalents of *batzarea*, *uribilgura*, and *uribulgura*. The last two of these (which are merely dialectical variants of one another) are nowhere to be found in Azkue. Were they, then, merely figments of Larramendi's imagination? Also excluded from Azkue's dictionary are *bilguma* ("city government") and *bilgunteguia* ("town hall") as well as *bataria* and *chacarra* (both of which could be used to translate "university" in a rural setting). For the porch of a church (*anteiglesia*), Larramendi supplied the Basque equivalents of *eleizaurrea* and *eleyzaurea/eleizaurquea*. Azkue, on the other hand, provides no definition of the term consisting of a compound word containing the element of *eleiza*. Instead, the good Bizkaian father gives us *elizate*. The same phenomenon is observed with other specialized and consuetudinary legal words. According to Larramendi, there are words that express the concepts of community (*baquidargoa* or *anizquidargoa*) and municipality (*iricaya*). He also accepts that there is a Basque equivalent of "confederation" (*bilgumaquida* or *balleraquida*). Azkue, on the other hand, gives us *bakiak* for "meetings"—and nothing more.

We have a serious problem here. To what point are Larramendi's translations pure invention? How excessive were Azkue's omissions? It is obvious that not all of Larramendi's work can be dismissed as pure invention. And Azkue appears to have omitted certain material for merely subjective reasons.

To a considerable extent, the Basque lexicon of words in common use two hundred, three hundred, or four hundred years ago is simply unknown to us. Only those words used in religious texts tended to be preserved for posterity. Yet, even in these cases, we cannot be sure that the writer has not created new words as a matter of necessity.

Continuing for a moment our discussion of vocabulary of terms related to the institutions of the ancien regime, we can see that Larramendi accepted commonly used Basque terms that closely resemble their Spanish equivalents. Thus, he included the word *alcatea* (*alcalde* = "mayor") along with a number of its compounds. Similarly, he gives us *sindicua* for *síndico* ("syndic") and *juradua*. On the other hand, Larramendi supplied the Basque *juradua* and *sarianta* for *alguacil*, even though *alguacilla* has long been used (and still is used) in Basque. For the equivalent of "jury," he gives us *cineguiña* (*zin*). From an institutional standpoint, the term is important. However, Azkue does not include it (despite the fact that he does include *zin egin* ("to swear"/"to take an oath"). There are likely many people in Spanish-speaking areas even today who know what "to swear" means, but who do not know what a jury is. Larramendi accepts *erregidorea* as the Basque equivalent of "prefect" (*regidor*), *erregentea* and *erondia* for "regent" (this last term not included in Azkue's work), and both *gobernatorea* and *bazcazalea* for "governor." All of these forms are, in my view, legitimate, and ought to be reclaimed for the Basque lexicon since, in addition to their obvious usefulness, they conform to a phonological pattern seen in the case of other loan words.[7] It is important to always be mindful of the historical and cultural value of the words under discussion here. As regards the old divisions of the country, we have already discussed the terms of *señorío* and *reino*. Yet there are other examples as well. For example, all of us are familiar with the notion of province or provinces, principally in the context of the three historical Basque provinces. Even at the turn of the century, the inhabitants of Iruñea-Pamplona spoke in general terms of *provincianos* when referring to Gipuzkoans, Bizkaians, and Arabans. Larramendi retained the word *provincia* as the Basque equivalent of the identically spelled word in Spanish, while for *provinciano* (i.e., "provincial," used as a noun) Larramendi supplied the Basque adaptation of *provinciarra*, which certainly seems to have been used in his day. Along similar lines, we can rightly conclude that there is no reason to eliminate words such as *boilandea, coroea,* or *coroa* as equivalents of "crown" (Spanish *corona*).

As regards the administration of justice and certain aspects of civil society, Larramendi also provides ample context, at least in my view. For "judge" he gives us *jueza* as well as *ecadoya*. For court, he gives us *ecadoiteguia* and for the verb "to judge" he gives us *ecadoitu*. None of these translations are provided by Azkue, who also does not accept Larramendi's *letraduna* or *anzijarraya* for "lawyer," although he does supply *anzi* as the equivalent of "legal action/lawsuit" (*pleito* in Spanish). For "witness," Larramendi provides all of the following options: *daquirasa, talazta, cinollea, lecucoa,* and *testigoa*. Azkue, on the other hand, and citing Humboldt, provides only *talazta,* accompanied by a question mark indicating his uncertainty as to its accuracy.

Yet, for all the undoubted virtues of his work, Larramendi also included a number of patently ridiculous claims regarding the purported origin of Basque terms. For example, he contended that the verb *escribir* ("to write"), as well as its Latin cognate, were of Basque origin. The truth of course is the exact opposite: the Basque *izcribitu* (or its variant, *escribitu*, also cited by Larramendi) is derived from the Latin *scriptum*. Recognizing this does not mean that the words in question should be banished from the Basque lexicon, and more than a number of other words used to denote a "scribe," and that are derived from the same Latin root. Such words include *escribañua, escribaria* (or its variant, *escuardea*), *escubania,* and *escribaquintza*. Such words are important in light of both the large number of Basque "men of the quill" and the large number of houses in both towns and rural areas called *Escribenea, Escribanea,* and *Escribenekoborda,* and so forth.

III

Even a purist like Azkue was not able to exclude commonly used words derived from Spanish, such as *eskola* ("school") and *maisu* ("teacher"), and he even included the respective variants *maister* and *eskolau*. These words are derived from the Latin words *scholae, magistrum, magister,* and the Spanish words *escolano* and *maeso*. All of this is nothing more than *erderismo* (i.e., "use of non-Basque words") in the extreme, although certainly no less so than the kind displayed in Larramendi's *izcribitu,* which Azkue excluded.

Larramendi contended that the Spanish *maestre* ("professor," "ship's mate," or a degree) was derived from the Basque *maizter* or *maister*. Yet this is the least of the problems with his work. A far greater problem is that Larramendi's dictionary includes an extensive list of words related to *maisua* and *maistrea*. Some of these words had definitions related to the concept of *maestre* and its derivatives. In Spanish, *maestro* is a very colloquial word, while *maestre* sounds quaint and antiquated. The same is true of the Basque derivatives of these words supplied by Larramendi. In the etymologies that he supplies, Larramendi refers to occupations that have largely disappeared since his time, but that were familiar in the ancien regime, both to those who spoke Spanish and those who spoke Basque. On the basis of *maisu*, he formed the words for "schoolmaster" and "master of the chapel" (the Santesteban chapel of Donostia-San Sebastián was, during the nineteenth century, called *Maisu Zarra*), as well as "master of ceremonies." On the basis of *maistrea*,[8] Larramendi formed words designating the "ship's mate," "army chief of staff" (*maestre de campo* in Spanish), "cargo master" (*maestre de plata*), "provisioner" (*maestro de raciones*), "chief waiter" (*maestresala*), and "cathedral dignitary" (*mestrescuela*). It is beyond doubt that many of these occupations and offices were once well known in the Basque Country, although they had largely disappeared by the nineteenth century.

What is clearly needed, then, is comprehensive review of the Basque vocabulary that encompasses all of the facets of social and cultural life reflected in Larramendi's dictionary, since the work of this Gipuzkoan Jesuit reflects to a conception of life and of the world that has disappeared since he compiled his dictionary in the eighteenth century.

IV

Such a revision cannot be based on a simple "updating" of Larramendi's work. Still, the task at hand does involve a careful study of not only his dictionary but of other old texts that contain some material or other that is relevant to the enterprise.

We now turn to a subject that has not been addressed as commonly as certain other issues, even though it has been considerably modified from the eighteenth century until our own times. In his dictionary, Azkue included the Basque word *mirari* ("prodigy," "miracle") as a usage current in Bizkaia and Gipuzkoa. (Its derivative, *miraritu*, means "to be surprised.") This is clearly derived from the Latin *mirror*. Previously, Larramendi had included the word *miraquindea* (meaning "magically" or "that which surprises/causes wonder"). This adapted root was used as the basis for forming the following terms: *claria* ("artificial magic" or "white magic"), *beltza* ("black magic"), and *miraquin beltza* ("magical charm"). One does not find anywhere in Larramendi the vocabulary related to sorcery and witchcraft that is much more familiar to us today. Sometimes, Larramendi's coinages seem to be based on a parallelism with Spanish. For instance, in Old Spanish, the words *estrellería* and *estrellero* were used for "astrology" and "astrologer" respectively. Larramendi included the corresponding *izaraquindea* (literally, "the wisdom of astrology") and *izarjaquiña*. Neither of these words is found in Azkue's later work.

As regards technical vocabulary, it is well known that the vocabulary related to particular technical activities is generally not very "native" but is instead created on the basis of words from the languages of the people responsible for the invention or discipline in question. Of course, there are also those instances where foreign words have been phonetically adapted into Basque. Let's have a look at a few examples, beginning with nautical vocabulary.

Larramendi gives us *galeoya* for "galleon." This form perfectly reflects the way Basque adapts those words containing the Spanish suffix –*on* or the Latin suffix –*onem*. Thus, *leonem* yields *leoi* or *leoe*. *Galeoi*, with no article, is entirely correct. Larramendi attempted to show that the root of this word (present in the words *galeaza*, *galeota*, and *galera*) was of Basque origin. Basque shipbuilders used these words, and in certain documents, the form *gallara*, which appears to have been common at one time, is also used. As regards the names of large seagoing vessels, we have the Basque *ontzi* or *untzi*, which are used for the equivalent of the Spanish *navío*, *nave*, and *nao*.[9] In other instances, the Spanish word is conserved. One example of this is the Basque *carabelá* for "caravel" (Spanish *carabela*). In yet other cases, the Basque word that was formed was peculiarly descriptive in nature. Basque sailors used the word *bergantiña* (brigantine), as attested by the well-known song of the ship's captain. But Larramendi refers to "*amar edo amabi arraunaco* ontzia." A "storeship" in Basque is *goitala*, a word that does not appear in Azkue's dictionary. According to Larramendi, the Spanish word *zabra* (referring to a type of small vessel used on the coast of Biscay) is of Basque origin. This word also does not appear in Azkue's dictionary, despite the fact that the *zabra* was commonly used in the Basque Country. For "frigate," Larramendi provided not only *zabra* but also *azabra* and *gudonci*. He also contended that the Spanish *lancha* was of Basque origin. He made the same claim for the Spanish *barco* and *barca* ("ship" and "boat" respectively). For "barge," (*barcaza* in Spanish) he supplied the Basque equivalent *barcatzarra*. Larramendi clarified that the flat and wide boats were referred to respectively by the words *ala* and *gabarra*.[10] The Basque etymology of *gabarra* is quite colorful.

A brief exploration of those words used to designate the parts of boats reveals interesting information as well. For "ship's wheel," Larramendi offered the Basque equivalents of *lema*, *eraquilla*, and *timoya*. Azkue included only *lema*. For "anchor," Larramendi had *aingura* and *angora*, once again claiming a Basque origin of the Spanish equivalent *ancla* and, in this case, supplying interesting supporting evidence. Larramendi supplied the Spanish *gavia* as the Basque equivalent of "main topsail" and claims that this word too is of Basque origin. For the noun "sail" (*vela* in Spanish) he supplied both *vela* and *aizapia* (the latter not found in Azkue), including expressions containing those words as well as derivations. For "capstan," *giragora* is found in both Larramendi and Azkue. The word for "compass" (*itsasoaratza*) seems to be a calque of "navigation needle."

In general, it is striking how little published material there is (i.e., dictionaries, lexicons, collections of folklore, etc.) when it comes to nautical vocabulary. From the dearth of such material, one might even get the impression that the Basque Country itself is landlocked. While it is true that marine vocabulary tends to draw upon a shared international vocabulary, it is still necessary to study its historical development. For "pier," Larramendi gives the Basque equivalents of *caya* and *caiguiña* (both accompanied by the article). Azkue supplied the same equivalents, including a question regarding the obvious relationship with the French *quai*. *Portua* ("bay") also does not deserve to be excluded. The same goes for other sailing terms, such as *popa* ("stern," in Larramendi) and *proa* ("prow"). Larramendi provided the following Basque equivalents of "prow": *branca*, *branquea*, and *upaita*. Azkue included only *branca*. Larramendi tells us that the Basque for the Spanish *babor* ("port") is *esquereronz*, and that *estribor* ("starboard") is *alde escuya*. For *remo* ("oar") he offered the alternatives of *arrauna*, *errauna*, and *borcaya*, and included a number of common expressions with these terms that are certainly useful. As regards smaller sailing vessels, Larramendi indicated that *chalupa* is a Basque word, and for *bote* ("boat") he offered *bote*, *botea*, *botazea*, and *ontziaren botea*. At times he provided interesting technical terminology. For the gunwale, he supplied the Basque equivalent of *latalquia* (which was not included by Azkue). *Escotillas* and *escutas* ("hatches") are, according to Larramendi, Spanish words of Basque origin, and are synonymous with the Basque *atapeac*. *Sirga* ("tow line") comes from the Basque *txirga* and the verbs *txirgatu* and *txirga eraman* are derived from it. He further tells us that the *arbol de popa* ("stern mast") is called *mesaná* in Basque, and that masts in general are called *masteac*. "To mast a ship" is, in Basque, either *apaindú* or *edertú*, and to "furl masts" is *ontzia zuaiztu*. He gives *goitarguia* for the Spanish *faro* ("lighthouse"), although this smells of a possible neologism. Yet in other cases, Larramendi sticks closely to the facts. Thus the Basque terms for "first mate," "captain," "dockyard foreman," and "helmsman" are all similar to their Spanish equivalents. These should all be preserved for posterity, as should expressions such as *ontzi capitana* or *lenaigua* ("flagship"), and either *almirantearen ontzia* or *almirantá* for "vice-admiral's ship" (*almirantá* in Spanish). Also worthy of rescue are Larramendi's *upela* and *asupela* for the Spanish *grua* ("crane"), and *ontzi mutilla* for the Spanish *grumete* ("cabin boy"). Once more, Azkue expresses his doubt about the Basque *itsaslapur* as the equivalent of "pirate" (which he references in Añibano). Yet *itsaslapur* does appear in Larramendi, as do derivative words referring to piracy and the commission of acts of piracy. Larramendi also included in his work many more words referring to navigation than did Azkue, giving *berridoncia* for "packet boat" and *baleazalea* for "whaling ship."

It is possible to reconstruct the entire nautical vocabulary of Larramendi's time on the basis of a careful examination of his dictionary. Taking just the letter "b" (i.e., for the Spanish entries in the dictionary) we have the following: *barlovento* ("windward") = *aizaldea* or *aizalboa*; *barraganetes* ("futtocks") = *urnicioac*; *batel* ("small boat") = *batela*; *bauprés* ("bowsprit") = *zuaitzearra* or *baupresá*; *bolina* ("bowline") = *vela cearra*; *borda* ("gunwale") = *sayetsa* or *aldamena*; *botalón* ("boom") = *botaloya*; *botamen* ("casks") = *botamena, potamena, botadia*, or *potadia*; *brafoneras* (armor used to coat the arm) = *burniezcatac*; *brulote* ("fire ship") = *suotzia*; *buque* ("ship" = *bularca*. In Larramendi, both *calafate* ("caulker") and *cámara* ("chamber") are the same in Basque as in Spanish, while *camarote* ("cabin") = *ontzigelo*; *carena* ("repairing") = *artequistea* or *bularca*; *carraca* ("carrack") = *ontzizarra*; and the list goes on.

V

There are still other areas that require systematic research for the purpose of restoring to the general Basque dictionary other forgotten words that have lost their meaning in modern societies. When a particular function disappears within a society, when something is lost from among a society's cultural assets, it is difficult for words associated with those things to be retrieved.

This is the case even if we concede that there are cases in which Larramendi invented words that reflected the world in which he lived. Others have done the same thing, and not nearly so gracefully. Is there in fact any need for an entry in a contemporary dictionary of common usage for the word *genetliaco* ("genethliacal"). Larramendi included this word, translating it as "one who can foretell the fates" and giving the Basque equivalent of *patujaquindea*. Azkue, noting his uncertainty and citing Iztueta as a reference, gave the Basque *patu* as the equivalent of "fate" or "destiny." Who would have invented a word in such a way?

As regards the strata of the society of the ancien regime, the dictionary provides some very interesting information. For the Spanish word *escudero* ("shield-bearer," "squire"), Larramendi supplied the Basque *ezcutaria*, which is quite obviously derived from the Latin *surtarius*.[11] Yet there is also the fact that, in Larramendi's time, noble ladies had *escuderos*. The men who served this function were referred to in Basque by the less Latinized word of *escudaria*. For the Spanish *hidalgo* ("nobleman"), Larramendi gives the Basque equivalents of *aguiria*, *lexuntia*, *noblea*, and *aitonen semea*. He also supplies various other Basque terms related to the concept of *hidalguía*, among them *jatori garbia*. This is a term that likely has little meaning to us today. Azkue later excluded some of the words that had been supplied by Larramendi, but did include *aitonen semea*, referencing Urte. Among the Spanish words that would have been familiar to Larramendi were *mesnadero* (a non-firstborn son of a *ricohombre*), *infanzón* (Aragonese equivalent of *hidalgo*), *caballero* ("gentleman"), *collazo* (a kind of sharecropper), and *siervo* ("serf" or "servant"). Larramendi considered the Spanish *dama* ("lady") to be of Basque origin. For the Spanish *mayorazgo* ("primogeniture"), he gave the Basque equivalents of *nabugoquia* and *legoquia*, and for *mayordomo* ("steward"), he gave *ocentaria*. Azkue systematically excluded all of these words from his compilation. The idea of *baile* or *bailío* ("bailiff") was represented in Larramendi by the Basque *bailea* and *baitzallea*. Larramendi also had no shortage of words that refer to parties or factions (*bandos*). *Bandoa* was apparently used in Basque, as was *berezquia*. For the Spanish *banderizo* ("partisan"), Larramendi gave *bandaguillea* and *berezguillea*. The splinter group of a faction is called an *aldedaridea* and a member of a schismatic group is called an *aldedaria*.

Larramendi's dictionary also made important contributions to the vocabulary of commerce. For "tradesman," he supplies the following terms (including derivatives of each): *mercataría*, *tratalaria*, and *salerostaria*. Azkue supplies the same Basque equivalents. The two lexicographers also don't differ greatly from one another regarding the Basque words for *mercado*, *mercader*, and *mercancía*. But Larramendi does include a number of words related to certain kinds of trade that are not included in Azkue. Thus, the Spanish *buhonería* ("peddling") is, in Basque, *bizcar denda*. He distinguishes among various classes of *abacería* (a shop where different food items are sold), giving the Basque equivalents of *janariteguia* and *jaquiteguia* for the generic term, *arateguia* for a place where meat was sold, and *arrandeguia* for where fish was sold. A tavern was an *ardandeguia*, *txaya*, *arnoteguia*, or *daferna*, and a tavern where cider was sold was a *lentategiria*. Paño ("cloth") was *oyala*, a *pañero* ("clothier") was an *oyalaria*, and a cloth merchant was an *oyalmercataria*. As regards fabrics, Larramendi's work reflected products of his time that are no longer referred to in either Spanish or Basque. The woolen cloth that was called *anascote* in Spanish was called *anascotea* in Basque. Yet Larramendi does not use the Spanish word then current (*contray*) for very fine cloth. The linen of Ruan was *ruana*. *Terciopelo* ("velvet") was *irulleta* and there was *brocadua*, *brocatela*, and *cambraya* (from Cambray). Larramendi held that the Spanish word *sarga* ("serge") was a of Basque origin, and for *seda* ("silk") he gave *ciricua*, which sounds as if it is derived from *sericam*. *Damasco* ("damask") was *damascoa* and *grana* (a fine scarlet cloth) was either *suteoa* or simply *graná*. *Vellori* (most likely "copper" —ed.) was another word held by Larramendi to be of Basque origin, and he supplied the equivalents of *belloria* and *billoria*.[12]

As regards arts, industries, and occupations that no longer exist, Larramendi's work is also a gold mine of information. If we take one of the Basque Country's paradigmatic industries—the armaments industry—we see that Larramendi refers to those who manufacture arquebuses with the Basque term *alcabuzguillea*, while a *ballestero* ("archer") is a *ballestaria*, an *escopetero* ("gunsmith") is an *escopetaria*, an *espadero* ("swordsmith") is an *ezpataquiña* or *izpataguillea*, and a *lancero* ("maker of pikes") is a *lanzateguia*. From Larramendi, we also learn that there were *boneteros* ("bonnet makers") in the Basque Country, and that they were called *boneteguilleac*. *Bordadores* ("embroiderers") were *bordariac* or *bardatzalleac*, *cordoneros* ("ropemakers") were *cordoiguilleac* or *esgarriguilleac*, and *cedaceros* (those who sell or make sieves) were *bai-*

guilleac, baeguilleac, baiquiñac, or *cetabeguilleac.* A *guantero* ("glove-maker") was *achorreguillea, escularruquiña,* or *guanteguillea,* while a *guadamacilero* (a maker of printed leather) is either *navarluquiña* or *navaluguillea.* A *guarnicionero* ("harness maker") is a *gordacaiguillea.* *Chapinería* (a shop where clogs and pattens are made and sold) is a *txapinteguia* or a *gordoinquiteguia.* A *cabestrero* (a maker of halters and collars) is a *cabrestuguillea, cabrestuquiña,* or *zalquiquiña.* A *calcetero* (one who makes, mends, or sells stockings) is a *galtzetaguillea,* and a *tintorero* ("dyer") is a *tintelaria, gambusteguia,* or *coransteguia.* A *tundidor de paños* ("shearer of cloth") is a *ulanlea* or *ulantaria,* and a *curtidor* ("tanner") is a *larrutzulea* or *narrutzalea.* These occupations appear alongside others that will be more familiar to contemporary readers. There is no specific word for "guild" as such. The Basque towns, with their tradition of medieval craftsmanship, were centers of other kinds of activities not traditionally represented by guilds, and which were expanded in scope and refined in execution over time.

Larramendi, who was a man of his time, incorporated the word "chocolate" into his dictionary, providing the Basque equivalents of *chocolatea* and *godaria,* and also supplying the derivatives *chocolataria/godariguillea* ("one who makes or sells chocolate"). He supplies no separate Basque words for *confitería* ("confectioner's shop") or *pastelería* ("pastry shop"). *Bizcocho* ("cake/pastry") is another of the many words that Larramendi contends to be of Basque origin, and he defines one particular kind of pastry, *hojaldre* ("puff pastry") as *gantzorea.*

When it comes to food, the Spanish words supplied as entries by Larramendi are often archaic and pure. And so it follows that the Basque equivalents are also archaic and pure. Today, hardly anyone knows what *sopas abahadas* ("steamed soups") are. The Basque equivalent is *zopa itoac,* and Larramendi explained, "*Eltzeá edo catilluá estali ta eguiten diranac.*" ("Pot or mug that are covered.") He identifies the Spanish word *cecina* ("dried and salted meat") as a word of Basque origin (the Basque equivalent of which is either *ceciña* or *ceceiña*). For *acitrón,* he gives the Basque *acitruya.* For *agujas de pastelería* ("pastry tubes"), he gives the Basque equivalent of *ogui orratzac. Alajú* (a paste made of honey and nuts) is *oraeztia. Alexijas* (a kind of barley puree) is *garagarraya.* The Spanish *alfeñique* (a kind of sugar paste) is *orasucrea. Almojábana* (a cheese paste) is *gaztataloa* or *gaztopilla,* while *mantecadas* (small rectangular sponge cakes) are *oraguria.* Larramendi thought that *arrope* ("boiled wine") was a Basque word. He also saw *badulaque* ("a ragout of stewed livers") as a word of Basque origin, in addition to attesting its use in the Basque language.

A number of observations are in order in closing. Larramendi included in his work a large number of Spanish words derived from Arabic. A glance at the pages of entries beginning with "al-" suffices to prove this point. Larramendi contended that some of these words had become incorporated into Basque, including the following: *albornía* ("a large glazed jug"), *albornoza* ("bathrobe"), *alcabalá* ("excise"), *alcandora* (which, according to Larramendi, is a men's shirt, whereas an *atorra* is a woman's blouse), *alcarabea* ("caraway seed"), and *alcarraza* (an unglazed, porous jug). He supplies Basque etymologies for some of these words. In other instances, he derives an etymological relationship with Basque words on the basis of phonological similarity. Examples of this are Spanish-Basque pairs in which the "l" of the Arabic preface "al-" is dropped in the Basque variant. Thus *almidón* ("starch") in Spanish becomes *amiruna, almirez-amireza,* and *almizcle-amizclea.*

I have made similar observations elsewhere with regard to legal vocabulary, penalties, punishments, and crimes. In sum, Larramendi's work constitutes a treasure trove waiting to be mined by both historians and linguists.

7
The Basque Country and Dialectology

Homage to Prince Louis Lucien Bonaparte

In the year 1869, a French-language book was published in London with lithograph illustrations that bore the title *Carte des sept provinces Basques montrant la delimitation actuelle de l'euscara et sa division en dialects, sous dialects et varieties* (Map of the Seven Basque Provinces Showing the Current Delimitation of Euskara and Its Division by Dialect, Sub-Dialect, and Variety). The author of this work was Prince Louis Lucien Bonaparte. Another map drawn by this same man was published around the same time, although he had completed it in 1863. One of the maps showed the population distribution according to dialect spoken, while another map showed the variations of each dialect, and also delineated mixed zones.[1]

In 1869, the prince also published *Le verbe basque en tableaux* (Basque Verb Tables), an earlier edition of which had previously been published.[2] In the two works, he presented the results of the vast research he had conducted during his extensive travels in the Basque Country. He began these travels in 1856–1857. In other words, about one century ago, the fourth child of the most able and independent of Napoleon's brothers traversed the Basque territories conducting seminal research that remains an indispensable resource even in our own time.

It is beyond question that studies of dialectology have sparked renewed interest in recent years. Yet, at the same time, in my opinion other needed research areas that ought to be conducted with the same vigor lag behind and suffer from a lack of support. This is true not only within the Basque context, but also with respect to other areas of the peninsula. I am referring here to the general field of historical geography. We continue to lack a standard reference of the geography of the Iberian Peninsula as it was in antiquity. This is because the work that Professor Schulten wrote during his final years was far from being completed at the time of his death, at least as far as I know.3 The best reference published thus far, in general terms, continues to be *España sagrada* ("Sacred Spain") by Enrique Flórez and his successors. There is an even more urgent need for a good treatise of medieval geography, given that the Middle Ages saw the fixing of boundaries of kingdoms, regions, and districts that have long had a profound meaning within the context of Spanish life. We will not at this juncture go into too much depth as regards those kingdoms, regions, and districts. I should only like to make mention of the fact that there are two Basque dialects—Gipuzkoan and Baztanese (a variant of Northern High Navarrese). What we need to know—or at least try to learn—if we want to lay the foundation for serious research in the future, is the historical-cultural meaning of the entities of those regions that we are referring to: in the present examples, Gipuzkoa and Navarre (and, within Navarre, the Baztan Valley).

If we fail to do this, we may end up with a very rickety linguistic foundation that does not take sufficient account of time and space as relevant variables, and this in turn can only lead to a series of dead ends.

What I would like to take up here are a number of issues related to Basque dialectology in relation to historical geography, taking as my point of departure the research conducted by the great Bascologist whose memory we now honor. My purpose here is to call into question the broad generalizations taken as incontrovertible truths regarding the immutability and impermeability of Basque, and to place the study of its dialects on a firmer foundation than that typically found in modern works. The remote origins and earliest studies of our language are undoubtedly important. Yet, in my view, these should not constitute an exclusive focus when it comes to striving to attain a broad-based understanding of the Basque language.

Basque Dialects

The awareness that the Basque language (or *Euskera*) has dialectical variations goes back a long way. It can justly be said that every speaker of the language gains such awareness as soon as the speech of Basques from other regions is heard. This difference among distinct ways of speaking carries with it a value judgment—that is, a comparison among the different variants and an assessment as to which of them constitutes the purest form of the language (and, conversely—on the basis of more or less sound criteria—of which dialects are the "worst" or "most corrupt"). It should be noted that such value judgments also have an ethical aspect. For example, it was once said in eastern Gipuzkoa that the Basque spoken in other regions—especially in the French Basque Country and in Navarre—was an appropriate communication medium for those with a perverse affinity for witchcraft and the black arts.[4]

The identification of the principal Basque dialects goes back to Axular, who wrote the following in the *Guero*: "Badaquit halaber ecin heda naitequeyela euscarazco mintçatçe molde guztietara. Ceren anhitz moldez, eta diferentqui mintçatcen baitira Euscal herrian, Naffarroa garayan, Nafarroa beherean, Cuberoan. Lappurdin, Bizcayan, Ippuscoan, Alabaherrian, eta bertce hainitz lekhutan."[5] The examples of variation cited by Axular are for the most part lexical in nature.

Dialectical differences within the Basque language based on nothing more than phonetic variation were also recorded. Some of these purported differences seem to be based on dubious assumptions regarding synonymity. In other cases, the geographic identification of the dialectical variations is suspect.[6]

Joannes d'Etcheberri (d. 1749), a follower and admirer of Axular, indicated the possible influence of *erderismos* (i.e., Latinization) in dialectical variations: with influences from Spanish in Araba and Bizkaia, and from Bearnese or Gascon in Zuberoa (Soule).[7]

Etcheberri was also well aware of certain explanations that are adduced even today to explain other dialectical variations,[8] and of the fact that varieties of Basque existed that pertained to sectors of the population that were smaller than those he identified, that is, the Baztan or Erronkari (Roncal) valleys.[9]

A much more famous contemporary of Etcheberri, Father Manuel de Larramendi (1690–1766), attempted to lay more solid foundations of Basque dialectology[10] in his *Corografía de Guipúzcoa* (Chorography of Gipuzkoa), pointing to the existence of a number of different dialects: Zuberoan, Lapurdian, Bizkaian, Navarrese (with many sub-variations), Araban (which, according to Larramendi, "is generally the same as Bizkaian, although not entirely"), and Gipuzkoan.

Within Gipuzkoan, which is the dialect that Larramendi was most familiar with, he distinguished the following subvariants:

1. The Beterri variant, with the following subregional variants: (a) from Irun to Errenteria (Rentería); (b) from Donostia-San Sebastián to Tolosa; (c) from "the port" to Mutriku (Motrico).
2. The Goierri (Goyerri) variant: with an axis running from Tolosa to Azpeitia.
3. A variant bearing a similarity to the Bizkaian dialect, encompassing Elgoibar, and especially Eibar, Soraluze (Plasencia), Bergara (Vergara), Arrasate (Mondragón), Aretxabaleta (Arechavaleta), Eskoriatza (Escoriaza), Gatzaga (Salinas), and Oñati (Oñate).[11]

Books published in Basque from the sixteenth through the eighteenth century, and which were primarily of a religious character, had been utilized by Larramendi to establish the most important differences among the dialects. Prince Bonaparte, prior to carrying out the aforementioned work of synthesis, ordered the translation and publication, at his own expense, of many texts (which were also for the most part religious) of variants spoken in particular localities that he thought were either representative or not well known.[12]

The prince established the following well-known system of groups and dialects:

The Basque Language

1. Eastern group:
    1) Zuberoan
    2) Low Eastern Navarrese
    3) Low Western Navarrese
2. Central group:
    4) Lapurdian
    5) High Northern Navarrese
    6) High Southern Navarrese
    7) Gipuzkoan
3. Western group
    8) Bizkaian

Among the eight dialects, Bonaparte enumerates some twenty-one subvariants.

His classification was accepted by Vinson, Campión, Azkue, and also by younger Bascologists.[13] In subsequent years, Bonaparte's classification was promoted and modified by men such as Irigaray, Koldo Mitxelena (Luis Michelena in Spanish), Irizar, and others too numerous to mention.

Today, we have the good fortune to possess not only a number of different general schemas and paradigms, but also examples of the speech of lands in which Basque is no longer spoken, such as the Ilzarbe Valley, south of Iruñea-Pamplona, and generally speaking, the other areas where High Southern Navarrese had been prevalent. In addition, we have examples of Erronkariera and other dialects.[14]

Here we also see the need to provide a renewed impetus to the theoretical study of dialects, taking as a point of departure the inquiries of the prince as well as of his predecessors, and adhering to the following criteria:

1. Phonetic criteria that reflect variations of some importance and generality in the pronunciation of the same words.
2. Lexicological criteria that reflect, on the contrary, variations in the use of words.
3. Syntactic criteria that reflect variations in the action and coordination of words.

Ancient Divisions of the Basque Lineage

Each aspect of Basque dialectology is significantly problematic. It is only after the problems have been clarified that proper responses to general questions can be supplied. And it is precisely these general questions that we have to ask ourselves in light of our awareness of the existence of Basque dialects. One of these questions clearly refers to their historical origins. In one of his writings, Larramendi compares the Basque dialects to Greek dialects.[15] This comparison may be useful for establishing an initial general criterion of historical research. Said criterion would be along the lines of the argument that some of the dialects spoken long ago in very restricted areas may have resulted from schisms within lineages that were originally united, and the geographic location of those lineages in specific territories. It is here that we come to see the importance of historical geography.

The task of determining the boundaries of the peoples that lived in the territories of Gaul and the Iberian Peninsula during antiquity has provided a great deal of labor to Spanish and French scholars ever since the Renaissance. Scholars in the Basque Country (or, at any rate, scholars who have ties to it) have also worked hard to determine the degree of similarity between the region's ancient and modern administrative and ecclesiastical boundaries. The results of such inquiries have neither been completely affirmative nor entirely fruitless. This is as it always is. When it comes to such matters, there is no such thing as a general rule. Instead, there are only specific cases that at times contradict one another.

Modern Navarre covers somewhat less territory than ancient Vasconia. In addition, the three current Basque provinces do not correspond to the borders of these same territories in ancient times. And yet traces remain of these divisions that are linguistic rather than administrative in nature. In the seventeenth century, French Basque historian Arnaud Oihenart Etchart postulated the following equivalences between the peoples known to have existed in ancient times, and those that spoke Basque in his own time, as follows:

1. French Basques = Aquitanians
2. Gipuzkoans and Arabans = Varduli
3. Bizkaians = Autrigones[16]

Such reductive schemas are not only inadequate, but also inaccurate, since only the extreme western portion (which is not itself completely Basque) of Bizkaia was occupied by the Autrigones. In addition, the parts of Gipuzkoa and Araba that belonged to the Varduli was in the east, while the western areas were occupied by Caristii and Caristes.[17]

Taking into account more highly specified boundaries, Arturo Campión averred that that the peoples of Gipuzkoa, who lived in what had once been territory occupied by the Vascones (according to the Ptolomaic Tablets), no longer spoke the Gipuzkoan dialect but rather a variety of High Northern Navarrese.[18] Campión also contended that the part of Bizkaian territory where Basque had not been spoken for centuries was the same land that had been occupied by the ancient Autrigones.[19] On the other hand, the boundary between the Bizkaian and Gipuzkoan dialects did not correspond to the current provincial borders, but instead more or less conformed to the boundary between the hordes of Varduli and Caristii.[20] In other words, along some of the dialectical boundaries where Basque has survived in the north of the peninsula, it appears that there remains a trace of the ancient gentilitious divisions. This is indeed interesting. In the southern part of the country, in Araba, it seems that during the Middle Ages and modern times there was a period of Bizkaian ascendency (or, if you will, a progressive "Bizkaianization"). This can be said, because of the high significance of the fact that some names that, at the beginning of the eleventh century, appear in texts such as the *La reja de San Millán*, and which reflected a central or eastern variant of Basque, later appeared with a distinctively Bizkaian (i.e., western) cast. We thus have *Harizavalleta* and then *Arechavaleta*, *Narbaiza* and then *Narbaja*. It is possible to trace other elements that confirm that in another time, to the east of a line that would have been located from north to south across the current province of Araba through Trebiñu (Treviño), "*Trifinium*" (or the point of contact of three different ethnic groups), Basque speech had a more "western" character and that this western form cut across the boundary between the Varduli the Caristii.

In sum, the hypothesis is that the Vascones were a people who originally spoke Navarrese dialects, that the Varduli spoke a Gipuzkoan dialect, and that the Caristii spoke Bizkaian, with the expansionist momentum of the latter carrying it south of the gentilitious boundaries. In Aquitaine, we only have to go back as far as the Late Roman Empire to find a population that was designated by the name of *Lapurdum*, a name that, according to most authors, was derived from the land of "Labourd" or "Lapurdi,"[21] where Lapurdian was spoken. The origin of "Soule" ("Zuberoa" or "Ziberoa") was also sought among a name recorded in Roman times: the Sybillates, which was certainly related to the medieval place names of *Sibillatensis* (*pagus*) and *Subola*.[22] In other words, it is possible to establish a relationship between French Basque dialects and ancient place names.[23]

Enigmatic Settlements

Thus, there seems little that remains to do in order to place the historical geography of the country during ancient times within the framework of the most important known dialects. This in turn opens up two new paths of inquiry. One would be to delve into the past and to study Basque and its various dialects in relation to other languages that were spoken in larger geographical areas: especially Aquitainian and Iberian. This is a matter that of course exceeds the bounds of dialectology. Yet some remarks are in order regarding such an undertaking. The latest studies demonstrate two things: the first is that there is a greater degree of similarity between Basque and Aquitainian than between Basque and Iberian (i.e., the language spoken in the eastern part of the peninsula as a whole.[24] The second path would take as its point of departure the fact that, in the territory of the Basque provinces and Navarre, the percentage of Latin inscriptions with Basque or "Basque-like" names is very small indeed. Those in Araba (where the most such inscriptions have been found) reveal that the Varduli and Caristii were related in some way to the Cantabrians and Asturians. This forces us to once again address the problem of what we could call the Cantabrianism of the peoples of the northeast littoral, which rigorous criticism seems to have negated altogether. Based upon the Ptolemaic tablets (which is the most reliable source we have of ancient historical geography), it is impossible for anyone to now deny that the Cantabrians (as identified by Ptolemy) can be considered, when all is said and done, those who inhabited what we currently know as the Cantabrian Mountains.[25] But a good many (even if not all) of the previous texts, and even some of the more recent texts, lead one to believe that those who lived between the mountain and the boundaries with Vascones and Aquitainians were also known as Cantabrians. In their struggles with Caesar's lieutenants, the Aquitainians would, for example, turn to these Cantabrians for support.[26] The state of affairs as indicated by Ptolemy in the second century AD may reflect a fissure of the Cantabrian peoples. Such a phenomenon has often been seen in other societies governed by a lineage system in which, following the passage of a certain number of generations, different branches take on their own names, the factions and subfactions divide,[27] and wars between factions are far from rare. Ancient references to the difficulty and obscurity of Cantabrian words and names are similar in content to what has been said in more recent times regarding the Basque language.[28] Yet, before moving on, it is important to point out that the names that have come down to us from ancient texts (e.g., the aforementioned Ptolemaic tablets, the Antonine Itinerary, and epigraphic inscriptions) of peoples and individuals who were settled in all of these lands do not really have much of a Basque flavor.

If we turn to the Cantabrian territory in the strictest sense of the word, Adolf Schulten has shown the presence there of a variety of names that he characterizes as Ligurian, Celtic, and Iberian, contending that Iberian was superimposed upon the former two languages. Antonio Tovar, on the other hand, who focused on languages that are more Indo-European in character, believes that what happened was the exact opposite, and that it was the Indo-European languages that were more modern, and that were later superimposed.[29] Whatever element of Basque remains is minute indeed, even though its presence is detectable. It appears that the linguistic Romanization of the Cantabrians and Asturians occurred at a very early stage. One way or another, it is beyond doubt that the ancient peoples who spoke the Vasconian language were in contact—perhaps intimate contact—with those peoples who spoke a language that we cannot clearly identify. It is apparently due to such contact that we are able to observe the following phenomena: the Basque word for "horse" (*zaldi*) may be related to the Asturian *thieldo(nes)*; in original Asturian mining vocabulary, the word *arrugia* was used, while the Basque language has the word *arragua*.³⁰ Similar examples exist. In the end, though, the data are lacking, and I do not want to force an interpretation.³¹

Let us now turn to more modern times, during which the geographical extension of the Basque language assumed its current shape.

We know that, when the Romans conquered the Cantabrians, Asturians, Vascones, Aquitainians, and other mountain peoples, they forced them to leave their ancient mountain homeland and to live instead in the plains or other lower-lying lands.³² It is likely that, during the era prior to the Roman conquest, the territorial boundaries among "peoples," lineages, and blood groups were not on high ground, and that the valleys constituted the nucleus of the gentilitious possession. Instead, populations resided on the peaks and slopes of the mountains themselves, with boundaries among different entities running through lowlands, and marked by natural topographical features such as rivers, streams, lines of channels, valleys, and mountain passes. Such settlement patterns are still commonly seen in the mountainous zones of North Africa.³³

The nature of the changes that this enforced resettlement wrought in the lives of the inhabitants of the land was not merely economic, but also linguistic. From a very early date, we can see that cities were established in the southern Basque territories (e.g., Araba and Navarre). The idea of a *civitas* gained ascendance over other conceptualizations, such as those of *populi*, *gentes*, and so on. Yet urban settlement decreases in importance the farther southward we look, with the gentilitious systems (with their factions and subfactions) retaining their importance. This system has been thoroughly studied within the context of Cantabrians and Asturians. Yet there are also remnants of Roman organizations that were typical of rural environments. In the French Basque Country, not very far from here, we find that, between the third and fifth centuries before Christ, there was a fairly important rural system of courts called the *magister pagi*), which was cited in the famous inscription of Hazparne (Hasparren), which is now considered authentic, and which also informs us of the autonomy that had been attained by the Aquitainian peoples of the southeast vis-à-vis the Gauls. These peoples also possessed what could be called their own "urban capitals" (i.e., markets and developed fortresses) which were in many cases the precursors of the modern cities that exist on those same sites today, and that conserve the gentilitious name. This is something that is frequently seen in France.³⁴

The *magister pagi* must have exercised his authority upon those who were referred to by the generic term of "peoples" (*populi*) and on geographical territories. In mountain lands such as these, and at a time when settlements had achieved a certain degree of stability, it must have been easy to establish clear boundaries among these different populations. This ease of establishing borders would have been due not so much to the topographical feature of mountains (as had previously been the case) but to their opposite—valleys (*vallis* in Latin, *aran* and *ibarr* in Basque).

Those who resided in the valley would have been distinguished by certain common interests, obligations, legal practices, and so forth. If there is any truth to the theory that the current population of many places within a country has its origin in settlements of the type represented by the Roman *fundi* or *villae* (and I believe that there are grounds for having a high degree of confidence in such a theory), the *magister pagi* was one of the most distinguished residents of such *fundi* and *villae*. The degree of Romanization of such settlements would have fluctuated depending on the historical era in question as well as other circumstances.[35]

The Middle Ages inherited the Roman tradition. During the Visigothic and Merovingian eras, the concept of *pagus* came to be employed in the most general of terms. This is something that can be seen in the work of Gregory of Tours.[36] But the idea of "valley" was employed with an ethnological meaning. The pays de Soule was called *vallis Subola* in a text written by Fredegario that referred to the year 645.[37] Other works, which referred to earlier periods (e.g., the year 572), refer to *Rucones*, who seem to have been inhabitants of the Erronkari (Roncal) Valley (referred to as *Runcale* in a Gipuzkoan song[38]). During later periods, the names of the valleys recur in various texts. We can conclude that during the first centuries of the *Reconquista*, these valleys had the same kind of significance as geographical and administrative entities that they have today, especially in the east. Thus, Father José de Moret and other historians did not hesitate to conclude that the boundaries of the ancient kingdom of Navarre were the same as the Navarrese territorial boundaries of their own time. The reference point for the ancient boundaries was for the most part those indicated in texts such as the census of 366 (soon to be published by Don José Javier Uranga[39]), which is one of the most important documents we have upon which to base a study of life in late medieval times. I do not see Moret's presentation as particularly farfetched. At the same time, a study of the dates when the names of these valleys and entities first appeared is certainly in order, and would not be a particularly daunting task.[40]

If we trace a modern map over the traditional divisions of Navarre, we discover something that has profound linguistic and historical-cultural implications: the line of maximum expansion of the Basque language, which is historically well known and well documented, conforms nearly exactly to the line that indicates the division of valleys. South of this line, the population centers are cities and towns that have territories that are rather less defined. To the north of the line, however, there are a series of divisions that are characterized not only by their geography, but also by legal, administrative, and cultural characteristics. The Errokari, Baztan, and Burunda Valleys each have their distinctive customs. Linguistically speaking, it should be acknowledged (or at least admitted as a useful working hypothesis) that, in each valley, a variant of Basque is or was spoken that is each worthy of separate study.

In order to assure the proper progression of dialectological studies, we need to not only know the characteristics of the dialects, subdialects, and varieties identified by Bonaparte and his successors, but also to have a clearer idea of the particular speech of each valley: that of Errokari, Zaraitzu (Salazar), Aezkoa, Baztan, and Ultzama—in addition to the speech of Larraun and the Lower Basaburua. The ideal would be to "at least" have a grammar and vocabulary of each of these variants in order to preserve them for posterity in a future linguistic atlas. In addition, such works would be of profound historical importance. Enterprises of this nature might also qualify to a degree some of the sweeping generalizations of Prince Bonaparte. For example, when one hears Basque spoken (by those who still know the language) in the valleys of Atetz (Atez) and Imotz (Imoz), and in towns such as Beratsain (Berasáin) or Muskitz (Muzquiz), and bearing in mind the speech of the five towns, the concept of "High Navarrese" in the far north of Navarre would seem to be rather imprecise, from both a phonetic and a lexicological point of view.

Basque and Latin: Some Hypotheses

The Romance languages evolved from Vulgar Latin and eventually gave rise to standardized written languages such as Spanish, French, and Italian which have become further developed, differentiated, and refined through their great and glorious literatures. We all know that Basque does not have a comparable tradition. Yet does this mean that the Basque language is so immutable in character, and so bereft of flexibility, as some have alleged? I am personally inclined to believe that the general dialectical fragmentation from the very beginning are a reflection of the gentilitious divisions of ancient times, as we have seen. Yet I also believe that Basque has endured profound transformations during the same period that Romance dialects have evolved, when the geographical organization centered on valleys was at its height. This is something that is difficult to prove. We do not have evidence that a process occurred with Basque that was similar to what happened with Latin and the Celtic tongues. What we do have, however, is a collection of data that do demonstrate broad-based transformations—including more modern transformations.

At least until the beginning of the eleventh century, it can be said that even the western and southern dialects that were spoken in close proximity to Spanish, such as Araban, conserved the aspirate sounds of "h" and "j." *La Reja de San Juan*, which I mentioned earlier, provides strong evidence of this.[41] But the findings that are now considered valuable in terms of dialectology occurred later. In contrast to the eastern French Basques, who derived *fagu-a* from *fagus*, the Basques of the central zone pronounced the word *bagu-a*, while those of the western zone pronounced it *pagu-a*, introducing an unvoiced consonant, the initial "p," which Schuchardt had previously demonstrated was of foreign origin.[52] The dialectical forms of the word *ecclesia* are also highly differentiated, ranging from the Bizkaian *elaja* or *eleja* to *elieza* or *eliza* and the French Basque *elissa*. What this means, I believe, is that the dialects continually "re-created themselves" during very different eras, and that, even when it comes to the pronunciation of words that are not of comparatively recent origin, it is important to discover the comprehensive influence of the different Basque variants. The differences among the variants are, at times, rather troubling. For example, one wonders why western Basque took the Latin *molinum* and derived from it *bolin*, *boliñ*, *bolu*, *borin*, and so on (which gave rise to Bolibar [Bolívar], Borinivar, Bolinaga, etc.), while eastern Basque retained the forms of *rotam*, *rueda*, and even *errota*, along with all of its components and derivatives.

Also worthy of close dialectological study are the different forms of biological and spiritual relationship, of names of objects, and of facts related to religious practice, law, medicine, technology, borrowed nouns, or nouns of medieval origin.

The matter of locative suffixes would also be clarified to a greater extent than is currently the case, in the light of the application of both dialectology and historical geography. Thus, just as texts provide us broad-based information regarding entities and people, the study of smaller settlements can only be conducted in light of toponymy. Many years ago, Justo Gárate published a list of suffixes grouped in a particularly illuminating way.⁴³ This enterprise was later vigorously carried forward, and reached completely opposite conclusions in a number of cases. Gárate himself, along with Isaac López Mendizábal and others, have criticized some of my own hypotheses regarding the meaning of certain Basque place names, and of various suffixes pertaining to said place names. Others have defended my views. Although I will not reproduce a detailed version of my views here, I would, in conclusion, like to say something regarding both my hypotheses and the criticism to which it gave rise, since both are relevant to the subject at hand.

One of the suffixes that has been most frequently discussed has been "-ain," which I have assumed is related to the Latin suffix "-anu." When I presented this idea before the Toponymy Congress in Brussels, both phoneticists and comparative linguists, such as Foucbé and the younger Johannes Hubschmid expressed their opposition, with the latter contending that "in Basque" the ending "anu(m)" gives rise to "au" (as reflected in the case of *garau* (which is derived from *granum*). To me, such an example demonstrates nothing other than the ease with which "phonetical" laws can be conceived on the basis of partial evidence, and without taking into account the complexity of dialects. Thus, one example was presented as proof of some supposed law but, at the same time, sufficient account was not taken of other instances, such as *albain*, which means both "sieve" (*vannus*) and a strand of thread (*filum vanum*) of an elegant cloth (*apain* or *aphain*), which appears to be derived from *apannus*. There are still other variants from oriental dialects. And, as if this were not enough, other instances relevant to the issue seem to have been forgotten, such as the fact that Etcheberri, in his works written in Lapurdian, used the form *capitain* for *capitán*,⁴⁴ a use which was also seen in the song of the viscount of Belzunce, which was written in Low Navarrese:

> *Belzunce bizcondea*
> *Hain capitain andia*⁴⁵
>
> (the Viscount of Belzunce,
> Such a great captain.)

The typical tendency of most Bascologists to dismiss obviously Latinized forms out of hand has been and will continue to be conducive to a good many overgeneralizations. Yet I myself continue to believe that names such as Beraskoain (Belascoain), Gendulain, Baternain, and so on are typical names of the ancient possessions, and that they are formations based upon the Latin suffix -*anu(m)* that are used mainly in the eastern zone, especially in Navarre, during one historical period. Other names reflecting this same suffix are Amillano, Arriano, Catadiano, Legutiano, Luquiano, Vitoriano, and so forth. Yet the words of this latter group have been subjected to a distinct phonetic process from which still other processes (e.g., the dropping of the intervocalic "n") can also be derived.

My own point of view is at least as historical-cultural as it is linguistic, if not more so. In essence, it is my view that we should not isolate Basque historically from the community of Western European peoples. Let us not turn Basque into even more of a Robinson Crusoe than it already is. It is truly a rare phenomenon that, within a small territory, a language such as Basque, a language in which scholars such as my dear friend Professor Lafon has discovered ancient similarities with the Caucasian tongues, has been preserved from extinction over the course of centuries. We of course should not take this unquestionable fact and then adorn it with inflated claims of the influence of the Basque tongue, such as Larramendi, Juan Bastista de Erro, Pablo Pedro Astarloa, Juan Antonio Moguel, and Elias D'Iharce de Bidassouet did, with their assertions that words such as *arima*, *kurkubita*, *lukainka*, and *potua* came into Latin from Basque, rather than the other way around.[46]

It is important to normalize the views of both Basques and outsiders with regard to the Basque language and its problems, and with respect to the country and its inhabitants. If history shows us that the Basques at some point experienced, in one way or another, the effects of Romanization; if we can also establish that, at a later stage, they governed themselves by means of institutions known by surrounding peoples as well; if we can see that they conducted trade via both land and sea, and that they devoted themselves to the industrial and technological pursuits, introducing over the course of centuries new developments that seemed the most advantageous to them; and if they so thoroughly assimilated a system of beliefs such as Christianity; then the following question must be asked: How can anyone possibly believe in an absolute linguistic isolation, or a "linguistic paralysis"? Just as the true personality of individuals is best appreciated by observing all of an individual's tendencies, and by in some way taking account of all their accumulated knowledge, so the personality of peoples and languages must be studied in light of a broad-based analysis, and not by simply listing strange coincidences that may or may not be valid. It really makes as little sense for us to continue to say what the previously cited Bascologists once affirmed as it does for us to uphold a view of a centralist and radical stripe of the kind common during the bitter period at the end of the nineteenth century (within an entirely different historical context, to be sure). Love and hate can often be equally conducive to the propagation of lies. But surely it need not be the case that love lead to mendacity. In sum, the more open Basque linguistics is to suggestions and ideas originating in other sciences, the richer and more productive will be the fruits of its labor.

Part 3

Economy and Society in the Basque Mountains

8

The Historical Bases of a "Traditional" Economy

Change in Rural Society

During the first half of the twentieth century, rural life could be viewed as having been static, at least for the most part. Some anthropologists, folklorists, and philosophers have asserted that villagers and rural dwellers really did not have their own history. What they meant by this was that their lives transpired, generation after generation, without much variation, and that those who lived in such a way could not be considered anything more than "survivors," comparable in many ways to primitive and prehistoric man.[1] It has frequently been the case that ideas that conform to a particular line of research, but that are not backed up by sufficient evidence, have exercised a high degree of influence. Yet facts themselves are far more powerful than such unsupported ideas, and it is the weight of facts that have obliged those of us who are conducting research today to abjure adhesion to the theory of rural mental immobility, and to other related theories.

It is no longer possible to sustain the theory that great historic events that were of vital concern to the ancient historians, such as international military battles and conflicts, did not affect those living in the countryside, either directly or indirectly. Moreover, other events, such as important technical and cultural changes in artistic styles, fashions, work methods, and the utilization of primary materials, also exercised their influence. The countryside does indeed suffer change. And, thus, it has its own history. It may be important or obscure but, in the end, it is history. Those of us here in Europe, citizens and village dwellers, rich and poor, the erudite and the unlettered, are all subject to historical transformation, whether we are aware of it or not. The villagers of Castile during the time of Charles II were not, in important respects, the same as the villagers who lived during the time of Philip V.[2] The changes that took place in rural life between the end of the fifteenth and the beginning of the seventeenth centuries are also revolutionary in character.[3] Those changes that occurred during the eighteenth century were especially important. Today, we are witnessing the disappearance of the ways of life that we grew up with. And yet, although this phenomenon can be seen, directly or indirectly, by reading books and magazines, a good deal remains unknown about this process—at least at the level of specific details. It is in order to remedy this deficiency that I have undertaken the research described herein.

Let us begin with a small corner of Spain, for quantity will not adversely impact our qualitative calculations. This is because the matter at hand concerns being able to see how quantity manifests itself within a relatively small area—in other words, how "big things" act upon "little things." Within the present context, what is being explored is how the image of traditional life differs depending upon on whether one views it through a traditional or traditionalist lens, on the one hand, or whether one approaches it through historical, rational, and (where applicable) scientific research, on the other.

Those of us who have lived more than half a century are better equipped to conduct research of this nature than our younger colleagues. This is because so many important changes have occurred during our lifetime. We were born during a period in which changes in rural life were taking place, albeit at a very slow rate. We have been able to observe the rapid changes that have occurred prior to our reaching the age of fifty. Thus, when we embark upon a historical inquiry, we have the right to question what we were told was traditional, what many people in previous generations would not have hesitated to characterize as immutable. And, as I've already said, if we take any part of Spain as an example, we have a right to deny this notion of immutability, especially as regards the northern lands, which are typically considered bastions of ultraconservative and traditional values. Let's now examine, as an instance of what we are talking about, the peoples of the far north of Navarre.

In Navarre, as in other territories of northern Spain during the seventeenth and eighteenth centuries, important social and economic changes took place, changes that are clearly reflected in demographic data alone. Partial and sometimes total land surveys and censuses had been taken in Navarre ever since the fourteenth century. Yet at least as instructive as a comparison between an old census and one taken in the seventeenth century (e.g., between the years 1366 and 1612) is a comparison between a census of the middle of the seventeenth century (say, 1646 or 1647) and another taken at the end of the eighteenth or the beginning of the nineteenth century. The data of these censuses were published in general texts. The increase in both population and in the number of housing units that is reflected in these later censuses could not be clearer. Also in evidence in the later data are changes in crops and techniques.

These were times of change and movement. I say this, without investing these words with any kind of optimistic and evolutionary connotations, as was the custom of researchers of fairly recent times—researchers who wrote with a clear and sometimes overconfident sense of their vision's correctness. In this connection, it should be clearly stated that the kind of moralizing and dogmatizing inherent in the thesis that we continue to either live better and better, and to increasingly approximate perfection, on the one hand, or on the other, that we are progressively degenerating, should be beyond the purview of any objective researcher.

Let us conduct our inquiry, then, in the spirit of Heraclitus's ancient maxim that "You cannot step twice into the same stream." The flowing waters of history leave their distinctive imprint, for good or for ill.

During every historical period, change in the physical environment has given rise to different expressions of the ideals of human existence. Thus, our task as ethnologists and social historians is to continually refine our studies, applying a variety of methods, from those that we might consider more materialist to others that we might think of as more spiritual (at least according to the conventional wisdom—which I don't endorse—which sees spirit and matter as an important dichotomy in human existence). Let us now explore a specific example of what I am talking about in order to focus upon the task at hand, taking as our point of departure a physical and material concept.

The Material Decline of Peoples

There is a system that explains the decline of peoples on the basis of clearly defined social causes. This destructive decline first affected castles and fortifications, which in Spain, following the conclusion of the Peninsular War, had steadily lost any importance or specific function, although they had retained some importance during the first civil war. Afterward, the decline proceeded to affect rural artisans—iron workers, weavers, potters—as well as places where other products were manufactured. All of these places continued to retain a certain vitality even as late as the nineteenth century, as can be seen from a glance at Madoz's dictionary. The decline made itself felt, on a secondary plane, in the dwellings of absentee *hidalgos* and nobles, because many of the properties they owned came to be poorly maintained, or to be let out at low rents. The same deterioration then began to affect the houses of farm laborers and the lands they tilled, planted, and harvested, after having first struck windmills, hermitages, and other buildings that quickly ceased to have any public use. This rural landscape, first humanized and then dehumanized or eroded, we find time and again wherever we go in Spain—in the north, south, east, and west. In small villages, social functions disappeared, more or less gradually, first losing their meaning in military and strategic terms. The towers of lineages either fell or deteriorated in the face of the pressure of royalty and the municipalities. Afterward the castles and town walls fell, due to their irrelevance in large-scale wars.

Artisanry declined as a result of the development of industries and the growth of distribution networks for manufactured products. Agriculture and cattle farming also fell victim to the effects of commerce and the economic pressures of states that had experienced a comprehensive economic development. It is not our task here to apply value judgments, whether optimistic or pessimistic, to these obvious facts. All the same, it is clear that, given that the lands seemed to have become infertile due to various natural causes, human creations also seemed to be suffering a similar decline as a result of the passage of time, and to have deteriorated in purely physical and material terms. Such was the state of affairs, at any event, from the standpoint of the critical historian. But instead of asking when all these things began to deteriorate, it also needs to be asked when these things had also previously flourished. And this is a question that needs to be asked without letting oneself be blinded by prejudices regarding what was "primitive," or what merely had "survival value" in terms of the life of rural towns, and also without letting oneself be carried away by the obsession of some folklorists who continue to search for the distant and primitive past by doing nothing more than exploring present rural life.

Origins and Demographic Growth of a Town

For our purposes, we need not hark back to prehistory or protohistory. This is because we can find during historical periods closer to our own the foundations of our current economic and social life. So, without further ado, let's examine a town in the mountains of Navarre, Bera, in the middle of the fourteenth century. What kind of organization do the documents of the era reflect regarding this town? Unquestionably, the organization that emerges from such documents is fundamentally different from current forms of organization, even though many past forms are preserved in the present. Thus, in documents of the bishopric of Baiona (which included Navarre until 1566), there are already references to the Bortziriak (five towns) that comprised (as they still do) an Archpriest's parish: Lesaka (Lesaca), Bera, Etxalar (Echalar), Iantzi (Yanci), and Arantza (Aranaz).[4] On certain other occasions, however, there is only a reference to "the land of Lesaka," a town that, from the fourteenth through the sixteenth centuries, gained an increasing number of privileges. In the end, what emerges from the record is an administrative division of the Navarre mountains' five towns, in which Bera constantly struggled against Lesaka to achieve parity with it. Lesaka had previously secured, among other privileges, a fair and a market (that still exists today), along with tax exemptions for exhibitors at the fair, the privilege of exercising jurisdiction in criminal cases, and so on.[5]

It is important to note here that this longstanding rivalry, which was documented in a legal dispute dating from 1615 that was studied by Navarrese archivist Florencio Idoate in one of his scholarly articles on Navarrese history, has lasted right up until the present time, although it is based on facts (or supposed facts) of an entirely different nature.[6] This is an example of tensions that endure over the course of many years, even though their particular motives or reasons change over time. Prior to the date of the legal dispute, there were surely reasons why the two towns were in conflict with one another. A number of factors seem to have been at the root of the conflict: a lord of the lineage of Zabaleta ruled Lesaka, while a lord of Alzate ruled over Bera. There would have been a natural enmity between these men, since the lord of the Zabaleta lineage belonged to a faction that was allied with the Oñacinos, while the lord of the Alzate lineage was allied with the Gamboinos.[7] The social organization that prevailed during the fourteenth century is one of factions, with the dominant lineages, nobles, and lineages of peasants, as well as plebians of various classes (e.g., craftsmen) in a state of rebellion. This is something reflected in Navarrese documents of all kinds, especially the *Libros de fuegos** that are referred to above.

---

* Literally, the Books of Fires (hearths or homes), records of taxes levied on homes in the Middle Ages. —ed.

One of the most complete census documents is the *Libro de fuego* of 1366, in which the population of Navarre is classified according to *merindades*, valleys, and other administrative and geographical divisions, as well as by social classes. The first section of the book provides an idea of the population of nobles, while other sections of the book provide totals of farm laborers, craftsmen, and the "general" population (the latter signifying the lowest possible category at that time). And yet, for a number of reasons, it does not seem likely that the census took sufficient account of the total population. Still, it appears clear that, according to this document, in 1366 Navarre was very sparsely populated. Thus, Bera was home to only five nobles and their families. The population of farm laborers and craftsmen was also very small given that, if one adds together the combined number of households of Bera and Lesaka, they total no more than fifty-two[8] households, and it can be reasonably inferred that an equal number of both houses and families can be added to this figure, for a grand total of between 250 and 300 persons. As is well known, the fourteenth century was of critical importance in the demographic history of Europe. We don't have at our disposal anything resembling the 1366 data for the fifteenth century, because the "book of households" for 1427 does not, for whatever reason, mention either Lesaka or Bera (although it does give figures for the other three mountain towns which, ecclesiastically, belonged to the archbishopric of Baiona).[9] We know that, by the sixteenth century, the population had increased, and that there were about 300 inhabitants in Bera and Lesaka, while there were no more than 100 to 150 in the other three towns.[10]

And this was the state of affairs despite the civil wars that had taken place, and that had brought the Navarrese monarchy to an end. Official texts indicate that, during the 1480s, towns such as Uharte Arakil (Huarte Araquil), Leitza, Murillo, Amunarritz (Munárriz), and Lesaka decreased in population from 150 to 90.[11] Wars, both major and minor, wrought their devastation. Yet these same wars seemed to promote later growth. Bera, which was on the border until the annexation of the kingdom by two neighboring kingdoms (i.e., Castile and Aquitaine), suffered a great deal because it became, from the time of its annexation, the first town in the possession of the Spanish crown that bordered France.[12]

Yet, even though fires were recorded there in 1550, and ongoing offensive actions took place there both before and afterward (1542, 1557, 1576), progress was later clearly evident.

The census of Bera for 1607 lists 181 houses that were valued (by their owners) at something more than 15,307 ducats. Some of these houses have the same name now as they did at that time, while others do not. What has changed to a greater degree are the surnames of the locals and residents. Yet there are a number of surnames from the seventeenth century that still survive.[13] What appears to have changed the most, in comparison to documents from previous periods, is the economic organization of this society, an issue we will soon examine. For now, let's continue with our demographic analysis.

Another population census was carried out in 1645, which indicated a marked decrease in the population (i.e., it recorded a total of 141 residents). This was understandable because, on July 16, 1638, Bera was set on fire by French soldiers.[14] Seven years later, the effects of this fire were still evident, even though a good many houses had by then been rebuilt, as can be seen when observing the facades of many of these houses that still exist today, which have dates and, in two cases, inscriptions regarding these events.[15] Leaving aside the effects of wars, there was an increase in population after the fire. And during periods of marked general decline, the population of Bera had increased by 1678.[16] It increased again in 1726.[17] The 1802 *Diccionario* of the Spanish Historical Academy indicates that the population of Bera at that time was 1,509, with eighty-nine inhabited houses and four windmills.[18] By the year 1828, Miñano increased these numbers to 338 property-owning households and 1,879 non-property-owning households.[19] This figure was reduced in Madoz (following the First Carlist War) to 346 property-owning households and 1,704 non-property-owning households.[20] The population once again increased, this time quite sharply, at the end of the nineteenth century and in the first decades of the twentieth century: from 2,352 inhabitants in 1888, to 2,710 in 1900, to 2,504 in 1910.[21] I don't think these figures increased any further. A geographical text that was published in 1923 gave an estimated population of 2,525 inhabitants and 416 buildings.[22] Afterward, other publications referred to the census of 1920, which gave a figure of 2,628.[23] I obtained the most recent available figures, which represent an increase in the 1920 population, from the town hall of Bera itself, although it should be noted that this increase represented a rebound after a slight previous drop in population.[24]

Social Transformations

Despite plagues and national and international civil wars, the modest settlement of Bera did increase to a great degree between the fourteenth and the twentieth centuries. We should now say something regarding the economic and social conditions that formed the backdrop of this increase. We will leave the economic data for last and will initially make a few comments regarding the social systems.

In the fourteenth century, in 1368, when the town had already been in existence for some time, we see that Bera, along with Lesaka, turned over no more than 381 libras per year to an outside lord that the king had imposed upon them. This despite all of the income, profits, jurisdictional privileges, ironworks, meadows, mountains, and other assets possessed by the town. This was because the king himself had assigned an income of five hundred libras to the lord, Mosén Tercellet de Anecourt, and because this lord was required to contribute 119 and 10 *sueldos* to the total product of the two villas[25] in order to make up the sum.

A difficult period followed, during which the kings of Navarre attempted to bolster the population on the border town, granting it privileges and then increasing the privileges whenever Bera suffered losses as a result of wars. The privileges granted in 1402 were clearly intended to serve such a purpose. Also illustrative, both in this regard and in other respects, are the Lesaka ordinances of 1429.[26]

It is our view that the pressures exercised by society are part and parcel of any society at a highly primitive stage, and that systems employing pressure, repression, and coercion were in fact instituted in the far distant past. And yet, while all this is true, when we study specific kinds of societies, we can also see that the codification of what is to be repressed varies with the passage of generations, and that repressive actions also change over the course of time. We can see evidence of this in these modest municipal ordinances of Lesaka, which were drafted in 1429. A review of this document reveals that, in addition to the usual provisions touching upon the economic life of that time, there are other provisions regarding civil life (i.e., that deal with relations among persons), religious life, public health, and public order. Everything that is to be avoided and prohibited within the community is categorically specified. The punishment imposed upon anyone violating an ordinance is proportionate to the severity of the violation. In such a medieval society, it is certainly no surprise that the crimes that were punished most severely were those against religion—actions that were inconceivable to many people in past centuries. These crimes, as well as their associated punishments, would eventually disappear throughout the course of history.

The *rollo* or *picota*, which was called a *pilliric* back in the fifteenth century, brings to mind the French *pilori* as a system of municipal justice. Persons were locked into the pillory as a means of public shaming. Those who blasphemed God would be pilloried, and would also have a nail driven through their tongues. Other infamous punishments were less severe. Of course, the time came when the municipality no longer had the authority to mete out such punishments.

At a later stage, there were a far larger number of municipal ordinances in Bera, which was also granted new exemptions and new privileges. Neighboring peoples brought suit against one another for water and pasturage rights, and over other matters as well. But the old-fashioned municipal and legal form of justice was, eventually, no longer practiced.

Apart from its strategic and geographical significance as a border town, a factor that made Bera somewhat important in the economic life of the old kingdom was the iron industry, which (in modified form, of course) continues to exist today. Ironworks appear to have functioned during the Middle Ages, and were later modified at the beginning of the modern era. Of the thirty-two ironworks in the Atlantic Mountains of Navarre in 1535, three were in Bera: Marzadia, Osinola, and Xemeola.[27]

And yet there was only a small number of ironmongers (and also a small number of artisans and craftsmen), as compared with farm workers. It is clear that local lineages (rather than the foreign lords of previous eras that were mentioned earlier) were imposed upon this sector during the fifteenth century.

The town of Bera today has a settlement concentration in the neighborhood of Altzate. This neighborhood is recorded as having been a seigniory between the years 1366 and 1399.[28] The influence of the lords of Altzate on Bera was continuous throughout the fifteenth century, and was reflected in the following powers which they held:

1. Right of patronage over the parish church of Bera. Proof of this is seen in the petition for increase presented by four beneficiaries, which was drafted in 1483, at the time that Rodrigo de Alzate was lord. It should be noted that the four beneficiaries, as well as a rector, continued to hold this privilege until our times.[29]
2. Rights over the windmill of Bera, granted by the king to Martín López or Lópiz de Alzate, son of Juan, in compensation for several armed retinues, in 1377. Later, in 1426, another king granted a concession to another Alzate lord for the income from the windmills of Lesaka, in order to finance a war with the lord of San Per (Senpere/Saint Pee) in Lapurdi (Labourd).[30]

The decisive role of this family can be appreciated by considering the figure of Rodrigo de Alzate, who was married in Lapurdi, and who had descendents who had been firmly established for some years in France. At the same time, the town, like so many others, began to have greater and greater needs until finally, in 1685, a number of its residents purchased the last of the assets and rights of the lord of Alzate from Andrés de Urtubia y Alzate, viscount of Urtubia, bailiff and captain general of the Lapurdi. Later, in 1688, the residents of the town acquired patronage of the church.[31]

All of this happened during a period when many other towns were either doing the same thing, or instead taking legal action against the old lords and "palace men." On the other hand, the social organization of the residents of Bera was changing. The letters patent of nobility that were issued by the five towns, along with weapons (as noted in the *Libro de Armería* [Book of Arms] of Navarre) indicated, following the lawsuit of 1615, that the residents of these towns wanted to be granted the right to fully exercise the rights of residence and of collective nobility, rights that already existed in Baztan and other Navarrese valleys.[32] As an outcome of its legal action, Bera came to have undisputed possession of its own flag, which it could display in parades and at other festivities. The flag of Bera continues to be displayed during the feast of Corpus Christi.[33]

The letters patent of nobility, or the granting of weapons and privileges to the five towns, as approved by Juan Alfonso de Guerra y Sandoval, master of arms for Philip V, is a document typical of a time in which masters of arms exercised a unique role on behalf of those who requested and paid for their services. The kinds of written records that had previously been used for such purposes were no longer employed. Instead, they were replaced by the half historical, half legendary testimonies of authors of the fifteenth through the seventeenth centuries whose accounts were more or less trustworthy, men like the Prince of Viana, Lázaro Díaz del Valle, Mosén Diego Ramírez Dábalos de la Piscina, Esteban de Garibay, Rodrigo Méndez Silva, and others.[34]

The instrument, countersigned by an employee of the monarchy, serves to establish a historical tradition that replaced (beneficially, in terms of the needs of residents) the old royal history. This was how the egalitarian social fabric, much beloved by Basques and Navarrese, was first established and later grew. The fourteenth century, with its lords and "courtesans," nobles, and commoners, gave way to the seventeenth century, with its "mountain hidalgos" and, a little earlier, the *francos*,[35] who wanted to minimize as much as possible the influence of the "courtiers"[36] and to erase all memory of an era when the nobility, and those outside of the nobility, constituted two distinct social classes.

So now it became a matter of defending collective rights and privileges—the rights of property-owning households and the nobility—in a rigid manner. The municipal ordinances and the parish documents governed rights and duties in both material and spiritual terms. Thus, the valley having first acquired the right of patronage of the church, the church lands were then equally divided among the houses of residents. It is important here to grasp the fundamental link between house and tomb in order to understand traditional rural life. Yet such a link implies a static number of both houses and tombs.

In this regard, the custom in Bera was the same as that of a great many towns in Navarre, Gipuzkoa, and elsewhere. It is thus understandable that laws needed to be enacted to complement and regulate this relationship, given the increase in population referred to earlier. The rights of property-owning households provided a source for a great deal of ancient regional legislation, as well as the later legislation derived from it.[37] The application of such laws was most severe in the northern valleys of Navarre, due to their limited resources.

These valleys have long been home to populations greater than they have been able to sustain. An egalitarian system of succession, in which all of the children of a rural family have the same rights and receive the same inheritance, has predictable results. There is a high degree of rural fragmentation after a number of generations, as can be seen in Galicia as well as in some areas of Navarre (e.g., Burunda).

Yet in Navarre, the ancient legislation tended to avoid such problems through the application of particular combinations of laws. The law of free choice of heirs is the primary such law, which has remained in effect until the present time. Another is the *donatio propter nuptias*[38] (a marriage settlement required by law of the husband or his family). We will later examine the current crisis in the application of this law.

Yet before this, in the seventeenth century, for example, there were, in addition to the two aforementioned laws, other laws that were very severe, laws that limited residents' rights and that even prohibited the construction of new buildings in a particular territory. This is what happened in the Baztan Valley (just after the lawsuit between "palace men" and "property-owning households"), as Juan de Goyeneche pointed out in a very important text:

All territory is divided equally among the property owning households, with each house holding the quantity of land that seems necessary for its upkeep. But because of the increase in houses, and the consequent excess of number of inhabitants in relation to the harvest yielded by the associated lands, it has become necessary for the people to apply themselves to mechanical occupations that are somewhat alien to the natural proclivities of the Nation, and that also run counter to the high aspirations with which all are raised, and which have preserved them to this day. There is thus in effect a law, which is zealously enforced, to the effect *that no new houses are to be built*, in order for there to be no further increase in property-owning households.[39]

Each resident can either increase his own house, or "construct farm houses to facilitate the proper maintenance of the land he holds." But nothing else.

What we have here is a prescription for the maintenance of a permanent status quo. But, as is always the case, rigid laws can be amended and subject to casuistic interpretations. The demographic situation of that valley, as well as of others with similar laws, was very different in the seventeenth century from what it had been in the Middle Ages. It changed even more in the eighteenth century. During the time that Goyeneche (1656–1735) wrote, the number of property-owning households was clearly increasing. This is evident from an examination of censuses and other related documents. This occurred not only in Bera, but throughout the basin of the Bidasoa River.

The growth occurred in accordance with a number of different systems. One of these involved a resident setting up one summer house and another winter house for his family and children. Another involved setting up an auxiliary house on the same property as the main house, for the use of a younger family member. Yet another involved the shared use of an auxiliary house. There were many different examples of each of these systems, since they were not only a product of individually contracted arrangements, but of longstanding custom.

Some Remarks on Cultural Morphology

As has previously been noted, and as was the case for many dwellings in Basque areas, each house in Bera had a "foundational name" that reflected either the name of its original builder or his occupation. In the census of 1366, a number of different classes of craftsmen were mentioned: peltmongers, furriers, shoemakers, and even masters. Later censuses, which specified the names of houses (i.e., those taken from 1612 onward), show a number of different kinds of designations:[40]

1. Many have the suffix *-enea* following a given name, surname, nickname, occupation, or a special use of the house (whether ongoing or for holiday celebrations);
2. Many are formed with the component *baita*;
3. Within a town, there some names of houses were formed with the word *borda* (with even more examples like this outside of towns);
4. Some names are formed with the suffix *-tegui*;
5. Still other names are descriptive, topographical, or indicate a greater or lesser degree of antiquity.

Thus, if someone named Juan ("Juanish") at some point established a house, it would continue to be called *Juanishenea*. If another with the surname of *Echandi* (which in itself means "large house") established a house, it would be called *Echandienea*. If someone with the nickname of *Chamburro* constructed a house, it would bear the name of *Chanburrenea*. There are other examples consisting of combinations of given name, surname, and suffix (e.g., *Juansancenea*, formed from "Juan Sanz" + *-enea*). Other houses bear the names of certain kinds of craftsmen and masters: *Arguiñenea* (from *arguiña*, "stonecutter"); *Barberenea* (from *barbero*, "barber"); *Arotzenea* (from *arotza*, "carpenter"), the list goes on. There were also the vicar's house (*Vicarioenea*) and the priest's house (*Apezenea*). The meaning of some names, such as *Erregenea* (i.e., "the king's house"), stems from customs and traditions that are no longer observed, and such names are common throughout Basque-speaking Navarre.

Yet it is clear that a stonecutter no longer lives in *Arguiñenea*, and that a barber no longer occupies *Barberenea*. The same can be said regarding names containing the element of *baita*, a word which is found the Basque Pyrenees and that has been the subject of considerable discussion among linguists.[41] It appears in names of houses, and has the same meaning as the suffix "*-enea*." Thus, we find in Bera the names *Juanishbaita, Juanishenea, Arbelaizbaita,* and *Martinbeltzbaita* as examples of the use of the word with a given name, surname, or nickname. Yet we also see *Sastrebaita* and *Tablajerobaita* (indicating houses founded by a *sastre* ["tailor"] and *tablajero* [possibly: "meat seller," "royal tax collector," "scaffold-maker," or "ticket taker"] respectively), and *Apezabaita* ("priest's house"). What is the difference among the three suffixes *-enea*, *baita*, and *-tegui*? It is difficult see any difference at all. And, to muddy the waters even further, we have houses named *Arosteguia* and *Apezteguia* (mansions of a stonecutter and priest, respectively).

The use of the word *borda* is more clearly understandable, since it signifies a construction or house that is dependent on another house. Thus, if a town has a house that is called *Trunquenea*, there may be another house outside of town that is called *Truquenecoborda*. Similarly, *Sastrebaita* could have a corresponding *Sastrebaitecoborda*. The house containing the component *borda* in its designation was usually smaller than the low-roofed rectangular house, with a single floor for the family and an attic. Yet the layout of houses varied with changing styles and eras, as we will soon see.

Few houses currently remain that have a close relationship with their respective *bordas*. In contrast, in towns that are located deeper within the interior of the Atlantic basin, we find instances conforming to one of the systems cited previously, in which a family spends part of the year (i.e., the winter) within town and the other part of the year (i.e., the summer) in the *borda* outside of town. This can be seen in the town of Zubieta,[42] for example. This is different from what one sees in the case of nearby towns, such as Elgorriaga, in which most of the population do not possess isolated country houses, but rather installations that house sheep (i.e., *ardi-bordak*) or storage facilities for hay, or other agricultural products.

The families of Zubieta that have winter houses in town and summer houses (i.e., *bordas*) in the mountains, seem to spend more time in the latter than in the former. Yet at times, especially when the older and younger generations don't get along well, the older family members will live in the city while the younger folk will live in the country. The designations of houses in Zubieta follow a pattern similar to those in Bera, Lesaka, and the Bidasoa region in general. Thus, for example, if the house in town is called *Shubitia*, then the house in the mountains will be called *Shubitiecoborda*.

As regards those houses that were originally built with the intention to divide them later, with an outside door leading to each separate living area, it is important to note that there are many such examples in the eighteenth century in the mountains of Navarre, from the Burunda to the Bidasoa. In this zone, there are number of examples with a lovely facade of Elgorriaga or Ituren stone. Such structures are less common in Bera, although large country houses constructed along similar lines appear to have been built there. On the other hand, it should be borne in mind that variations in the implementation of a style or general technique within a region or zone may be due to very specific material circumstances, rather than any legal prohibitions.

In Bera, it is obvious that the fire of 1638 resulted in later construction along the lines of a style that is typical today of the streets of the town, but that was also applied well into the eighteenth century in newly constructed *bordas* and country houses. Only in rare instances does one find elements of Gothic construction in some of the lower floors. Yet in Lesaka, such elements are frequently seen, with the lineage towers that were so prevalent in the fifteenth century, as well as a style of tower from an even earlier era, continuing to be preserved.

In contrast, among the five towns of Navarre, Etxalar has the most houses in its urban center that bear inscriptions on their doors. The style of these inscriptions is fairly uniform, although they vary in age, going back to the times of Philip V, Charles III, Charles IV, and Ferdinand VII. Some bear the name of the house and the date of its construction, while others bear the name of the house and the person or persons who rebuilt it (who are typically are not the same). This latter observation is important for the purpose of confirming our assertion that houses conserved their own character: their names were not changed by virtue of later ownership or occupation. Such was the case even for the large eighteenth-century palaces, which also were extremely important in Basque-Navarrese towns. There are two houses of this kind in Bera: *Arosteguia* and *Larrache*. There are also such houses in Lesaka, in addition to other houses that have old towers.[43] Yet it is in the valleys of Doneztebe (Santesteban), Bertiz, and Baztan where they are seen most frequently. The reasons why this is the case will not be detailed here. Briefly, they have to do with the fact that, at the end of the seventeenth century and throughout the eighteenth century, there were many families residing in those areas that accumulated vast fortunes as merchants, as state contractors, and as high-level public functionaries.[44]

Consequences

What I have attempted to show here, on the basis of a very small and specific example, is that history—including classical history, in the broadest sense—is a vital factor in rural life and small towns, and that "tradition" is something that, for rural inhabitants, has a very specific and "utilitarian" character, in the service a particular social group.

What we have seen here is a town that emerged in the Middle Ages, as part of a group that comprised four other towns, and which collectively constituted an archpriest's parish of which it is no longer a part. The earliest historical records reveal that this town was governed by an outside lord, and was governed by a feudal system that depended on the favor of the king of Navarre. We have seen how it afterward it came under the influence of the dominant local lineage during a long period of civil wars. Later, we witnessed the disappearance of this influence, and the emergence of an "association of residents" that enjoyed the rights of collective nobility, rights that were later accepted as universal, and as having existed "from time immemorial."[45]

Each of these past eras has left its mark on the present—whether materially or linguistically—to a greater or lesser degree. This is all a far cry from the immobility that supposedly characterized rural life, societies, and thought! During every "historical moment," what is called "structure"—conceived as an intricate web of related functions—continues to undergo inexorable transformations as a result of numerous different external forces. All the talk of isolation, self-sufficiency, and so on, is, in the end, a matter of putting the cart before the horse. Everything changes, whether in large cities, tiny villages, or towns, with a deceptively tranquil appearance. And this is also the case in terms of the lives of rural dwellers who are "stuck in the past."

9

The Structure and Functions of the House

On the Idea of Structure

Within the field of social anthropology, there has recently been an emphasis on structuralism following a period during which functionalism was a theory very much in favor. The anthropology that was learned by students in the 1930s from men like Radcliffe Brown and Bruno Malinowski (each of whom had his own distinctive point of view) was functionalist.[1] There is today perhaps an even more zealous advocacy of structural anthropology. Thus, we see that a number of linguists have declared themselves structuralists, and that many younger anthropologists have followed in their footsteps. This younger generation looks to Claude Lévi-Strauss[2] as their mentor and guide. This despite the fact that there are ways of dealing with structures different from those recommended by the famous French anthropologist.[3] Even though I have a great deal of interest in, and respect for, anthropological theories, I cannot say that I am a functionalist, structuralist, or any other kind of anthropologist. I make this statement because I do not believe that the so-called structural models have, in either space or (especially) time, the scholarly validity that some claim for them. In other words, I believe those structural models that have been presented to us as "social structures" are always somewhat more enigmatic, contradictory, and less structured than is commonly supposed. This is the case the case for those who live within them, with their own code of social order, but also as regards those who offer finished studies of them, written in scholarly—or generalized—terms. Supplying definitions is generally a pleasant activity for pedagogues. Disagreements about definitions seem to be necessary among those who are less directly involved in teaching. Be that as it may, historians of European societies, or historians (like myself) dedicated to the study of the life and history of ancient European peoples, frequently come up against this problem of structures and find the abovementioned definitions to be rather unhelpful. And these historians find even less helpful examples involving distant and more or less primitive peoples—peoples about whose historical development we know little, and who have been the subject of a great deal of speculation. In other words, the recent writings do not offer much more in the way of understanding structures than the little that can be gleaned from a reading of Emile Durkheim, from Fritz Graebner's *Struktur der Kulturgruppen* or from other authors from previous eras.[4] One such writer was Fritz Krause, who formulated what he called *Strukturlehre* in 1912.[5] Although more modern anthropologists have done more observation and fieldwork than those of previous generations, they seem to me to have been less fruitful when it comes to devising methodologies and formulating theories. When closely examined, the most recent theoretical versions of the functionalism originally introduced by Bronisław Malinowski seem to have lost something. Other highly astute observers of life in more recent times are, when it comes to theorizing regarding functions and structures, really little better than mediocre. In any case, it is my belief that the apostle of structuralism himself, the aforementioned Radcliffe Brown, who established an important distinction between social "structure" (considered as concrete reality; in other words, as the sum total of relations existing at any given moment, and that unite a given number of human beings) and a general or normal "structural form" of relationships, abstracting from variations in particular cases (even though such cases are taken into account in studying structural form).[6] This distinction has been debated and even denied[7] by some. I myself believe that this distinction is valid and important, as I've already said. But I also believe that such a distinction applies to human beings who live within a society, within a "structure" to which they have to ascribe interpretations that are always—or nearly always—different. Such interpretations often go against the grain of the so-called structural form when this is understood as a norm or in a general sense. To illustrate what I am saying, I would like to carry out a specific study of various kinds of Navarrese families that we can consider as conforming to a great degree to the social "structural form" understood as normal and typical in Navarre over the course of centuries.[8] The reference here is to how the house and those belonging to it were an inextricable part of the fabric of the lives of men and women over the course of many generations. Taking a single case as an example, examining what exactly happened over the course of years and even centuries may be useful for the purposes of determining the scope of certain structural or structuralist conceptions. Comparing various cases of similar houses might prove even more useful. The present essay will focus on two specific cases: (1) A study of the vicissitudes of a specific house from the seventeenth through the nineteenth centuries; (2) A study of the history of another manor house—a house that was also located near the same mountain in the Bidasoa. I think that what I have previously written in my initial study will suffice for providing an understanding of the general structure or norm that applies in these cases.

As part of the methodological underpinnings of these preliminary remarks, I also would like to point out here that, within the context of these very specific cases, one might find a justification for defending the thesis that "structure" is an extremely static concept, and that "function" is, on the contrary, a dynamic notion. This point has previously been made by a famous theorist about thirty years ago.[9] One way or another, what has become increasingly evident to me is that the anthropological concepts derived from the study of primitive peoples are inadequate and dangerous when they are applied to peoples who have a long and rich history.

On the Characteristics of the Physical Area

It seems appropriate at this point to say something regarding the physical geography of the land where the houses that are the subject of this essay are located. They are situated in the northernmost region of Navarre, a region that has geopolitical borders in three different directions. The climate of the region is Cantabrian, and thus typical of "rainy Spain." This region is more closely linked to Gipuzkoa and to the French Basque Country than it is to the rest of the former kingdom of Navarre. This characteristic is even more marked (if that is possible) in Bera that in the other mountain Bortziriak (five towns).

This region, then, is characterized by its land as well as by its distinctive organization of settlements into clusters of two, three, or five. This organization is well documented and goes back many centuries. It is also reflected in place names. According to Pliny, there were groupings of Celtic towns in Aquitania that were known as *pinpedunni*—in other words "five settlements (with *pinpe* meaning "five" and *dunon* meaning "town" or "settlement" in physical terms).[10] Afterward, in the Middle Ages, there is also a record of other groupings of five villages (i.e., other than those of the mountain) in the *merindad* of Lizarra (Estella)[11] and in Aragon (the latter constituting perhaps the most famous grouping).[12] This kind of organization is also documented farther south in rather enigmatic fashion. Thus, there are places named Cinco Villas in Guadalajara,[13] a village in the province of Madrid,[14] and a deserted area in Badajoz.[15] In addition, there is a place in Segovia named the Cinco Villas de Fresno[16] and Cinco Aldeas (i.e., in Córdoba).[17] On the other side of the Pyrenees, in France, there are Troisvilles, Tresville, and Treville,[18] all of which are located in the former territory of Aquitaine. This last-named town was made famous by a captain of the musketeers during the reign of Louis XIII.

There are clear differences among the Roman or early medieval *villa* as a hereditary seat of a family, and named after its founder (e.g., Antoñana—after Antonius) or Leciñana (after Licinius), the *villa* of Visigothic and later times, as reflected in names such as Villadiego or Villarramiel (which have their Basque equivalents), and the *villa* of the late Middle Ages. But in order not to get too far off track, we will take as our starting point the most modern of these notions.

From the physiographic point of view, we know that the three largest towns in this district—Lesaka (Lesaca), Bera, and Etxalar (Echalar)—were in relatively open valleys and that the two less developed towns—Lantzi (Yanci) and Arantza (Aranaz)—were on higher ground, on craggier and narrower land. This can clearly be seen by looking at Map 65 (Scale 1:50,000) of Spain of the Geographical Institute. This map also clearly depicts the isolation of this area in relation to the rest of Navarre, since it can be seen there that between Sunbilla (Sumbilla) and the fields of Lantzi there is a long and narrow, sparsely populated and cultivated gorge, through which a road passes that was constructed fairly recently.

Of the valleys of the five towns, the most open of them is obviously the Bera Valley, within which various sectors and neighborhoods can be identified, with the Bidasoa River as the boundary, and the tributaries and subtributaries of this river being areas where population centers were located.

The section of this area that we will be examining was urban and densely populated and developed along the rivers. Such was the case in both Bera and Altzate. The rural sector of the population was dispersed and homes in that sector were not located along roads. Instead, the rural population of Bera and Altzate lived on the slopes of mountains above the rivers or streams.

The Structure and Function of the House

Figure 9.1. Itzecoborda, Bera, Navarre.

Figure 9.2. Martinborda, Bera, Navarre.

Figure 9.3. (I) Alquegui-garaya, (II) Alquegui-echeberria, and (III) Alquegui-berea at the foot of Mount Labiaga.

The settlement comprised a number of principal houses as well as a number of smaller satellite houses, in a number of old texts, a division into different neighborhoods is noted. These neighborhoods have the same name as some of these houses (Dornaku, Elzaurdia, etc.). Principal houses (or fortified houses) and dependent, satellite houses, *bordas* or shepherds' huts, and poorer houses, can be distinguished from one another on the basis of mere external appearance. Fortified houses are large, with a more or less rectangular base, but with a wide frontage. The poorer houses usually have a narrow base and frontage. A comparison of figures 9.1, 9.2, and 9.3 will suffice to illustrate this. During the era when these estates assumed the names that they currently have, they were surrounded by lands dedicated to the cultivation of grains that were bordered by *robadas*, groves of apple trees or chestnut trees, and ferneries. These areas in turn were bordered by *peonadas* and uncultivated land. At that time, there were also flocks of animals that we still see today (cattle, pigs, and sheep) as well as goats, which hardly exist in our time. These houses usually had workhorses that were used as a means of transportation. The figures supplied for these lands and animals in various documents from the beginning of the seventeenth century differ sharply from one another. This variance may in part be due to the fact that the owners concealed (to a greater or lesser extent) part of their property. Yet there is no doubt that, at that time, the crops of the Basque Country were much more rudimentary than they later became, after the introduction of crops of American origin, such as corn (the potato was introduced at an even later stage), and orchards. Swine, milk, chestnuts, millet bread, and goats were the basis of a diet that differed greatly from what we are familiar with today, which includes potatoes, beans, tomatoes, and so on.[19] But let us return to our examples:

Figure 9.4. Alquegui or Alquegui-garaya.

Figure 9.5. Alquegui-berea or Alqueberea, eastern facade.

Figure 9.6. Alqueberea from the north and west.

Figures 9.4 through 9.7 depict *baserri* that are the subject of specific study in what follows herein. What will be specifically examined is the estate as both the "container" and the "content," that is intimately related to another four or five estates that are located near it. Given this relationship, one could well say that, over the course of centuries, houses, property-owning residents, and relatives constituted an organic community that lived within the estate, not always harmoniously. Those that were part of the estate lived within its structure and, at times, in spite of its structure. In this connection, one should bear in mind that a social system and its rules is entirely different from the moral order and its rules.

Figure 9.7. Alqueberea from the south.

Developments in One House from 1647 to 1742

Figure 9.4 represents the location of the estates that I've referred to in relation to one another. Leaving aside certain modifications, it can be stated, in general terms, that these estates are conserved in the form in which they were built during the seventeenth and eighteenth centuries—at any rate, following the fire of 1638, the effects of which they suffered as a result of being located along the royal road from Navarre to Lapurdi.

It is also in the seventeenth century that we first see the surname Alquegui, as well as three houses that contain it as a component: Alquegui-garaya (figure 9.3), Alquegui-berea, and Alquegui-echeberria (i.e., "the Alquegui house on high ground," "the Alquegui house on low ground," and "the new house of Alquegui," respectively; nos. 1, 2, 3 of figure 9.3). It seems that it can be inferred from this that, from a single stem family household, two others arose that were, in legal terms, considered part of the original family household—this as a result of avoiding increasing the official count of property-owning residents of a valley or municipal entity. Within a short time, however, these three houses appeared to include inhabitants of another stem family household. Still later, the lineages combined to form two different houses: Alquegui-berea and Alquegui-echeberria. By the beginning of the seventeenth century, the owner of the latter house was no longer someone with the surname of Alquegui. In fact, on March 29, 1607, when the appraisal of the Bera properties resumed, the following entry was made: "21 Said Martin de Garayar, owner of the house mentioned hereinunder. He claims ownership of that house, as well as of two and a half *robadas* of land for making bread, one grove of apple trees of seven *peonadas*, twelve *peonadas* of uncultivated land, and an orchard of one *peonada*, four cows and five sheep. He does not own any other properties. He declares that the value of his two and a half *robadas* to be twenty-five ducats, the grove of apple trees to be five ducats, of the uncultivated land to be twelve ducats, of the orchard to two and a half ducats, of the cows to be twenty-eight ducats, and of the bees to be thirteen and a half ducats."

It is the papers of this house that we will now be examining.[20]

The first document of this collection is dated March 20, 1647, in which the curate of the parish of Bera, Pedro de Elzaurpea and Miguel de Bicuña, representatives and executors of the late Martín de Alquegui, who name as his heir his son Sebastián de Alquegui, on the condition that he make payment of his due obligation and give each of his sisters—María Catalina and Domenja de Alquegui—beds after they become married. This short document presents a case of the free will of the heir, with the terms of said will to be carried out not by the father or mother (or both together) but rather by the executors of the deceased that have been empowered to do so. The male line of succession is not broken here, and there is no other break with tradition either, despite the posthumous naming of the heir. Sebastián de Alquegui, however, did not always live off the income generated by his property. Another document, the second of the collection, which is dated February 2, 1651, shows him practicing the profession of arquebusier and being sued by his brother-in-law, Juanes de Irazábal, a property-owning resident of Hondarribia (Fuenterrabía), who had married his sister María. The grounds for this suit were that Sebastián had not given the ten ducats due to María as her lawful inheritance, as stipulated in the 1647 document. Here is an example of the kinds of disputes that arose regarding the payment of dowries, disputes that were just as common in the middle of the seventeenth century as they later were at the beginning of the twentieth century.

The third document, referring to the selfsame Sebastián de Alquegui, is dated February 19, 1653, and bears reference to a tax collection, something that was very common at that time. As a result of this action, Juan Pérez de Irazoqui "purchased" (this is the word used in the deed) Martín de Alquegui's house, which was called Alqueguiberea "along with everything belonging thereto, with payment due in full within ten years," for the sum of fifty-six ducats, thereupon renting the house to Martín for thirty *reales* per year. Thereafter Martín and, when he died, his son Sebastián, made payment of the rent. But at the time that the 1653 document was drafted, Sebastián wanted to be granted an exemption from the taxes (the document states) and, even though the ten years granted for the payment for the house had long since passed, Martín de Irazoqui, stonecutter and executor of the late Juan Pérez de Irazoqui, received, as consideration "for his beneficent actions and works" on behalf of Sebastián, the sum of fifty-six ducats. This deed is ambiguous and, as in many similar cases, reflects the considerable delays often associated with financial operations—delays that would be considerably remedied in later years. The principal house was thus saved by nothing less than an act of goodwill. We will later see how this goodwill could be violated—even within the same family, lineage, and related houses.

The fourth document refers to one of these same related houses and is a good example of continuity between past and more recent systems. What we will see here is a protocol that is worth drawing attention to. On January 27, 1688, a meeting was held between the fathers of a couple that had been married for fifteen years.

One of them was Juanes de Echenique and the other Juanes de Elizechea. The purpose of their meeting was to legalize the *donatio propter nuptias** of the former on behalf of his son Baltasar and on behalf of the latter's daughter, Gracia. Juanes de Echenique thus, first and foremost, made a donation from his estate. This estate was initially called Alquegui-echeverria (written with a "v"). The name meant "new

---

* A marriage gift or settlement required by law of the husband or his family. The Roman emperor Justinian required that it be equal to the wife's dowry but it was permitted to be made after and used for expenses of the marriage. —ed.

house of Alquegui." The name of the house was later changed to Iacagorri. The donation included the following:

Arable land, "part of which of which borders the royal road, the lower part of which borders a section of the house of Alqueguiberea, and the upper part of which borders a section of the house of Alqueguigaraya. And, in addition, the house with its three quarters of a yoke of that section (note the expression continued to be used among the farmers of Bera who spoke Basque).

- Another half yoke of land, including a grove of apple trees;
- A grove of chestnut trees "located in the town commons, with a right to the ferns within it";
- Two other ferneries;
- Two cisterns, manufactured by the donor, measuring twelve and six *robos* respectively;
- A barrel for making cider; and

Two beds ("in terrible condition" by the way).

But this irrevocable donation ["which the *dro* calls protter nupcias (*sic*)"] and which must have been given as such in 1673, did not take effect until the donor was deceased. This indicates that a higher degree of prudence was exercised in this instance than in other cases of "donation." Moreover, in consideration for such property, it was obligatory to provide the donor the burial and offerings befitting "persons of his station" (this is a formula that one repeatedly encounters). Alacrity was not one of Juanes de Echenique's strong suits. I say this because the donation also established that his children from his second marriage (who were halfbrothers of Baltasar only), named Martín, María Miguel, María, and Graciana, were to receive twenty ducats as their legitimate inheritance "within four years counting from the date of the death of said donor." In addition, Juanes did not include all of the property that he owned in the *donatio*. This other property that was not included consisted of holdings that his second wife was to have received as a dowry, including a grove of chestnut trees and monies as settlement for the family of his second wife (and also for her dowry). Yet this delayed *donatio* included still more. For his part, Juanes de Elizechea and his wife promised to give property worth thirty ducats as a dowry for the daughter who had married fifteen years earlier—fifteen ducats in four years and the other fifteen ducats in eight years. So the total delay in the payment-in-full of the dowry was some forty-five years! One can see that the concept of *donatio* was interpreted in a very flexible manner. In the present instance, the dispensing of the *donatio* did not constitute a hardship for the parents, as was the case in other instances. From a financial standpoint, it once again needs to be stressed that the money involved was paid out over a long period of time in dribs and drabs. The managing of money, both then and now, constitutes the most serious problem for estates. This is also the case for those houses that were considered "strong"—such as Alqueguiberea apparently was. We will now continue to follow the history of this house.

Martín and Sebastián de Alquegui were succeeded by a third owner, whose given name was also Martín, and whose first marriage (in 1696) was to Ana María de Miranda. This couple lived in Alqueguiberea. In the meantime, in Alqueguiberria or Iacagorri, Baltasar de Echenique had a son named Juan Martín. All the aforementioned persons lived at the end of the seventeenth and the beginning of the eighteenth century.

After the death of his first wife, Martín de Alquegui remarried. Afterward, on December 9, 1723, the marriage contract was signed for the nuptials of the daughter of one of the older couples, Catalina de Alquegui, and the son of the other older couple, Juan de Echenique. A *donatio propter nuptias* was now bestowed by Martín de Alquegui that, in accordance with the wishes of his second wife, María Asencia de Elizondo, designated Catalina as heir while excluding her sister María Josepha. The groom was from a neighboring area. What is interesting in this connection is the following:

1. Martín de Alquegui chose as the heir of his house one of the two daughters of his first marriage while excluding the other (i.e., María Josefa), while the daughters, as well as a son, of the second marriage (i.e., Magdalena, María, Catalina, and Martín de Alquegui) are designated as having a legal right to inheritance that they are to receive when they marry—and not before—in the amount of "twenty ducats for each, as well as a chest or safe for each of them."

2. The new husband, a self-made man, brought a dowry to the marriage (which is cited at the beginning of the marriage contract) that consisted of one hundred ducats of credits acquired as a result of his own work and application, plus five head of cattle, as well as eighteen sheep. The marriage contract includes a promise to turn over these monies to his father-in-law in two equal install-

ments: fifty ducats in one year's time, and the other fifty in two years. One can see that things moved faster in this instance.

3. As regards the property listed in the *donatio*, we see that Alqueguiberea possessed greater wealth than Alqueguiecheberria. The possessions of the former were listed as follows:
   - The house called Alqueguiberea, with its residence rights;
   - Orchard;
   - Stove;
   - A "cider barrel";
   - "All of the furniture, clothes, beds, safes, furniture, and other items belonging thereto";
   - "Plus all of the arable land for sowing seed, as well as the groves of apple trees belonging to the same house and adjoining it, below the fence thereof, and bordering the fences of *Alqueguigaraya* and *Bastida*";
   - Another grove of chestnut trees lying below the cultivated land of the house of Miranda, and facing a grove of chestnut trees belonging to J. M. Echenique;
   - Another grove of chestnut trees with a fernery, in Guiartecoerreca;
   - Another grove of chestnut trees with a fernery, lying below the grove of apple trees in Gorostipalo;
   - Another in the place called Alqueguiondo;
   - Another fernery called Yralecuberri;
   - Another in Mirandacoarrobia and Elarbunota.

4. The donor reserved one hundred ducats of his own dowry, the sheep that he had in his home, a cow and its calf ("acquired and tamed during his second marriage"), and another of his cows from his second wife, but not three beehives and one sow.

5. In return for the donated property, he demanded the following consideration, for both himself and his wife: his burial expenses, an offering, commemorative masses in the days following his burial and then, thereafter, on the anniversary of his death, each year. He also demanded dowries for his remaining children: seventy ducats for María Josefa, twenty ducats for the daughters of his second wife (with each of the foregoing to also receive a chest). These dowries were to be given them when they got married. If one of them were to die prior to marriage, it was established that the funeral expenses were to be covered by the donated property.

6. What we have here is a contract that has the purpose of regulating family life that deserves to be cited in full: "This contract was made between the following parties: Martín de Alquegui and his wife María Asencia de Elizondo, and the future bride and groom: These persons are to live together in the selfsame household of Alqueguiberea, helping one another to maintain the household, provide food [?], sustenance, and clothing, and meet other responsibilities and obligations of said house. Should any disagreement arise, said Martín de Alquegui reserves the right, during his life, to command, direct, and enjoy all of these said goods donated with all of their corresponding charges and responsibilities. . . ." Should María Asencia become a widow, he reserved for her "a section of the lower floor of the house" along with a yoke of arable land, a section of the grove of apple trees, and the first grove of chestnut trees listed above.
7. The successors of the contracting parties were obliged to honor the same principle of indivisibility of property, as well as the corresponding legally obligatory inheritance rights.

So what we have here is a clear case of the designation of a daughter as heir for the purposes of consolidating the property in conjunction with a relatively powerful son-in-law during a time that—as one can clearly see—money was in short supply (although not as scarce as it had been previously). The fact that Juan de Echenique had some money at his disposal seems to have to do with the fact that we was a master stonecutter by profession and, as such, had apprentices in his service. This is indicated in documents dating from 1723. However, eighteen years later, in 1741, Juan de Echenique had not paid his father in law the entire one hundred ducats that he had promised to pay him within four years. The latter sued for what was owed him and, on September 20, 1741, the deputy mayor of Bera ordered Echenique, under threat of imprisonment, to pay the thirty ducats that were still outstanding. The following year, on January 18, Martín de Alquegui, along with his daughter (but not with his son-in-law) purchased a half a yoke of arable land for fifty ducats from Domingo Garmendia, owner at the time of Alqueguigaraya. Forty of the fifty ducats were used by the son-in-law to liquidate his debts. Four-fifths of the land remained in the possession of Martín, and the other fifth in the hands of his daughter. The former owner became a landlord, renting the property for two ducats a year "assuming all responsibility for damages resulting from ice, rocks, drought, or flooding" and making proportionate payment to father and daughter (seventeen *reals* to him and four to her). This sale was conditional on the seller being able to return the fifty ducats. So what we have here is the kind of revocable agreement that is nowadays common. The fact that Martín de Alquegui conducted family business with a very firm grasp of the legal and financial implications involved can be seen in other documents in this collection. On February 29, 1728, Martín paid his brother-in-law, Juan de Tellechea, owner of Yamotenea, sixty ducats from his sister Catalina's dowry, as had been agreed twenty-eight years previously. In other words, while he sued his son-in-law for payment of a dowry after eighteen years, he himself waited twenty-eight years to pay his brother-in-law.

On the other hand, within the same family and in the same neighborhood, and during the lifetime of Martín (who likely died around the middle of the eighteenth century; only a fragment of his last will and testament survives) a number of tensions and quarrels arose that are reflected in documents that retain a certain interest.

Tensions and Disputes within the Family and in the Area

Let's have a look at what happened. In 1714, the owner of the house of Erausatea (spelled Eraustea now), Francisca de Irazoqui, who was gravely ill, dictated her last will and testament. She was an only child and had never married. We have already seen that second marriages were rather common. Francisca was the daughter of Domingo de Irazoqui and Catalina de Miranda. When Catalina died, Domingo remarried and had four children with his second wife, two sons (Martín and Juan Manuel) and two daughters (María Josefa and María Teresa). The mother of these children was Ana Josefa de Echenique. It appears that Francisca lived peacefully with her father (a self-made man who had married into the family house), her stepmother, and her half-brothers. Thus, she left her half brothers twenty ducats (half in cash and half in cattle, payable when they married) and the usufruct of Eraustea while they lived and even if her stepmother were to survive her father (as long as she did not remarry). As regards the final inheritance of the house, two possibilities were left open:

1. That one of the children of her maternal aunt, María Josefa de Miranda, and her husband Martín de Echegaray—Martín Esteban or Pedro Esteban—would be designated as heir.
2. Or that she would choose between the two daughters of her other maternal aunt, Ana María de Miranda, and her husband

Martín de Alquegui of Alqueguiberea. The names of these cousins of Francesca were Catalina and María Josefa de Alquegui, whom we have already met. She preferred that the Echegarays be the heirs, but they were both quite young. She thus delegated the authority to designate a future heir to Don Juan de Celaeta, a church elder, to Martín Irazoqui, owner of Irazoquiberea, and to Martín de Elzaurdia, owner of Ojanenea, who in due course were to convene with Martín de Echegaray and jointly make a decision. On November 30, 1744, the scribe Martín de Leguía issued a certified copy of this last will and testament specifically for the parties of Alqueguiberea. This seems to indicate that what was envisaged was the distinct possibility of Catalina (as opposed to her cousins from Zalain) inheriting the house of the unmarried aunt, who had died thirty years previously. There is no further documentation regarding this matter.

An even more tangled web emerges from the examination of a will made by a widow by the name of Graciana de Oyarzabal. The will in question is dated December 17, 1727 and she died in 1732. This widow designated as her sole heir a certain Don Pedro de Borchea, a priest attached to a curate in Bera, who was her nephew. She left him "the interest and principle of a number of credits" for different tracts of lands and houses on the condition of his covering the expenses of her burial. In addition, she left a lesser quantity of money (five ducats), to be divided among her sister Susana de Oyarzábal, her niece María, the daughter of this sister and of Juan Martín de Echenique. She imposed the additional obligation of an offering on her behalf after her death that would also come from the inheritance monies.

And yet we see here that the widow made no mention in her will of the fact that she also possessed five chests that, after her death some years following her dictation of her last will and testament, she provided for disposal of as follows: the smallest was to go to her niece María Asencia de Echenique; another, in poor condition because it was old and worn, was to go to Juan Martín de Echenique and his wife Susana de Oyarzabal (Graciana's brother-in-law and sister); another to Pedro de Borchea, and the two remaining chests to her nieces Agustina and María de Echenique so that they could share the cloths therein with their mother (the aforementioned Susana). Once all of these chests were opened, it was discovered that, in the one bequeathed to Agustina and María, there were not only cloths but also "a fair sum of money that had not been mentioned previously either in any written document or by word of mouth" by the decedent. And thus a dispute arose, because Pedro Borchea, the heir, claimed that this money rightly belonged to him, while Agustina de Echenique was so perplexed about the matter that she consulted a number different parties.

The first of her consultations was with a Jesuit priest from Iruñea-Pamplona, Father Inurre, and another was with a priest of the Order of Mercy, Father Plasencia. Father Inurre responded to her rather vaguely on July 10, 1732. This response appears even vaguer to us now, given the fact that the paper on which it was written has severely decayed over the course of time. But an opinion regarding the matter that was signed on July 10, 1732 by Don Miguel de Olazagutía and Don Joseph Hernand de Pagola concluded that the money rightfully belonged to the Borchea, since he had been designated the sole heir.

It is because the Echeniques and the Alqueguibereas were blood relatives that this matter was addressed in the papers of the latter family.

We see other matters in which conflicts arose among relatives as a result of money. We also see instances in which serious disputes arose among neighbors regarding money as well as other matters. The dispute that we will turn to now arose in 1737, and involved conflicting claims between the owners of, on the one hand, Elarraldea and Salderresgaray and, on the other, the owners of Alqueguigaraya, Alqueguiberea, Yracelaya, and Yagocagorría regarding the water pipes and water courses along the royal road between Salderresgaraya and Elarraldea. On July 27 (i.e., when the river was at its lowest height) the mayor and aldermen of Bera held a meeting for the purpose of resolving the matter, and they determined that the parties to the dispute were obliged to accept the manner in which the water was transported prior to the difference, in accordance with decrees dating back to 1629 and 1699. In addition, it was ordered at this meeting that a small aqueduct be opened for the purpose of supplying water for the houses of Alqueguigaraya and Alqueguiberea. This decision was committed to writing the following day.

Other documents reflect other incidents that arose in the house of Alqueguiberea between the years 1730 and 1740. In 1746, Juan de Echenique "Alqueguibere," who at that time was owner of the house (and who did not have a father-in-law), brought criminal suit against his neighbor Domingo de Garmendia, who had sold a piece of land to his father-in law). From records we have, we know that the relations between these two neighbors did not conform to the standards widely expected in the Basque Country. On October 7, Domingo de Garmendia was in the company a number of workers in his employ, in the area called Machigarzarra, cutting down some ferns on the town commons. He signaled to one of these men to continue cutting when, suddenly, just at the time the wagon holding the cut ferns was to be hauled off by oxen, Juan de Echenique appeared and asked Garmendia who had given him the authorization to cut the ferns. The discussion between the two men grew heated and Echenique "violently and without provocation" disengaged the cart and threw the ferns to the ground. He then stalked off and, when Garmendia and his son Juan Francisco again attempted to haul the ferns onto the cart, Echenique returned with a hooked stick and attempted to strike Garmendia in the head with it. The two men ended up struggling on the ground and rolling down a hill. Garmendia, despite the fact that he appears to have suffered one or more broken bones and a broken rib, did not want his son or any of his men to detain Echenique. However, he did later present a criminal complaint against him for harm and damages—among other things for the cost of a physician's services over the course of the thirteen days that he was bedridden.

The animosity that found such violent expression had previously existed. Yet we don't know the result of the criminal complaint brought against Echenique, and of which he was notified on November 12, 1746. A short time after this episode, we no longer see mention of Echenique or his wife in the records of the house. Instead, there is mention of new owners: Juan Bautista Errandonea and his wife María Asencia de Alquegui (whose last name really should have been Echenique). What this shows us is that the fifth succession over the course of about one hundred years, counting from 1647 was, as in the previous case, through the female line.

Events in Later Times (1752–1864)

On December 21, 1752, the *cabildo* (municipal authority) of Bera, comprising Don Juan Bautista de Garmendia, rector of the parish, and the curates Don Juan Esteban de Garzezuría, Don Pedro de Borchea (mentioned before in connection with the inheritance of the chests), Don Carlos de Leguía, and Don Pedro Joseph de Lizardi declared that the goods pertaining to the chapel of María de Aramburu had census taxes and duties of 4 percent, one hundred *ducados* on the people and goods of Juan de Echenique and Catalina de Alquegui, by writ of July 26, 1731, and which the *cabildo* had collected from the current current owners of

Alqueguiberea, Juan Bautista Herrandonea and María Asencia de Alquegui, his wife.

María Asencia was likely the daughter of Catalina de Alquegui and Juan de Echenique, and she was named after her mother's stepmother. What this means is that the family harmony that was stipulated as a condition in the marriage contract of her parents had not been seriously disturbed, at least on the female side, and that the female heir of Alqueguiberea had used the maternal surname, and not the paternal surname, both as an expression of inheritance rights and because it was a family name that carried more weight in Navarre.[21] For his part, Juan Bautista de Errandonea (or "Herrandonea") seems to have been a husband who was a self-made man, born on a fortified house in a nearby neighborhood, Dornaku, a name that is applied to the neighborhood as a whole even today. He apparently was a very religious man of some importance in the council of Bera who, along with his wife, appeared on the scene well into the eighteenth century.

Juan Bautista appears to have had some disagreement with his father-in-law Juan de Echenique, judging by a receipt signed on May 18, 1760 by Juan Esteban de Yrazoqui in which a specific dispute is referred to. Juan Bautista Errandonea appears in two different documents of 1767 as the treasurer of fees collected in the town of Bera that year. In one of these documents, he assessed a fee of one third of the rental value of various lands, and in the other he assessed a fee for wood that was also the property of the town. More instructive than these municipal documents are others dating from 1780 and 1782 which refer to something very important in the domestic and public life of Basques in general: the manner in which marriages were contracted and the devotion to the memory of the deceased. Around the year 1780, it appears that Errandonea and his wife had a number of daughters of marriageable age. At least two of these daughters did indeed contract marriage, one of them, named María, with a certain Juan Esteban, a young man who had been born on the estate of Gorostipala. Earlier, however, the parents had thought of marrying her off to a wealthy man who had returned from the colonies, Esteban de Irazoqui, also of the same neighborhood, and who later returned to Montevideo. Errandonea appears to have written him with news of the wedding, and offering him another of his daughters, with her consent. However, Irazoqui responded on April 9, 1780 indicating that he did not want to contract marriage with a woman he had not met, and also saying that, since he had already been disappointed by one daughter, that the other might end up disappointing him as well.

This letter reflects the authority that parents had over their daughters when it came to marriage. It also showed how, as regards marriage, there was a wide berth given to the possibility of "marriages of convenience" given that, in his letter, Irazoqui recognized that his rival from Gorostipala was "a very well-born young man" and implies that the marriage in question had been arranged without the couple having become acquainted. The document or documents from two years later, in 1782, indicate that the marriage of the Errandoneas had taken place under similar circumstances. Alqueguiberea was not buried in the church, and this was unusual for someone born to one of the houses of the neighborhood.

On March 7 that year, the parish vicar of the bishopric of Iruñea-Pamplona, Dr. Mateo Joseph de Areizaga, issued a document granting the request of Errandonea and his wife that a sepulcher be opened in the place that the latter had purchased in the church of Bera, which was "a woman's seat in the tenth row of the part of the Epistle" declaring that it was suitable for such a purpose and that it would not in any way harm the structure of the church itself. In addition, he stipulated that the parish priest of Bera was to make known this authorization at the time of the reciting of the mass on a holiday, and that the burial vault be placed at the disposition of the owner of Alquequiberea, without prejudice to any third parties, once a designated sum in alms had been paid to the church. This same document provided that an entry be made regarding this transaction in the book of those who had made offerings to the church. This was apparently done on March 14. Once the alms had been given to the foreman of the workshop, and "María Ascencia de Echenique had been bestowed said title in the selfsame Church and shown the burial vault that she had obtained, she sat upon it, lit a beeswax candle, placed it upon the vault, extinguished it, and remained there, having performed this rite, in quiet and peaceful possession of the use of said sepulcher." This ceremony took place in the presence of numerous witnesses, and was officially documented by the scribe Martín de Leguía. Subsequently, on April 1, a document was drafted that complemented the one just referred to. María Esteban de Camio, widow of Joseph de Borda, owner of Betrobaita, who was the actual owner of the woman's chair in the church that had been granted to the owner of Alqueguiberea, definitively transferred said space. Errandonea and his wife promised that "From the moment that the said María Estaban de Camio passes away, she will be admitted to perpetual participation in the light of said sepulcher."

This document is very telling because of both its legal and religious content. The woman who made the donation to the church is associated with the family—or, rather, the house, of Alqueguiberea in the most intimate sense, and this is what gives her the right to a light in the new sepulcher.

There are still more documents concerning Alqueberea, yet the remaining material does not provide a comprehensive account an entire single generation. On June 4, 1833, about fifty years following the donation of the burial vault, Juan José Errandonea, "minority owner" of Alqueguiberea, purchased a grove of chestnut trees from José Francisco de Goicoechea, owner of Amurusbaita for twenty-seven *pesos fuertes* in "authentic coins of gold and silver." This appears to be the same man who, on December 31, 1864, bought a section of the commons from Bera for the purposes of cultivation. At the time, Juan José Errandonea y Ezponda was sixty-six years old. In other words, he had been born in 1798. The fact that, in 1833, he was described as a "minority owner," leads one to think that he was yet another self-made man who became part of the family by marrying a granddaughter of Juan Bautista Errandonea (and thus part of his lineage). The surname "Errandonea" is very common in the town of Bera even today.

These persons represent the seventh generation of inhabitants of Alqueguiberea, a line that began with Martín de Alquegui, who lived at the beginning of the seventeenth century, some two hundred years previously.

General Observations Regarding the Data Just Presented

From the last-named individuals until the date of the writing of the present essay (1968), another four or five generations have passed. But let's pause for a moment first. During the seven generations that passed from 1633 until 1833, we see the following kinds of succession: three father-son; one father-daughter; one mother-daughter; and yet another by a daughter (in this latter case it is unclear whether the succession was from the mother or father). The principle of free choice of heir was applied quite freely. The *donatio propter nuptias* was applied repeatedly, albeit belatedly and in convoluted fashion in certain instances. All the same, it is clear that between the social "structure" within which these six generations of male and female owners of houses lived, and the "structural form," there are striking differences that are determined not so much by changes in time as they are by personal relationships among those who preserve, adhere to, and submit to said form. I myself prefer to call this form a "system" or "regimen."

From a descriptive and ethnographic point of view, we can reduce all of the foregoing concepts to the clear principle of the local laws[22]—or common law—in addition to "systems" of religious beliefs and practices regarding burial. Seen in this light, some might consider such a system good in terms of assuring continuity of property, family work, and so on. But can we also infer other consequences of the "structural form"? The examples we've reviewed here don't allow us to do so. And it would be even less justifiable to offer an apologia from a moral point of view. The physical structure of the house was the primary determinant of the many possible functions of family and of work. In light of the cases we've reviewed here, we can well understand *how* this form came to be. With respect to *why* it came into being, however, we need to be rather more cautious. We could possibly accept Wilhelm Emil Mühlmann's proposition that, in the final analysis, the word "structure" reflects a category that is static (and perhaps even aesthetic) while the word *function* contains a category that is, above all, ethical in nature. It is even possible to contend that structure is something that is a given in the lives of human beings, and therefore as something within which—or in spite of which—they must necessarily function according to their nature. In this connection, we should also not lose sight of the fact that there may be a series of mutually contradictory structures that simultaneously impose themselves upon individuals and groups.

In effect, and in a very literary—perhaps even theatrical—vein, we find ourselves confronted with a scenario and arena of action that must necessarily be experienced by human actors. Who are these actors? A timid man, perhaps. Or a rapacious man. A man who expands his property holdings. Another who reduces his holdings. One who expends more energy in matters of the spirit than in building his estate. One who gets on well with his neighbors. Or perhaps one who ends up killing his neighbors. One who gets along with—or perhaps hates—his in-laws. And what about the women? How do they adjust to the givens of their existence, either under normal circumstances or in times of crisis?

When we undertake folkloric research, we often find more or less common sayings or expressions that reflect common patterns in distinctive ways. The haughty daughter-in-law assuming the role of *etxekoandre* is understood in one way.[23] A meek man is understood in quite a different way. The number of commonplaces multiplies accordingly. Yet it is perhaps even more interesting to observe the impact or reflection of legal customs or burial practices in physical forms (i.e., in so-called material culture). For many years, antique dealers have been procuring the chests of Navarrese houses. As we have seen, chests and beds are emblematic of married life—and are passed down along with a certain amount of cash as part of the legally due inheritance of daughters. Recently, funerary stelae and offering tables (*arguizaiolak* or *bildumenak*), which have a very plain style in Bera, have become collectible items.[24] Burial cloths are at least equally coveted items. The artistic sense of the rural populations became wedded to practical function, and religious belief and legal custom thus received joint expression in these objects. Everything is interrelated. The assertion that everything is "structured," however, is another matter altogether. And such an assertion seems even more dubious now than in previous historical periods. In sum, it is my personal belief that the word *structure* should not be used in the ways it has been used in recent times by certain philosophers and sociologists, because the stasis that it implies seems simply ill conceived.[25]

But let's now have a look at another example.

The History of a Manor House

Manor houses (i.e., the manor houses with coats-of-arms) have observed the same regimen of succession as the houses of land-owning residents or of rented satellite houses. In this regard, the case of Reparacea, a famous palace in the Bidasoa, in Oieregi (Oyeregui), in the valley of Bertiz (Bértiz or Bertizarana) is significant. Reparcea was situated within the parish of Narbarte (Narvarte). In the census book of 1366, Juan de Reparaz is mentioned as a prominent resident.[26]

During the following century, we see that the *Erreparaze* family was the owner of the house: Machin Bértiz (or "de Bértiz"), squire, and his wife María de Oyerequi. Machin died in the town of Roa, in service to the king of Navarre, and his house was burned and his family was ruined. In consideration of this fact and of the services that had been rendered by the decedent, the king exempted the widow from the obligation to pay both the three *quarteles* that had recently been assessed, and any other payment that she might be subject to henceforth, except for those payments assessed for the marriage of Navarrese princesses. Each *cuartel* (or *quartel*) was worth the sum of twelve *sueldos carlines*. This royal favor was authorized in Iruñea-Pamplona on September 18, 1414 according to the copies that survived in Reparacea (three in all; two from 1758 and another from 1780).[27] A second, identical royal favor was granted to the house in 1477, at which time the Infanta Doña Leonor was lieutenant general of the kingdom, and when Martín de Bértiz and Juana de Subizar were owners of the same house. The official document in which this favor was granted was drafted in Tutera (Tudela) on October 13 of the same year, and indicates that Martín de Bértiz was a "a nobleman who many have followed, and who has gone, in the company of noblemen of the mountains, and through his industry, or through his diligence, the Royal Crown has been greatly served." As a consequence, "he has bestowed upon him and his house, in consideration of the fact that his house was burned and destroyed because of said service" a special royal favor. This was reaffirmed by Don Pedro, cardinal infant of Navarre (and also viceroy [*visorrey*]) in Iruñea-Pamplona on July 18, 1480. It is certain that, at the time that Reparacea was burned, it was a tower-house, like others in the same vicinity in Larraiotz (Arráyoz), Irurita, and other places. But once the civil conflicts were over and Navarre was annexed, the military use it had had in the fourteenth and fifteenth centuries likely no longer applied. The palace house of head of the lineage—in spite of this title—was, during the sixteenth and seventeenth centuries, a rural house that was larger than other houses and one[28] that enjoyed certain exemptions, but that was essentially dedicated to agriculture and livestock farming.

Donations

Martín de Bértiz, governor of Altzorritz (Alzórriz), and his wife had a son who succeeded them as owner of Reparacea. This son, Marticot de Reparáz, married Catalina de Apestegui. Martín had another son, Juan de Bértiz Reparaz, who married María de Arizcun. These sons were in turn succeeded by Marín de Videgui y Reparaz and Catalina de Reparaz (or "Reparace"). Then, well into the sixteenth century, we see that the inheritance of the palace passed through the female line, with Catalina de Reparace (who dictated her last will and testament on November 3, 1592) as owner and heiress, and Martín Videgui as a "self-made husband" (*marido aventicio*), as the expression went in the lands of Zuberoa and Lower Navarre. We also see that this couple had two sons (Miguel and Juanes) as well as two daughters (Catalina and Juana de Videgui). The mother Catalina invested her husband with the authority *to designate the heir* of his choice, and to establish in his will that, while he, the father, was still alive, he was to be considered the "lord and master" of the palace. Nine years later, on March 18, 1601, we see that the father chose his daughter Catalina as heir (rather than his sons). Catalina in turn became owner under the terms of the marriage contract established by Videgui (by then a widow) and Miguel Audadi and María Joan Goyeneche. Catalina de Reparacea (who took her mother's surname) subsequently married Joanes de Audadi y Sarrate, with the groom's husband stipulating the primary dowry to be provided, by means of *auriches* (a second dowry). The dowry was to consist of fifty ducats, along with twenty lambs, two young bulls, a cup worth twelve ducats, twelve ducats to supply clothing for Martín de (Videgui) Reparaz, and a sow and its litter. Half of the ducats that were part of this dowry were to be converted into cattle. It should be noted here that Miguel Audadi was a stonecutter and that, in clause six, he promised to provide up to twenty ducats for works to be carried out at Reparacea. The second Catalina was succeeded as owner by another woman, as stipulated by a marriage contract dated June 27, 1635 between María Juan Sarrate y Reparaz, daughter of the house, and Pedro de Gaztelu, of the Capallarena de Gaztelu house, and son of Juan de Gaztelu and María de Ursúa. Two men in succession followed María as owner, through the use of the *donatio propter nuptias*. In fact, on April 9, 1674, a marriage contract was drafted for the nuptials of Juan de Gaztelu, heir of Reparacea, and María Ana de Bértiz. This was followed on August 26, 1697, by another marriage contract between the son of the aforementioned couple, Pedro de Gaztelu, and Graciana de Albirena, who had an only child, María Francisca de Gaztelu, who was the indisputable owner of the palace. María was baptized on April 17, 1704, and she married Juan Bautista de Uztáriz in 1717, who had been baptized on January 10, 1696. Beginning with this marriage, the lineage of Uztáriz was established in Reparacea, and when the old palace of the leader of the lineage acquired a different character.[29]

Change of Social Statute

The mountain branch house—in effect—soon took on the character of a residence of the economic upper bourgeois. This following the obtaining of aristocratic titles in the seventeenth century. For example, Doña María Francisca de Gaztelu chose as the heir of her house her oldest son Juan Miguel de Uztáriz, who was born in 1720. Juan Miguel attended the University of Salamanca, was a Knight of the Order of St. James, and a man who conducted business in Madrid and Cádiz. It appears that, for a time, he was inclined to accept the designation as heir. But later documents indicate that the designated heir of Reparacea was the second son, Juan Bautista, who was Count of Reparaz, also a

Knight of the Order of St. James, a shipowner, and a businessman who was born in 1728 and who died in 1810 in Jerez de la Frontera. Juan Bautista, in turn, ceded his rights to the house to his younger brother, "Juan Miguel the Younger" (called thus to distinguish him from the first-born son), who was born in 1746.[30] The second cession referred to here was recorded in Mexico, on September 25, 1776. From the death of Juan Miguel the Younger to the present owner of Reparacea, Doña Concepción Uztáriz y Micheo, there were two male heirs. These were Andrés José[31] (son of Juan Miguel the Younger) and his son Eugenio. At present, and for the first time in centuries, the principle of indivisibility and the *donatio propter nuptias* are no longer applied. But let us return to the issue of structures and functions.

Between the property of Alqueguiberea, in Bera, of the mid-seventeenth century and the property today, there have been substantive changes. Yet as regards Reparacea, from the time of the fortified house of the fifteenth century, the farmhouse of the sixteenth and seventeenth century, the manor house of the eighteenth century (figure 9.8) and bourgeois mansion of the nineteenth and twentieth centuries, there have been at least twice as many important changes, despite the fact that the legal and social concept providing that, within the framework of local Navarrese law, the manor house was included, and also despite the fact that the defining features of a manor house had not changed. How, then, is it possible to compare the family that live in Reparacea at the beginning of the eighteenth century, which lived within the framework of a simple *baserri* economy,[32] with the family of some fifty or sixty years later, which zealously pursued aristocratic titles, and which converted the tower house into a Baroque mansion?[33] And what does any of this have to do with the lives of its residents and owners today?

It seems that there are distinct kinds of structures. Legal structures and economic structures are not always expressed in parallel fashion. In addition, the existence of one kind of structure does not necessarily indicate the correspondence with the other kind of structure. This observation, which any law student will recognize as self-evident, is not necessarily obvious to certain modern ethnologists. What family histories show us as regards the vicissitudes of fortune also forces us to recognize that social structure and structural form are two things that are even more different from one another than Radcliffe Brown believed when he formulated the distinction cited at the beginning of this modest study. These family histories also lead us to reflect on the possibility

Figure 9.8. Reparacea.

that structure as a static category—as an excessively static category—may end up deceptively leading us to wrongly label different things as similar that are in fact quite different from one another.

Certain words, as well as particular legal and social concepts seem to always have the same content. Yet this perception turns out to be fallacious, something I will attempt to show in my essay on concepts of honor and vengeance in Spain from the Middle Ages to modern times.[34] It is also fallacious in the case we are examining here, for the general idea of "house" and "stem family household" not only varies in content over the course of centuries, but the very idea of "house," considered in material terms, is subject to such obvious variations,[35] that it is the historian in the end who must always have the last word—the humble historian who puts things one after another, like they are given to him.

10

Agriculture and Cattle Raising

The social and economic history of the Basque people and the Basque Country could be conceived as the product of two different historical processes. The first of these is of very recent origin, is most important within the larger context of the economic history of Western Europe, and has to do with the problems that come to the fore when we reflect upon the iron industry, naval architecture, and urban settlements in general. This has been a short and rapid process, because it began at a relatively late stage of the Middle Ages, and we can now feel its menacing immediacy, unaware of what it may hold in store for us.

Along with this mercurial current in our history, which has been radically transforming the surface of the country ever since the nineteenth century, there is another, slower historical process within which our agricultural and shepherding ancestors lived their lives. This involves the settlement of families in small groupings, with their own distinctive way of life, and their physical, anthropological, and cultural characteristics—characteristics that have made the Basque people so interesting, from both a human and scholarly point of view. In other words, there is a fundamental dichotomy between the vertiginous whirlwind of economic history that we can call technology, and the placid existence of the rural inhabitants of the Basque Country from time immemorial. And yet, we must be ever mindful that this far more profound current in our history contains its own phases, periods, and problems and that, even though it is obvious that there has been a high degree of preservation of the past, we must not lose sight of the modifications that have also occurred in time and space, and of which we are only dimly aware.

Every work of Basque ethnography has a few paragraphs dedicated to linguistic inferences regarding the names of some of the agricultural implements that were fundamentally important to rural life (e.g., the words for "axe" and "spade"). We've all read something regarding the meaning of the Basque word *aitz* (i.e., "rock") in compounds such as *aitzkor* ("knife"), *aitzur* ("hoe"), and so on. This might lead us to conclude that, in terms of the Basque conceptualization of primitive tools, there is a transition from the world of stone to the world of metal. We might also make a number of inferences regarding words like *laya* (a two-pronged instrument for turning up ground), that unusual tool that was so common in certain Basque areas until recently.

We'll leave this to the linguists, because it is a matter that involves a number of problems that haven't yet been resolved. Yet we should observe how, when studying Basque rural life, a master like Jose Miguel de Barandiarán made a number of positive inquiries that showed that, in places like the Goierri (literally, "highlands," a region in Gipuzkoa —ed.) and other areas of highland rural settlement (frequently associated with the placement of a dolmen) where there were ancient burial grounds, country houses were established afterward. This phenomenon lends credence to the transition posited in certain general schemas of ancient economic history from a pastoral economy to a rural economy. Yet, although this may be accurate from a particular point of view, it is also important to remember that, in the north of Spain, there is another technical tradition that is evident not from the findings of archeology, but from ancient texts (first and foremost the work of Strabo), which suggests that, in many towns in the north of the peninsula, there was a kind of agriculture and horticulture that was the exclusive province of women. In other words, while men were engaged in other activities, women cultivated the fields in distinctive manner, practicing a nonlivestock agriculture that made prominent use of the spade and the *laya*. This was an agriculture that had nothing to do with ox-powered plows. This feminine agriculture—or rather horticulture—is found among many ancient peoples all over the world, as well as in relatively modern civilizations that reproduce this ancient pattern.

An interesting aspect of this agriculture is that it is not associated with any kind of large-scale herding. In other words, the keeping of animals in this kind of civilization was often related to forms of matriarchal law, and not to intensive animal husbandry. Pigs and goats were raised, but not other animals that would later play such a vital role in our country.

We lack the extensive documentary and archeological information that would enable us to fully depict and reconcile these two different transitions—from the prehistoric tending of flocks on the highlands to the modern farmhouse, and then to more modern forms of settlement, with the transition from a horticultural economy (documented in texts) to a more modern form of agriculture based on use of the plow. In the absence of any documentation to the contrary, we can once again seize upon linguistic information that, even though it is far from adequate, does provide us a good deal of knowledge regarding the nature of certain human settlements in general, and especially those settlements involving shepherding, agriculture, and extractive industries, such as coal mining and woodcutting.

As regards the names of certain settlements, it is evident that, in the southern part of the Basque Country (i.e., the south of Araba and the central and southern zones of Navarre), it is possible to discern that, at least in Roman times, there was a system of large estates and country houses—that is, of agricultural activities similar to those seen in other parts of Spain, and in France and Italy—which were designated by the names of their founders. The Araban town of Antoñana and Leciñana (which gave its name to two towns) derive their names from an "Antonio" and "Licinio" respectively (i.e., the men who founded them). This is surely the case for other towns as well, where settlements were established, and where labor was organized along the lines of the large country estate, with tools and animals. This was a pattern that was common throughout the Roman Empire.

In some of these place names, a given name that was common in the land of the Ebro (e.g., Antonio, Licinio, Montano) was added to *villa* (either before or after the name, as was the case with the French *ville* during particular historical periods). Thus, on the one hand, we have Villabezana and, on the other, names like Genevilla or Berantevilla or Lunivilla, which correspond to the French names that include the component of *ville*. This pattern suggests the development of agricultural settlements such as those found in France, and which has been thoroughly studied by historians of French rural life. By studying the methods of these researchers, we can glean ideas that are useful—as I've indicated—for the southern region of the Basque Country (although there are some cases where similar settlements are found farther north as well).

It is evident that the increase in rural settlements occurred here in a similar way, over the course of about a thousand years, from the first century AD until the tenth or eleventh century. One sees that the system of baptizing a settlement (which today might be a more or less large town) with the name of its founder—the person who first plowed the ground to prepare it for farming, and who set boundaries on and exploited the land—was done by using Basque designations. Near Bilbao, there is a town by the name of Enekuri (Enécuri), where it is clear that the word *uri* is joined to a given name (i.e., Eneko, the Basque form of Iñigo). Similar place names are seen in Araba and in Upper Rioja (which seems to have been reconquered or at least repopulated by Basques who spoke a Bizkaian variant of the language). Thus, an Obekuri (Obecuri) (town of Obeko) was established in Araba, and Obekuri was later established in Castile and León. In Herramelluri, the personal name is Herramel or Ferramel. There is an evident concern that the integrity of the large estate or country house that was formed preserve a distinctive name. This was evident in later stages, judging from the personal names. Thus, the time comes when we no longer see names like Antonio or Licinio, as in Roman times, but rather typically medieval names, such as we observe in many names of Navarrese towns with the suffix "*-ain.*" Thus we have Gerendiain (Guerendiáin), Beraskoain (Belascoáin), and Baternain (Paternáin), which were clearly founded by men by the names of Gueren, Velasco (Blasco), and Paterno respectively. These three names were all very common in the registries maintained by monasteries.

In a considerable proportion of the toponymy of the Basque Country, we thus find settlements that conform to linguistic and chronological patterns that are seen elsewhere in the Western world. In addition, we find many settlements today that are phytonyms (i.e., names of plants) that represented plants typical of the area where the settlement was founded. It has often been said that Basque place names are fundamentally characterized by descriptive elements of this kind. When it comes to such theoretical considerations, it is important to consider relative proportions and not to impose a rigid system that does not bear close scrutiny. It is evident that place names containing an element of the name of a tree (e.g., chestnut, oak, walnut, evergreen oak, alder, river trees, mountain trees, birch, etc.) are extremely important for reconstructing the agricultural landscape of the Basque Country. Yet it is also important to take into account that the other kind of designations that employed given names and technical activities can also be used to derive a good deal of information regarding past eras. While it is clear that those designations based on the names of plants, trees, and other natural elements can eventually give an idea of the landscape, if we fail to conduct other kinds of research, our reconstructions will have diminished chronological utility. In addition, there remain a number of other social and economic problems that need to be clarified. More detailed information is needed regarding both the history of property ownership and of the technology that was employed in the Basque Country.

As regards the history of property ownership, it is necessary to take as our point of departure the fact that, within the very center of the Basque Country (i.e., the territory that in all respects can be considered as having the strongest specifically Basque character) *baserriak* were primarily *exploitative* rather than *productive* in character. This can be said because there are many regions of Navarre where there are a great many properties farmed by families of tenant farmers whose lineage stretched back many centuries, as did that of the lords they served. We might even go so far as to conclude that there are farmhouses whose diminishing returns have led to a fall in social status for their occupants or those people who work for them. For example, in the Baztan Valley there is the neighborhood of Bozate, where the proprietors of houses clustered together are the famous and, until recently, highly unfortunate Agotes who were dependent on noble landed estates. The case of the Agotes is rather extreme, but we also need to take account of the fact that, in comparison to other parts of Navarre and Gipuzkoa, there are in the Baztan Valley a good many *baserriak* that have been owned by prominent Basque families for many centuries. We are referring here to figures of the caliber of the Counts of Oñate, who owned property in this area that for so long retained a fair measure of independence. Other men of prominence who have owned property in the Baztan are the lords of Lazcano, the Dukes of Granada de Ega (or their relatives, from the Narros family), and others. Until recently, these families were in possession of a large proportion of the lands in the valley. In Araba, expressions such as "lands of the Count," "lands of the Duke," and the like are attested at a very early date. When it comes to Bizkaia, for me personally, the problems grow murkier still. In order to clearly understand the history and function of *baserriak*, and the extent of their autonomous character, a study of vast and free-standing properties in Bizkaia would most certainly be in order.

There are also areas where *baserriak* belonging to families have existed for a very long time. In my opinion, an evaluation of the history of family property in light of the idea of freedom held by Basques over the course of centuries would constitute a fruitful topic of future research.

The notion of freedom among property owners vis-à-vis lineages is an ideal that has progressed considerably since the fifteenth century, and that has led to the embracing of concepts such as "collective nobility" (*hidalguía colectiva*) and the established form of "residents' rights" (*derechos de vecindad*). In Navarre, the problem of collective nobility is seen most clearly at the time when entire valleys in the border region, such as the Baztan, Erronkari (Roncal), or Lana Valleys, began to be granted such rights, and then proceeded to forge a particular character within the context of Navarre. This character was indeed so distinctive that, at the same time that collective nobility was being established in the mountains, along the riverbanks, the largest and most lawless fiefdoms in the history of the kingdom of Navarre were being established. This state of affairs shows that any kind of linear and evolutionary approach that studies the transition of one form of organization into another is in reality the most rickety of foundations upon which to establish research, at least in the absence of due consideration of the actual physical and economic conditions of the Basque Country as a whole. In southern Navarre, the irrigated and fertile land, and the favor of kings toward their kinfolk or "entourage" led to the creation of large fiefdoms, such as those held by the Count of Lerin and the Lord of Azkoien-Peralta. In the meantime, collective nobility rights were being established in the highlands—rights that propelled the Basque Country in an entirely different social and economic direction.

As regards Gipuzkoa and Bizkaia, the problem is perhaps less complex and ambiguous, at least to a certain point. Yet problems were evident in these two provinces as well, given that the notions of property and freedom were perhaps more divergent from one another there than anywhere else.

As regards shepherding, we also need to make distinctions in methods of sheep-raising in different areas of the Basque Country. In the kingdom of Navarre, for example, there was one particular shepherding method that was applied in the eastern region, from the northern reaches of the area of the Basque Pyrenees in the Erronkari, Zaraitzu (Salazar), and other valleys, to the southern lowlands that could not be more different in every way. The shepherding employed there conforms to a pattern of classical transhumance. It was this transhumant shepherding that was characteristic of the high Pyrenean valleys and the banks of the Ebro (and when grazing land there was scarcer, that was also employed in the short grasslands of Aragon). In Navarre, this method of shepherding led to the creation of *cañadas reales* and *ganados reales* (i.e., sheep walks and cattle trails, respectively, and which in some cases were the exclusive property of a single estate). It also led to the creation of a council that resembled the Castilian *mesta*. The word *mesta*, which seems to be a

Spanish word, has been used in Erronkari Basque, and the authority of the Navarrese *mesta* seems to closely resemble that of the Spanish *mesta*. In other words, what we can see here is a system of shepherding that may in part have grown out of the *Reconquista*, and in which various important interests were at stake, given that the sheep walks were often used as cattle trails as well. In medieval Navarrese documents, it is surprising to find that, just as there is the Extremadura del Duero in Castile, and later the Extremadura that is today associated with a vast province in southwest Spain, and just as in Portugal, there is both an Estremadura and an Estremo, in the kingdoms of both Navarre and Aragon, there were also territories designated as "Extremadura" (i.e., in the far reaches of each of these kingdoms).

The necessity to traverse a territory ranging from the Pyrenees to the far south of the kingdom of Navarre is what led to the particular kind of cattle-raising that we see here, a method of cattle-raising that is partially Basque in character. Until the end of the nineteenth century, some of the men engaged in this activity spoke the Basque language. This method of cattle-raising also made extensive use of words derived from Arabic, which may have been spoken at one time in Tutera (Tudela), or farther south within Navarre. This kind of relationship between the north and the south is fundamentally important for understanding other aspects of life in the extreme east of Navarre, such as the trade in rafts, the transportation of trees, and other typical activities. In other areas of the Basque Country, we do not see such a marked degree of transhumance, a phenomenon that over the course of history has been increasingly limited by agricultural interests. In any case, in the Basque place names of areas that are mainly agricultural, we see terms and names that indicate the existence of ancient paths and ancient cattle trails. In the codes of law of the French Basque territories—specifically, in Zuberoa, as well as in certain texts of the Zaraitzu Valley and elsewhere—there is a constant reference to *altzubide* or *altxubide*, which is similar to the Spanish *alzada*: *Altzubide* or *altzuguren* or *altzugarai* is the path, area, or point of high pasturage—in other words, it is a pastoral term that indicates the activity of pasturage on high ground. In these Basque-speaking areas, the entities designated by the words *seles, korak, saroi,** and so on have been studied, but we don't have a particularly clear idea of cattle trails in terms of the

---

* Type of pasturage, *sel*, has survived in Spanish as a cattle pasturage, referring to a circular pasturage. Of *korak* no exact meaning was determined. *Saroi* is a sheep fold or shepherd's meeting point. —ed.

form that they would have existed in the fourteenth, fifteenth, and even sixteenth centuries. We also are not certain of how cattle were specifically raised at that time. What we do know is that herders practiced a different kind of transhumance, driving their herds from south to north—from the high sierra of the watershed to the milder climes of the coastal valleys. This constituted a kind of transhumance that is still reflected in barely perceptible ways in the practices of some peoples. For example, in my hometown of Bera, cattle drivers will guide their herds from the colder barren scrublands in the mountains to lower ground in the spring, or at some other time during the year, in order to secure access to more lush pasturage.

Such considerations could profitably result in cartographic research on distinct areas and provinces. If such research took account of chronology, it would be more useful still.

As regards specifically agricultural problems, we ought to clarify a number of issues related to succession and other legal matters, specifically as regards the ability of women to inherit property, whether that of the family or of leased lands. We also need to clarify some technical matters, and to resist any overgeneralizations regarding the supposed archaic character of Basque agriculture that seem prevalent in certain ethnographic texts. We have already noted that the *laya*, the hoe, and the agricultural and horticultural cultivation carried out by women reflect the existence of an archaic society. But although there is no question that this is true regarding agricultural methods, there are other factors to take into account as well. More than eighty years ago, for example, Dr. Telesforo de Aranzadi y Unamuno, who served as an early ethnographic mentor for Barandiarán noted that it is possible to discern in a number of the technical elements of the work of Basque farmers certain characteristics that could be called Nordic or central European. For example, head yokes and certain other critically important implements, such as a certain kind of plow, are similar to those used in Nordic and Western European lands. Other elements, like the *laya*, are peculiar to the Basque Country. Still others (e.g., certain kinds of carts that are familiar to some of us from our childhood, but that have now been relegated to museum displays) appear to bear a similarity to those used in the Mediterranean world. Yet, as regards carts, it should be pointed out that there was a marked difference between the distinctive form of the wheels on the carts used in the western Basque Country, from Enkarterri (Las Encartaciones) to a large section of Araba, and the wide heavy wheels typically used on carts in the eastern Basque country.

This is a subject that should be studied within the context of European ethnological cartography. Yet, turning from morphological similarities to matters of functional importance, a more pressing need is to analyze how the economic structure of rural Basque settlements dramatically evolved during the seventeenth and eighteenth centuries, and even afterward.

If we examine the population censuses and rolls of the seventeenth century, we see property registered in terms of number of cattle, trees, area of meadows, and so on. This notion of property is very different from that of the eighteenth century. I have seen this difference most notably in reference to the towns in the highlands of Navarre. In some of these cases, census data is available over the course of many years. This makes it possible to see, for example, how at one time, horses and goats held a place of importance in Navarrese mountain valleys. This is strange in light of the present situation in that region. In addition, we also see how, during previous periods, sheep had an importance that they no longer have, and that there were a lot of wild cattle—wild cows and bulls—as well as wild horses. In addition, we begin to see how more land is devoted to pasturage, a growing use of stables, a higher level of interest in using fertilizers, as well as a change even in animal species. All of these changes have been fundamentally important in the economic development of the Basque Country.

There is no question that such changes occurred as a result of two different processes: the personal experience of farmers as well as actual planning, as reflected in the minutes of the Sociedad Económica Bascongada (Basque Economic Society). In other words, for example, we see that a particular crop was introduced at a certain time in particular towns. At some other time, we see that the Sociedad Bascongada de los Amigos del País (Basque Society of Friends of the Country), or perhaps some other institution, were involved in promoting the expansion of meadows, the use of fertilizer, importing particular animal species. In short, considerable planning was in evidence. But, given that not all aspects of a society develop at the same pace, it is also important to study legal issues that have heretofore been neglected. The struggle for residents' rights (*el derecho de vecindad*) in many valleys during the eighteenth and nineteenth centuries was of dramatic importance. This was because the former privileges of the lineages began to be replaced by those of residents. Thus, people who entered a particular area from other valleys began to have increasingly limited possibilities.

On the other hand, the severe economic crises at the end of the eighteenth century and during the entire nineteenth century resulted in many people exploiting those who leased their lands by creating forms of sharecropping as well as housing that would soon result in destitute and overcrowded conditions.

But at this point everything is in crisis. To us, the *baserri* seems like something from the ancient past.

I for one am unable to provide, or even suggest, possible solutions to this situation. Yet I do believe that we all, collectively, have the obligation to let it be known—and to insist—that we need to put a stop to what is going on, and to advise that portion of our population involved exclusively in industry that they are not the only persons in the Basque Country who have problems, even though the industrial sector is of primary importance from an economic standpoint.

As I stated at the outset, it is the Basque Country, and not the Basque people, that has declined in importance—that has, in effect, shriveled. The Basque Country does not have the strength of the Basque people. Can a people live happily in a small and declining country? Whatever economists, technicians, or optimistic sociologists might say, I don't think this is possible. And I believe that it is the task of those of us who are not technicians, economists, or men who work with numbers to demonstrate to technicians, economists, and men who work with numbers that we also have our arguments—scholarly, quantitative, and numerical arguments, in order to challenge their position, and to refuse to accept the notion that progress is solely determined by those factors that they identify. This is because, first, there are so many other functions and, secondly, in light of a consideration of the collective future of the country, there are functions that they don't consider in the least. Some might characterize such a peroration as rather archaic or reactionary for this short course on the social and economic history of a country and a people. Yet it is my sober contention that there is nothing in the least archaic or reactionary—or anything that could be characterized by juvenile minds with even worse epithets in my contentions here.

I think that we need to recognize and denounce the danger involved in only paying attention to one form of culture—what we might call a "short-term culture," a culture that is fleeting, and in which time and space seem to lose all importance. Instead, we ought to defend the value of those gifts which have been bestowed upon us by nature—those things which endure over the course of centuries and which, from what we can see as a result of our recent experience, appear to be the object of scorn on the part of certain kinds of modern men who are prepared to do away with them. It would most certainly be paradoxical if the energy that nature has provided over the course of millions of years—through forests, oil, iron—were exhausted in a few hundred years. Seen from the standpoint of the historian, this is indeed one of the most dramatic developments that is currently taking place in the world. I do not think that because one is a historian and expresses such ideas, that he is either more or less reactionary than any self-satisfied and oblivious accountant, common laborer, or oblivious and self-satisfied engineer.

Part 4

The Basques, Other Peoples, and Other Worlds

11
Regarding the Basque Shipbuilding and Iron Industries

The Shipbuilding Industry

During the last centuries of the Middle Ages, the political and economic history of the country was dominated by a race to the ocean and what the sea signified for the Basques and their neighbors. In classical antiquity, references to seas and oceans involving the Basque Country are rare, although it has recently emerged that Romans exploited the iron deposits of Oiartzun—near what was conceived of in ancient geography as the border between Gaul and Hispania or Iberia—by way of the sea lanes. Pliny more or less vaguely points to Bizkaian iron deposits, and they must have played some role in maritime commerce with Gaul and the lands to the north. This is understandable, since the geographical characteristics of the Basque coast are inherently conducive to the development of direct trade relations with northern peoples.

Then there is a long period of historical silence, followed, around the ninth century, by the establishment of a settlement of great navigators called Lapurdum—from which Labourd or Lapurdi is derived near Baiona. These arrivals were Normans who, as is well known, at some point expanded southward toward the Mediterranean from the northern Atlantic. These navigators—who were seen as pirates—were feared as great threats to places they landed. They established a long-term settlement in Baiona, and left a lasting legacy as they transformed from ethnically distinct and rootless pirates into settled people practicing traditional economic commerce.

Medieval pirates seem to have gradually become transformed into legal traders. Still, the idea of a lawless sea where anything was permitted continued to form an important part of the mindset of the inhabitants of the coast. Thus, the transition from Norman piracy to traditional medieval commercial activity is very difficult to trace via anything other than questionable speculation.

It is clear there was contact between Basques and Normans. There was a murky period involving contact between the seafaring peoples of northern Iberia with those of Gaul, but it is only from the Middle Ages onward—when the fuero of Donostia-San Sebastián was established—that we have a more solid basis for studying the commercial and seafaring activities of different Basque settlements.

Since the Minoan civilization, the sea has been a symbol of order and royal power. It was thought that the sea was the property of royalty or the powers of the state. However the sea also represented extreme *disorder*: specifically, the havoc arising from piracy. Practically, the sea was both a source of great wealth that drove the force of collective enterprise. The sea also caused the most extreme situations of impoverishment, penury, and sorrow—those taken captive and made slaves serving in the galley, the *naufragios* and castaways who returned to their homelands with wild tales of enchanted realms, and so on.

There are now, and there always have been, highly diverse forms of navigation and very distinct forms of naval power. Is it legitimate to speak of a Basque thalassocracy, in the same way as one speaks, for example, of Portugal, England, and the ancient Cretans? Can we speak of a great Basque maritime power with specific characteristics? Or, are there important qualifications? Is it proper to consider Basques as men of the sea in the fullest sense? Or only in a specialized sense? Or are all of these characterizations legitimate depending on the era in question? How much of a difference are the answers to these questions depending on the differences between coastal trade and extended voyages? The activities of fishermen are far different from those of the great admirals, or pirates, or shipwrecked castaways.

Basque sailors have always possessed a limited territory—a very shallow hinterland. Basque ports were also quite small until relatively recent times, and suffered from limited local natural resources that made it impossible to truly compete with the great European thalassocracies. Despite these limitations, however, Basque seafarers have played a leading role in many oceanic adventures and enterprises.

In the Basque Country, there has also been constant contact between the Basque hinterland and coastal activities. In short, the inland depends on the sea to sustain its commercial and other relationships. Furthermore, at certain points in history, powerful monarchies' enterprises of expansion exerted great pressure and required the deployment of a considerable proportion of available Basque vessels.

We have already proposed the schematic characterization of Basque social and economic history as an oceanic race: an overriding concern for deriving the maximum benefit from seafaring and for maritime ports. If such indeed were the case, then we must also infer that the conditions of Basque shipping were fundamentally determined by a series of exigencies that weighed more heavily than a limited concern for the development of the Basque Country itself.

Basque catches, the "product" of ocean fishing, were sold in distant lands. And merchandise that arrived at Basque ports had a provenance in the distant interior of the peninsula and was shipped to faraway destinations. We also find that the transformation of navigational enterprises has always been associated with war, and that these activities constantly resulted in mistakes. The medieval chronicles, roughly beginning with the Castilian kings of Ferdinand III and his son Alfonso X, make numerous references to the activities of Basque sailors and sea vessels: on behalf of the Castilian monarchy, to conquer Seville, in African enterprises, in political missions of various kinds, and in the struggles between the Christian kingdoms. Kings were in a position of having to rely on Basque shipping. But there was always a fundamental problem: the ships constructed in Basque shipyards—constructed by Basque workers and financed by Basque entrepreneurs—were built for commercial or industrial purposes, yet they were often pressed into military service. The separation between the merchant marines and the military marines, which became fundamental in the modern era, was rather blurred in the Middle Ages. This fundamental tension resulted in the blockading of ports by various monarchs, and pressure on ship owners, builders, and seafarers to often act against their own interests.

Various medieval and modern texts refer to this tension and explicitly address the arguments of each side. Indeed one of the fundamental justifications sometimes given for the fueros needing to be scrupulously respected was the significance of Basque naval power. For if the fuero were not complied with, the shipping industry would collapse—at least according to one Basque historian writing in the time of Charles V. There are reports regarding tensions and bitter disagreements between navigators and royal ship owners during the time of Catholic monarchs Charles V and Philip II, and there is a reference to inquiries that were carried out to study ways of resolving such issues. One such inquiry was conducted by Esteban de Garibay in his dual role as a man who loved his own country and as a functionary who represented the royal house.

Despite this tension, the Middle Ages and era of great discoveries were the historical periods of greatest relevance for Basque seafaring within a larger European context. During this time the sensations of restlessness, decadence, and foreboding that appeared in later periods did not exist. This may be for any number of reasons. The Basque Country generally and its coastal region in particular have highly distinctive characteristics in the era prior to the Age of Discovery. To simplify, we can consider the Basques at this time as southern Europeans who looked to the northern maritime powers as seafaring examples, especially in light of its long-standing contacts with—among other peoples—the Normans.

This meant that, even in the traditional vessels like the small fishing boats known as *traineras*, northern styles were much more prevalent than Mediterranean models. But the conceptualization of this northern style often combined the northern tradition with elements that were more typical of the south, using touches that were borrowed from the Mediterranean tradition.

The Basque people were most strongly associated during this era, and even later, with coastal shipping—commercial shipping—which involves craft putting to sea without ever venturing too far from the coast, voyaging from trading port to trading port in heavy, deep, and wide vessels.

It is possible to follow the technological tradition of coastal sailors. Juan Garmendía Larrañaga indicated the prominent role of Basques and what were considered to be "Bizkaian" or Basque products in Italian ports of the fifteenth century, including Genoa. Basque ships served as a bridge between Italy and Spain. Coastal seafaring carried Basques to the Eastern Mediterranean and even Constantinople, and Basques were active in the cities of Flanders, England, Scandinavia, and the great German ports. Carmelo de Echegaray researched the archives of the Netherlands in order to identify and publish anything dealing with the Basques.

The history of Basque seafaring has had its share of both triumphs and tragedies. To get to the truth of the matter, it is necessary to penetrate the rhetorical patina that has accrued over many years—a patina that has resulted from an overemphasis on the discoveries, conquests, and colonizing of the Indies and other areas. It is only natural that these latter activities have in the past sustained a good deal more interest than purely economic activities. The historical record contains many Basque sailors, admirals, and other men who distinguished themselves in various eras in seafaring enterprises. There are an enormous number of disquisitions, as well as comments in dictionaries and other works devoted to seafaring activities. The works of Fernández de Navarrete are particularly important in this regard. There are also specialized technical volumes and written records in local histories that have been compiled regarding heroes and men of distinction within the realm of Basque seafaring activities. And yet, even though it might be interesting to tell or retell the story of an admiral like Oquendo, or some of the other heroic Basque with respect to particular enterprises, I think that it would be more interesting, in terms of the evolution of our country, to study Basque sailors, Basque technicians, and Basque seafaring activities with an emphasis on the shipbuilders, owners, admirals, and other actors.

A number of texts by non-Basque writers treat technology and naval construction, as well as the relationship between the technology of a given time and any military or economic successes or failures. References to the activity of Basques can be found in the classic accounts of naval construction. Basque superiority in comparison with other peoples within the realm of coastal navigation has been fully acknowledged. There are references to the kinds of constructions, the form of the constructions, and to differences in construction techniques. There are also references to crises that occurred when particularly unscrupulous characters, who were more concerned with profits than quality, resulted in both navigational setbacks and the construction of ships of inferior quality.

It can be fairly said that sea captains in the Basque Country were often also great shipbuilders and navigational theorists. Men like Zubiaur, whose collected letters were published many years ago, is one of the most prominent Basque figures in terms of technical accomplishment. Despite the fact that there are more than enough documents to write a detailed biography about him, nobody has yet seen fit to undertake a study of his ideas and life circumstances during an eventful existence that included success and failure in equal proportion. Zubiaur viewed the sea as a technical problem. He was a great sea general as well as a great technician. As a soldier, he engaged in actions that at times were brilliant and at other times unfortunate. He spent a good deal of time in an English prison. While in England, he observed the technical position of the enemy with particularly keen insight, and came to understand that, at the time that the naval power of the Philippine monarchy appeared to be highly formidable, there were reasons—and not only reasons, but solid scientifically grounded arguments—to foresee the possibility of failure and defeat. The reference here is to the period encompassing the end of the reign of Philip II and the reign of Philip III. Zubiaur was a figure who was largely ignored. His collected letters, as well as his warnings and observations, were not given their just due. Thereafter, what is most interesting is to observe how other technicians found themselves in the same circumstances and expressed the same concern, and how they also compared the situation of the Basque Country (which was of critical importance during the Habsburg monarchy and empire) with what was going on with the navies of England, Holland, and France. It would not be appropriate to characterize this as technological pessimism and yet we can, I feel, legitimately speak of a *critical pessimism*—an outstanding characteristic among Basque seafarers from the end of the sixteenth century through the seventeenth century.

There are families that are known because of a tradition of fathers, sons, and brothers dedicating themselves to construction, engineering, and wood-based shipbuilding. This sometimes gives the impression that the men practicing within such a traditional and hereditary framework lacked the flexibility of approach needed to adapt to changing circumstances. However, three successive generations of the Echeverri family—who lived and worked during the reigns of Philip III, Philip IV, and Charles II—authored a number of short but highly critical documents regarding the state of the navy—especially as regards what they saw as a lack of flexibility in conception and construction at a time when nations such as England, Holland, and France were making strenuous efforts to modernize their naval forces in order to be able to compete with other powers and, above all else, to provide the navy with a continually improving scientific basis.

Basque expansion proceeded apace during the seventeenth and eighteenth centuries despite—or in the face of—many obstacles and setbacks. It is perhaps this dramatic aspect of our historical development that has given rise to a high degree of dissatisfaction with bureaucratically constituted powers. Basque sailors, who could clearly see that the empire greatly depended on their actions, yet also knew that the empire's bureaucrats were uncooperative and trapped in a life of blinkered routine, could justifiably be seen as tormented souls. Such men were, like Zubiaur, able to see what England was doing and, like the Echeverri, what France and Holland were doing. Such men might also have come to the realization that their most important sources of theoretical and architectural inspiration had an external provenance.

This was the case for Admiral Gaztañeta, a man who, during the late seventeenth and early eighteenth centuries, gained renown as one of the best and most important shipbuilders of his time. Gaztañeta made the important contribution of introducing the French school of construction in Spain. A rivalry would later develop between those technicians who had an English view of the sea and those who had a French view of the sea. The time came when the fleet, which Gaztañeta was in charge of, began to take on characteristics similar to those seen today, with the fleet divided into a war squadron, war navy, merchant marine, and navy dedicated to conducting peaceful missions.

Be that as it may, as long the maritime prowess of monarchies—whether of the Habsburgs or the Bourbons—endured, the technical role of Basque sailors and ship owners was fundamentally important. Of the many decisive moments of this tradition, which began in the Middle Ages, which reached its zenith in the sixteenth century, which temporarily fell into decline in the seventeenth century, and which rebounded to attain an even stronger position (yet not without difficulties) during the eighteenth century, we must recognize the definitive crisis, one of fundamental importance for the Basque Country. Much has been written of Trafalgar and of the devastation wrought during the Peninsular War. Varied opinions have been offered regarding the economic collapse during the time of Charles IV of Spain. This crisis arose after the war launched by Charles III of Spain against England resulted in the near total collapse of Spanish finance, along with a steep decline in naval construction. Thus, it can be inferred from a very brief reference in Jovellanos's diary of his trip to Bilbao in 1791 that shipyards were a thing of the past. By the Peninsular War the entire naval tradition of large-scale construction had disappeared, ships were old, and financial backing for new construction was lacking. This crisis affected not only Basque coastal maritime commerce, but also trade with the Americas. When the empire collapsed, Basque relations with the newly emerged nations took on a distinctive and ambiguous character.

The nineteenth century could be characterized as something of a romantic era of small-scale trade, a small merchant marine, and a few shipbuilding companies that conserved something of their former prestige. Yet the nineteenth century could not compare with the previous golden era of the great admirals and shipbuilders. However, one constant never disappeared: the *arrantzale*—the fisherman—was still there, living as he had lived from time immemorial. There was also the *mariñel*—sailor—who shifted his position in the ocean. The bibliography regarding the fishermen of the ancient coast of Terranova and other areas is vast indeed. There are also many references to the fishermen's way of life in texts written in various eras, including in monographs published at the beginning of the twentieth century. These works are critically important for understanding fishermen's lives during epochs that have today been entirely forgotten, even by their own descendents. As things stand now—if I may offer an observation regarding matters of my own particular interest as a folklorist and ethnographer reflecting upon the lives of common folk and of classes that are most closely associated with what is distinctively Basque, including the Basque language—it seems to me that the Basque history vis-à-vis the ocean is now completely ignored.

If we look at a modern Basque dictionary, like the Azkue dictionary, we find that it yields no information whatsoever regarding the Basque equivalents for any number of words: for example "pirate," "galley," "galleon," and so on. Azkue offers but one linguistic example of the rejection of any word that did not sound purely Basque. But if one consults the dictionary of Larramendi, which was written during an era of great maritime expansion, all of these words, whether in their pure or impure form, but reflecting the way they were actually spoken in the Basque Country, have their place and can be found. In the cultural-historical world in which we now live, we need to conduct soundings—expeditions into the field of linguistic matters—and to construct technical vocabularies.

For example, if you think of the turbulent times of Philip IV of Spain, when taxes were imposed on salt, this kind of revolution cannot be explained without reference to maritime activity. For those who were in revolt, salt was fundamentally important for preserving the fish that they traded. If we think of forests, foundries, or other components of Basque industry, we always find the ocean lurking in the background. And yet, in recent times, many books of Basque ethnography and history—especially treatises—seem to give the impression that Basques have been nothing more than peasants, farmhands, and shepherds who lived inland. For me, however, the greatest enigma and the prime mover of Basque history has been the Basque relationship with the ocean. At present, when I think of where the strength of our country—and perhaps where the greatest threat to our country—lies, I necessarily think about the great ocean ports and the coast. I do not in this respect think of the interior and its quiet and tranquil life—even though I personally find this aspect of our land the most appealing. It is this force which the history of our country possesses vis-à-vis the sea that helps explain the constant drama of a people that, as I said at the outset, has followed two separate lines in its development—two lines that are as contradictory as they are inexorable: the way of technology and technological progress for its own sake, and the desire to remain in harmony with the natural environment.

Iron and Other Industries

Among the clichés and common expressions that one often hears in Spanish is one that speaks of *"llevar o traer hierro a Vizcaya"* ("bringing iron to Bizkaia") to refer to any gratuitous or superfluous action. In reality, the geographical connection that the Basque Country has with iron dates back to ancient times. There is a reference in book 34 of Pliny's *Natural History* that refers to enormous iron mines, which must surely refer to the mines of Bizkaia.

We also have a number of references to sites in different areas where iron and other minerals were mined. The mines of Oiartzun, as we have already seen, were an important Roman center for export of generally raw mineral to Gaul and the coast of Aquitaine. We have little conclusive information regarding ancient metallurgical methods, but as is well known, the Basque Country had two mining centers, each with its own separate export destination: a northern center that for the most part traded with Aquitaine and the Gauls of southwest France, and a southern center on the southern border of what is today Navarre. There are a number of references to this deposit in the regions of Moncayo, the Jalón, and Tarazona. It also appears that there was not only a highly developed armaments industry, but also an extensive iron industry in the border regions of the Basque Country as far back as the time of the Sertorian War. But these are all very remote and unconnected antecedents that don't really tell us a great deal about the later development of the iron industry. Medieval documents from Navarre, Araba, and Bizkaia tell of the iron workshops of small villages for domestic and local use. We also know that, during the Middle Ages, iron was subject to transformational cycles for small-scale use. Thus during a period when there was a threat of war, agricultural implements that were useful during peacetime were melted down and remade into weapons. When the threat of war passed, weapons were once again converted into implements of daily use. Such a cycle of transformation shows that iron was used for very limited purposes during a critical time for the history of industry.

The most important question here, as it was with respect to the naval industry, has to do with the fact that the collective emergence of the Basque and Navarre territories as important iron-producing regions was a quite a late development. In addition to being a late development, it is also a datum that engendered diverse social and economic conditions within the Basque Country. Thus, the situation in Navarre was different from that in Bizkaia or Gipuzkoa. The history of each of these provinces unfolded in its own distinct way.

When the people of Araba witnessed the marked increase of villas constructed on their land, which occurred at the same time as the marked increase of ironworks (which in the thirteenth century benefited from a technical revolution in Western Europe), they attempted to place limits on and halt the expansion of this kind of urban and industrial development. At the same time, other ethnic groups were encouraging these selfsame developments.

What we find in Navarre toward the end of the Middle Ages is the emergence of an upper class—the *infanzones*, who were distinguished not only by their socioeconomic class, but by their ties to industry. This was because, around the year 1420, there arose what were called the *Señorio* (seignior—master or lord) of the ironworks. This was a class of nobility that was also found in other areas of the country, as well as in Alsace and other lands, and that was always seen in areas where the iron industry flourished during the transition period between the Middle Ages and the modern era. In Navarre, which was politically organized as a monarchy, there was also what were called royal ironworks. Charles III of Navarre (Charles the Noble), whose life spanned the end of the fourteenth and the beginning of the fifteenth centuries, was the seignior of twenty ironworks within his domains.

The fates of the ironworks varied considerably during these times of great upheaval and internal struggle. Ruining an ironworks that belonged to the enemy—or to an enemy lineage—was something that was fundamentally important for the different factions. For the kings, on the other hand, it was fundamentally important that the ironworks prosper so they granted a large number of exemptions and privileges for iron producers. At the same time, we also observe something analogous to what has occurred numerous times throughout the economic and technical history of the nation. In order to resolve technical questions, men from other lands came to Navarre at the very beginning of the fifteenth century to explore minefields bearing iron and other minerals. Even in the remote five mountain towns (Bortziriak or Cinco Villas) of the Bidasoa, there is documentation of German miners working there, the equivalent of today's mining engineers.

This is not the only time that outsiders came to the Basque Country for their technical expertise. On other occasions as well, it can be seen that the reputation of the Middle Ages as an era of isolation and inwardness in which each person lived in his or her own particular setting without much awareness of other settings is not an entirely accurate depiction of reality. The Middle Ages is apparently inward looking, but in reality great changes and important technological revolutions occurred then, just as they have occurred during other times. So what we find is that the Basque Country and the Basque people are not an exception to the rule of a general diffusion and mobility that characterized the Late Middle Ages. But inventions are one thing, and the pace at which inventions are diffused is quite another. In the sixteenth century, and even as late as the eighteenth century, there were ironworks that could be called highland. These highland ironworks, which are referred to by writers such as Garibay and Baltasar de Echave, and later by Padre Henao and even by Villarreal de Bérriz, are the oldest ironworks known. These are also the ironworks that, in terms of Basque toponymy, gave rise to two different designations containing the element *ola*, and both of which signify a factory or ironworks par excellence: *Ola* by itself sometimes refers to any ironworks in general. *Agorrola* is a term for a dry ironworks, while *aizeola* is an open-air ironworks. *Agorrola* or *aizeola* are establishments that are unable to make use of either hydraulic pressure or any other energy than human power and the wind.

The old highland foundries were located on high ground, near the mines themselves. They were also near the vast woodlands that comprised the old forests of Vasconia.

Highland foundries consumed an enormous amount of these wild forests. This consumption of wood from the end of the Middle Ages until the eighteenth century resulted in great change for the Basque landscape. Once characterized by dense forest growth, the Basque mountains were increasingly devoted to pasturage, or consisted of meadows, ferneries, areas of secondary growth, or even worse. At times, it was the inhabitants of an area themselves who saw to it that foundries (both highland foundries and other kinds of foundries) were installed so that iron workers could strip a territory bare for the purpose of converting it into agricultural land or pasturage, and also to rid the area of large animals such as bears and wolves. When the Marquis of Iturbieta, an *arizcun* (businessman) of the eighteenth century had disputes with the municipalities where he obtained wood specifically for the Iturbieta iron foundry, the inhabitants of the area revealed what their primary motivation had been for allowing the massive exploitation of wooded areas: It was simply a matter of the people wanting to become more pastoral and agricultural in character, as well as their desire to protect their haciendas from the attacks of animals who most naturally resided in the forest.

Deforestation is important to Basque history, and its significance shows that it is not only in contemporary times that primary materials can become endangered. Wood is an ancient primary material, but a primary material nonetheless.

In any case, the Industrial Revolution came to the country at a later stage than the period during which the highland foundries—whether *agorrola* or *aizeola*—flourished. It was only after the development of water-powered foundries that there was a true consolidation and technical systematization of foundries. Hydraulically powered foundries were to a large extent a part of a revolution whose effects were initially felt most strongly in the thirteenth century, and that later gathered further momentum in certain areas. This revolution had to do with the application of the principle of the watermill, that is, a hydraulic wheel comprising planks or other components, a current of a body of water, and the harnessing of the movement of this hydraulic wheel, not to move millstones, but to move hammers, bellows, or other equipment. When the hydraulic wheel was employed in industry, not only for grinding, but for making cloth, for crushing minerals, and for pulverizing various other substances, then powder mills and sugar mills appeared. The notable expansion of hydraulic energy in industry had a number of unforeseen consequences. The old foundries would survive for a very long time. For example, there were hillside foundries in Zegama (Cegama) in the seventeenth century. Yet during the last years of the Navarrese monarchy, in 1417, we know that there were foundries in Navarre with dams and mill ponds that required repairs, and these water-powered foundries were described by writers as having already been developed by means of a kind of "air kiln" (or *aizearka*, as it was referred to in a number of documents). These foundries assimilated technological advances or, at the very least, reflected the results of debates regarding technical matters among industrial enterprises that at different times studied the properties, advantages, and disadvantages of every system.

As regards exploitation methods, I have previously mentioned the seigniors of the foundry, who first appeared in Navarre in the fifteenth century, and who also of course took part in all of the wars among different factions in Bizkaia and Gipuzkoa. The seignior of the foundry was one of the most important actors in the country's social and economic life, within the various factions and in the struggle among the various lineages. One of the worst aspects of these conflicts was the destruction of foundries and factories that were the greatest source of wealth for each of the factions. As a result of these struggles, in the Old Law (fuero) of Bizkaia, in the statutes of the Brotherhoods of Gipuzkoa, and in other nascent legal codes, there was a constant and vehement insistence on imposing punishment on those who destroyed foundries and dams, on those who inflicted abusive treatment on ironmongers, and on anyone who engaged in actions that adversely affected the value of foreign industrial assets in a significant way.

What this reflects is a highly important feature of the history of the factions: an industrial competition that was going on at a time that was still considered preindustrial. Yet it is clear that, during the era of lineages, industrial competition was occurring. Competition among companies is not limited to the important capitalist enterprises of the modern era, but was something also seen in these much more archaic and primitive societies. This earlier competition was, on the surface, a good deal more barbaric. The reality, however, is that it was no more barbaric than what has been seen more recently, when the ugliness of reality is often been concealed by deceitful rhetoric.

Our toponymy reflects names that are richly visual in nature, names that are meaningful and picturesque to the ears of the country's inhabitants. There are houses, palaces, and old structures that are called *Olajaunena*, *Olajaunzarrena*, *Olajaunzarrea*, and so on. *Olajaun* reflects an important reality of this world of seigniories tied neither to the land nor to specific persons, but instead to iron and factories. Foundries thus functioned during those times as apart from entailed estates, and when there was a social class equivalent to the English rural nobility—the gentry or rural seigniors were not tied to rural activities.

Navarrese documents show that royal and other foundries were administered through leasing and subleasing arrangements. There are also records of the division of the inheritance of a foundry, which provided for their administration along the lines of tracts of irrigated land in the south—with reference to the sharing of water hours used by two or more heirs. There are also an astounding number of notarized documents regarding such arrangements, such as work contracts and apprentice contracts for ironmongers. The economic functioning of this class—which cannot yet properly be termed a "social class" but is instead a class of workers consisting of ironmongers (*olaguizonak*) who, within

Basque society, displayed a number of highly distinctive traits, and who have left a mark, however faint, on Basque folklore and traditions.

Unquestionably the best description of the life of ironmongers was provided by Mogel. In his *Corografía*, Larramendi also provides a number of colorful and striking sources that enable us to see how larger and smaller foundries functioned. "Larger foundries" were thus designated because of the volume of their production. The description provided below pertains to the form of organization used in these larger foundries. As you will see, what we are referring to here is a very important industry and yet one that, compared to the industries of the modern world, is in reality microscopic in scale. This can be seen in the fact that the foundries that we are talking about were headed by a master (an *arotza*) who was the welder. The welder-master (in Basque, *urtzailea*) took care of the welding. Below him on the hierarchy of the foundry were two men who held the title of "laminators," who were also referred to as "iron pullers" (usually referred to by the term of *isheliak* or *ijeliak* (meaning "those who thread" or "those who align"). Beneath them was a kind of apprentice who did whatever he was told to do—someone who "took up the slack," so to speak, and who was therefore called a *gatzamalea*. In the smaller foundries, the person in charge was called the *achicador* ("maker of smaller things"; *txikitzale* in Basque). This was the basic organizational structure of the ironmonger's workshop, comprising a total of six or seven workers. The ironmonger (*olaguizon*) was, in folklore and social history, represented as possessing certain traits. At some point in the past, you must surely have come up against the problem of the *machinadas*,* a matter that has not yet been sufficiently clarified. In folklore, for those of us who are most interested in the somewhat mysterious aspects of life, it is striking to observe how, up until our own era (specifically, until 1920), peasants held a rather negative and hostile opinion of ironmongers. Peasants were generally of the firm belief that ironmongers were in fact heathens (*gentilak bezala*) at heart, and therefore men who were not really Christian, who were not like others, men who—perhaps because of their craftsmanship and their handling of iron—had a mysterious, if not demonic, aspect. Taken as a whole, this view of ironmongers has existed for a very long time, and was held in various societies—from the *Nibelungen* to the most advanced cultures of the Niger River—of nearly everyone who worked with iron and other metals. The ironsmith,

---

* Eighteenth-century revolts taking their name from Saint Martin "Machín" the patron saint of ironworkers. —ed.

the man of iron, the manufacturing man, was everywhere an object of suspicion.

We must now describe the process of transforming and converting the raw metal into something different. It is here that we encounter a series of derivative industries that arose in the Basque Country at a particular time, and that are most closely associated with certain river basins, as well as with activities that can be seen to have analogues in naval history.

Steel and munitions are the most important derivative industries that arose in many towns of both Gipuzkoa and Bizkaia (e.g., Durango, Ermua, and smaller towns such as Elorrio). As I pointed out earlier, these industries gave rise to conditions that have their analogues in the naval industry. Thus, for example, at the time of the Catholic Monarchs, extremely harsh laws and provisions were enacted to facilitate the confiscation of weapons as well as the accelerated production of certain kinds of weaponry in response to the needs of the armorer. Later, there was an ongoing struggle over control of production, which also led to political crises. Concomitantly, grave problems arose as a result of the relatively advanced foreign production technology as well as the technological crisis in general. In the Basque Country, one of the subjects that we find most deserving of further study, and of which the historical record provides no more than a few passing references, is the transition from sharp and projectile weapons to modern firearms. This was a transition that occurred over the course of a rather extended period of time, perhaps beginning in the fifteenth century and ending in the sixteenth century. One of the results of this transition was the reduction in the manufacture of such a staple of medieval weaponry as the crossbow and the commencement of the production of harquebuses and muskets, among other armaments.

The crossbow continued to be produced until the seventeenth century as a luxury item for recreational use, just as the bow is used today. The crossbow itself is still seen today in towns where crossbow competitions are held, but its use is more folkloric than practical. In any case, the transition in production was spurred by the innovation and competition of foreign manufacturers. In this connection, we once again must look northward, to German crossbow manufacturers. The transformation of firearms that occurred during the era of Charles V of Spain, and its attendant crises, are important. The old weaponry, along with the time-worn conceptions of the armaments industry, came to be seen as passé, and it was imperative that they be transcended.

It is important to have a fundamental grasp of the history of technology in Western Europe in order to understand what occurred in our country. Regarding the history of technological progress, the Basque Country formed a more integral part of Europe, and was more aligned with European concerns, than in reference to any other aspect of our history. The Basque Country lived, moved, and had its being in dynamic relationship with the technological and economic development of the rest of Europe—rather than with that of any region within Spain. During this era, weapons—muskets and harquebuses in Soraluze (Placencia de las Armas); knives in Bergara; harquebuses and *beatillas* in Eibar and Elgoibar; sword decoration in Durango; pikes in Elorrio—became a fundamentally important feature of Basque identity both inside and outside the Basque Country. It is interesting to note the cultural and technological analogues with naval history. In general terms, the most important crises and the greatest contributions arose as a result of the relationship with northern lands. But, in certain specific respects, the relationship with the southern manufacture of luxury goods profoundly influenced the kinds of weapons produced by the Basque homo faber.

In fact, it is impossible to understand the damascenes of Eibar without knowing, on the basis of documentary evidence, that Eibar, Arrasate (Mondragón), and in fact all of the areas of Gipuzkoa and Bizkaia where arms were manufactured had close relationships with the armaments manufacturing areas of the interior of Spain (e.g., Toledo). One might even plausibly conclude that many Bizkaians and Gipuzkoans who conducted business in the Spanish interior dealt in swords, harquebuses, and other weapons. Garibay's life is a good example of this phenomenon. The historian had links to Toledo because of his business interests in Arrasate, and his name also appears in many different lists of armorers with Basque names (whether in documents, on swords, or on other weapons kept in places like the Royal Armory of Madrid).

A number of monographs have been written about this luxury aspect of the iron industry and, in fact, this part of the history is considerably better documented than other sectors. But other aspects of the iron industry have received less attention, and little is known about them. In terms of economic history, it is important to clarify these other aspects. I am referring mainly to the mass production of farm implements and other tools. Such production had nothing in common with the cyclical production of goods in medieval times. Instead, it involved the manufacture of hoes, spades, rakes, and all kinds of other farm tools made of iron. In addition, it involved the production of knives or plow rakes in mass quantity for sale and export.

We know that a considerable proportion of the wrought iron products of this kind that were manufactured in the foundries of the Basque Country ended up in the Americas. We also know how important Basque foundries were—until the first years of the present century—for Spain as a whole. There are not many Spanish cities in which Araban, Bizkaian, or Gipuzkoan surnames are not connected with iron manufacture or commerce. But the volume, significance, and scope of what amounted to a kind of Basque monopoly is, from the standpoint of the history of the Spanish Americas, unexplored terrain that deserves detailed and quantitative study.

In addition, there are other related subjects that are specifically connected with the crisis of the Americas—the crisis in relation to the peninsula in general and to the Basque Country specifically. And there is yet another subject that I would like to raise before concluding, and that is the economic effects of the revolution of 1830 on Navarre, Gipuzkoa, and Bizkaia. I am referring here to the so-called liberal revolution that occurred during the reign of Louis-Philippe of France. This revolution resulted in steeper tariff barriers between France and Navarre and the other provinces, which led to a sharp decline in the iron industry, especially in the eastern Basque Country. This occurred at the same time as the dawn of the iron industry of Bizkaia, which began in 1832 and continued to grow steadily until 1902.

There are contradictory movements, as well as technological and political crises that are not always taken into consideration in modern accounts of industry. I therefore believe that it is impossible to produce a social or economic history of the country without considering situations that are, in some aspects, contradictory.

12

The Basques and the Sea

Critical Situations and Famous Enterprises

Commercial and privateering enterprises occurred with more or less equal frequency during the last part of the fifteenth century. At the same time, there were occasional seizures carried out by the monarchy, which were designed to promote the state's military activities. Documentary evidence indicates both that letters of marque continued to be enforceable, and that the art of navigation continued to be refined. All of this took place within a climate of considerable tension. Life on the seas has always been difficult, and always will be difficult.

At the beginning of the sixteenth century, the shipyards of Bizkaia were functioning full force. Shipbuilders were constructing vessels that they often later sold, often to foreign buyers. In 1501, a royal decree attempted to put a stop to such commerce. Many years later, as a result of the consequences of that law, highly serious writers who were notably biased toward the interests of the monarchy vehemently criticized that law. The great enterprises of discovery and conquest had barely gotten underway before the first symptoms of a bureaucratic bottleneck manifested themselves—symptoms that had dire consequences. Francisco López de Gómara, in his *Crónica de los Barbarrojas* (Chronicle of the Redbeards),* recorded both the ruin of the Catalan galleys that occurred

---

* The *Crónica de los Barbarrojas* recounts the history of two Moorish corsairs and was Gómara's first history, although it remained unpublished until 1853. Gómara is more famous—or infamous—for his *Historia general de las Indias* and *Historia de la conquista de México* (1552; General History of the Indies and History of the Conquest of Mexico) both being attacked by Bartolomé de las Casas and others for their negative view of Native Americans and close personal ties to Hernán Cortés. See Germán Bleiberg, Maureen Ihrie, and Janet Pérez, eds., *Dictionary of the Literature of the Iberian Peninsula*, vol. 2 (Westport, CT: Greenwood Press, 1993), 960–61. —ed.

as a result of the poor advice given to the Catholic Monarchs, as well as the collapse of Bizkaian and Gipuzkoan shipping. The latter occurred for two reasons: (1) the failure of the crown to pay the crews of the vessels, and (2) a failure to prioritize according to the tonnage of the vessels. Gómara thus concluded that the Basques "do not want to either build ships or engage in the art of navigation, even though they are the world's best and bravest sailors, and the most prolific constructors of vessels." According to him, there were not, at the time that he wrote, a sufficient number of large ships, the two maritime provinces had become impoverished, and the proximity of rival nations posed a grave danger. Gómara concluded thus: "This entire situation would improve somewhat if those privileges and favors of former kings were restored." The political significance of such an assertion has perhaps not been sufficiently emphasized. What is beyond doubt is that, during the course of the sixteenth century, a series of actions were aimed at rectifying this "sluggishness." Thus, for example, between 1568 and 1569, Hernán Suárez de Toledo, with the assistance of Don Esteban de Garibay, drafted a report "on the reasons why not as many ships are being constructed now as there were in the past." Other documents do not reflect the same degree of pessimism as this report, which Garibay himself would later refer to in his highly interesting memoirs.

Men of the sea were characteristically rowdy and dangerous. The violence of seafaring life was hardly conducive to the development of political pragmatism. On the other hand, it did spur certain developments in the sciences and the arts. Life on the seas also acted as a stimulus to both the development of myths, and to the creation of narratives that were for the most part fantastical in nature, and whose origins were rather obscure.

In this connection, it is important to note that, just after his discovery of America, a rumor was making the rounds that the caravels of Columbus had been led to the New World by a strange sea animal. The nature of this sea animal, which was initially shrouded in mystery, later became the subject of wild speculation in various contradictory accounts. As one might well imagine, given the Basque nautical tradition, it was already said in the sixteenth century that it was a Basque vessel (others said it was an Andalusian or Portuguese ship) that first arrived on American shores, and that Columbus had received word of the discovery at Madeira.

Don Esteban de Garibay reported a tradition that he had heard from others and that made its way into various texts that gave the name of the Bizkaian captain of the ship.

Let's set this matter aside for the moment. Let's also set aside the details of both Columbus's relations with Basques, and his use of ships that had been constructed in the Basque Country—of which there were a considerable number in his second voyage. From the very beginning, it should be added, there were reports of Basques who had settled in the islands and then, shortly afterward, of those who had settled on the American continents.

For both geographical and commercial reasons, the focal point in Spain of the discovery of the New World was Seville. The journeys that led to the discovery were conducted by men of varied origins. Extremadurans, Andalusians, and Castilians were notably represented. But transport and navigation to a large extent was handled by northerners, although we don't have a clear idea of exactly who these men were. Despite the tensions and rivalry between Spain and Portugal, some of these were Portuguese.

A good example of this was the composition of the crew of Magellan's fleet of five ships of varying tonnage. This crew was assembled with considerable difficulty, and comprised sailors from Portugal, Italy, France, Germany, England, Flanders, and Greece. Juan Sebastián Elcano of Getaria (Guetaria) was on the crew of the *Concepción* with a lowly rank of "master." He was accompanied by thirty-nine other Basques. The role of master (in Basque, *ontzico maistrea*) grew in importance as the journey progressed. But from the technical and economic point of view, it is also important to note that a large proportion of the supplies on Magellan's fleet had been acquired in Bizkaia, according to the written accounts of Don Martín Fernández of Navarrete. This included artillery, gunpowder, crossbows, springalds, coats of armor, guns, shields, and darts, as well as various nautical tools and instruments, such as harpoons, three-pronged harpoons, bellows, anvils, and nozzles.

It can thus be seen that the foundries, as well as the munitions and tool factories of the Basque Country provisioned the Indies for a considerable period of time. The accounts of Magellan's landmark expedition are among the thousands of accounts of expeditions to the New World, and recorded for posterity in the General Archive of the Indies.

Magellan's first circumnavigation of the globe began on August 11, 1519 and ended on September 7, 1522. During the voyage, there was no shortage of disturbances and plots, in which even the famous Guipuzkoan sailor was involved. The account of the voyage is well known. In terms of the history of geographic discoveries, it is the return of the ship *Victoria* that holds pride of place. Elcano returned with only one ship and eighteen men. A few days later, he was received by Charles V Holy Roman Emperor in Valladolid, who presented him a coat of arms that depicted a globe underneath the inscription *"Primus circumdedisti me"* ("You circumnavigated me first"). The return of their fellow countryman Elcano has faithfully been commemorated ever since then by the sailors of Getaria with a presentation of a more or less theatrical recreation of the event. Yet it is important to recognize that there was no one who was less theatrical than Juan Sebastián Elcano. This can be seen in the fact that, in the second expedition, he was content to serve as the captain of the ship *Sancti Spiritu*, which set sail from La Coruña on July 24, 1524, under the supreme command of García Jofre de Loaysa, and that Juan Sebastián died of scurvy in the middle of the Pacific Ocean on August 4, 1526. His testament was undersigned by Basques, some of whom later became famous. Shortly before his death, the general of the fleet had died, and Elcano had been appointed to take his place. The fleet disintegrated, and endured various tragedies including the poisoning of Martín Iñiguez de Carquizano of Elgoibar by the Portuguese, as well as the vicissitudes of Andrés de Urdaneta of Ordizia (Villafranca), who would later make a name for himself.

Cod Fever

So far we have seen history on a grand scale. Not only did Basque sailors venture forth from the shores of Iberia. They also crossed the Atlantic and sailed the Pacific. And yet, while all this was going on, the old commercial and fishing tradition continued apace. Basque seafaring activities were so noteworthy that an experienced shipbuilder, Tomé Cano, in his *Arte de farbricar naos* (Art of Constructing Ships), published in Seville in 1611, declared that the Portuguese and *vizcaínos** were the best shipbuilders, with the Portuguese holding the advantage when it came to long-distance navigation. The fact of the matter is that the activities of both these groups were highly diverse, and were determined by the nature of the country itself, as was pointed out by the highly astute Venetian diplomat

---

* Literally, Bizkaians, however often used to mean Basques in general in source texts. —ed.

A. Navajero in his travels in Spain during the years 1524–1526, where he made the following declaration: "The Basques frequently take to the seas because of their many ports, and because they have constructed a great many ships at very little cost, and also because of the vast quantities of oak trees and iron that they possess. On the other hand, the limited territory of the region, together with the large number of people within its borders, force them to go elsewhere in order to make a living." These few lines say a great deal more than lengthy treatises (whether from the pen of friend or foe). A small country, with a reputation as being agriculturally poor, and yet abundant mainly in two essential raw materials, one of which became scarce because of the enormous quantity of wood consumed by the foundries. Deforestation is not only a contemporary matter. The population had grown in comparison to other regions of the peninsula, and emigration became a matter of general necessity. This high degree of mobility resulted in the presence of Basques in the most remote reaches of La Alpujarra, and in Seville and Cádiz. It also led to the growth of Basque colonies in Lisbon, Basque brotherhoods in a number of cities of the Low Countries, and Basque sections of major European ports such as Hamburg. In terms of global toponyms, it led to a "Biscayne Bay" on the Florida Coast, as well as a "Biscay Bay" in Newfoundland. We also have both a "Biscayne" and a "Key Biscayne"—both once again in Florida. And this brings us once again to the lands of the New World, which would become a new source of wealth for Western Europe.

Some of the lands that were discovered have been written of more frequently than those who discovered and subdued them, and this led to the creation of both golden legends and black legends. We have a far vaguer notion of other lands of the New World.

Leaving aside for the moment the murky origins of the discovery of Terranova, which we have previously discussed, it is evident from contemporary records that, by the middle of the sixteenth century, there was a veritable torrent of Basque fisherman who set sail for that vast island for the purpose of cod fishing. Many years later, the founder of English utilitarian thought, Francis Bacon, would write in one of his essays that the fisheries created by these pioneers were of greater human worth than all of the mines of Peru. It is thus understandable that Newfoundland was a territory coveted by various European powers—as well as by the fishermen of diverse lands. During the time of Philip II, there was a veritable "cod fever," which led to cod becoming a staple of the diet of poor people. It is thought that the word for cod in Spanish (*bacalao*, *bacallao*, or *bacallu*) is of Basque origin. J. Corominas makes such a case in a scholarly article devoted to the word in his magisterial dictionary. Whatever the truth may be regarding the word's etymology, it is important to point out that the words for "dried cod" in German and French (*laberdan*), English (*laberdine*), and Russian (*labardan*) are derived from *laburdano* or *laburdino* (i.e., of, or pertaining to, Lapurdi). This is something that brings to mind the hostile portrayal by Pierre de Lancre, who conducted a massive witch-hunt in Lapurdi, of the life of sailors who landed in Newfoundland at the beginning of the seventeenth century, leaving their women behind in a state of wretchedness that led them to engage in a variety of aberrant behaviors. It seems possible, however, to read too much into this text. I think that I hardly need to explain such a dubious observation as resulting from the massive witch-hunts that were carried out in the mountainous lands of the European interior. Documents dating back to the period 1540–1574 reflect this polarizing tendency. One such document, signed by Cristobal de Barros in 1574, indicated that the whaling ships set sail in the middle of June and returned in either December or the beginning of January. He further stated that ships that set sail to fish for Newfoundland cod left earlier, at the end of March or the beginning of April, and that these returned in the middle of September or even as late as October. In contrast, according to Barros, the merchant fleets that set sail for Flanders with cargo that had been loaded in Burgos made two different voyages. The first of these set sail either at the end of April or the beginning of May, and the other set sail between the middle of August and September, and were of shorter duration. Sailors, who in these voyages could be seen as analogous to warriors, had to take advantage of the spring and summer, just like certain animal predators. Such activity on the part of Basque sailors and fisherman reflected more reckless courage than sobriety of judgment. These men were characterized by their vigorous activity. Yet in another respect, one might conclude that spiritual and cultural elements were conspicuously absent on numerous occasions and that this absence, which was aggravated by political powerlessness, was a characteristic that became increasingly more pronounced during the period beginning with the reign of Philip II and concluding at the end of the seventeenth century.

Eminent Persons

But what concerns us here are far more prosperous times. The era of discovery and conquest is striking for the large number of more or less well-known Basques who played a part in it. Almost all who played a noteworthy role were men of the sea—men of action. We really do not need to get into the question here of whether this action was carefully planned, or whether it was in one way or another problematic in nature. Around the great epoch of discovery, there were conflicting accounts of what was happening, from both uncritical enthusiasts and implacable enemies. I have no interest here in trying to be a moralist. Ernest Renan wrote that the fifteenth and sixteenth centuries in Italy were terrible times that were, nevertheless, accompanied by an awakening of the human spirit. He went on to add that storms are not necessarily bad for the growth of tall trees: Things of great beauty can emerge during very difficult times. This applies to other countries as well, although perhaps without the enthusiasm of Renan regarding the necessity of colonization and the role of certain peoples in that process.

In this instance, as in others, it may be useful to draw a Kantian distinction between efficient causes and final causes. Efficient causes of human action are impelled by various factors, but the old Greek idea of necessity, or *ananke* is rather precisely defined, and propels man in a certain specific direction in any given instance. In Basque, the word *bear* or *biar* graphically expresses this idea, and the abstract term used by the common folk—*biarra* or *bearra*—is frequently used. Larramendi was already using it in his day. It was this necessity that inexorably spurred seamen and fishermen, just as it spurred camel-riding nomads in their own particular environments. Explaining their lives in terms of final causes, moral theory, or other similarly abstract terms doesn't seem particularly useful for understanding the truth of what was really going on. An examination of efficient causes is more than satisfactory in this regard. The life of a Basque sailor in the sixteenth century was, like the lives of other men, governed by efficient causes. And it was these efficient causes that gave rise to eminent persons. Some of these men, like Andrés de Urdaneta (1498–1568) and Miguel López de Legazpi were inseparably associated with one another. These men collaborated in the discovery and conquest of Poniente Islands (literally, "islands of the west wind" —ed.) which later came to be called the Philippines. The two men undertook this enterprise when they were both well on in years: both of them wrote letters and memoires about their activities. Legazpi died in 1572 having received the honorary title of *Adelantado* ("Advanced"). And once he was dead, the struggle with Chinese corsairs grew ever more fierce. Basques sailors were very much involved in this struggle. On the other hand, China came to be more or less directly known, and a permanent system of navigation was established between Mexico and the

Philippines. The activity of Basque sailors in these enterprises is also well documented.

We should mention in passing a few prominent figures. It is important to show that some men, like the two aforementioned, were not only men of action, but also keen observers who were able to write about what they observed. Such was the case with Pascual de Andagoya, an explorer who wrote various accounts that contain very interesting ethnographic information. Other men distinguished themselves as warriors. One of these was Domingo Martínez de Irala. The Ibarras were also notable in this regard. For a long time now, Basque historians have been compiling lists of famous sailors. The sheer length of such lists is what is most noteworthy about them. At the beginning of the seventeenth century, Martínez de Isasti summed up the role of Gipuzkoans alone as follows: "[Gipuzkoans] have navigated most of the vast expanse of the ocean: Florida and the Indies, Norway, England, Ireland, and other islands. They are highly skilled captains and are intimately familiar with the sea." There was at that time a classification of seamen according to their function as captains, warriors, or shipbuilders.

Cosmographers, Naval Architects, and Warriors

This leads to not only a number of different and complex questions, but also highlights the fact that the life of each of the men under discussion here was lived within a collective historical context that was imbued with great meaning—including philosophical meaning.

Ship pilots—or at least the greatest of the pilots—have always been those who have closely studied the tides and ship routes, and who have been cartographers of the seas and islands. It would seem interesting to remember in this connection that, although he had previously been a resident of both Santoña and of Puerto de Santa María, Juan de la Cosa, a close associate of Columbus, was often assumed to be from Bizkaia and, in one document, he is even referred to as "Juan Vizcaíno." Various maps of sea routes have been attributed to him. The best known of these is the planisphere depicting the coasts of the recently discovered islands. Not all such works acquired the same degree of fame. For example, Isasti, in his catalog of captains, refers to "Jaimes de Zamorra" of Lezo, who wrote a treatise titled *Mareas derrotas* (The Course of Tides). This work was widely used by the ship pilots of his time. Alas, no copy of this once-important text survives today. We will soon see how, in the areas of both geodesics and cartography, which were quite advanced in the eighteenth century, the cosmographers of the Basque Country played a very important role.

From both the technical and economic point of view, the construction of ships involves a great many facets and complications. We have already seen how it gave rise to struggles and pressures during the fifteenth and sixteenth centuries, which continued into the following century. It could well be said that these struggles and pressures grew increasingly tense for very obvious reasons. On the one hand, ever since the Age of Discovery had begun, naval power had become an arena of rivalry among various states, with England in the forefront of the race for dominion of the seas. On the other hand, the power struggle was accompanied by emulation among the rivals when it came to intellectual and technical effort applied to navigation—and especially to naval architecture. During some years, the Basques held their own in terms of this rivalry. Afterward, a period of decline—of "technical pessimism"—began, which is reflected in various texts that have been written by Basque sailors and shipbuilders. This period may be clearly seen as having begun with the destruction of the Invincible Armada in 1588. But let us first look at what happened before that momentous defeat. From the theoretical point of view, we must point out first and foremost the significance of the fact that, among the books on the art of navigation printed in the sixteenth century, there was one that was written by a Bizkaian author and printed in Bilbao in 1587. It is also significant that various texts of this kind, from the same or the following era, appear in the form of dialogues between "an inhabitant of the mountains" and a "Bizkaian." Some of these kinds of books, such as the one authored by Diego García de Palacio, *Instrucción nautical para navegar* (Manual of Sea Navigation, 1587) provide instructions regarding how to build ships of varying tonnage for use in different bodies of water. It should also be pointed out that General Don Antonio de Urquiola, who died in Madrid in 1600 and who was a native of Getaria, composed an "opinion" (1589) in which he gave instructions regarding the building of galleons and the recommended measurements of those weighing three hundred tons. It is difficult to provide even a vague idea of the extent of the writings authored by Basques during the reigns of Philip II and Philip III regarding the best construction methods. Many of these writings were polemical and critical in nature. Many of them also went against the grain of the tendency of the Royal Court to stymie private initiative and to require the construction of more warships than cargo ships, imposing relative proportions with respect to the two types of ships that did not even come close to meeting the needs for the latter, according to critics. Among such critical writings is an argument presented to the king on behalf of Gipuzkoan shipbuilders that was authored by Juan del Puerto and Juan de Echeverri, yet this text appears to be a defense of the interests of the builders in question, and it is difficult to determine exactly which side the authors favor. Design specifications also survive from that same era (and from the later reigns of Philip IV and Charles II) that were drafted by Bizkaians and Gipuzkoans. These are highly interesting documents.

Yet it is important here to emphasize a particularly important phenomenon: The most authoritative writers from the period beginning with the end of the reign of Philip II indicate that a marked decline has taken place with respect to both the Basque mercantile shipping fleets as well as in the application of technology, which appears to have stagnated. In the meantime, first England and later Holland continued to make important advances. These same problems were noted by the aforementioned Tomé Cano, who wrote of the precipitous decline that set in between 1585 and 1609, and who insisted on the inflexibility and the bureaucratization of seafaring activities. General Zubiaur made similar observations in his personal letters, which reflect a high degree of pessimism that resulted from his direct knowledge of what was going on in England. Conversely, the writings of Englishmen during this same period reflect a haughty confidence of their own superiority, an attitude that can be seen in a document authored by Francis Bacon in his old age (1634), a document that Cardinal Richelieu ordered to be translated into French at the time that he began his long and ultimately victorious struggle with Spain.

An important revolution in the manufacture of naval armaments had begun as early as the reign of Henry VIII of England. This revolution is reflected most notably in the construction of welded canons that were more powerful than their predecessors. At the same time, progress continued to be made on the construction of lighter and more streamlined vessels. These two advances were evident during the expedition of the Spanish Armada. Yet even after that event, Spanish shipbuilders for the most part continued to cling to the old methods, leading one author who wrote during the reign of Philip IV to lament that, while all of the northern nations had forsaken the high quarter-decks of the large ships and galleons, which they had determined were harmful, these structures continued to form a part of the design of Spanish ships. Be that as it may, shipbuilding in Spain continued apace, as can be seen in the treatises of the history of shipbuilding that have come down to us. One of these, which continues to be of great value, was authored by Don Gervasio de Artiñano.

These were years of great conflict, encompassing the disaster of the Spanish Armada as well as the rivalries with both France and Holland. The names of the Basque captains of this era are not associated with the same unambiguous aura of glorious heroism as those of their predecessors of years gone by. The fate of these men was rather more tragic from a historical point of view, because their efforts and their adventures were not also crowned with success, and because their failures revealed fundamental technical problems. Much has been written about these men, and their actions have given rise to a good many rhetorical expressions. Here are the names of some of these men: Juan Martínez de Recalde, a *bilbotarra*; Martín de Bertendona, a Bizkaian; Miguel de Oquendo, "the Old Man of the Invincible Armada"; Don Pedro de Zubiaur; and Miguel de Vilazabal. Later, there were Don Carlos de Ibarra and Don Antonio de Oquendo. Space does not permit an account of even a biographical sketch of these eminent sea captains who had varying degrees of success and failure. Yet it would be interesting today to publish the writings that some of these men have left, in which they recorded their impressions and experiences in a systematic and organized fashion.

Commercial Activities

What is perhaps most interesting for contemporary readers (especially the younger generation among them) than the individual lives of the aforementioned men, are the vicissitudes of maritime commerce, and of the institutions and interests created by that commerce during the period of time under consideration here. The steadily increasing political tension on the part of the Habsburgs, which continually weakened the Spanish position, had clearly discernable effects on trade in general and fishing in particular. It was the exigencies of trade, after all, which had led to the initiation and development of navigation, as we have seen. It is clear that maritime trade is clearly related to trade conducted by land transport. It is the products that are being traded that in the end determined the creation network of roads, the founding of towns, the identification of sea routes, the establishment of the distant ports utilized by Basque agents, and the development of both civil institutions and religious brotherhoods. From the fourteenth through the sixteenth centuries, there were important advances in each of these respects. And from the sixteenth through the eighteenth centuries, it was colonial expansion and imperialist enterprise that unquestionably determined the development and refinement of navigation. Right up until the beginning of the nineteenth century, it can justly be said that the priorities and methods of the ancien régime were implemented, albeit in distinct phases.

As regards both these phases, and the problems that were encountered, it is important to note the crucial importance of the wool trade with England. The overland trade routes resulted in the concentration of wool being transferred from centers such as Burgos and Vitoria-Gasteiz to Cantabrian ports. Bitter rivalries were a part of this process, especially after the founding and initial phase of growth of Bilbao. Thus, amphibious trade routes for merino wool, along with the functioning of the controversial institution of La Mesta, were developed. Later, trade in iron, armaments, and agricultural implements also gradually developed. This trade essentially resulted in Bizkaia becoming renowned for its importance, in both the Atlantic and in the European ports of the Mediterranean Sea. Yet the manufacture of armaments gave rise to the same kind of questions as the condition of the fleets in general. For example, in 1483, when the Catholic Monarchs attempted to protect Sicily, which was being threatened by the Turks, they commissioned Diego de Soria to provide a designated quantity of arms, and assured that Basque foundries were devoted to the manufacture of objects such as iron spears, pavises, Lombardy guns, and culverins. Afterward, during the colonization of the Americas, the tools that were transported to the New World from Seville were almost exclusively of Basque origin. The important technical problems that arose as a result of the reformation and modernization of the iron industry in general and of the armaments industry in particular are beyond the scope of this essay. Yet it is important to point out that these problems should always be studied in relation to the shipbuilding industry. There were also sea routes for the export of dried fish, even though such trade was generally conducted via overland routes. Conversely, wheat was among the most commonly imported goods, and sometimes arrived from very distant lands. Other common imports were wine, oil, and cloth from Flanders, France, and England. The Basque Country is considered deficient in basic foodstuffs, and poor in general terms. The image of a rich and prosperous country was limited in its validity to a particular historical era. It is also important to remember that, during each era of prosperity, there were also very serious problems and crises.

The religious and political movements that arose during the Renaissance decisively influenced the methods employed in Basque maritime commerce. The Reformation, considered broadly, resulted in a gradual decrease in trade with northern lands, particularly Germany and Scandinavia. The second half of the sixteenth century is characterized by a retreat in the face of the Protestant powers of the north, which increased with the rise of England and Holland to the northwest. This resulted in the collapse of the entire old system of maritime relations. Catholic Spain assumed a defensive posture, and this stance was reflected in interesting ways in its ports. Fears of Protestant infiltration, and of what was popularly called "bad books," resulted, for example, in representatives of the Holy See conducting thorough searches of ships that anchored there. Thus was established a ban of books, a ban that, as always, could be circumvented by clandestine means. There is nothing new under the sun, especially when it comes to the exercise of authoritarian power.

13

The Feeling of Belonging in the Basque Diaspora

I

National history seems to have its own peculiar rhythms, while regional and local histories have their own particular leitmotifs. The venerable independent kingdom of Navarre ceased to be autonomous after the forced annexation carried out by the Catholic monarch Ferdinand—a watershed in Navarrese history. According to most historians, Navarre's loss of autonomy coincided with the pinnacle of Spanish history in general. Yet before it lost its independence, Navarre had played an important role in Spanish history during the time of Sancho the Great and his successors. It also flourished afterward, and had influence with the Spanish royal house, during the seventeenth and the first half of the eighteenth centuries—a time that, according to universal agreement, coincides with the decline of the Spanish state. Medieval Navarre has been studied by a series of brilliant medievalists. Chief among these scholars in our time is Don José María Lacarra. Not many of us know a great deal about Navarrese history during the final stages of the Habsburg dynasty and the first Bourbon ruler. More research on this period is needed, just as we need to know more Andalusian and Murcian history during this period. In general terms, there is a deficiency of knowledge regarding the social and economic history of Spain between the years 1680 and 1750—a period that more or less coincided with the life span of Friar Benito Jerónimo Feijóo y Montenegro,* one of the outstanding figures of his era.

Some eras can lay claim to excellence, while others cannot. The first part of the eighteenth century has not been extensively explored,

---

* Friar Benito Jerónimo Feijóo y Montenegro (1676–1764) was noted for encouraging scientific and empirical thought to debunk myths and superstitions. —ed.

although the more clear-sighted among our contemporary historians have begun to take an interest in that era deliberately ignored and discredited, for the more traditionally popular Romantic Era through the end of the nineteenth century. Given that nearly everyone today, when referring to the 1700s, only refers to the second half of that century, it is now important to rediscover and clarify what transpired during its first half. Yet, in the end, can we really think of an era that has had a more profound influence on our fathers, grandfathers, and great-grandfathers? We are what we are—for better or worse, in large part as a result of what our forefathers of the beginning of the eighteenth century were. Perhaps in Navarre more than anywhere else, one can say that the first part of the eighteenth century laid the foundations of life for the generations that followed. Any minimally attentive tourist who travels the length and breadth of this province will notice the vast quantity of lordly mansions, palaces, stem families, town halls, and both secular and religious edifices in general that date back to that period. This period was initially characterized by Baroque architecture, which was employed more conservatively in secular buildings than religious buildings. In rural (or, perhaps more accurately, rustic) settings, this style was used to create edifices of extraordinary beauty. Let's set aside the splendid Romanesque architecture of Navarre of the center and southern regions, as well as the later Gothic and Renaissance styles, and begin our discussion at the end of the seventeenth century.

Furthermore, rather than beginning in Navarre itself, we will begin our historical exploration in Madrid, the capital of a declining empire that had markedly diminished during the era of Philip IV, but that was still more or less intact in the West Indies, despite the continuous fighting that occurred in that region. On July 7, 1683, the day of San Fermín, the Navarrese residents of Madrid decided to found a congregation, the constitution of which was drafted by various dignitaries of the royal court: nobles, councilors of the king, friars, officers of secretariats, doctors, and market merchants. This group was joined by a second rank of individuals comprising renowned members of the aristocracy who had at least some connection to Navarre.

The full name of this body was the Royal Congregation of San Fermín de los Navarros, and it still exists today. Dr. Pío Sagüés Azcona, O.F.M. has written a well-researched and scholarly history of this institution.[1] Once the constitution of the order was approved, its congregants dedicated themselves not only to honoring their patron saint, but also to carrying out intensive charitable activities in hospitals and prisons. They were following the example of other congregations in Madrid that had been founded by various other ethnic groups. In 1579, a hospital dedicated to St. Peter and St. Paul had been founded by Italians. Later, a group of Flemings founded the Congregation of St. Andrew. This was followed in 1606 by St. Anthony's (Portuguese), in 1613 by St. Louis (French), and in 1635 by St. Patrick's (Irish).[2] We can thus see that, like the other groups that founded congregations, the Navarrese considered themselves a "nation," (as used to be said), although the word did not have as much political significance as it does today.[3] The congregation comprised a considerable number of men and women—its rolls listed 327 members, all of whom became members prior to the end of the year 1684.[4] It is a shame that we don't know the profession of each and every one of them (apart from the members of the secular and regular clergy, monks, and women in general). Otherwise, this Madrid congregation would provide the key to a great deal of what would later be said regarding the influence of the Navarrese in Spain and the Indies. And we indeed can see that, on August 19, 1685, these Navarrese who lived in Madrid decided to solicit help for the congregation from those of their countrymen "who are occupied in the service of His Majesty"—specifically in the Indies.[5] Later, in 1695, the congregation granted permission to those residing in the Indies to request alms, and the list of those who proceeded to do so is filled with names accompanied by titles, and by nobles, captains, clergy, friars, and so on scattered throughout the Spanish Americas.[6]

II

The successful collection of funds for this enterprise also constitute evidence that, in the various viceroyalties and colonial courts, there were influential Navarrese colonies, that these colonies were generally prosperous, and that they had a special connection to the Navarrese community in Madrid. In other words, both because of holding official positions and because of business connections, there was a considerable contingent of powerful Navarrese in the domains of Charles II of Spain (*el Hechizado*, "the Hexed"). Some of these family names were already long known by that time, while others were bursting onto the scene at that very moment.[7] The fact that they all lived very close to one another, and that there was a high degree of solidarity among them, can be inferred from examining a seventeenth-century text from the beginning of the reign of Philip IV; it is a fictional dialogue between a Basque and a Castilian in Peru, in which the latter confronts the former with the fact that so many persons from the

French Basque Country were in the Spanish Americas—protected there because of kinship and geographical ties by Spanish Basques (who were primarily Navarrese Basques).[8] In this dialogue, the following words are put into the mouth of the Castilian: "Furthermore, in the Indies, the majority of those who have Navarrese names are from France, since the majority of this kingdom is in French territory, and because the territory—though [politically] divided—is united, it can be assumed that the majority of the people is from the area represented by the largest proportion of territory." What we see here is a pontificating man who in fact is going off half-cocked—as the common expression goes—regarding the relative sizes of Spanish and French Navarre. Yet this text—which likely was written in 1624, remains significant all the same.[9] We will soon see—for example—that in the time of Charles II of Spain, a man of Lower Navarrese origin attained an important position in Madrid. The anonymous author of the previously cited text also seems to have been unaware that at least part of the old kingdom of Navarre (which, in his time, was already linked to the crown of Louis XIII, and which comprised Lower Navarre—or "Benaparroa") had a population with "residency rights" in the domains of the Spanish crown—specifically in Castile—in accordance with rulings issued by the Chancellery of Valladolid in 1597, 1604, and 1622[10]—and that, in lands of Donibane Garazi (Saint-Jean-Pied-de-Port), Spanish was spoken so commonly during the sixteenth century that one of the great men of Spanish letters of that era was born there. I am of course referring to Dr. Juan Huarte de San Juan.[11] But let's proceed. Navarre, like the Basque provinces, are countries with very strict inheritance laws, and it therefore obliged those who were not chosen to inherit the family estate to seek their fortune in the world. The monumental event of the discovery and conquest of the Americas provided a welcome outlet for such young men who had no future in their own country. On the other side of the Pyrenees, in Béarn, in the lands of Zuberoa and Lower Navarre, the so-called cadets also needed to venture forth. These men were even poorer—if this is possible—than the Basque-Navarrese noblemen that we will be discussing in due course. The results of this process were similar in both cases, because many of those younger brothers in the Paris of Louis XIII, Louis XIV, and Louis XV attained great wealth and status, while the firstborn who stayed at home often never amounted to much. Many years ago, Mr. Jean de Jaurgain recounted both the true life of Mr. de Troisville, a native of Oloron, Béarn, who was born in 1598, as well as something about the life de Artegnan of Gascony, who was born in Lupiac, shortly before Dumas presented him as a full-fledged dashing troublemaker, along with his three inseparable companions.[12] These men experienced a kind of adventure in their lives that was worlds away from their contemporaries and near-contemporaries who stayed in Navarre—which would remain linked to the Spanish crown. But those upon whom Dumas's great work has left its mark should note that the real d'Artagnan is not particularly flamboyant and larger than life. Instead (according to the account of Gatien Courtilz de Sandras) what he was in reality was a good soldier, eager to both ascend the ranks of the military and to marry a rich heiress or widow (who was valued for her wealth more than anything else) and then to make the lead the very best life possible with his newfound wealth.[13] Many other military men—and not only our Gascons, Bearnese, and Navarrese—had similar aspirations.

The men in these areas also had to venture forth from the lands of their birth, as has already been indicated above, for they lived in valleys where the right of residence was severely restricted, and where indivisible family estates could expand, but where it was impossible to create new houses owing to rigid local laws. The following text, in regards to the Baztan Valley comments upon these particular facts of life, and refers to one of the leading figures that we will soon be discussing in some detail:

> The entire territory is divided among property-owning residents, with each family holding an estate sufficiently large to meet its needs. But because the number of houses has increased, and therefore the number of inhabitants has exceeded the capacity of the land to provide for them, it would now be necessary for the people to lower themselves to the status of common laborers, which is entirely alien to the genius of our nation, and to the elevated aspirations with which our people have been raised. Thus a law—strictly enforced—was instituted to the effect that new houses cannot be constructed. This so that the number of property-owning residents does not increase, thus disturbing the order of society. The forefathers of old decreed said law to conserve the land in all its glory.
>
> It is thus legal for any property-owning resident to build houses that reached high into the sky, build extensions to their houses, fortify them, and embellish them according to their tastes (and within their means). It is also legal to build country houses to meet the needs of estates. But it is not legal to construct residences that expand the property resided upon. This in order to avoid the unsightliness and lack of space that often results from the presence of an excessive number of persons.[14]

The Navarrese congregants in Madrid, among whom was the author of the above text, themselves were part of this excess population of their respective valleys, village councils, and country estates. Goyeneche thus wrote that, in Baztan, "not all are born with the means to display their nobility in all its grandeur, and it is thus necessary that many acquire said means by dint of hard work, and that they venture forth to foreign lands to seek their fortunes."[15] Of course, the idea of "seeking one's fortune" here needs to be qualified by the reality that there was a vast support network among the Navarrese, with (for example) uncles supporting nephews, wealthy market merchants preferring to do business with their fellow countrymen in order to help them out financially, and so on. Family ties could also be established by means of marriage, and as was the case in all traditional societies. One can well imagine that agnatic ties were a determining factor in terms of who did and did not enter a particular sphere of activity. Goyeneche wrote that the inhabitants of the Baztan Valley comprised "a single family—a single house."[16] He himself clearly indicated that he felt this to be the case. The "house" was a defining concept in Navarre over the course of centuries. Property was transferred from one party to another, from one married couple to another, either through the wills of older generations or through the application of *donatio propter nuptias*. From the various children, a man or woman was chosen "for the house." And it was not necessarily the oldest son or daughter who was thus designated. We will soon see that there were numerous examples involving inheritance of houses through the female line, with the later male owners being referred to in certain French Basque legal texts from Zuberoa as "adventitious husbands."[17] Yet this should not be seen as a vestige of "traditional" mores, but instead as a system that allowed a woman to provide stability and within which a husband found himself in a situation in which he took a more active role—either because of his enterprising nature or because well-to-do relatives in distant lands called upon him for help because they trusted blood relatives more than outsiders. Women sometimes stayed "in the house" for the purpose of managing its economic affairs. Sometimes it was an unmarried uncle (who may have been well on in years) who married his niece, who then became the *etxekoandre* (the "woman of the house"). Sometimes cousins married one another, and sometimes marriages were formed by men and women from the same or neighboring valleys. Outside of Navarre, the Navarrese tended to intermarry—or to marry other Basques. The mechanism tends to remain the same, whether a man attains a considerable fortune or whether a situation involves the inheritance of a simple country house with renters and sharecroppers. Those of us who have passed the age of fifty can remember seeing this system in operation when we were children. Yet it is no longer as common today. The old colonist in Mexico or Argentina would sometimes summon his young nephew, and then make him his business partner or heir. Other times, he would return home to marry his niece. Others would either summon a girl from the same region in order to marry her, or arrange for a marriage-by-proxy in Navarre itself.

The 1920 departures and returns of Navarrese occurred according to the same customs that had reigned some two centuries earlier. Yet historical circumstances were different then. The notion of an exodus within that earlier historical context was also a good deal clearer. However, we should remember some of the explanations offered for these exoduses—explanations that imply a high degree of disrespect for the northern lands. The following is a testimony from a contemporary of Goyeneche: "May God rid me of this miserable land, with which the sky becomes enraged and darkens at any moment." These words were written by a Castilian who had gone off to transport Marie Louise of Orleans in 1679. The specific reference here was to the Basque provinces, although it could very well include the Atlantic region of Navarre as well. This man (like other Castilians) had an elevated conception of his native land's magnificence. He continued his unfavorable assessment of the cloudy and craggy Basque Country as follows:

> Father Luis Perino . . . told me that he had a friend . . . who, in an argument with another person, said angrily, "I hope God grants me the wish of seeing you inherit an estate worth six thousand ducats in Victoria [Vitoria-Gasteiz] with the provision that you have to live there all the time. This is my curse upon you, for that place is the complete opposite of Old Castile. Unlike so many other places, in Victoria all you see are trees instead of sky, and cliffs instead of habitable land. If you live there, you better know how to get around by walking. I maintain that the reason that so many Castilians have left Madrid, Seville, Valencia, Granada, Córdoba, and other large cities and, have returned to back to those places without establishing themselves elsewhere, is because they have not found a place with more wide open and fertile spaces than their own homeland. On the other hand, the Bizkaians, Gipuzkoans, and Arabans set out for the Indies—these great soldiers and sailors . . . great merchants and everything else one can imagine, and they don't come back home because their lands are so very wretched. Instead, they

strive mightily to establish themselves elsewhere, and work for a measly four *reales*."[18]

But didn't this individual just say that the Basques are so attached to their land that they don't believe there is any better place? As for the matter of a large number of families, palaces, charitable foundations, and the like, we will examine this issue later. For now, it needs to be said that, to a large extent, the evidence shows that the exact opposite occurred. At the same time, there were indeed a considerable number of persons who permanently detached themselves from the land, and who even ceased to follow the fundamental legal principles of the land. One really cannot generalize about these matters. Let's return now to our main subject.

The origin of some Navarrese families' prosperity, and which Goyeneche himself refers to, seems to have fundamentally derived from their participation in the fighting among different armed bands that occurred at the end of the period during which Navarre was an independent kingdom. As is well known, at the end of the fifteenth century, this kingdom was divided into two parts: that of the *agramonteses* (with close ties to the French crown) and that of the *beamonteses* (which, during the time of the Catholic monarchs, had ties to Castile). After the annexation of Navarre, the *beamonteses* were compensated in various different ways, while the *agramonteses* were persecuted to a great extent (and even—despite claims to the contrary—exiled[19]). These events coincided with the great enterprises of the colonization of the Indies, and more than one young man of *beamontes* origin sought his fortune in the New World under official or state protection. A typical example in this regard is Pedro de Ursúa, a gentleman from Arizkun who undertook an expedition to Eldorado[20] after having undertaken other expeditions in collaboration with his relative Miguel Díez (de Aux) of Armendariz, who also essentially considered himself *beamontés*.[21]

The life of Pedro de Ursúa was both tragic and romantic. He was the ancestor of men who prospered in the Indies and received titles in Castile, and who ended up being rather alienated from their native Navarre. In fact, among the illustrious progeny of the Baztan Valley mentioned by Goyeneche is Pedro de Ursúa—the same man who participated in the voyage to Eldorado. Others that were mentioned included a seventeenth-century captain named Don Pedro de Elizalde y Ursúa, defender of the Changre Castle, and another Don Pedro de Ursúa, whose descendents were granted the title of Count of Gerena by Philip IV.[22] Yet this lineage, which originated in Baztan, appears to have also produced other noblemen who themselves were natives of a Navarrese valley much farther to the south—that of Orba or Valdorba, as is attested in this locale's list of nobles, published in 1714 by Don Francisco de Elorza y Rada, abbot of Barasoain. This work has recently been reprinted,[23] and includes a rather large section dedicated to recounting the military feats of Don Martín de Ursúa y Arizmendi, who later became Count of Lizarraga Vengoa.

It is interesting to see on the list (dated June 30, 1695) of those authorized by the Congregation of San Fermín de los Navarros de Madrid to collect alms, a sergeant major with this name, with a listed residence in Mexico.[24]

The valley itself was ungenerous to its inhabitants; within its borders one had to live a severe and restricted existence. One had to escape its confines to seek one's fortune, either by land or by sea. It was the church and the military who were the primary dispensers of honors and favors during the sixteenth and seventeenth centuries. And so was the royal house—according to a well-known proverb.[25] And thus there were three official means of "seeking one's fortune": (1) the church, which attracted large numbers of men and women as members of the regular and secular clergy, exercised considerable influence in traditional societies—and not only in terms of those who attained the rank of bishop, canon, or provincial. Sometimes, even a humble friar could exercise a fair degree of power—even economic power;[26] (2) the sea, which enticed a good many young men, even those from inland towns and cities. In terms of our present subject, we know that some fortunes gained by those in the Atlantic region of Navarre came from a combination of seafaring, military, and commercial activities; and (3) royal service, which in the Basque-Navarrese world played a crucial role. We will soon see how the most distinguished men that form part of the group we are studying were, in disproportionate numbers, secretaries, treasurers, and trusted advisors of kings. In sum, there were instances in which each family had a person engaged in each of these activities. It is therefore unnecessary to accept the kind of thesis posited by Captain Marryat regarding his native England, according to which that nation's naval prosperity could be explained by the fact that each illustrious family and sent off its dimmest son to the navy.[27]

III

But the people of northern Spain also had a longstanding affinity for industry: especially the iron and shipbuilding industries.[28] Basques and

Navarrese were especially prominent in commerce. It should therefore not be particularly surprising that the Basque who had made his fortune in the colonies was represented in literary works (i.e., following his return, either in the court or in Seville). We see such representations in novels of manners written during the reigns of Philip III[29] and Philip IV. Such individuals were also represented in plays. Lope de Vega, for example, in *El premio del bien hablar* (The Prize for Speaking Well), tells the story of Don Juan, a nobleman who defends the honor of women above all else. He falls in love with the daughter of a "Bizkaian" who has made a fortune in the colonies (to be understood as someone who speaks Basque) and puts the following words in the mouth of the brother of her betrothed:[30]

"¿Que trate	"What's the meaning
mi hermano por interés	of my brother's interest
con esta Indiana casarse?	in marrying this girl from the Indies?
Que ¡vive Dios! Que me han dicho	Who—as God lives!—they have told me
que vendió en Indias su padre,	that her father sold in the Indies,
carbón o hierro, que agora,	charcoal or iron, that now
se ha convertido en diamantes;	has been converted into diamonds;
que puesto que es vizcaíno,	given that he's a Basque
para el toldo que ésta trae	for all of his vanity
son muy bajos sus principios."	his principles are very base."

To which Don Juan replies:

"—Los que saben	"—Those who know
que en Vizcaya a los más nobles	that in Bizkaia the highest nobles
se les permite que traten,	are allowed to wear,
con hábitos en los pechos,	the simplest priest's habits,
no dicen razones tales."	do not say such nonsense."

The merchant's daughter, when she hears of this dispute, adds:

"Es de mi padre solar	"My father's lineage
el más noble de Vizcaya:	is the most noble of Bizkaia:
que a las Indias venga o vaya,	if to the Indies he comes or goes,
¿qué honor le puede quitar?"	what honor can that take from him?"

Thus, we can see, long before the prejudices arose in Castile on the part of noblemen against men who engaged in commerce and related occupations that—as Father Larramendi pointed out—men who lived in the north did not have to struggle against such attitudes. And this was the case not only in Gipuzkoa,[31] but also in Navarre. And various members of the families that we will soon be speaking of were, in the interior of Navarre, fighting against a certain pervasive suspicion against commerce and industry—and all the while engaging in commerce and accumulating favors and noble titles. Both family and ethnic solidarity, along with the great economic enterprises that were being undertaken, were all important aspects of the life of Spaniards—both at home and in the colonies. There were intense rivalries in Potosí, Peru, between Basques and Navarrese, on the one hand, and Castilians, on the other. The former held economic power, as well as the majority of positions within government. They were proud of what they had achieved, in comparison to other emigrants who were less able or fortunate.[32] Tensions arose for the same reason: a near absolute dominant economic superiority on the part of the Basques and Navarrese, who emigrated in an organized fashion right up until the time that the colonies achieved their independence, according to written testimonies in the nineteenth century.[33]

But, on the other hand (and as usually happens) these ethnic divisions did not constitute an insuperable barrier when it came to dealings among individuals, whether business dealings or romantic relationships. Similarly, the borders of the Spanish empire were not entirely closed to foreign merchants, as has been repeatedly pointed out. In the memoirs of Raimundo de Lantery, a merchant from the Indies who worked in Cádiz, the second part of which (covering the years 1673–1700) has survived and been reprinted, is one of the most interesting documents of the era, despite its clumsy prose. Reading it, we discover the predominance in Cádiz of prosperous merchants from Genoa, France, England, Holland, Flanders, and Hamburg. In the meantime, the Spanish were in the minority and the Basques, generally speaking, had a distinctive presence, and it is evident that Lantery (who was from Nice, a territory belonging to the Dukes of Savoy) got along well with them.[34] He got along so well with them, in fact, that he arranged for the marriage of one of his daughters with a Basque (whom I believe was from Navarre) by the name of José Antonio de Iriberry (apparently a very energetic man who died young).[35] He also consented to the marriage of one of his sons with the daughter of a Navarrese accountant from Mexico, Don Juan Francisco de Zabalza, who was not at all impressed by the match for reasons of "race" and region of origin. It appears that Zabalza got on famously with Iriberry, but not very well with his son-in-law[36] Thus, apart from being "a man who was difficult to put up with,"[37] he represents an elitist attitude that would frequently be seen in the coming years.

This elitism was reinforced to a great extent, at least initially, by the fact that, at the beginning of the eighteenth century, the Basque-speaking area of Navarre extended well south of Iruñea-Pamplona. The previously cited abbot of Barasoain, in the genealogy of his family, wrote: If the Orba Valley, whose offspring converse in (conserve) the Basque tongue, forms a book of *Certificaciones de Armas* comprised of a district of only five hundred houses—a small section of the *merindad* of Erriberri (Olite), then what books would be sufficient to describe the kingdom and its nobility?"[38] The houses, which were easy to count in each valley, formed a contingent of men who protected one another. For these men, venturing forth to Madrid, Seville, Cádiz, or America was a path paved with gold.[39] The idea that the Navarrese constituted one large family was firmly entrenched in the seventeenth century, as shown by the founding of the Congregation in Madrid. This large Navarrese family in turn felt itself part of an even larger Basque family. Don Francisco Espoz y Mina, who was a formidable soldier in his youth and much later a liberal anti-Carlist military leader wrote the following in his highly interesting memoirs regarding the War of Independence: "The Gipuzkoans, Bizkaians, and Arabans, who in the interest of upholding their rights and in preserving national solidarity, have always marched shoulder to shoulder with the Navarrese, of course ought to be on the same side during this war."[40] Thus, it was only later that internal conflicts led to the collapse of a system that remained in force from the time of the annexation of Navarre in the sixteenth century, through the seventeenth and then into the eighteenth century. This is something that is corroborated in other documents. Don Francisco Fernández de Mendivil was a lawyer from Iruñea-Pamplona who attained a high position in Madrid, and who was charged with drafting a new constitution for the Congregation of San Fermín. In a letter of July 3, 1756, that he attached to a draft of this constitution, he referred to the well-known advantages that could result from merging the Navarrese congregation with the Basque congregation of St. Ignatius, advantages arising from "the strong ties and the powerful effects of shared geography, language, and customs, a traditional alliance, common religious principles.[41]

Part 5

The Basques Yesterday and Today

14
The Basques Yesterday and Today

More than anything else, the Basques have elicited a fair measure of general academic interest on account of their ancient tongue, which is so completely different from the languages of other European countries. Apart from their distinctive language, it has also been determined that Basques have certain distinctive physical characteristics. Their ethnographic traits are also an object of curiosity, as is the "historical rhythm" to which the Basque people have been subject—which is also highly distinctive. We will now attempt to clarify these issues, each of which is problematic in its own way.

As is well known, a rather small area of the Iberian Peninsula, and an even smaller area in the far southwest of France, are both home to a people that calls itself *Euskaldun* or *Euskalduna* (the final "a" constituting a singular article). *Euskaldun* is someone who speaks *Euskara* or *Euskera*, while one who does not speak this language is called *erdeldun*. Depending on which side of the Franco-Spanish frontier the person resides, *erdera* or *erdara* is used by Basque speakers to refer to Spanish/Castilian or French/Gascon. This fundamental linguistic distinction between those who speak Basque and everyone else who speaks some other language is still observed among many rural folk, and has also been applied to groups who are thought to have their own special jargon. It has been said, for example, that wizards and witches have their own special language (*sorguin-erdera*, "the witches' tongue") that has deliberately been designed to be confusing. There have also been contemptuous references to a "frog language" (*sapo-erdera*), and so on. All other languages and jargons are seen in reference to the Basque tongue—which is thought to be "*the* (normative) language." Thus, one is an *Euskaldun* if one speaks Basque, and one does not enjoy such a status if one does not speak the language, even if the person lives in the

Basque Country and has Basque surnames. This is a commonly held and time-honored point of view. It perhaps arose from a more intellectually grounded opinion regarding the existence of a homeland for the Basques (*Euskaldunak*; the suffix "*-ak*" merely indicates the plural article). This land is called *Euskal-erria*. *Erri* can be translated by the German *Land*, as used in many toponyms—including *Baskenland*. *Erri* is a word that signifies the homeland of a specific group of individuals, or a homeland with specific physical characteristics. The Basque province of Gipuzkoa is divided into three zones: the coast (*Kostalde*), the lowlands (*Beterri*), and the highlands (*Goyerri*). Yet there is also a term for the land of the dead (*ilerri*)—the term used to designate a cemetery. There are also terms to designate lands populated by Agotes (*Agoterri*) or by an abundance of birds (*Txorierri*). Basque poets of the nineteenth century, led by Iparraguirre, the author of "Gernikako arbola" ("The Tree of Gernika"), celebrated the glories of *Euskal-erria*.

This is not the place to delve into issues regarding Basque's characteristics and theories regarding its origin. Germany, which has produced great philologists, has made a decisive contribution to the propagation of the so-called Basque-Iberian thesis, according to which Basque is the last vestige of the language of the ancient Iberians. Wilhelm von Humboldt was the most rigorous of the Basque-Iberianists. More recently, Hugo Schuchardt has defended this same thesis. For now, we will leave aside these academic matters, including issues regarding the possible connection of Basque with Hamitic, Caucasian, and other languages. In sum, it is most likely the case that, in the dim mists of history, the Basque language was spoken where it is still spoken today: along the Pyrenees eastward, and in the southwest of Gaul (in Aquitania). Peoples who spoke Indo-Germanic tongues undoubtedly hemmed in those who spoke Basque during various phases of the Middle Ages.

The connection of the Basque language with a "racial type" is something that investigators have sought to establish in modern times. The Basque anthropologist Telesforo de Aranzadi, following the lead of other renowned and brilliant researchers, attempted to objectively define Basque traits in anthropometric terms. Afterward, sero-anthropological studies also seem to indicate distinctive Basque racial traits. Finally, ethnographers and folklorists have conducted painstaking research for the purpose of collecting any information relevant to constituting the "popular culture" of Basque rural inhabitants. It is clear that they have obtained satisfactory results in this regard. I really should say: *We* have obtained satisfactory results, for I am a part of this group of researchers. Among this group of ethnographers and folklorists are many distinguished figures. Among those still alive is J. M. de Barandiarán. Among those no longer with us are R. M. de Azkue and J. A. de Donostia. The group comprises both Spanish Basques and French Basques.

It has almost always been a pleasure to write about the Basques from the standpoint of folklore and ethnography. From the sixteenth century, when Don Esteban de Garibay began writing about a number of Basque customs, until the present, there has been a tendency to emphasize certain Basque mores—namely, those that could be considered the most "archaic" or "primitive." There exists in our own time a group of artists that, taking their inspiration from such research, have attempted to create a "Basque art" and a "Basque aesthetic." The myths of shepherds and the peoples who dwelled in the highlands, the ideas of those who lived in homes in isolated areas, and the expressive prehistorical world have been fused to create a thoroughly modern form of expression. Oteiza, Basterrechea, and others are exponents of this school.

Folklore is one of the aspects of "primitiveness," but there are others as well. This is because a people so intimately connected to the sea, and strategically situated in western Europe, were never able to live an entirely isolated and self-absorbed existence, and because of uncanny and unexplained connections with others in their practices and customs, techniques and arts, games, dances, and the like. Why are there certain musical similarities? Why are there still other similarities in wood-based architecture? And, on the other hand, how have the Basques given particular expression to Catholic culture since medieval times? These are all important issues that need to be addressed, along with others such as the maritime connections with the peoples of northwest Europe.

Despite all this, the Basque expression of those elements held in common with western European culture reflects a Basque rural life of extraordinary creativity and evocativeness, and which over the course of centuries has redefined itself.

So, on the one hand, we see rural and even primitive existence that continued until a very late date. And, on the other hand, we see a world that constantly renewed itself. And it is precisely this clash of two contradictory historical forces that has constituted the great tragedy of the Basque people. The history of this clash is complicated and dramatic, and we must have some understanding of it in order to understand the current difficulties and complexities of Basque society.

The "historical rhythm" that I referred to earlier reveals that at the end of the Upper Paleolithic Age the Basque Country, as well as neighboring areas, was populated by accomplished hunter-gatherers who experienced a period of cultural splendor. Afterward, there were periods characterized by less dazzling cultures. And then came the period of dolmen expansion, as mysterious as it is visually compelling. All of this was followed by a very long period of silence, during which other peoples entered and populated the peninsula. Then there was the intensive Romanization of what is now southern Navarre and Araba. In other areas, there was a lesser degree of Romanization. Afterward, we see a resistance to the Visigoths, Franks, and Muslims—a resistance that always had a more marked effect on the frontier areas of the Basque Country. Meanwhile life in the interior continued to be characterized by a disquieting silence and hermeticism. And then, finally, the time came in which the territory came to be divided along the lines familiar to modern man.

And yet a great deal of history came to bear upon this division—the weight of all of the ethnic tensions that were mentioned, as well as certain important contacts with other cultures, such as that of the Basques with the Normans in Baiona.

In the Dark Ages, some time after the Muslim Invasion of Spain, a kingdom arose in the Pyrenees—the kingdom of Navarre, which eventually came to control part of the territory that the Vascones had occupied in ancient times. Back in the ninth century, the term "Vascones" was still in use. Afterward, it disappeared and one only sees references to "Navarrese." At the same time, other gentilitious designations were also disappearing, and one began to see references to a land bordering Navarre—the county of Álava. Afterward, the domain of Bizkaia gradually took shape, as did a smaller territory characterized by a complex and obscure form of organization—Gipuzkoa. Over the course of many centuries, the fates of these three territories were tied to the kingdom of Navarre. They were also tied to the fate of other domains located north of the Pyrenees, in what is now known as Lower Navarre (*Basse Navarre* in French, *Benaparroa* in Basque), Lapurdi, and the Valley of Zuberoa. Two of these French Basque territories, as well as a considerable part of Gipuzkoa, seem to have been Christianized at a very late stage—somewhere around the ninth century.

In medieval society the monarchy did not have the degree of power that it would subsequently attain. And the lineages and factions never attempted to defend the principle of political unity. Other ideas, propagated in certain Spanish history texts, regarding the struggle against the infidel as a collective ideal did not at the time they actually circulated have the dogmatic flavor suggested in such texts—which might be best characterized as "historical rhetoric."

At the same time, it is true that Navarrese, Arabans, Bizkaians, and Gipuzkoans acted together during this time. Afterward, the Navarrese were separated from the others, which each in its own way came to recognize the kings of Castile. In the meantime, in French territory, the Lower Navarrese merged with the kingdom of Navarre, while the Lapurdians and Zuberoans did not. Matters grew increasingly complex over the course of the next several centuries. Navarre's borders came to encompass a Basque core, along with a vast southern zone that was retaken from the Muslims at a rather late stage and where a Muslim population remained, but where Basque was spoken. Monarchs encouraged the construction of urban settlements and new towns through special laws designed to attract merchants, artisans, and other townspeople. These monarchs were, to a large extent, from the south of France, and they had a great deal of antipathy toward the indigenous population. So new and larger towns were founded (first and foremost along St. James' Way) that more or less followed the Helenistic principle of synoecism—the grouping of villages to form city states—only with many centuries difference. Jewish families in the towns would later produce figures of great historical importance, especially in the large settlement in the extreme south of Navarre, in Tutera (Tudela)—a city that, generally speaking, did not have a particularly Basque character. The kings of Navarre eventually applied similar principles in Araba, thus fanning the flames of resentment among the rural population, led by the heads of lineages, toward the upstart settlers of the new urban settlements. This would seem to be one of the reasons why the Navarrese monarchs lost Araba.

Bizkaia and Gipuzkoa began to acquire a marked degree of economic importance from the twelfth century onward. This was because, even though they were considered lands that were backward and rural in physical terms, they produced large numbers of sailors and fisherman, as well as a notable contingent of metal workers. What is often written so pompously in the history books in descriptions of the conquest of Seville (for example) regarding the "Castilian Navy" actually refers, to a large extent, to Bizkaian and Gipuzkoan ships that set sail from modest ports that would later become crucially important in the colonization of the Americas.

The way of life in medieval times allowed the Basques to enjoy a form of "self-government," even though they were also constantly threatened by the ongoing internal conflicts among factions and lineages.

During the fourteenth and the fifteenth centuries, these conflicts grew out of control all throughout northern Spain. The fierce mutual hatred that existed between the *agramonteses* and the *beamonteses* resulted in the latter joining forces with the kings of Castile in order to bring down the Navarrese dynasty and kingdom at the beginning of the sixteenth century. Gipuzkoans struggled shoulder to shoulder with Castilians in this enterprise. Unity within the Navarrese kingdom came to an end with Charles V, and developed within the peninsula and empire as a whole under Philip II. By then, the medieval era had drawn to a close and, economically speaking, life was organized along very different lines. In Navarre and the Basque provinces, this led to a number of different effects that sometimes contradicted one another.

It can hardly be denied that during the ancien regime (i.e., from the sixteenth through the eighteenth centuries) many Basques and Navarrese were loyal servants of the "absolutist and patriarchal monarchy." I am deliberately using this term, which I read some time ago in a book written by Vierkhardt, because I feel that it is particularly useful and evocative. As sailors, warriors, accountants, secretaries, counselors, and confessors (the latter being men who knew how to keep a secret, and who general did not say much themselves) the Basques were a prominent presence in the courts of Charles I and Philip II. It is said that the emperor eventually learned Basque (which, if true, may be a reflection of his greater affinity for Germany than for Spain). Don Esteban de Garibay, the chronicler of Philip II and Basque to the core, placed special emphasis on this collaboration of Basques with the monarchs. During the decline of the Habsburg dynasty, Basques retained their prominent position in the royal court. Basque influence did not diminish during the reign of the first Bourbon, Philip V, a time that also had a distinctive Navarrese-Basque influence (i.e., on the part of Navarrese from the Basque-speaking zone of Navarre, who served with distinction as shipbuilding contractors, economic advisers, and promoters of industry, and all of whom clearly sought to place the Spanish economy on a sound footing). The first Spanish economic treatise was written by a Basque. Yet, along with these Basques who loyally served the crown with distinction, it also needs to be acknowledged that there were other Basques who held very different stations in life, and this duality would continue over the course of centuries.

Throughout Europe, the ancien regime was very respectful vis-à-vis both local freedoms as well as the laws of the ancient kingdoms, fiefdoms, and other units that it absorbed. But as centralized and centralizing ideas gained increasing ground, a certain distrust developed of the diversity of territories that comprised a single monarchy, with their different laws, practices, and customs. Royal advisors, minions, and ministers made efforts to either change these laws or to circumvent them. The fact that different peoples from different regions of the Iberian Peninsula lived together in the Spanish colonies (especially in the Andes) over several centuries was not necessarily conducive to mutual benevolence and understanding. This shared experience of "the Spanish," conceived as a unified nation sometimes led to the development of group solidarity while, on many occasions, it resulted in conflicts, double standards, and mutual recrimination.

The first clear indication of this state of affairs—one of a clearly adverse character—was evident as early as the seventeenth century, during the decadent reign of Philip IV of Spain, prior to the separation of Portugal and the war with Catalonia. During that time, there was unrest in Bizkaia because the Gaspar de Gúzman, Count-Duke of Olivares, a disgraced rival of Richelieu, attempted to introduce stamped paper, something that was generally considered a violation of privilege. A Basque attached to the court (one of the numerous Basque "secretaries") identified as instigators of the unrest those elements of Bilbao's commercial bourgeoisie who were related to foreign families, and who had displaced the former heads of lineages—the medieval nobles—as influential figures. In reality, a process could be traced back to that time (or perhaps earlier) that aimed at Basque egalitarianism, whose foremost theoretical exponent was the Jesuit priest Larramendi, the famous author of the *Diccionario Trilingüe castellano: Vascuence y latín* (Trilingual Castilian, Basque, and Latin Dictionary) and *El imposible vencido: Arte de la lengua vascongada* (The Impossible Tamed: The Art of the Basque Language). Both of these works were seminal for those later European philologists who studied Basque language and culture. Larramendi was also the author of *Corografía de Guipúzcoa* (Chorography of Gipuzkoa, unpublished during his lifetime), a brief summary of ideas that were widely accepted at that time, and a work that established the principles of original racial purity as the basis of the collective and egalitarian nobility of the Basques—as opposed to the acquired and hierarchical nobility of the Castilians, an upstart and modern people whose main source of pride was their supposed descent from the Goths. It was not a particularly great leap from that kind of attitude to a theocratic republicanism. And thus we see that Larramendi, in depicting Gipuzkoans of his era (i.e., during the first half of the eighteenth century) and reflecting upon the staunch religiosity of the Basques, held a scornful attitude toward what he saw as the pretensions of the traditional lords of the Basque Country, calling them "small lords" (*jauntxoak*) or "little big men" (*andikiak*) while, on the other hand, praising the sailors, ironmongers, and humble farmers—in contrast to all of the ideals of royalty and of class that were common at that time.

It is crucial to understand this stance in order to fully appreciate the particular ideological viewpoint that took shape, and that still exists in our own time, as seen in the accusation leveled by some in Franco's regime (who would have thought it!) that the Basques adhere to a kind of Nazi ideology. Nobody would deny the fact that the notion of "racial purity" is reflected in some of the laws of Gipuzkoa and Bizkaia, which prohibit Moors and Jews, as well as their descendents, along with (at a later stage) Cagots and Gypsies, from living in those territories. During the period of colonization, Africans, Native Americans, and mestizos (i.e., those who might have been brought back to the Mother Country as servants by prosperous colonists) were also forbidden to live in those two provinces. Such local laws did not allow for exceptions. And local laws also established that, with respect to taxes, the location of Castilian custom houses on the southern Navarrese border, as well as on the borders of both Araba and Bizkaia (but not, as today, on the French border). Some ministers of Philip IV and Philip V, and later monarchs, sought to modify arrangements that, from their centralist standpoint, were abusive. But the trusted royal advisers previously referred to—both Basque and Navarrese—squelched such efforts. Generally speaking, it was precisely when an influential Basque and Navarrese element was no longer present in the royal court when the local laws were most seriously threatened, both in theory and practice.

A long time before this, signs of mutual hostility among the different peoples of the decaying monarchy were evident. Pamphlets appeared accusing the Basques of being unfaithful subjects. Some of these were written by Galicians (as in the case of the notorious *El buho gallego* [The Galician Owl], which dates from the time of Philip IV), and some by Castilians. Some of the most violent of these writings grew out of the civil war in Peru. Responses to such attacks were written, such as *El tordo vizcaíno* (The Bizkaian Thrush), which was written shortly after the appearance of *El buho gallego*. There were also a good many popular jokes making the rounds in which "Bizkaians" (at that time, the term of reference for all Basque speakers) are portrayed as clumsy, hot-tempered, and intellectually impoverished. The "collective pride of the lineage" among Basques gained strength with the passage of time. I do not think that it would be wrong to say that a special kind of "practical religiosity" within the Basque Country was the result of its having produced a figure of such prominence and enduring influence as St. Ignatius of Loyola. Following his canonization, Ignatius was designated as the patron saint of the Basques, who were organized in brotherhoods both within and outside the Basque Country. St. Francis Xavier likewise became the patron saint of the Navarrese.

At the same time, the idea that a community of interests united the natives and residents of the ancient Navarrese kingdom and the three Basque provinces was steadily gaining ground. This was evident not only in the strenuous efforts to preserve local courts, liberties, and privileges, but also in shared tasks that brought these peoples together during the course of the eighteenth century. Basques founded the Gipuzkoan Company, and Navarrese participated in the administration of this enterprise. Basques also took part in the colonization of the Philippines, as well as in other similar enterprises. When the first Basque Economic Society was created (with the motto of "three in one," referring to the three Basque provinces), many Navarrese joined it as well. At the same time, it should be noted that the principle of loyalty to the monarchy remained a fundamental element in the constitution of this same society, the statutes of which formed the basis of the creation of many other similar societies throughout Spain.

Tough times would soon follow. At the end of the eighteenth century, during the reign of Charles IV—in Goya's Madrid—a scholarly apparatus was being constructed by royal officials that aimed at a partial dismantling of the system of local courts. This project was undertaken on the basis of the principle of "enlightened absolutism," as understood within a Spanish context (and, we could also add, within a bureaucratic context). A group of experts in paleography, diplomacy, and other related disciplines were charged with the task of collected documentation that would prove that Basque and Navarrese laws ultimately derived from no source other than royal favor and that, therefore, any ideas such as original or natural freedom were illusory. Thus, what the king had done he could now undo, if he so wished. During the reign of Charles IV, five books of medieval documents were published that aimed to prove this thesis. In addition, a geographical-historical dictionary based on this same thesis was compiled. Both of these works were published at government expense. We can now profit from studying these books, but at the time they were written they were like an explosive charge that had been specially prepared for evil purposes.

Both the French Revolution and the Napoleonic Wars that followed shattered the foundations of the ancien regime. Also contributing to this process was the collapse of the Spanish empire, with the associated annihilation of the Spanish navy. During the brief period between 1792 and 1814 both the wood-based shipbuilding industry and the old hydraulically powered iron industry—the chief sources of the eighteenth-century prosperity of the Basque provinces and Navarre—collapsed. As if all this were not bad enough, there was also, as in any crisis, an ideological polarization. The young soldiers of the late nineteenth century often became either progressive liberals or diehard royalists.

We should clarify here that the majority of Basque and Navarrese youth embraced royalism or absolutism. These territories were fundamentally Catholic, and the French Revolution had frightened the more or less wealthy families of noble lineage who may have briefly flirted with the Encyclopedist movement and other trappings of the Enlightenment. Both the lay and regular clergy firmly believed that the liberals and revolutionaries (whom they thought of as masons with republican tendencies) would, if they triumphed, put an end to the old laws.

Matters were not that straightforward for those Basques and Navarrese who loved their country but who also considered themselves liberals. This is because they viewed the potential triumph of absolutism as a return to an age that was much harsher than anything represented by either enlightened despotism or the Enlightenment—a return to the hideous barbarism of the Inquisition, and to the administration of local law by petty rural chieftains and illiterate village priests. It was precisely these fears that led to the strange circumstance of a large part of the Spanish army associating itself with "the cause of Freedom." Many Basque and Navarrese youth who had fought in the Peninsular War and/or in the Americas were military men with liberal convictions. Foremost among such men was the Navarrese Espoz y Mina. Yet it must once again be emphasized that the majority were, first, royalists and absolutists and, afterward, Carlists.

The time has now come to address the roots of the Basque problem in our time. Nineteenth-century Spanish liberalism was a very special kind of liberalism. This was because it had to deal with the ever-present reality of, on the one hand, a force of armed men loyal to the king and, on the other, rather anarchical popular masses. For its part, Carlism always had the character of a complex and problematic position liable to change with circumstances—whatever others might say. At one time, the motto of the Carlists throughout Spain was "God, Country, and King." It was the different ways of interpreting this motto that led to different shades of opinion regarding "the Cause," (the famous term by which Carlism came to be known). First and foremost, the Carlists raised the issue of legitimacy in light of the Salic Law, which prevented women from ascending the throne of Castile, Navarre, or any other kingdom.

During the sixteenth and seventeenth centuries, the application of the contrary principle (i.e., that women could ascend the throne and possess kingdoms) had in France, and in Navarre itself, been considered something specifically Spanish. The eminent men of Navarre who had proclaimed Isabel II queen had in fact declared that the Salic Law was not applicable or recognized in the old kingdom. Yet this declaration had no discernable effect on the majority of Navarrese. Less problematic than the application of an obscure law were those of God, Country, and the King (or the recognized pretender to the throne). For many Basques, God was the *Jaungoikoa* of the popular imagination—the "Lord Most High." It was even said (sometimes seriously and sometimes in jest) that He had spoken Basque with Adam and Eve in Paradise. (Whether the Almighty spoke Basque with the serpent as well is not recorded.) For the Basques, the king (*errege*) or pretender was a human being of flesh and blood—a figure about whom little was known at the outset of the Carlist conflict. Yet the monarch was a figure that priests garlanded with all kinds of divine and human favors. For many Carlists—including many of their leaders—the country clearly was the land where one lived (in other words, the Basque provinces and Navarre, where the initial conflicts first arose.

The Basque Country was home to a military organizational genius by the name of Tomás de Zumalacárregui, was a somber and reserved Gipuzkoan who was recognized as a great strategist not only by those he commanded, but also by his enemies and by foreign experts. Germans can read what Baron von Rahden and General von Goeben wrote of him. But Zumalacárregui consistently refused to fight outside of Navarre and the Basque provinces, and at the end of his life was fed up with the coterie assembled around the king with its slavish bureaucratic adulation, friars and ignorant nuns, and constant court intrigue. When he died, Carlism began to enter into a period of decline. It was during this decline that a clear division could be observed between two groups that had uneasily united previously—a Basque and Navarrese group, on the one hand, and a Castilian one, on the other. The Basques and Navarrese were more rooted in local laws, and theocratic in orientation, while the Castilians were more bureaucratic and centralist. There were always generals like the Navarrese Elío who advocated the creation of a Carlist Basque-Navarrese state.

This regional, internal hatred was one of the main factors that led to the Bergara Accord, and to the end of the so-called Seven-Year War (i.e., the First Carlist War). This war resulted in both the political and military triumph of the victorious Liberal general Espartero. Contemporary historians view this progressive general as a mercenary with a severely deficient character and imagination. All the same, it is important to recognize that, as regards the resolution of Basque-Navarrese issue, he was a good deal more effective (or, perhaps, had a more able group of followers) than later politicians.

Both Basque and non-Basque Carlists claimed that this accord was not only a betrayal on the part of its signatories, but also that it constituted a major setback to Basque and Navarrese freedoms. In reality, Navarre went from being a viceroyalty to being a province, and its local courts were reduced in number and came to constitute what was termed a "contrived legal system" that has remained in place until present times. A similar development occurred in the Basque provinces.

Centralists were also not happy about the solution—a solution that, in my view, seemed quite well balanced in terms of what was realistically possible and implemented by an able group of jurists. Of course, the law is one thing and feelings and passions are something else. Many Navarrese, Gipuzkoan, and Araban Carlists were left with a sense of frustration: Some were merely disappointed; others plotted revenge. A poetic idea of "the lost cause" took shape. Those who retained a memory of the military and court intrigues of Don Carlos, and of this monarch's weaknesses, chose to turn a blind eye to them and that prince continued to be viewed by the masses as a living saint and possible future redeemer—a king whose return was foreordained by God. The real nature of Don Carlos was really irrelevant. In fact, he seemed to be quite dim-witted.

The political mysticism of peoples is difficult to understand. The spirit of revenge took firm root and remained a vital force between the years 1839 and 1870. Parents gave this spirit to their children, who bestowed it upon theirs in turn.

The Revolution of 1869, which brought the reign of Isabel II to an end, had just broken out when the Carlists began to show new signs of life. The second civil war was perhaps less violent than the first. Carlism did not have men such as Zumalacárregui in its service, and the conflict ended in a series of small compromises. At the same time, a number of liberal generals showed themselves to be quite inept, and suffered severe setbacks.

The end of the second conflict coincided with the Alfonsine Restoration, and with the decisive and direct action of its architect: Don Antonio Cánovas del Castillo. This leader of the Liberal-Conservative party was called "the monster" by his followers. He was very self-satisfied and clearly able. Yet I also believe that, in the way he went about resolving the Basque-Navarrese problem following the war, he was far clumsier than Espartero. Men who speak and write little have the advantage of having their errors discovered less than those who speak and write a lot. Cánovas belongs to the second group. Other exasperated centralists spoke more and worse in the Cortes that he led around the year 1876. One deputy, a certain Marquess of Sandoval, ended up saying that the Basque language should disappear, and that the ignorant people who spoke it, and who constituted a threat to peninsular unity, should also be wiped out. Newspaper and "cultural" campaigns, which were launched in Madrid, propagated the pedantic slogan *Carthago delenda est*. The pagan poet Rutilius Namatianus saw in Judaism the *radix stultitiae* that eventually produced Christianity.* It could similarly be said that the *radix stultitiae* that led to Basque nationalism was, to a large extent, a crass extremism in the Spanish press, the Cortes, and various congresses. Sometimes, this extremism was expressed in liberal circles, and other times in antiliberal circles. The kind of rank idiocy and gross insults that have been expressed (at times with the approval of the authorities) regarding Basques, Catalans, and other groups from 1876 until the outbreak of the third civil war is absolutely despicable. But let's not get ahead of ourselves.

The Second Carlist War (in spite of the vast number of books, newspapers, flyers, etc. that the Carlists produced in support of "the Cause" after it was over) led to feelings of disgust and discontent on the part

---

* *Carthago delenda est* ("Carthage must be destroyed") was the Roman slogan driving the later stage of the Punic Wars and a reference to the incitement of popular passions. *Radix stultitiae* is translated variously as the root or stupidity, folly, madness, or silliness. —ed.

of the general population. Carlism lost much of its former strength in the Basque provinces (as well as in Catalonia and Valencia). It remained strong in the center of Navarre, a region where Basque was no longer spoken. The Basques continued to be a very religious people who were very attached to their land. The old slogan of "God, Country, and King" was revised to eliminate the third element. The "Country" would simply be *Euskal-Erria*—no more and no less. It would soon no longer include the concept of the physical land so cherished by those of us who lived there, and would instead refer to the hypothetical state called *Euzkadi*. What brought about this change? The process was both rapid and complex, as is the case in all such mutations.

As previously mentioned, the slogan of the Basque Royal Economic Society of Friends of the Country was, during the Enlightenment, "Three in One" (*Irurac bat*). At the end of the reign of Isabel II, in a regional exposition that was held in Iruñea-Pamplona, it seems that this slogan was suddenly changed (in the face of some objections) to "Four in One" (*Laurac bat*). Shortly afterward, a number of Navarrese scholars propounded the thesis that the principles of Basque-Navarrese autonomy should be founded on the basis of racial unity (which at that time meant more or less the same thing as linguistic unity). This thesis was a response on the part of the most conservative element of the population, Catholic to the core but not Carlist, to the rhetorical excesses of the Cortes of 1876, in which Basques, Navarrese, Carlists, and reactionaries were all lumped together for the purposes of collective condemnation—in the name of unity as well as of liberty and modernity.

So another couple of decades passed before the fateful year of 1898, when Spain lost Cuba and the Philippines. The Spanish government fell into extreme disrepute. It began to be said that Spain was a country on its last legs. At the same time, however, there was a high degree of industrial prosperity in Catalonia as well as a thriving iron and steel industry in Bilbao and its environs. Before continuing, we need to first note two parallel phenomena. During both the first and second civil wars, Catalan and Basque Carlists had shown their antipathy toward the large population centers of their respective provinces. Bilbao, the capital of Bizkaia, which endured two sieges in which the Carlists were defeated, was considered the liberal city par excellence. Barcelona was home to a Carlist minority. Iruñea-Pamplona, Donostia-San Sebastian, and Vitoria-Gasteiz (capitals of Navarre, Gipuzkoa, and Araba respectively) were never controlled by the Carlists. The ancient biblical opposition between "wicked Babylon" (i.e., the city) and the religiously and moral upright country folk who are faithful servants of God was something that was very much a living reality in the minds of Carlists, whether Basque or Catalan, as a result of regular sermons and harangues that prominently featured this idea. It is interesting to note that, at the end of the nineteenth century, Barcelona felt that it was superior to Madrid, and Bilbao began to see itself as a city with a distinctively Northern European character (and therefore as the antithesis of the lazy and dirty inland regions). The reason why many elements of the Catalan middle class saw Barcelona as the ideal capital of a future Catalan state that was thoroughly European and Mediterranean in character is easier to understand than the reason why the foundations of Basque nationalism were forged in Bilbao. The role played in this regard by Don Sabino Arana Goiri in the constitution of this Basque nationalism was decisive. Arana Goiri created the motto "God and the Old Laws" (*Jaungoikoa ta lagi zára*). This motto was soon written according to the new Basque spelling system. Where would the ideal expressed therein receive fullest expression? In *Euzkadi*.

It should be recognized that nationalism embraces—more synthetically and intuitively than analytically and historically—the old theocratic tendency that had previously found expression in Larramendi's work, joined to an egalitarian thesis that stressed the notion of "the people." A people, that is, united in the service of God.

It could be said that the period between Arana Goiri's initial formulation of this ideology until World War I constituted the first phase of Basque nationalism. It is my view that the end of that war ushered in a new theoretical development. When, following their victory, the allies set themselves the task of dismantling the political structure of the Habsburg Empire, the idea that the new European nations should be founded on the basis of shared language, culture, and race quickly gained ground. This state of affairs was like wind in the sails in terms of the political aspirations of Basques and Catalans. Many publications of the era reflect this reality. Later, the Irish independence struggle greatly influenced the nationalist party, despite the Anglophilia (and in some cases even Anglomania) of many Basques. Yet a certain modus vivendi was soon reached—one that endured for many years—between nationalists and Carlists, who found common ground in their shared antipathy to the dictatorship as well as in Basque student congresses. Other Basques, however, went their own way.

I've previously pointed out how, from the sixteenth through the eighteenth centuries, many Basques held important positions in Spanish public life at the same time that hostility toward Basques as a group was gaining ground. It should be emphasized that, while nationalism was ascendant, another important development was taking place: In Spanish life, and especially in Spanish letters, men of the first rank were emerging who were full-blooded Basques. In 1869, Don Miguel de Unamuno was born in Bilbao. In 1870, the painter Ignacio Zuloaga was born in Eibar. In 1872, my uncle Pío Baroja was born in Donostia-San Sebastián. The Araban Ramiro de Maeztu and Bizkaian Juan Echevarría were born shortly afterward. And there were other men of talent who lived and pursued careers in various parts of Spain. Some of these men, such as Dr. Achucarro (who was part Norwegian) were of mixed blood, while others, such as R. Baroja, an engraver and painter, were born outside the Basque Country. These names have been invoked in arbitrary and wrongheaded ways by those advocating quite different positions. This use of their names is yet another indication of that conflict between ethnocentrism and integrationist tendencies that has led some to claim that St. Ignatius is the archetypal Spaniard, and others to claim that he was the purest expression of the Basque soul. Let's leave such matters aside for the moment.

The clerical orientation of the nationalism of those who were known as *Bizkaitarrak* (in the same way that "Bizkaian" was used by Castilians throughout the sixteenth century to refer to Basques) began to take shape during the 1920s. Nationalist newspapers such as *Euzkadi* helped lay the foundations of this particular brand of traditionalism. However, as has previously been pointed out, from the proclamation of the Second Republic in 1931 to the closing of the Cortes of the Republic, the balance among Carlists, nationalists, and other Catholic groups (generally considered "right-wing") largely held. Afterward, it would collapse. Basque nationalists soon appreciated that it was the leftist parties who were more sympathetic to their aspirations for autonomy. The Carlists, on the other hand, considered themselves essentially supporters of the monarchy, and thus defenders of the unity of religion and the Spanish state. Mutual hatred between the two groups became abundantly clear after the Civil War broke out in 1936. Basque Catholic nationalists had to throw in their lot with the parties of the left. The Carlists and defenders of the fueros, on the other hand, joined forces with the most diehard centralists in all of Spanish history: the Spanish Falangists, who derived their ideology in part from the Italian fascists (e.g., the notion of a dogmatic *Hispanidad* that reflected Mussolini's concept of *Italianitá*) and an army characterized by unbending centralism and royalism.

Elsewhere, in the meantime, there was a flirtation with liberalism.

In Navarre, Carlism attracted people from all socioeconomic classes during the conflict—including barons of the liberal Alphonsine monarchy, bedecked in their *requeté* berets.* The commonality of interests among Basques and Navarrese, which was widely assumed during the eighteenth and nineteenth centuries, no longer held true. The forces that marched out of Navarre marched victoriously into Gipuzkoa and Bizkaia. The victory, which in large measure could be credited to Navarrese and Carlists, meant the suppression of economic arrangements that had held through the Second Carlist War with those two provinces. Yet the accords with Araba and Navarre still held. And thus, what happened was seen as a punishment. The law that enacted the aforementioned suppression was among the most ill conceived in all of Spanish history. Some old Basque Carlists thought that the law would be nothing more than a provisional measure that had been conceived in order to "teach a lesson" to nationalists and "reds." This very impolitic idea of teaching a lesson will be familiar to most Spaniards—one can hardly deny it.

Many years have passed since the conquest of Donostia-San Sebastián and Bilbao, as many as had passed between the First and Second Carlist Wars. We can see that Basque nationalism is today quite formidable, whatever anyone might say and however uncomfortable this fact may make some people feel. It is even stronger than Carlism, which ended up being vanquished by the same parties that had cheered it on during the conflict—as well as by social and demographic factors that I will not go into here.

Readers of a certain age are able to discern the results of the political and military actions of forty years ago, as well as the economic transformation of the postwar era.

In general, it can be fairly said that the country is unbalanced. Some parts of it—the narrowest parts, such as the industrial zones of Gipuzkoa and Bizkaia—are very densely populated. The working districts created from the incessant arrival of immigrants have been very intensively developed, with a density of seven to twelve thousand people per square kilometer. On the other hand, vast rural sections of the Pyrenees have become uninhabited. Basque-speaking areas have become restricted (in areas where there is still human habitation). Rural life, so treasured by ethnographers and folklorists, is languishing and drying up. At the same

---

* The *Requetés* (French *requête*, "hunting call") were a Carlist militia on the Francoist side during the Spanish Civil War. They regarded the war as a crusade. —ed.

time, a large number of troublesome industries have been created. And so, while there are groups of rural inhabitants who struggle to survive, there are others who, through speculation of various kinds, have amassed great fortunes.

The political conflicts are very well known, as a result of the violence that they led to. New things were happening that disoriented those who clung to old ways—new things that have parallels in our own time in those areas where there are serious racial conflicts. And thus we see the effects of a new mutation in this respect.

Historians fear the possibility that the magnitude of events will again overwhelm people's capacities to confront their effects. I refer here to the problem of Basque autonomy, with its centuries-long historical burden. And, in a similar vein, those who advocate centralist conceptions of the Spanish state, and those who have actively carried out this project, also have their own centuries-long burden. Nowadays, the age-old distinction between universalism and particularism is dead in the water. Madrid—the venerable bureaucratic Madrid—cannot justly claim to be far-sighted in its outlook, and instead reflects the laziness and self-absorption that is so typical of individual government functionaries. And, it should be added, an explosive situation cannot be resolved by mere conceptual games.

Endnotes

Introduction: The Life and Work of Julio Caro Baroja

1. Caro Baroja, "Una vida en tres actos," 589.
2. Ibid.
3. Caro Baroja, "Una imagen del mundo perdida," 112.
4. Caro Baroja, "Semblanzas ideales," 11–13.
5. Caro Baroja, *Los pueblos del norte*, 30 and 9.
6. Caro Baroja, *Los pueblos de España*, 12.
7. Caro Baroja, *La vida rural vasca*, 350.
8. Ibid., 16.
9. Ibid., 350, note 1.
10. Caro Baroja, *Etnografía histórica de Navarra*, 21–22.
11. Caro Baroja, *Las formas complejas de la vida religiosa*.
12. Caro Baroja, *La casa en Navarra*.
13. Caro Baroja, *La estación de amor*.
14. Caro Baroja, *El estío festivo*.
15. Sánchez Harguindey, "Prólogo," 5–12.
16. Caro Baroja, *Los vascos y la historia a través de Garibay*.
17. Caro Baroja, *Los Baroja*.
18. Caro Baroja, "Género biográfico y conocimiento antropológico," 29.
19. Caro Baroja, *Los vascos y la historia a través de Garibay*, 30.
20. Ibid., 30.
21. Caro Baroja, *La vida rural vasca*.
22. Caro Baroja, "Género biográfico y conocimiento antropológico," 25.
23. Ibid., 31.

24. Ibid., 21.

25. Ibid., 28–29.

26. Ibid., 30.

27. Ibid., 37.

28. Ibid., 32.

29. Kant, "Anthropologie du point de vue pragmatique," 17–27.

30. Greenwood, "Julio Caro Baroja," 263–284.

31. Caro Baroja, "El último Avencerrejo," 51–68.

32. Caro Baroja, *Las brujas y su mundo*; Ibid., *Vidas mágicas e inquisición*.

33. Caro Baroja, Los *judíos en la España contemporánea*.

34. Caro Baroja, *Las formas complejas de la vida religiosa*.

35. Caro Baroja, "Problemas psicológicos, sociológicos y jurídicos en torno a la brujería en el País Vasco."

36. Caro Baroja, "La vida rural vasca," 57.

37. Ibid., 351.

38. Caro Baroja, "Mundos circundantes y contornos histórico-culturales," 40.

39. Caro Baroja, "Cosas humanas y tiempos de ellas," 27.

40. Caro Baroja, "Situación actual de la antropología," 18.

41. Caro Baroja, *Introducción a la vida económica y social del pueblo vasco*, 93.

42. Ibid., 94

43. Caro Baroja, "El mar en situaciones tópicas," 65.

44. Caro Baroja, "Mundos circundantes y contornos histórico-culturales," 32.

45. Caro Baroja, "Sofismas en torno a la mitología," 205.

46. Caro Baroja, "Mundos circundantes y contornos histórico-culturales," 32.

47. Caro Baroja, *Etnografía histórica de Navarra*, 21–22.

48. Caro Baroja, "Ciclos culturales e identidad vasca," 9–34.

49. W. Koppers, " Individualforschung unter den Primitiven in besonderen unter Yamana auf Feuerland" 365 in *Festschrift P.W.Schmidt*. Wien: Mechetharisten Congregations-Buchdrukerei 1928.

50. G. Balandier, *El desorden* 227. Barcelona: Editorial Gedisa.

51. Baroja, *La dama errante*, 252.

52. Ibid.

53. Caro Baroja, *La vida rural vasca*, 352.

54. Ibid., 19.

55. Literally, "the noisy cart," the traditional Basque cart, thus known for the sharp sound of its axles.

56. Ibid., 352.

57. Caro Baroja, *Etnografía histórica de Navarra*, 10.

58. Caro Baroja, *The Basques*, 199, 120 fig. 50.

59. Ibid., 145.

60. Caro Baroja, "Una vida en tres actos," 587; Caro Baroja, "La crisis del caserío," 133.

61. Caro Baroja, "La crisis del caserío," 133.

62. Ibid., 139–140.

63. Ibid., 141.

64. Caro Baroja, "Sobre los vascos (Reflexiones de 1967)," 142.

65. Ibid., 143.

66. Ibid., 146–147.

67. Ibid., 151–152.

68. Ibid., 154.

69. Douglass, *Oportunidad y éxodo rural en dos aldeas vascas*, 111–146.

70. Caro Baroja, "Sobre los vascos (Reflexiones de 1967)," 159–160.

71. Ibid., 161.

72. Ibid., 156.

73. Caro Baroja, "Prólogo" of *Sobre la religión antigua y el calendario del pueblo vasco*, 8. Donostia-San Sebastián: Editorial Txertoa 1980 2ª ed.

74. Caro Baroja and Temprano, *Disquisiciones antropológicas*, 84.

75. Ibid., 106.

76. Ibid., 106.

77. Caro Baroja, "Prólogo" a *Sobre la religión antigua y el calendario vasco*, 8

78. Caro Baroja, *Introducción a la historia económica y social del pueblo vasco*, 69–70.

79. Caro Baroja, "Sobre los vascos (Reflexiones de 1967)," 153.

80. Lahire, *El hombre plural*, 272–273.

81. Ibid., 272.

82. Rothacker, *Problemas de antropología cultural*, 141.

83. Ibid., 146.

84. Ibid., 152.

85. Ibid., 159.

86. Ibid., 154.

87. Caro Baroja, *Los Baroja*, 548.

88. Ibid., 11.

89. Caro Baroja, "Una vida en tres actos," 587.

90. Caro Baroja, *Palabra, sombra equívoca*, 63.

91. Caro Baroja and Flores Arroyuelo, *Conversaciones en Itzea*, 270.

92. Julio Caro Baroja, "El Baroja perplejo," *El Correo*, August 19, 1995.

93. Caro Baroja, *Palabra, sombra equívoca*, 63.

94. Caro Baroja, "Una vida en tres actos," 583.

95. Caro Baroja, "Prólogo" to *De la superstición al ateísmo*, 10.

96. Ibid., 9.

97. Ibid., 14.

98. Caro Baroja, "Una vida en tres actos," 583.

99. Caro Baroja, *El laberinto vasco*, 113.

100. Ibid., 139.

101. Lledó, *El epicureísmo*.

CHAPTER 1. **Neighboring Peoples and the Historical-Cultural Context**

1. Julio Caro Baroja, *Etnografía histórica de Navarra*, vol. 3 (Iruñea-Pamplona 1972), 457–64 (epilogue).

2. *Kritik der Urteilskraft*, ed. Karl Vorlander (Hamburg 1968), 223–28.

3. "Medium" was initially used to translate the German *Umwelt*. Later, a distinction was made between *Umwelt* and *Merkwelt*.

4. The translation of *Ideas para una concepción biológica del mundo* (Madrid 1922) had an unfortunate influence on some who read the book, and who saw in it nothing more than an attack against evolutionary theory. Shortly afterward, Jakob von Üexküll's essay, "La biología de la ostra jacobea," was published in *Revista de Occidente* 9 (March 1924): 279–331.

5. See examples in von Üexküll and Kriszat, *Streifzüge durch die Umwelten von Tieren und Menschen* (Hamburg 1956), 19–101.

6. *Historia de la literatura inglesa*, translation of *La España moderna*, 2nd ed., vol. 3 (Madrid [no year]), 20–29.

7. A great deal has been written in this regard. For a general orientation, see Pablo de Gorosábal, *Noticia de las cosas memorables de Guipúzcoa*, vol. 1 (Bilbao 1967), 171–75 (chapter 5, section 2), although there are later texts that present other original documentation. The name, which first appeared as "Ipuzcoa" and in similar forms, has been construed in a number of different ways, although there is no consensus regarding its meaning.

8. As regards the method for studying these boundaries, which have been written about extensively, the most authoritative work continues to be that of Claudio Sánchez Albornoz, "Divisiones tribales y administrativas del solar del reino de Asturias en la época romana," *Boletín de la Real Academia de la Historia* 95 (1929): 315–95. In his *Etnología de la Península Ibérica* (Barcelona 1932), 604–61, Don Pedro Bosch Gimpera systematically presented the geographical data, and later authors proceeded to cover much the same ground.

9. Regarding this point, see my forthcoming *Sobre el mundo ibérico-pirenaico*, a one-volume work containing studies of the ancient history of Spain. [Editorial Txertoa, 1988 —ed.]

10. Strabo, 3, 4, 10 (161); Ptolemy, 2, 6, 67.

11. Polybius, 3, 35, 1–3; Libio, 21, 23, 1–2, etc.

12. Royalty was highly developed among the Ilergetes. There is a historical record of an Ilergete ruler as early as 218: Polibio, 3, 76, 7. This was likely the famous Indibil, although he was referred to as Andobales. Figure 1.5 is based upon Müller and Dübner's edition of Strabo.

13. According to Strabo, 2, 5, 27 (127), the Celts border Iberia on the east, with the Pyrenees constituting the boundary between the two peoples. But the blood relationship between Iberians and Celts is continually repeated as if it were an unquestionable fact.

14. Zonaras (8, 21) later wrote that various peoples lived in the Pyrenaic valleys, and that these peoples had *diverse political organizations as well as different languages.*

15. Julio Caro Baroja, *Cosas humanas y tiempos de ellas.*

16. Von Uexküll and Kriszat, *Streifzüge durch die Umwelten von Tieren und Menschen*, 88–92.

17. See *Etnografía histórica de Navarra*, vol. 3 (Iruñea-Pamplona 1972), 378–84; "Notas de etnografía histórica de Navarra," *Revista de Dialectología y Tradiciones Populares* 28 (1972): 3–38.

18. Historians of the sixteenth century (Zurita, Garibay, etc.), and then Moret, offered conjectures regarding these place names.

19. The importance of toponyms as tools of historic-ethnographic knowledge has never been sufficiently appreciated.

20. Figure 1.6 represents a depiction on the basis of historical documentation. See also J. M. Lacarra, *Aragón en el pasado* in *Aragón I* (Zaragoza 1960), 127–343.

21. Even though the settlement in the lands of Tudela was of long duration.

22. "All of our writers nevertheless are in agreement that Bizkaia and Gipuzkoa, as well as other regions, always remained in Christian hands. This was the case for the same reason that was stated earlier: because these provinces were in the far reaches of Spain, because of the inordinate labor involved in conquering them, and the few rewards to be attained as a result of any such conquest. For this same reason, the Moors made no effort in recent times to subjugate them" (Ambrosio de Morales, *Los otros dos libros undecimo y duodecimo de la Corónica General de España* [Alcalá de Henares 1577], folio 203r, book 12, chapter 76).

23. *Los vascos y la historia a través de Garibay (ensayo de biografía antropológica)* (Donostia-San Sebastián 1972), 13–39.

24. Many years ago, I wrote a monograph (which I never subsequently published) regarding the county of Álava, from which I have drawn the present general observations.

25. Towns such as those of the Mediterranean zone of Navarre (e.g., Lerin) are representative in this regard. Caro Baroja, *Etnografía histórica de Navarra*, vol. 1 (Iruñea-Pamplona 1971), 169 (figure 25).

26. Regarding the Mediterranean peoples of this type, various medieval descriptions can be consulted, such as those of Mármol Carvajal. These descriptions can then be compared with modern maps and photos.

27. *Los moriscos del reino de Granada* (Madrid 1957).

28. The boundary with respect to the types of roofs and terraces used was something that was carefully considered by a number of ethnographers with extensive knowledge of North Africa.

29. Miguel Asín Palacios, *Contribución a la toponimia árabe de España*, 2nd ed. (Madrid-Granada 1944), 83–94.

30. *Descripción geológico-minera de las provincias de Murcia y Albacete* (Madrid 1868), interleaf 2 (between 14 and 15). There are other drawings of the same map.

CHAPTER 4. **Origins: Basque-Iberianism**

1. One comprehensive, though not necessarily reliable, treatment may be seen in Enrique Eguren y Bengoa, in his *Estudio antropológico del pueblo vasco* (Bilbao 1914), 5–77 (first part). With respect to this work, it makes sense to draw a distinction between, on the one hand, those ideas that are based upon the observation of physical traits—ideas drawn from ethnological and cultural study—and, on the other hand, strictly linguistic observations. Such a distinction is rarely made in theoretical works.

2. See below the reference to the article by de Jean-Joseph Saroïhandy, as well the historical works of Manuel de Larramendi Garragori, Hervás y Panduro, and others. In *Mélanges de linguistique et d'anthropologie*, by A. Hovelacque, E. Picot, and J. Vinson (Paris 1880), 187–190, Vinson copies a text on Basque written in Latin by Marineo Sículo in his *Opus de rebus Hispaniae mirabilibus* (Alcalá 1533), which reads as follows: *Caeterum genus illud sermonis Hispani initium habuisse credendum est, non ab Iberis, non a Sagis nec a Phoenicibus, quos in Hispaniam quondam venisse quidam*

scripsesunt, sed a prioris illis Hispaniae cultoribus quos linguarum diversitas a patriae sedibus exulare coegit.

3. "Los XL libros d'el compendio historial de las chronicas y universal historia de todos los reynos de España. . .," vol. 1 ("Printed in Antwerp by Christophor Plantino . . ." 1571), 81–93. See especially book 4, chapters 1–4.

4. There is a presentation of the ideas of Morales in an article by J. Saroïhandy, "Ohienart contra Garibay y Morales," *RIEV* 13 (1922): 450–55; see especially the portion of this article that includes texts authored by Scalígero, Merula, etc.

5. "IO. Marianae Hispani- and Socie. Iesv. Historiae de rebus Hispaniae libri XX" "Toleti, Typis Petri Roderici. 1592. . ." 8–9 (book 1, chapter 5, "De Hispanorum linguis").

6. "Del origen, y principio de la lengva castellana o romace que oi se usa en España Por el Doctor Bernardo Aldrete Canonigo en la Sancta Iglesia de Cordoua . . ." "En Roma acerca de Carlo Welietto en el año del Señor 1606," 227–232 (book 2, chapter 10, "Diuersas opiniones de la lengua antigua de España se excluien por inciertas, muestrasse que fueron muchas."). This is an important reference.

7. On these two works, see Julien Vinson, *Essa d'une bibliographie de la langue Basque I.* (Paris 1891); 46–47 (n. 5: Poza), 48–50 (no. 8: Echave).

8. His work *Notitia utriusque vasconiae* (Paris 1638) was translated into Spanish and published in *RIEV*; see especially 17–1926; 329–37, chapter 15.

9. *Annales del Reyno de Navarra* (Iruñea-Pamplona 1766). [Quote from Madariaga Orbea, *Anthology of Apologists and Detractors of the Basque Language* (Reno: Center for Basque Studies, 2006), 318. —ed.]

10. "Investigaciones históricas de las antiguedades del reyno" (vol. 10, 2)

11. "*Diccionario trilingüe castellano, bascuence, y latín*, vol. I (Donostia-San Sebastián 1853). The extensive introduction of this book that had appeared in 1745 is devoted to the various arguments. See especially parts two and three of the introduction (51–205). In addition to this work, Larramendi also wrote equally polemical works against scholar Gregorio Mayans y Siscar, and against various other scholars who were opposed to vascoiberismo, and who restated with varying degrees of scholarly acumen the arguments of Bernardo Alderete and others.

12. *La Cantabria. Disertación sobre el sitio y extensión que tuvo en tiempo de los romanos la región de los cántabros. . . . Discurso preliminar al tomo XXIV de la España Sagrada sobre la provincia Tarraconenses* (Madrid 1768).

13. Op. cit., 134–43 especially (at 17).

14. Cited by Masdeu, *Historia crítica de España, y de la cultura española* XVII (Madrid, 1797; 79–80; suppl. 12 art. 1 at 13).

15. As inferred from Masdeu's defense in the volume cited above, 79 and 96–97 (suppl. 12, art. 2 at 27), with Masdeu's reply (97–101).

16. *Diccionario geográfico-histórico de España por la Real Academia de la Historia*, section 1, 2 (Madrid 1802) 151–66 (see "Navarre"; article 13).

17. *Historia crítica de España* II (Madrid 1784), 62–84 (book 2 at 1–11).

18. Op. cit., 2 84–86 (book 2 at 12). See, in the same book, "Ilustración IX. Naturaleza, construcción y origen de la antiquísima Lengua Bascuence" (277–93).

19. *Apología de la lengua bascongada o ensayo critic filosófico de su perfección y antiguedad sobre todas las que se conocen: en respuesta a los reparos propuestos en el "Diccionario geográfico histórico de España, tomo segundo, palabra Nabarra* . . . (Madrid 1803), 193–273. This work was consulted by Humboldt prior to its publication, and was the object of criticism that is irrelevant to the present chapter.

20. *Alfabeto de la lengua primitiva de España, y explicación de sus más antiguos monumentos de inscripciones y medallas* . . . (Madrid 1806). He later wrote a book that was even more confusing.

21. Masdeu (op. cit., 17, 1) writes: "Spanish scholars have been working for more than two centuries to decipher the text on our ancient coins." Masdeu then acknowledges, among those who have dedicated themselves to such labors, first Juan Andrés Estrany and Antonio Agustín, and then, among his own contemporaries, Luis José Velázquez and Francisco Pérez Bayer, as conscientious writers. The paleographer Terreros had already insisted that the inscriptions had to be deciphered by using Basque: "Spanish paleography, which contains all of the known modalities of writing in Spain ever since its beginnings and foundation, and until the present time . . ." "En Madrid: En la Oficina de Joachín Ibarra . . . Año de 1758" (133–42).

22. *Catálogo de las lenguas de las naciones conocidas, y numeración, division y clases de éstas, según la diversidad de sus idiomas y dialectos*, vol. 5 (Madrid 1804), 134. The work consists of six volumes. Even before that work, in a monograph that has a long name, *Preeminencias . . . del convento de Santiago de Uclés, y límites . . . de las antiguas Diócesis, Urcitana y Segobricense*, etc. (Madrid 1801) in which he lashes out against the Masdeu's system of Spanish "Celtism" (which had been expounded by the latter in his *Historia* XX [Madrid 1805], 451–510), Hervás wrote: "In this work, I present practical evidence of the fact that the names of the primitive towns of Spain had Basque names." Masdeu op. cit., 457.

23. Op. cit., 5, 3–133 (in Italy).

24. Op. cit., 5, 141–83.

25. Op. cit., 9 (Madrid 1804). The study of the peoples that are mentioned is apportioned as follows: Persians, Phoenicians, Carthaginians: 112–54; Celts: 154–243; Ligurians: 244–67; Greeks: 267–89; Romans, etc. and ending with Arabs: 290–300. Finally, he offers a particularly insightful exposition of the Iberian peoples of France (301–38).

26. The Ligurians had also been referred to by Risco in his *España Sagrada* vol. 32 (Madrid 1878). 7–11.

27. Op. cit., 5 (especially 184–208). He first cites the opinions of Lucio Marineo Sículo, Merula, Garibay, Ambrosio de Morales Mariana, Ohienart, Alderete, Moret, Larramendi, and Mayans before inveighing against the notion (propagated by eighteenth century Celtists) that Basque is a Celtic language). From a strictly linguistic standpoint, Hervás is primarily a follower of Larramendi.

28. *Prüfung der Untersuchungen über die Urbewohner Hispanicus vermittelst der Vaskischen Sprache von Wilhelm Von Humboldt* (Berlin 1821) 8–192 (in 4). The French translation of this work by M. A. Marrast, *Recherches sur les habitants primitives de l'Espagne à l'aide de la langue basque* (Paris 1866) 27 and 195, was based upon the faulty Spanish translation by Ortega y Frías. Spanish readers can now consult the accurate translation of D. Telesforo de Aranzadi in *RIEV* 25 (1934): 475–520; 26 (1935), 44–92, and 499–552.

29. E. Phillipon is an original author who wrote a book in which he attempted to show that the Iberians spoke an Indo-European language. In this remarkable work, he offered criticism that seems eminently applicable to all Basque-Iberianists. See his *Les ibères; etude d'histoire, d'archéologie et de linguistique* (Paris 1909), 6–8 and 2–22 (mainly criticizing Humboldt). Ironically, Phillipon's criticism is also applicable to his own work.

30. In the introduction to *Proverbes basques recueillis par Arnauld Ohienart suivis des poésies basques du meme auteur*, 2nd ed. (Bourdeaux 1847) 5–25, E. Michel provides a number of interesting bibliographic references in terms of where such matters stood at that particular time.

31. *Monumenta linguae ibericae* (Berlin 1893) 24–25, etc. The entirety of chapter two of the prolegomena (20–31) repays close reading for the historical background it provides. In chapter four (57–142) Hübner systematized all of his deductions regarding the Iberian language, which were based on his analysis of epigraphs.

32. *Die Iberische Deklination*, Sitzungsberichte der Kais. Akademie der Wissenschaften in Vienna (Phil. Hist. Klasse), 157 2 Abhandl. (Vienna 1907).

33. A list of the major works of Schuchardt has already been provided by Julio de Urquijo in "Estado actual de los studios relatives a la lengua vasca," in *Primer congreso de studios vascos* (Bilbao 1919–1920), 405 and 424. See also the following previously published works: "Iberische Epigraphik. Die Bleitafel von Alcoy," in *RIEV* 14 (1923): 507–11, response to Gómez Moreno, or "Das Baskische linguistisch-ethnologische Problem," in *RIEV* 19 (1928): 613, response to Bosch, etc.

34. *Zur Kenntnis der vorrömischen Ortsnamen der Iberischer Halbinsel*, in Homage to Menéndez Pidal vol. 3 (Madrid 1925), 475–99.

35. García de Diego, during a presentation in which he responded to a previous presentation of Urquijo, on the occasion of his admission to the Academia Española: see *RIEV* 21 (1930): 275–80.

36. *Retroceso del vascuence* in *Atlantis* 16 (1941), 35–62. I am indebted to my friend Ángel Irigaray for additional data regarding this subject, as well as a number of critical observations, which I will not respond to here, since they are not relevant to present discussion. The data concern certain towns in Aragon where Basque must have been spoken not long ago (perhaps as recently as the sixteenth century), conclusions regarding both the date in which it can be assumed that modern Basque dialects existed, and the identification of subtypes of said dialects.

37. It should also be pointed out here that the "de-Basque-ization" of the provinces of Araba and Navarre had a pre-Roman phase during which the Celts firmly estab-

lished themselves in certain regions, as pointed out below on the basis of particular evidence.

38. *Retroceso del vascuence*, 46–47 (re Aragon). Irigaray has informed me that Axular (in his *Guero*), after enumerating the varieties of Basque in the seven provinces where it was spoken during his time (four in Spain and three in France) declared: ". . . eta berze ainitz lecutan." He was in all probability referring to the valleys of Aragon.

39. One factor that does not appear to have been taken into account is the "Romanization of the Visigothic period," during which time it was evident that one of the reasons that the Basque language was better preserved in the north was that those who spoke it there never fell under the rule of the Gothic kings.

40. Strabo, *The Geography of Strabo*, translated by Horace Leonard Jones (Cambridge: Harvard University Press, 1919), vol. 2, book 3, chapter 3.

41. See the article "Cantabri" by Hübner in *RE* 3 2 (Stuttgart 1899), columns 1491–1494.

42. 149 s. 2, 934 (article *Cantibri et vardulli*), where there is a reference to English inscriptions. 149 7, 435, 1031, etc.: see index on page 337.

43. Tacitus *Hist.* 4 33, 3.

44. Zacarías García Villada *Historia ecclesiástica de España* I, 2nd parte (Madrid 1929), 89, where there is a reference to a Greco-Egyptian inscription at Gebel-el-Tuj that reveals the existence there, in the fourth century, of a garrison in which there were Asturian soldiers. On the participation of Asturian troops in the campaigns of Trajan, see M. Rostovtzeff *Historia social y económica del Imperio romano*, vol. I (Madrid 1937) 473 (note 27 of chapter 6).

45. These Celtic settlements apparently were important towns within the provinces of Araba and Navarre, such as Contrasta (in Araba) *149* 2; 2950–2957; Gastiain (Navarre) *149* 2 2970–2971, S. 5827–5831; Iruña (Araba) *149* 2 2935, etc. The tombstone of Marañon (Navarre) is an important piece of evidence in this respect (See J. de Altadill, *Navarra* I, in *Geografía general del país vasco-navarro* [Barcelona no year]) 671. It seems possible that these Romanized Celts, whose rustic lifestyle resembled that of modern Basques, were used as guards in the borderlands between the zones occupied by Romans and the territories of the Vasconic tribes. Toponyms such as the Deba (Deva) River in Gipuzkoa indicate an ancient Celtic influence in those regions.

46. Among the Autrigonians, *Deobriga* and *Uironias* = Briviesca were important names (Ptoltemy 2 6, 52). In addition, one must consider the archeological evidence.

47. *Forum Gallorum* is del iter *a Caesarea Augusta Benearno* de Antonino: *Discursos leídos ante la Real Academia de la Historia en la recepción pública de D. Eduardo Saavedra el día 28 de diciembre de 1862* (Madrid 1862), 78; *Itineraria Romana*, ed. Cuntz (Leipzig 1929), 69 (452).

48. G. Bähr, *El vasco y el camítico* in RIEV 25 (1934): 240–44 (this is a summary of an article written by Ernst Zyhlars).

49. *The Racial History of Man* (New York 1923), 161.

50. *La race, les races, mise au point d'Ethnologie somatique* (Paris 1933), 252 and (by the same author) *L'ethnie francaise* (Paris 1935), 125–37. Montandon's contention (in the latter work [126]) that in both anthropological and ethnological terms, the French Basques are more distinctive than the Spanish Basques is the exact opposite of the truth.

51. Spanish readers will greatly benefit from consulting the article of A. M. Tallgren, "Sobre el método de la arqueología prehistoric," *Altantis* 16 (1941): 68–79. This article contains a number of interesting observations regarding this issue—observations that also apply to Spain.

52. C. C. Uhlenbeck, "De la possibilité d'un parente entre le basque et les langues caucasiques," *RIEV* 15 (1924): 565–88. R. Lafon, "Basque el langue kartvèles. A propos des post-positions basques formées au moyen de –gan-," *RIEV* 24 (1933): 150–75.

53. See the detailed classification of Caucasian languages in R. Bleichsteiner, "Die Kaukasische Sprachgruppe" in *Anthropos* 32 (1937): 61–74.

54. Strabo, *The Geography of Strabo*, translated by Horace Leonard Jones (Cambridge: Harvard University Press, 1919), vol. 1, book 1, chapter 3, paragraph 21.

55. Stephanus de urbibus quem primus Thomas de Pinedo Lusitanus Latii jure donabat, v. observationibus scrtinio variarum linguarum, ac precipue Hebraicae, Phoniciae, Graecae & Latinae detectis illustrabat, (Amstelodami: Typis Jacbi de Jonge, 1678), 319. Original Latin, "Sed neutrum affirmari potest. Hae enim res excedunt ingenii humani aciem nec opus est ad commendandam Hispaniam antiquitatibus, ipsa per se satis commendatur." [Translation courtesy of Dr. Xabier Irujo –ed.]

CHAPTER 5. Historical-Cultural Problems of the Basque Language

1. "Caractère de la grammaire basque" in *RIEV* 2 (1908): 505–34. See also G. Lacombe and R. Lafon, "Indo-européen, basque et ibère" in *Germanen und Indogermanen . . . Festschrift für Herman Hirt*, vol. 2 (Heidelberg, 1936), 109–23.

2. "Vorlateinische indogermanische Anklange im Baskischen," *Anthropos* 35–36 (1941–1942): 202–07.

3. J. Caro Baroja, *Materiales para una historia de la lengua vasca en su relación con la latina* (Salamanca, 1945).

4. "Suffixes du basque servant à la dérivation des mots," *RIEV* 3 (1909): 1–16, 192–225, 401–30.

5. "La Linguistique" (Paris 1887), 156–72.

6. Del primero, "La langue basque et les idiomes de l'Oural . . . second fascicule" (Montagne 1866), 125–31.

7. R. Goutmann, "Lelo," *RIEV* 4 (1910): 305–18; see also, by the same author: "Essai d'un petit vocabulaire Basque-Ugro-Finnic," *RIEV* 7 (1913): 571–74. L. L. Bonaparte had previously written, *Langue basque et langues finnoises* (London, 1862), in which he claimed to have collected 250 examples.

8. "Finnisch und Baskisch," *RIEV* 5 (1911): 96; from "RB, 7, 571 ff.," *RIEV* 8 (1914): 169–70.

9. "Basque et ouralo-altaïque," *RIEV* 6 (1912): 412–14.

10. "La langue basque et les langues ouralo altaïques," *RIEV* 8 (1914–1917): 282–323.

11. Texts in Vinson, "Essai d'une bibliographie de la langue basque," vol. 2 (Paris1898), 711–12 (no. 1172).

12. "Delle relazioni tra il vasco e l'egizio" in "Archivio glottologico italiano. Supplementi periodici. Serie gen., 2, 15–96 (c.f. Vinson, "Essai . . ." cit., 2 [Paris 1898], 746).

13. "Zur methodischen Erforschung der Sprachverwandtschaft (Nubisch und Baskisch)," *RIEV* 6 (1912): 267–81.

14. "Baskisch-Hamitische Wortvergleichungen," *RIEV* (1913): 289–339.

15. "Zur angeblichen Vorwandtschaft des Baskischen mit Afrikanischen Sprachen," *Frühistorische Zeitschrift* 13(1932): 69–77; review of G. Bähr, "Basque and Hamitic," *RIEV* 25 (1934): 240–44 (in *Anthropos* 38 [1933]: 788–89.

16. "Objektive Kriterien in der Ethnologie" in *Korrespondenz Blatt der Deutschen Gesellschaft für Anthropologie, Ethnologie and Urgeschichte*, (1911), 71–75.

17. *The Racial History of Man* (New York 1923), 161.

18. *Le race, les races, mise au point d'Ethnologie somatique* (Paris 1933), 252; *L'ethnie française* (Paris 1935), 125–37.

19. *El Gerundense y la España primitiva* (Madrid 1879), 7–75.

20. *Literatur Blatt für Germanische und Romanische Philologie*, 13 (1892), col. 426 (see also note 33).

21. (Bologna, 1925), 163, 4th.

22. *Das Baskische und der vorderasiatischmitteländische Völker und kulturkreis"* (Breslau 1909), 52

23. *RIEV* 11 (1920): 62–66.

24. "Le Basque et les langues caucasiques," *RIEV* 3 (1909): 520; "Le basque el les langues caucasiques, 2," *RIEV* 4 (1910): 121–24.

25. "De la possibilité d'un parenté entre le basque et les langues caucasiques," *RIEV* 15 (1924): 565–88.

26. "Einführung in das Studium der kaukasischen Spruchen" (Leipzig 1928), 24–28.

27. "Beiträge zur kaukasischen und sibirischen Srachwissenschaft 4. Das Tschuktschische (Leipzig 1941), 42–51.

28. 11, 2, 16 (499).

29. 11, 4, 6, (502).

30. "Die kaukasische Sprachgruppe," *Anthropos* 32 (1937): 74.

31. "Introduction à la grammaire comparé des langues caucasiennes du Nord" (Paris 1933), 123–24. Similar reflections, but with no supporting evidence, may be found in an article by the same author: "Langues caucasiennes et basque" in *Germanen und Indogermanen*, op. cit., 2, 183–98.

32. Trombetti, op. cit., 157–59.

33. "Ueber den passive Character des Transitivs in den Kaukasischen Sprachen" in *Sitzungsberichte der Phil. Hist. Classes der Kais. Akad. Der Wissenschaften*" (Vienna 1896).

34. Trombetti, op. cit., 108–49.

35. Uhlenbeck, "De la possibilité . . . , 581.

36. It is believed that in names such as "Calagurris" there is an element that in Basque would have the meaning of height (a variant of which is "gara"). Regarding other compound names containing this component, see A. Dauzat, "*Cala* dans la toponymie gauloise et espagnole" in *Zeitschrift für Ortsnamenforschung*, vol. 2 (1926–1927), 216–21.

37. Grundriss der Sprachwissenschaft," 3, 2 (Vienna 1885), 1–47 (see especially page 18).

38. *La langue basque possède-t-ell oui ou non, un verbe transitif?* (Bordeaux 1890), 15 pages, in 8th.

39. "Baskische Studien I. Ueber die Entstehung der Bezugsformen des baskischen zeitworts" in "*Denkschriften der kaiserlichen Akademie der Wissenschaften in Wien, phil. Histo. Classe* 43, 3 (1893): 82, 4th. By the same author: "Baskische Konjugation," *RIEV* 10 (1919): 157–63.

40. "Les theories nouvelles sur le verbe basque," *Revue de Linguistique* 27 (1894): 95–111.

41. "Quelques reflexions sur le verbe simple dans la conjugaison basque," *RIEV* 5 (1911): especially 472–93.

42. "Puntos obscuros de la conjugación vascongada," *RIEV* 10 (1919): 83–97.

43. "Quelques observations sur la passivité du verbe basque," *RIEV* 21 (1931): 1–14.

44. Gavel, op. cit., 1–2.

45. Gavel, op. cit., 3–4.

46. Uhlenbeck, "Le caractère passif du verbe transitif ou du verbe d'action dans certaines langues de l'Amérique du Nord," *RIEV* 13 (1922): 399–419.

47. *Die Sprachfamilien und Spruchenkreise der Erde* (Heidelberg 1926), 124–42.

48. See, for example the article by Schuchardt that is also titled (like the article cited in note 13 above) "Zur methodischen Erforschung der Sprachverwandtschaft," *RIEV* 8 (1914–1917): 389–96.

49. Bosch-Gimpera, "Los pueblos primitivos de España," *Revista de Occidente* 3, no. 26 (1925): 178; by the same author, "Etnología de la península ibérica," 124–42.

50. Aranzadi, Barandiarán, and Eguren conducted research on the Basque area, while Pericot systematically organized what was known about both the Basque and Catalan areas in *La civilización megalítica catalana y la cultura pirenaica* (Barcelona 1925). The latest work by the same teacher (and personal friend of mine) is "Exploraciones dolménicas en el Ampurdán," *Ampurias* 5 (1943): 5–37.

51. M. Almagro, "Exploración de los primeros sepulcros megalíticos aragoneses" in *Actas y Memorias de la Sociedad Española de Antropología* 13 (1934): 271–79.

52. *El hombre primitivo en el país vasco* (Donostia-San Sebastián 1934), 72. [Selections from this book can be found in English in *Selected Writings of José Miguel de Barandiarán: Basque Prehistory and Ethnography* (Reno: Center for Basque Studies, 2007), 135–87. —ed.]

53. Barandiarán, op. cit., 77–78.

54. Diodorus, 5, 33.

55. "Negerafrika und Nordostafrika" in *Die Grosse Völkerkunde*, de Bernatzik, vol. I (Leipzig 1939), 266–67.

CHAPTER 6. **On the Basque Lexicon**

1. *Tesoro de la lengua castellana o española* (Treasury of the Castilian or Spanish Language), 1611; and *Diccionario de autoridades* (Dictionary of Authorities), 1726 and 1739. The latter was the first dictionary by the Real Academia Española (Royal Spanish Academy) and thus is the forerunner of the modern authoritative *Diccionario de la lengua Española* (Dictionary of the Spanish Language).

2. Arturo Campión, "Sobre el Nuevo bautizo del país basko (el nombre Euzkadi)," *RIEV* (1907): 148–53.

3. Works such as those of J. M. de Barandiarán, *El hombre primitivo en el País Vasco* (Zarautz 1934), *Mitología vasca* (Madrid 1960), and others are examples of what I am talking about.

4. *Diccionario vasco-español-francés. Dictionnaire basque-espagnol-francais.* 2 vols. (Bilbao-Tours 1905–1906).

5. *Diccionario trilingüe castellano, bascuence y latín.* 2 volumes. (Donostia-San Sebastián, 1853).

6. In addition to being used in the Lord's Prayer, it is also documented in other texts. For example, "Erreñuetaco usanza" is used in *Confesioco eta Comunioco Sacramentuetan gañean esacusaldiac, . . ."* de Juan Bautista Aguirre (Tolosa 1823), 260.

7. The following appears on the very cover of the previously cited work of Aguirre: *Iruñeco gure Apaiz naguriarencta cuengo Corregidorearen baimenaguerin . . ."* (To our father from Iruñea, with the permission of the *Corregidor*.)

8. The use of *mayçter* is well attested in a text dating back to 1167, where the word is used to mean "head shepherd." See L. Michelena, *Textos arcaicos vascos* (Madrid, 1964), 47–48. This word appears to be a direct derivation of *magister*.

9. In reality, these Basque terms are related to the concept of "vessel," which was used by those who wrote about seafaring activities.

10. There are many other words in Basque nautical vocabulary. A "bilander" is a *cargontzia* or simply a *balandra* (i.e., the exact same word used in Spanish [*navis vectoria* in Latin]). A "carrack" is an *ontzizarra* (*magae molis navis* in Latin). Larramendi believes that the term is based on the word *chalupa*, which he thinks is of Basque origin. He does not include the words *galizabra* or *felibote*. He indicates that the Spanish *pinaza* is also used in Basque, but provides the alternatives of *cymba* and *scapha*. *Patache* ("a tender attending a squadron") is itself a Basque word (derived from *patachea*) and its Latin equivalent is *modicus gaulus*). *Pingue* is the same in Spanish and Basque, and is equivalent to the Latin *navis operaria*. The Basque for *polacre* is *oncí mota*. The words *saebia* and *tartana* are the same in both Spanish and Basque (save for the addition of an accent on the final "a" in the latter word—*tartaná*—in Basque).

11. *Surtarius* has also been documented in the writings of Andramendi. Michelena, op. cit., 159.

12. Larramendi shows that many other different kinds of cloth were known in his time. In the following list, the Spanish word is followed by the Basque: *barragana* (or *beatilla*, both terms referring to a kind of fine linen) was either *meatilla* or *bentillamisa*. *Bombasí* (fustian) was *inaurteá*, and *brabanite* was *auqui brabantiarra* or *Brabanteco auquia*. *Bretaña* was *auqui bretañarra*, *alemanisco* ("Germanic") was *Alemaniaco zamanac*, and *chamelote* ("camlet") was *txamelote* or *gameleula*.

CHAPTER 7. The Basque Country and Dialectology

1. J. Vinson, *Essai d'une bibliographie de la langue basque*, vol. 1 (Paris 1891), 320–22 (no. 330).

2. J. Vinson, op. cit., 1, 324–25 (numbers 343b–343c).

3. A. Schulten, *Iberische Landeskunde. Geographie des Antiken Spanien*, vol. 1 (Strasbourg 1955), vol. 2 (Strasbourg 1957). Antonio Tovar has assumed responsibility for continuing the Spanish edition of this work.

4. In an essay regarding aspects of witchcraft published in 1618, Lope Martínez de Isasti wrote that Gipuzkoans "did not trust French and Navarrese foreigners (in other words, eastern Basques): *Anuario de Eusko Folklore* 11 (1933): 145.

5. *Gueroco guero* (Bayonne 1864), 20 and reprinted in Joannes d'Etcheberri, *Obras vascongadas* (Julio de Urquijo's edition; Paris 1907), 52 (special edition).

6. Axular, *Gueroco guero*, 21; Etcheberri, op. cit., 52.

7. Etcheberri, op. cit., 5: ". . . *halla nola Alaba herriac, eta Bizcayac Gaztellarequin duten mugaquidetasun hurbila dela causa baitituzte hainitz hitz cidaratic; Çuberoarrec bere hauço Biarnessetaric, edo Gaiscoinetaric.*"

8. Etcheberri, op. cit., 54.

9. Etcheberri, op. cit., 318.

10. In *El imposible vencido*, which was published in 1729, the arguments presented are very sketchy. See the edition of Donostia-San Sebastián (sons of Ignacio Ramón Baroja, 1886), 6.

11. *Corografía o descripción general de la muy noble y muy leal provincia de Guipúzcoa* (Barcelona 1882), 262–270. See the current edition of I. Tellechea Idígoras (Donostia-San Sebastián 1969), 300–1.

12. These are enumerated in the Vinson's *Essai* . . . , 1, 308–55.

13. J. Vinson, *Les basques et le pays basque* (Paris 1883), 67; A. Campión, "La langue basque" in *La tradition au pays basque* (Paris 1899), 415–17. Also by Campión, "La lengua baska," in the general reference work, *Geografía general del país vasconavarro* (Barcelona, no year), 196–98.

14. High Southern Navarrese is reflected in the Christian doctrine drafted by Juan de Beriain, Abbot of Uterga, which was published in Iruñea-Pamplona in 1626, a work that had been cited by Larramendi (*Corografía*, 267). Although Vinson did not cite this work in the relevant sections of his *Essai* . . . (64–65, no. 13 and 539–41, no 12 bis), he did cite therein another work by the same author, the *Tratado de cómo se ha de oyr missa* (Iruñea-Pamplona 1621). The foremost expert on the abbot and his work is Ángel Irigaray, author of *El tratado de oír misa euskérico de Beriayn, abad de Uterga*, in *Fontes Linguae Vasconum* 1, no. 2 (1969): 291–94.

15. Larramendi, *Corografía*, 246–47.

16. *Noticias de las dos Vasconias*, translated by P. Gorosterratzu (Donostia-San Sebastián 1929), 59.

17. This is something that had been fairly well determined at the time of the publication of *La Cantabria* by P. Flórez (Madrid 1768), as well by authors such as Aureliano Fernández Guerra, in work also titled *La Cantabria* (Madrid 1878). Later works provided new data in this regard. See especially Adolfo Schulten, *Los cántabros y astures y su Guerra con Roma* (Madrid 1943); Julio Caro Baroja, *Los pueblos del Norte de la península Iberica* (Madrid 1943).

18. Arturo Campión, *Euskariana (décima serie) Segunda parte, primer volumen* (Iruñea-Pamplona, no year), 52

19. Campión, *Euskariana* . . . , 69.

20. In this connection, the importance of reexamining the significance of rivers in relation to the ancient divisions should be noted.

21. The *Notitia dignitatum* contains the following text: "*In Provincia Novempopulana tribunus cohortis Novempopulanae Lapurdo.*" Dubarat, *Le missel de Bayonne de 1543* (Pau-París-Toulouse 1901), 3.

22. Pliny, N.H. (19), 108: "vallis Subola" in Fredegario 78. Oihenart, op. cit., 301–02; *España Sagrada* 32 (Madrid, 1878): 419.

23. Nevertheless, the name of *Baja Navarra* must still be seen as being of modern origin.

24. The study of Aquitainian was greatly facilitated by the important work of A. Luchaire, who wrote two splendid monographs: *Les origins linguistiques*

de l'Aquitaine (Paris 1877) and *Etudes sure les idioms pyrénéens de la region française* (Paris 1879). Others among us have followed in his footsteps. See the recent summary of Luis Michelena, *De onomástica aquitana* (Zaragoza 1954).

25. Ptolemy, 2, 6, 50: See the works cited in paper 16, as well as previous works, such as that of P. Bosch Gimpera, *Etnología de la peninsula Ibérica* (Barcelona 1932) and, especially, the article by Claudio Sánchez Albornoz, "Divisiones tribales y administrativas del solar del reino de Asturias en la época romana" in *Boletín de la Real Academia de la Historia* 95 (1928): 315–95.

26. Caesar, *Bell. Gall.*, 3, 20–24. Regarding this subject, see Raymond Lizop, *Le Comminges et le Couserans avant l'occupation romaine* (Toulouse 1931).

27. I have discussed the theory of lineages elsewhere, and have devoted to this subject part of a course that I taught in Coimbra.

28. See texts in Julio Caro Baroja, *Los pueblos del Norte* (82–83).

29. Schulten, *Los cántabros*, 49–50, etc.; Antonio Tovar, *Cantabria prerromana o lo que la lingüística nos enseña sobre los antiguos cántabros* (Madrid 1955), 12–33.

30. Regarding *thieldo*: Pliny, *Natural History*, book 8; and *arrugia*, ibid, book 38.

31. At first glance, one gets the impression that the Cantabrians were Romanized to a greater extent than the Asturians, and that the latter conserved more of the ancient Basque substratum. Names such as those of the *Gigurri* tribe (Schulten, *Los cántabros*, 95), and the *Arronidaeci* (c. 1, a. 2, 2679) as well as some given names (*Neconi*, c. 1, a. 2, 5718, *Andoto*, etc.) suggest a relationship with Basque similar to that of Aquitainian.

32. I discuss all of these issues, on the basis of trustworthy data, in a forthcoming study of the ancient territory of Alava. For now, see Julio Caro Baroja, *Los pueblos del Norte* (45). For the Aquitainians, see Raymond Lizop, *Les Convenae et les Consorani* (Toulouse-Paris 1931), 1–11, etc.

33. Julio Caro Baroja, *Estudios mogrebíes* (Madrid 1957).

34. J. Sacaze. *Inscriptions antiques des Pyrénées* (Toulouse 1892), 539–41 (number 468).

35. The Basque word *maister* is derived from the Latin *magister*.

36. A study of the use of the word can be found in Alfred Jacobs' appendix to the French translation of Guizot, *Histoire des francs. Grégoire de Tours et Frédégaire*, vol. 2 (Paris 1861), 287–311.

37. See note 21.

38. *España Sagrada* 32: 315–16, 414. The form *Runcale* was used in a song transcribed by Francisque Michel in *Le Pays Basque* (Paris 1857), 494.

39. He has already published a number of highly interesting fragments of this study. See "Fuegos de la merindad de las Montañas en 1350" in *Príncipe de Viana*, 15 (1954), 251–94.

For the boundaries of the kingdom of Navarre, see Moret, *Annales del reyno de Navarra*, 1 (Iruñea-Pamplona, 1766), 139–43. The appendix of that work is presented by way of illustration, and is based on data provided by the *Historic Geographical Dictionary of Spain* of the *Academia de la Historia* (in 2 volumes; Madrid 1802), as well as on the list of valleys and divisions coinciding with jurisdictional areas (*partidos*) and counties (*merindades*). He indicated those that represented administrative entities with an asterisk.

40. A series of writings pertaining to the Bishopric of Baiona that date back to the eleventh and twelfth centuries, but which were presented as being of earlier provenance, refer to a number of the Navarre valleys in the coastal region of the territory as important entities in terms of ecclesiastical territorial divisions. In the Call of Arsio, a bishop who served at the end of the tenth century, the text *Bast[a]ant[insium vallis, usque in medio portu Be[l]ti"* and *"[v]allis quae dicitur Lerin* (Dubarat, *Le missel de Bayonne* . . . , 31). The names *Bastan* and *Lerin* also appear in a bull attributed to Pascual II, dated 1106 (Dubarat, op. cit., 32). In a bull of Celestine III, dated November 1194, and which is considered authentic, one does not see the division of the five *villas*, but rather *Vallem que dicitur Lesseca* (i.e., the *villa* of Lesaca) (Dubarat, op. cit., 32). Other names of known Navarrese valleys, such as Larraun (*Larraum*) appear to be mingled with the names of simple towns (Aranatz, Labaien, Leitza, Areso, Ezkurra, etc.) in a document attributed to Sancho the Great (Dubarat, op. cit., 33). During the thirteenth century, the High Navarrese oceanic valleys of the diocese of Baiona constitute three Archpriest's parishes: (1) the Bortziriak or five towns (Bera, Lesaka, Etxalar, Arantza, and Igantzi); (2) Lerin (including the Bertiz and Lower Basaburua valleys); and (3) the Baztan valley (Dubarat, op. cit., 37).

41. I am currently preparing a study of the grille of San Millán and will thus refrain from further comment here.

42. It can rightly be said that Schuchardt made his debut as a Bascologist with the paper he wrote that demonstrated this, published in 1887 in the *Zeitschrift für romanische Philologie*, which I do not currently have at my disposal.

43. Justo Gárate, "Sufijos locativos," *RIEV* 21 (1930): 442–48.

44. Joannes d'Etcheberri, op. cit., 63.

45. Francisque Michel, *Le Pays Basque*, 265.

46. It would be useful to review all of the supposed loan words from Basque to Latin and other languages that are cited in Larramendi's famous *Diccionario*, since in my view they shed a bright light indeed on certain facts related to the passing of Latin words into Basque, a subject that has not been sufficiently studied.

CHAPTER 8. **The Historical Basis of a "Traditional" Economy**

1. Theories on the supposed equivalence between prehistoric peoples, current primitive peoples, and *campesinos* (i.e., "survivors," who some researchers even perceive as being childlike) are highly problematic. After such theories were employed by Frazer and other authors of his time in some of their research, attempts have been made to identify "a typical rural mentality." One writer involved in such an enterprise is E.K.L. Francis. See his article, "The personality type of the peasant according to Hesiod's Works and Days" in *Rural Sociology* 10 (1945): 275–95. I am not a big believer in

such ideas. For a discussion of these theories, see Robert Redfield, *The Primitive World and its Transformations* (Ithaca 1957), 26–53.

A summary of discussions of what has been called "rural society" have been summarized, with the inclusion of a useful bibliography, in Ake Hultzkrantz's valuable book (which constitutes the first volume of the *International Dictionary of Regional European Ethnology and Folklore*), *General Ethnological Concepts* (Copenhagen 1960), 206–7. I personally have the same reservations as Erizon and other Swedish authors regarding Redfield and other North American sociologists. More recently, an edited collection has been published (which includes a preface by G. M. Foster) that addresses the question of the life of *campesinos* from an anthropological point of view.

2. We will soon see how the period 1680–1750 is critically important in terms of internal Spanish history, in light of the wealth of research that has been conducted on social and rural history. For now, it will suffice to cite Jovellanos regarding the growth of agriculture during the War of the Spanish Succession in *Informe en el expediente de la Ley agraria*, *Obras* (B.A.E., L.), 81, a.

3. The introduction of crops from America and other areas is something that occurred continually from the end of the sixteenth to the beginning of the nineteenth century.

4. The oldest references, cited by V. Dubarat in *Le missel de Bayonne de 1543* (Pau-Paris-Toulouse 1901) are *The bull of Celestine III* (November 5, 1194), which includes, as part of the diocese of Bayonne, the *"Vallem que dicitur Lesseca"* (op. cit., 32, note 4) and the lists of the arch priest's parish that include the five villas (op. cit., 37).

5. The concession of the market to Lesaka dates from 1499. There was a market day twice a month, as well as two annual fairs that lasted a couple of weeks each. Privileges were granted in 1402 for both towns. See José de Yanguas y Miranda, *Diccionario de antigüedades del reino de Navarra*, vol. 2 (Iruñea-Pamplona 1840), 195–200.

6. Florencio Idoate, "El escudo de cinco villas" in *Rincones de la Historia de Navarra*, vol. 3 (Iruñea-Pamplona 1840), 251–56.

7. Regarding lineages, see Idoate, op. cit., 254–56; Yanguas and Miranda, op. cit., *Adiciones* . . . (Iruñea-Pamplona 1843), 16–17 ("Alzate"), 379 (Zabaleta). See also Jean de Jaurgain, *Chateaux basques. Urtubie* (Bayonne 1896) and Julio Caro Baroja, *Linajes y bandos* in *Vasconiana* (Madrid 1957), 15–61.

8. On October 25, 1749, the need for producing a copy of the census of 1366 was announced. This copy exists today in the Archives of Navarre, and is titled *Libro de fuegos de todo el Reyno de Navarra del año 1366*. Information regarding the five towns (between Etxarri-Aranatz (Echarri-Aranaz) and Baztan) may be found in folios "120 vto." And 164 rb. of the volume containing data regarding the "*Merindad* of Iruñea-Pamplona." In the census of *hidalgos*, population figures for the towns of Bera, Etxalar, and Igantzi are provided, while Lesaka is cited as having no population at all and Aranatz is referred to without being named. Here is the text:

"In the five towns. In the town of Lesaka, there is no one, because no hidalgo resides there. In Bera: Johan Martiniz, Lord of Alzate, with four florins. Martin García Muniz, with II florins. He lives in King's House and is actually quite poor.

Martin Ivanies Daguire, with two and a half florins. Michelco, son of Chariquo, with one and a half florins. Miquelez Vetea, with two and a half florins.

In Etxalar: Miguel Yvaines, with two and a half florins. Pedro Martiniz Tesorr, with two and a half florins.

In Igantzi: Johan Lopiz, lord of Zavaletta, with four florins. Johan Dirigoien, with two and a half florins. Martín Ferandiz, with two and a half florins. *Nichil*, because we haven't been able to find goods (*). Joahn de Echallarr, one and a half florins. Joahn Dirisarri, with two florins.

There are twelve households that each have two and a half florins, for a total of thirty florins.

As regards the other text, one can see in the index that the data for the "land of Lesaga" also refers to Bera (**). Here are the list of inhabitants "in the land of Lasaga":

Primo Joahn ochoa Dal [zaiaga] (Alcayaga?)	Johan Sanz de Zallain.	Petri Molso
Vettri Martiniz Dalzaiaga	Ochanda de Zalain.	Gracia Ladona de Ururre
Michelco de Goienechea [Dalzaiaga.	Petri Barrundina.	Johan Yvaines de Yzuza.
	Machin Sillarr.	Miguel Arizpellza.
Johanet Verrontrana.	Machin Jararte.	Johan Darrupe.
Martin Miguel de Picave.	Sancho Zamarr.	Musilla de Zavalletta.
Sancho Duarte Peilleitero.	Domingo el Pelegero.	Martín Miguel.
Musilla el Ferrero.	La Casa de Yriartecoa.	Ochotte el Maestro.
García Zapattero.	Miguel de Zugarramendi.	Miguel Sanz.
Martin de Velzaiaga.	(Zurgarramurdi?)	Guizona.
Miguel de Larrrauri.	Joahn Sanz de Iriverri.	Petri Dirivarrena.
Johanico./ (fol. 164 vto.)	Domicu Periz.	Chant Chipia.
Sant Decheverria.	Miguel Errandoiz.	Miguel el Chico.
Ochoa Verridi.	Pascoal de Francia	Sancho de Sarazuría.
Joahn Miguel de Elizalde.	Gasttea Dalzaiaga.	Machin el Zapattero.
Simeno de Veroan.	Sanchotte de Zallain.	Alvira Periz.
Miquel Capero.	García Azeariz de Zalain	Johanet de Zaldarraga.

Total of 52 households

(*) "*Nichil*" is repeated in the margin.
(**) Letter V.

9. The decrease in the number of inhabitants of Navarre and the harshness of life for farm laborers there are both consistently reflected in the documents of the era. Thus, in the census of 1427, in a counting of the residents of "Narvart et Dipullatze" (fol. 237 r.), we find the following:

Upon being asked, the foregoing inhabitants have indicated that they are residents of Bidasoa, and that, when they go to mountain pasturages, there is sufficient pasturage to feed three or four pigs or as many as there are in the neighborhood, but not those brought by others.

Asked how they support themselves, they said that, by the grace of God, they maintain enough bread for half of the year and *pomade* for the year and they live with their few cattle and the little that they have.

Asked about the decrease in the land of their place of residence, they said this decrease is due to the loss of six houses there because of the deaths of their inhabitants, during the past twenty-five to thirty years.

And they said that they pay quarterly six *Libras* and twelve *sueldos*. It appears that the people here are functioning on the bare minimum of resources that are available.

This questioning relative to hard times, ways of living, and decline are repeated insistently. Without doubt those questioned sought to pay the least amount to the tax collector, but even beyond possible dissimulation there remains a dramatic reality. This decline led to the complete abandonment of some small villages. The plague took over the entire country. There were epidemics in Navarre, according to Yanguas y Mirando, *Diccionario . . .*, vol. 2, 714–16, in 1348, 1362, 1380–1383, 1401, 1411, 1422, 1423, 1434, 1435, 1508 . . . On earlier outbreaks see Idoate "Peste y cólera morbo en Pamplona," in *Rincones de la historia de Navarra*, vol. 3, 703–8.

10. Idoate, *El escudo de cinco villas*, op. cit., 3, 254–55. But another work written by this outstanding scholar, *Notas para el estudio de la economía Navarra y su contribución a la real hacienda (1500–1650)* (Iruñea-Pamplona 1960), 3, includes a summary of figures for 1637, which indicates that Lesaka has 237 inhabitants and Bera only 119.

11. See P. Boissonnade, *Histoire de la reunion de la Navarre à la Castille* (Paris 1893), 8, note 1. Where he writes "inhabitants," it is "residents" that is meant.

12. Within the framework of discussion of peace in the Pyrenees, there was a great deal of discussion regarding this border. Pierre de Marca, who defended the French point of view, attempted to demonstrate (as he had tried to do in previous works) that the entire basin of the Bidasoa belonged to the ancient Gauls. For a discussion of this issue, see Manuel Risco, *España Sagrada* 32 (1878): 100–265.

13. From the Archive of Navarre: "Villa de Bera. Value of the potential sale of the houses of the town of Bera, determined by means of an order of the Tribunal dated November 10, 1612, via the testimony of Simon de Asco." This note is in a folder that contains information pertaining to the other five towns. In 1612, 179 houses were recorded. Yet the information of 1607 regarding houses was more specific.

14. A house in the neighborhood of Altzate (Alzate) bears the following inscription: In the name of our lord and savior Jesus Christ. In faithful service to his majesty, this town was burned on the 16th of july of the year 1638. In the name of God. On another, higher beam, the following inscription was found: This house was built in the year 1641. A house in Illekueta (Illecueta) bears the inscription seen in figure 1.

15. Inventory of the Archives of the Kingdom of Navarre, Volume 4: Statistics: file 2, folder 7. Census of residents and temporary inhabitants of the town of Bera within the *merindad* of Pamplona (1645). It gives a figure of no more than 131 houses in all of the towns, with 59 residents in Bera, 12 in Zalain [today a neighborhood of Bera], and 49 in the remaining towns. In folder 19 of the same file, there are figures pertaining to another census that was taken on September 25, 1646, and which lists 141 *vecinos* and 73 *moradores*. Included in the number of houses and "farm houses" are 65 burned houses The total number of houses listed is 212, along with two palaces: Aguirre (no. 27) and Alzate (no. 145). "It was evident that the Palace of Alçate had been burned and destroyed. An inhabitant lives there in a small hut." The effects of fire were evident in all of the houses.

16. In file 4, folder 16, there is another census for Bera, dated 1678. In 1726, yet another census was completed, and which can be found in file 5, folder 11.

17. Families greatly prospered in Navarre throughout the eighteenth century.

18. *Diccionario geográfico-histórico de España por la Real Academia de la Historia. Sección1*, 2 (Madrid 1828), 440, a.

19. Sebastián de Miñano, *Diccionario geográfico-estadístico de España y Portugal*, vol. 9 (Madrid 1828), 291, a.

20. Pascual Madoz, *Diccionario geográfico-estadístico histórico de España y sus posesiones de Ultramar*, vol. 15 (Madrid 1849), 668, b.

21. Julio de Altadill, *Provincia de Navarra*, vol. 2 (in *Geografía general del país vasco-navarro*. Barcelona, [no year]), 297. An increase in both emigration (as a consequence of the war in Cuba and the Philippines) and in fugitives and deserters (as a consequence of the war in Africa) were evident at the beginning of the twentieth century.

22. Luis Amorena y Blasco, *Síntesis geográfico estadística de la provincia de Navarra* (Iruñea-Pamplona 1923), 244.

23. See the article "Vera" in the *Enciclopedia universal ilustrada europeo-americana* 62 (Madrid-Barcelona-Bilbao 1929), 1338, b, which indicates that the census of 1910 assigned the town a population of 2,600, and that the census of 1920 assigned it the figure indicated in the text above.

24. After the war of 1936, there was a marked drop in population. On the other hand, the increases from 1960 onward were quite sharp—but not in the rural population.

25. Yanguas and Miranda, *Diccionario...*, cit. 2, 195–96.

26. Yanguas and Miranda, *Diccionario...*, cit. 2, 198–200 include a reproduction of the text of 1402 granting said privileges. The Lesaca ordenances, which had been displayed in the lobby of the town hall, are no longer to be found there. But there is a 1429 text granting privileges in the General Archive of Navarre. Florencio Idoate has supplied an extract from this later document in *Rincones de la Historia de Navarra*, vol. 2 (Iruñea-Pamplona 1956), 502–7 ("A través de las Viejas ordenanzas").

27. Yanguas and Miranda, *Adiciones...*, 134–37.

28. See note 8 above regarding the census of 1366, as well as Yanguas and Miranda, *Adiciones*, 16 on Martín Lópiz, lord of Alzate, in 1399.

29. I have in my possession a notebook titled *Extractos de la antigüedad y nobleza de la Villa de Vera, como del Patronato de su Yglesia*, written in elegant nineteenth century script by José Joaquín de Agesta, and which contains copies of the following documents: (1) 1463. Prerogatives conceded to the owners of the Palacio de Alzate (fol. 6r.); (2) Year 1483. Petition for increase presented by four beneficiaries, for the church of Bera (fols. 6 back.-7r); (3) Warrant of information of the Bishop of Iruñea-Pamplona (fols. 7r-8 back.); (4) Report of the permits by the commission holding jurisdiction (fol. 8r); (5) Division of the benefices and profits of the Church (fols. 8r-8 back.); (6) Installation of a rector and four priests, replacing a single rector, and the right to the shares that they deserve (fol. 8 back.); (7) Equal distribution of offerings (fols 8 back.-9r); (8) Right of presentation of the lord of Alzate as patron, and of the rector and beneficiaries of the institution of the bishop (fol. 9r); (9) Warrant of obligations and responsibilities (fols. 9r-10 back.). These documents are copied from a translation from the Latin, which was drafted on February 9, 1726 by Don Juan

Esteban de Sanjuanena, and countersigned by the notary Diego de Berecochea (fols. 10 back.-11 r.).

30. Yanguas and Miranda, *Adiciones*, 16.

31. Notebook cited in note 29 above, fols 11r.-12r.

32. Letters patent of nobility were published that established these rights throughout the seventeenth and eighteenth centuries. The first of these was written for Martín de Vizcay: "The natural right that the natives of the *Merindad* of Donibane Garazi (St. Jean-Pied-de-Port) have in the Kingdoms of the Crown" of Castile (Zaragoza 1621). Later, in 1685, a letter patent of nobility was written for Juan de Goyeneche (see note 39). Later, in 1714, another was written for the Orba Valley.

33. The shields make reference to either feats associated with the *Reconquista*, or to events in the remote past of the Navarrese monarchy.

34. I have in my possession a copy of this "Certificación de armas y privilegios de las cinco villas" drafted by Agesta himself in his notebooks which I've previously cited (Extractos . . . fols. 1r.-5 back.). The certification, drafted in Madrid, is dated December 5, 1735.

35. Idoate, "El escudo de cinco villas" in op. cit., 253.

36. This tendency can clearly be seen in the lawsuit brought forward in 1651 by the "valley" of Baztan against its "palace men." This lawsuit was studied by Florencio Idoate in *Rincones de la historia de Navarra*, 2 (Iruñea-Pamplona 1956), 260-268. The "palace men" asked to be seated in positions of prominence at meetings of the valley councils, and also asked to be consulted. The valley did not grant any preferred seating at meetings on the grounds of the preeminence of the "palace men" but rather as a matter of courtesy. They also refused to grant any other perks. This can be seen in documents beginning in the year 1437. But it seems that even afterward, the class of "gentlemen" continued to be given preference over ordinary residents. Such "medieval honors" angered the "property-owning residents" of the seventeenth century "to an extreme degree." In 1654, there was a ruling in favor of the palace men. In 1660, this ruling was revoked, and the rights of the valley were recognized. A number of other important cases in this struggle occurred afterword. Around the year 1677, there were cases of this nature involving Joaquín Francisco de Arizcun, Baron of Behorlegi (Béhorléguy), who, in the *Cortes* of Navarre, had referred to himself as the lord of Arizkun. Also involved in such a case was Juan Antonio Eslaba, who referred to himself as lord of Zozaia (Zozaya). The Baztan Valley obtained a ruling that prevented men from characterizing themselves in such terms. Thus, instead of saying "who possesses Arizkun" or "who possesses Zozaia" it was to be said "who possesses the palace or estate of Arizkun of Zozaia." These episodes aside, the struggle between the residents of the valley and the "palace men" continued throughout the eighteenth century, because the palace men continued to seek recognition of privileges and preferential treatment that the residents refused to recognize. See Pérez Goyena, *El valle del Baztán*, 117.

37. The admission of the rights of residence was regulated by the Lesaka municipal ordinances of 1429 by means of a payment of five florins. It was established that the person requesting said rights "retain the approval of the council, as required by the privilege. Should this approval not be granted, then none of the ordinances of the coun-

cil shall be applied." The request had to be presented before ten fellow parishioners, or men who had taken an oath, who gathered in an assembly on Tuesdays (Florencio Idoate, *Rincones de la historia de Navarra*, vol. 2 [Iruñea-Pamplona 1956], 504. A large amount of material has been published regarding residents' rights in Navarre. Yet the two most reliable references to date are two works by Yanguas and Miranda: *Diccionario* . . . cit. 3, 482–84 and *Diccionario de los fueros del reino de Navarra, y de las leyes vigentes promulgadas hasta las cortes de los años 1817 y 18 inclusive* (Donostia-San Sebastián 1828), 421–25.

38. Regarding the *donatio*, see Julio Caro Baroja, *The Basques* (Reno, 2009), 190–95, 265–68 and the works cited in the related notes, 407–8. For a case study of its application within a single "house" from the sixteenth through the nineteenth centuries, see chapter 9 "The Structure and Functions of the House" in this book.

39. *Executoria de la nobleza, antigüedad y blasones del valle de Baztán, que dedica a sus hijos y originarios Juan de Goyeneche* (Madrid 1685) fol. B2 of the introduction, according to the document of 1440, in which the men of Baztan are characterized as "free hidalgos and noblemen."

40. In *Rural life in Vera de Bidasoa* (Madrid 1944), 233–36 I published one list of names of houses in homes within the urban center of Bera (237–44), and another list of 493 houses in Lesaka, dated January 12, 1878. It is instructive to compare these lists with others supplied as part of studies of Gipuzkoan or French Basque towns in order to recognize certain patterns. One recent work in this area is that of Jean Forucade, *Trois cents ans d'histoire au Pays Basque. Urrugne, Socoa, Béhobie, Hendaye, Biriatou* (Toulouse 1967), 87–108 (on the names of houses in Urruña [Urrugne]), and 109–13 (on tombs in the church).

41. In *Los vascos* . . . ed. cit., 160, the *baite* of the Italian Alps are mentioned. Prince Luis Luciano Bonaparte, in *Remarques sur certaines notes, certaines observations et certaines corrections don't M.J. Vinson a accompagné l'Essai sur la langue basque par F. Ribáry* (London 1877, from the *Actes de la Societé Philologique*, 7, 2 5–115), 10, 22–23 maintained that the Basques had given the words to the Lombards. See also Azkue's *Diccionario vasco-español-francés*, 1 (Bilbao/Paris 1905), 126, b, s.v.

42. Zubieta is a town that seems to have fallen on hard times. It has solidly built, yet poorly maintained houses, with stone doors and keystones (61). What is particularly distinctive about these houses (apart from their exterior staircases) is their wooden balconies, with turned iron ledges (which sometimes protruded and had their own roofs), which were attached to the upper floors (figure 9). A few of these can be seen in Eratsun (Erasun), a reconstructed town on higher ground, as well as in other towns in the Ezkurra (Ezcurra) River basin. And there are a good many examples of such structures in the Ultzama Valley.

43. The "palace" of the seventeenth and eighteenth century (figure 18) is characterized as such because of its luxurious appearance and architectural character. This is what gave rise to the popular expression that a particular house "is a palace." Yet, until the seventeenth century, at least the *idea* of a "palace" had a particular legal meaning. In 1637, there were 197 palaces in Navarre, 72 of which were in the *merindad* of Iruñea-Pamplona, with another 72 in Zangoza (Sangüesa), 33 in Lizarra (Estella), 16 in Erriberri (Olite), and 4 in Tutera (Tudela). These were "palaces of armory command-

ers" whose owners were gentlemen—"commanders of lineages"—who were at one time exempt from paying *cuarteles* and *donativos*. A number of houses were elevated to the category of "palaces" for various different reasons:

1. Because their owners had provided services to the king. In this regard, I have in my possession a "Copy of the favor granted by King Carlos to Juan de Goñi, squire, that his house, called 'Larrayn nagusia,' be henceforth a Palace, and that it be titled and designated as a Palace." This document was drafted by Juan de Sada, royal notary of Iruñea-Pamplona, on March 19, 1544. The reason for this royal privilege dates back to 1525, and has to do with the adherence of the Goñi family (who claimed descent from Don Teodosio) and their possessions, to the side of King Carlos during a war being fought at that time. This palace received the name "Palace of San Miguel de Goñi" and its coat of arms included a reference to the legend of Don Teodosio.
2. Because a king had at one time slept at the house.
3. Because such a favor had been purchased by means of a *donativo* made to the impoverished Spanish State of the seventeenth century—a practice that continued into the eighteenth century. The old palaces enjoyed prerogatives identical to a medieval Right (for example, that of providing asylum to criminals, because of their immunity). See Yanguas and Miranda, *Diccionario* . . . 2. 100–502, s.v. "Palacios" and "palacios de cabo de armería." As already indicated, there are no traces of the Alzate palace in Bera. The Aguirre palace also no longer exists. The tower of Zabaleta remains in Lesaka (which was at one time considered a palace, and which appears on the 1637 list). It appears to be a lovely fifteenth century structure, and the oldest structure that is called a *Jaureguizarra* (figure 19).

The tower of Gaztelu was also built in Etxalar. This tower now belongs to the Marquis of Echeandía, who also owns a windmill, various other houses, country houses, and land in Etxalar. The tower has been renovated several times. On the side facing the river, it has Gothic-style walls. The facade seems to have been built later, and the shield is even more modern. The eighteenth century palaces that will be discussed later were different from these "palaces" or old manors (*jaureguiak*).

44. Examples of such palaces are Jarola in Elbete (Elvetea) and Sagardía in Ituren. Palaces with towers include Reparacea, near Narbarte, those belonging the Gastón family in Erratzu (Errazu) and Irurita, the Arizcun family palace in Elizondo (which has three different buildings), and Iturraldea in Arizkun. All of these palaces were established by families who attained wealth between the time of Charles II and Charles IV. They later fell into disrepair.

The palace of Zubieta, for example, is also an eighteenth century structure, and is now for the most part vacant. Other large houses dating back to the same era were not built with funds that were transferred by the state. This seems to partially explain why, when the wealthy families that constructed them later sold them off, they either fell into disrepair, or were converted into farms.

45. Thus, in the middle of the eighteenth century, when authors such as Father Larramendi believed they were making ironic references to the old lineages and "made jokes about the *andiquis* of Gipuzkoa," they were in fact restoring long-held truths

to their rightful place (*Corografía o descripción general de la muy noble y muy leal provincia de Guipúzcoa* (Barcelona 1882), 133–39.

CHAPTER 9. **The Structure and Functions of the House**

1. Many years ago, I wrote a book (one that was perhaps overly general in nature) regarding the ideas of these two important anthropologists: *Análisis de la cultura* (Barcelona, 1949), 83–87.

2. Claude Levi-Strauss, *Structural Anthropology* (New York, London 1963).

3. Ake Hutlkrantz, "International Dictionary of Regional European Ethnology and Folklore I" (*General ethnological concepts*) (Copenhagen 1960), 213–15 ("Social structure").

4. F. Graebner, *Methode der Ethnologie* (Heidelberg 1911), 148 especially.

5. Wilhelm Schmidt, *Handbuch der method der Kulturhistorischen Ethnologie* (Münster de W. 1937), 31–36.

6. A. R. Radcliffe-Brown, "On social structure," *Journal of the Royal Anthropological Institute* 70, no. 1 (1940).

7. Meyer Fortes, "Time and social structure: An Ashanti case study" in *Social Structure: Studies Presented to A. R. Radcliffe-Brown* (Oxford 1949) 54–84.

8. Julio Caro Baroja, *Los vascos*, 2nd ed. (Madrid, 1958), 131–47, with bibliography. A number of different theses are currently being prepared regarding this matter within the framework of social anthropology.

9. Wilhelm Mühlmann, *Methodik der Wölkerkunde* (Stuttgart 1938), 105.

10. Pliny, *N.H.* 4 (19) 108. There have been historians who have identified these settlements with the five towns of the Bidasoa. Luis Michelena, in *Apellidos vascos* (Donostia-San Sebastián, 1953), 56 (number 172), cites the existence of names such as "Busturi" within the same cycle.

11. Arturo Campión, *Euskariana* (7th series). *Algo de Historia (volume cuarto): Gacetilla de la Historia de Navarra. Mosaico histórico* (Iruñea-Pamplona), 6 (1333), 21 (the valleys of the five towns were: Azantza [Azanza], Amunarritz [Munárriz], Goñi, Urdanotz [Urdánoz] and Aizpun [Aizpún]).

12. Madoz, *Diccionario geográfico-estadístico-histórico de España y sus posesiones de Ultramar* 6 (Madrid 1847), 409, a.

13. Madoz, op. cit., 6, 408a–409b.

14. Madoz, op. cit., 6, 409a.

15. Madoz, op. cit., 409a–b.

16. Madoz, op. cit., 409b.

17. Madoz, op. cit., 408b.

18. Jean de Jaurgain, *Troisville, D'Artagnan et les trios mousquetaires* (Paris 1910) 13, 21, and 26.

19. The following five paragraphs, pertaining to houses that still exist today, are extracted from appraisals taken in Bera on March 28, 1607:
   1. "6 Said Martin de Liçardi, owner of the house of Alquegui, declares that he is the owner of that house, along with one and a half *robadas* of land for making bread, thirteen cows, thirty-five sheep and goats and he declared the robadas in his possession to have a value of ninety-one ducats, and the sheep and goats to have a value of twenty-four ducats . . ."
   2. 10 Said Joanes de Perugorria, owner of the house of Dornacu, says that he has in his possession that house, along with seven and a half robadas of land for making bread, and one grove of apple trees of eighteen peonadas, one grove of chestnut trees of 40 (?) peonadas, uncultivated land measuring one hundred twenty peonadas, and seven goats. He does not have any other property. He declares that the value of his robadas to be seventy-five ducats, of his apple orchard to be forty-five ducats, and of his grove of chestnut trees to be ten ducats. He declares the value of his barren land to be one hundred sixty ducats, and of his ten goats to be seven ducats . . ."
   3. "89 Said Joanes de Miranda, owner of the house of Echeberçea, declares that he possesses that house, along with seven robadas of sowing ground and one apple orchard of twelve peonadas along with seven peonadas of uncultivated land and an orchard of two peonadas, one cow, one workhorse, and bees. The value of the robadas of land being one hundred sixteen ducats and of the apple orchard one hundred six ducats, of the uncultivated land thirteen ducats, of the orchard seven ducats, of the cow seven ducats, of the workhorse four ducats, of the bees and goats twenty-four and a half ducats . . ."
   4. "176 Said Graciana de Minena, a widow who administers the house and manor house of Alçate and its belongings, has provided information regarding the value thereof. She declares that this house includes seventy-six robadas of land for making bread, sixty peonadas of uncultivated land, one orchard of one peonada, two mills for making flour, and seventy peonadas of ferneries. She has no other property. She states that the value of the robadas of the land that she owns is one thousand forty-six ducats, that the value of the uncultivated land is sixty ducats, that the value of the orchard is seven ducats, that she earns one hundred ninety ducats from fees for use of the flour mill each year, and that the value of the ferneries is eighty ducats.

   Some 181 declarations of this kind are recorded, and the sum total of the property thus appraised is 15,307 ducats and 3 *reales* (plus 12 maravedis).

20. The papers in question constitute a collection, some of which have deteriorated with age. These papers were generously given to me by my friend Luis Errandonea, a native of Bera who now lives in Donostia. These documents are as follows: (1) 1647: Designation of the heir of Martín de Alquegui. (2) 1651: Claim of legitimate right to his legacy by Sebastián de Alquegui. (3) 1653: Request for tax exemption by the aforementioned. (4) 1688: Marriage contract of Baltasar de Echenique and Gracia de Aizechea. (5) 1714: (copy of 1744) last will and testament of María Francisca de Irazoqui. (6) 1716: Baptismal certificate of Jacob de Echenique (July 5, 1689). (7) 1723: agreement between Juanes de Echenique, official stone-cutter, and Manuel Joseph de Yparraguirre. (8) 1723: marriage contract of Juan de Echenique and Catalina de Alquegui. (9) 1727: last will and testament of Graciana de Oyarzábal. (10)

1728: Certification of provision of legal inheritance entitlement to Juan de Tellechea by Martín de Alquegui. (11) 1732: Request of information by Agustina de Echenique and response of Father Ynurre. (12) 1732: Opinion regarding this same matter (estate of Graciana de Oyarzábal). (13) 1737: Resolution of dispute regarding water. (14) 1741: Payment of male dowry (from son-in-law to father-in-law: Martín de Alquegui and Juan de Echenique). (15) 1742: Sale of land from Domingo de Garmendia to Martín de Alquegui and his daughter. (16) (17) ... last will and testament of Martín de Alquegui (damaged). (18) 1746: Criminal complaint of Domingo de Garmendia against Juan de Echenique. (19) 1752: Receipt for taxes paid, authorized by the *cabildo* of Bera (1731), for payment made by J.B. de Errandonea and his wife. (20) 1752: Invoice and receipt for the aforementioned payment. (21) 1767: income of Bera estate. (22) 1767: List of lumber to be used for construction in Bera. (23) 1780: letter written in Montevideo, dated April 9, from Esteban de Irazoqui to J. B. de Errandonea. (24) 1782: authorization of burial in Alqueguiberea. (25) 1782: burial certificate for María Esteban de Camio. (26) 1833: deed for the sale of a grove of chestnut trees, by José Francisco de Goicoechea to Juan José Errandonea. (27) 1864: deed for the sale of land constituting part of Bera commons to Juan José Errandonea. (28) 1864: Various receipts from a different era. (29) Agricultural survey map and authorization of deeds. (30) Memorandum of indulgences conceded by Pope Pius V.

21. E. Munárriz Urtasun, "El cambio de apellidos en la vieja Navarra," *RIEV* 14 (1923): 401–3. But the standing rules in this regard are not discussed in this article.

22. Relevant references in this regard include authorized works regarding the subject, such as that of Fernando Arvizu, *Las donaciones inter-vivos en el Derecho Civil de Navarra* (Iruñea-Pamplona 1928). See also the review article by Bonifacio de Echegaray in *RIEV* 21 (1930): 269–73.

23. The emblem of female authority is the ladle for serving soup (the *burruntzalia*). *Ongui artadu burruntzalia* ("she knows how to handle a ladle") is a saying used of a new mistress of the house who displays a bossy air. See Julio Caro Baroja, *La vida rural en Vera de Bidasoa* (Madrid 1944), 131–32.

24. Regarding such items, see the pamphlet of Luis Pedro Peña Santiago, *La "argizaiola" vasca* (San Sebastian 1964).

25. Most of the content of Number 5 (May 1967) of the magazine *Esprit: Nouvelle série* is dedicated to an exposition of *Structuralisme. Idéologie et method*. The contributions of Yves Bertherat, Pierre Burgelin, Jean Conilh, Jean Cuisenier, Jean-Marie Domenach, Mikel Dufrenne, Jean Ladriére, and Paul Ricoéur give an idea of the importance that the term has in contemporary France. Yet, in general terms, it is difficult for a non-French reader to see why this should be the case. Reading such material also makes one think that the language he learned is somehow different from the language that is used today.

26. *Erreparatze, Erreparaz, Reparaz* (and even *Erepatzia*) is the name of a house in the Bidasoa area, where the surname Reparaz has long been known. *Reparacea* is the most famous manorhouse of all. But the surname stretches from here to the mountains. Michelena, in *Apellidos vascos* (62, no. 220) believes that it comes from *errege-beratz* or "the king's orchard."

In the census of 1366, the name *García Reparaze* appears in Santesteban (fol. 119r) and the name Johan Periz de Reparaze (with one guilder) appears in Bertiz (fol. 120r). The following names appear in Oieregi: "Martin Yvaines, three and a half guilders. Lope, two guilders. Johanguo, two guilders. García Martiniz, two and a half guilders. Narbarte appears as *Narvart* (fol. 119 vto). In the census of 1427 (fol. 238r.) the name of "Miguel Bertiz" appears in Oieregi as a nobleman. Either this man or his family were the likely owners of the fortified house that had existed before the manor house was built. A public document from 1910 indicates that the address of the current manor house is considered to be San Juan Bautista 20, in Oieregi, and that it measures twenty-six meters from side to side, and eighteen meters from front to back.

In an appraisal of the property conducted in Oieregi in 1607, we read the following:

"Catthalina de Reparazea, in the absence of her husband, declared that she is the owner of the house and Palace of Reparazea, and that this house includes an orchard of one-half *peonada*; ten *robadas* of land, a grove of apple trees, a grove of chestnut trees, and a fernery of forty *peonadas*, a workhorse and twenty head of sheep. She declares that the value of the orchard is four ducats, that the value of the land is two hundred ducats, the value of the groves of apple and chestnut trees and the fernery is sixteen ducats, the value of the workhorse is ten ducats, and the value of the bees is twelve ducats." She supplied evidence of the privileges to which the palace is entitled. In the appraisal of 1612, Juanes de Bértiz indicates that his house is worth 101 ducats (and half of its income).

27. I am grateful to Doña Concepción de Uztáriz, her daughters Doña Dolores and Doña Soledad Céniga, and her grandchildren and son-in-law for allowing me access to the archive of Reparacea in order to examine its papers for the purposes of researching the history of the palace and the family. In addition to the copies referred to in the text, there is an older copy of portions of the deeds of 1477 and 1480 that dates from 1694, and in which additional information is revealed.

28. On June 27, 1647, Joanes de Reparaz successfully requested an extension of the exemption from payment of the *cuartel* for the palace of Reparacea after having made various efforts in that regard. A brief written by Marcos de Echauri, Secretary of the *Cámara de Comptos* of Iruñea-Pamplona, wrote a note in the margin of the brief indicating that the palaces of Bértiz, Repáraz, and Oteiza were located in the valley of Bértiz, and that these were exempted from *cuarteles y alojamientos* in 1666. In 1717 and 1782, the *Tribunal de la Cámara de Comptos* was still issuing rulings regarding the Reparacea's "exemption from the quartel."

29. All of the following documents can be found in the archives of Reparacea: (1) Last will and testament of Catalina de Reparacea (November 3, 1592); (2) Marriage contract of Catalina de Reparaz and Juanes de Audadi (March 18, 1601); (3) Marriage contract of María Juana Sarrate y Reparaz and Pedro de Gaztelu (July 27, 1635); (4) Marriage contract of Juan de Gaztelu and María Ana de Bértiz (April 9, 1674); (5) Marriage contract of Pascual de Gaztelu and Graciana de Albirena (August 26, 1697); (6) Marriage contract of María Francisca de Gaztelu, an only child, and Juan Bautista Uztáriz (February 2 1717); (7) Marriage contract of Juan Miguel de Uztáriz (February 2, 1717); (8) Marriage contract of Juan Miguel de Uztáriz, the younger, and Antonia de Vértiz y Aldecoa (October 9, 1768).

30. All of the documents that record these events were in the archives of Reparacea. There is no doubt that the current palace was built in the eighteenth century. An official document from 1829 refers to the manor house of Reparacea and to "another house adjoining the manor house that is called the old manor house."

31. Juan Miguel de Uztáriz ("the Younger") died on February 12, 1812, at which time Reparacea was being used to quarter retreating French troops. His son died on July 15, 1878. From an official document drafted in Oieregi and dated February 18, 1861, we know that this son restored Reparacea around the year 1859 at a cost of 36,795 *reales* and 25 *maravedís*. The bill for said amount was drafted by the master builder José Joaquín Agesta of Bera. The house had suffered a great deal during the First Carlist War, when the Carlists appropriated lead and iron from it for military purposes.

32. When the marriage contract for Juan Bautista de Uztáriz and María Francisca de Gaztelu was drawn up in Oieregi on February 2, 1717, the "old owner" of Reparacea, Graciana de Alviena, established the following conditions in the *donatio*: "On the condition that the donor and recipients live together in said Manor House of Reparacea, sharing the same living space and taking meals together, and on condition of said donor enjoying usufruct, during the remainder of her life and so long as she so chooses, of said palace and of the donated properties, during which time she will provide sustenance, clothe and feed, in sickness and in health, said recipients as well as any children they may have. And when she no longer exercises this authority, the recipients themselves will assume expenses to sustain, clothe, and feed, in sickness and in health, said donor during the rest of her natural life and, in addition, to assume the expenses for her burial and related expenses, in accordance with persons of her station. In addition, should any disagreement arise among these parties as a result of which they are no longer able to share the same residence, said donor is to annually receive twelve *robos* of wheat, sixteen *robos* of corn, two *robos* where both hazelnuts and walnuts are planted, quantities of apples and chestnuts necessary for her diet, a suckling pig of nine or ten *docenas*, two *docenas* of oil, and all of the garden vegetables that she needs for her orchard. This in addition to the land necessary to plant seed on one half a *robo* of flax. Said land is to be in the same area where *pegantes* for the home are sowed, and the recipients are to provide her the land necessary for planting seed, and to give her the manure necessary for doing so. They are also to give her cider of the second pressing that they have in the house. In addition, they are to give her eight *reales* for her own personal use, as well as the lodgings of her choice for sleeping . . . ."

33. Here is the text of the property certificate for the palace in 1777, when Juan Miguel de Uztáriz became its owner: In Narbarte, on the twenty-second of April of the year one thousand seven hundred, seventy-seven. Rl. Ymfrasto, in compliance with the request of the Royal Court of this Kingdom in the decree of last seventeenth of March, grasp the right hand of Don Juan Miguel de Uztariz the Younger and escort him into the Palace of Reparacea. This after the previous inhabitants have left or been removed. I have, in addition, opened and closed doors and windows within the halls of said palace, and have also carried out other actions that signify the quiet and peaceful possession of said palace for all to see, know, and be mindful off, without any protest or complaint having been raised by anyone else. Witnesses thereto were Don Juan Antonio Zozaya and Don Manuel de Yriarte, both of the Priests of the Parish of Narvarte, the

first-named being also a rector thereof. All of the parties signed in witness whereof: I, Juan Miguel de Uztáriz the Younger; Don Juan Antonio Zozaya; Don Manuel Yriarte. In the presence of me, Pedro Geronimo Bengochea." Afterward, in the orchard, for the purposes of symbolizing the transfer of possession, Bengochea once again "took the hand" of the new owner and "cut leaves from the vegetables and cast them forth, and carried out other demonstrative actions symbolizing the true quiet and pacific possession of the property." He walked upon the freshly plowed land and "picked up clods of earth and cast them forth," proceeding to do the same in the ferneries (where he "plucked grass") and other lands adjoining the property. In the oak grove, he cut down branches.

34. "Honor y vergüenza" (Examen histórico de varios conflictos populares) in *La ciudad y el campo* (Madrid 1966), 63–130.

35. This note is based upon documentation in the archives of Reparacea:
In the last will and testament of Ángela de Juangonera, dated March 5, 1711, we can see that this lady was at that time the widow of Juan de Albirena, owner of the house of Dibeguirena de Legasa, where she dictated her will. This document also indicates that she had a daughter, Graciana (*), lady of the palace of Reparacea in Oieregi ("although it lies within the parish of Narbete [probably modern-day Narbarte —ed.]") and a son, Miguel, who was to be her successor in Bideguirena. Clause 4 reads as follows: 4. Item. I declare that my brother, currently in the kingdoms of the Indies, has written me that he will, as soon as he is able, send monies for the purpose of supporting me in my old age. Although I do not know how much money he will send, whatever is sent will be placed at my immediate disposition, as well as that of my late husband, who died one year ago (**). It is my wish that, upon my death, that my son Miguel de Albirena receive said house in its entirety, and that he make improvements thereto that are needed because of its age. For this purpose, I bequeath to him all of the large and small cattle of every species which I possess." This lady died on March 14, 1711, in Legasa.

By 1756, when her great-grandsons, Juan Bautista and Juan Felipe de Uztáriz, were about to become Knights of St. James, and were submitted to the inquiries corresponding thereto, the house appears to have been restored and in good condition. It therefore appears clear that Miguel de Albirena had received the money from the Americas and that, in addition, he had other money at his disposal. The fact is that factors that had nothing to do with communal and local life impacted the status of the house. This was as much the case in the eighteenth century, and in even early eras, as it is today. Some of those earlier eras are difficult to reconstruct. Yet documents reflect the realities that the house confronted in those remote times. The house of Bideguirena still exists today (although it is known by the name of "Bideinea") and it is interesting to compare its current form with the description of 1756 that was provided for the reason indicated above: "The house of Bideguirena, located in Legasa, the front of which faces North, has three floors, with three oval windows on each of these floors, and an arched door. The entrance on the right side also has a window, with an iron grating. . . .".

(*) Born in Legasa and baptized on February 1, 1669.

(**) March 18, 1710. He had married Ángela on July 24, 1661.

CHAPTER 12. **The Basques and the Sea**

This essay's narrative endnotes are presented here for the sake of consistency —ed.

Critical Situations and Famous Enterprises

Acts of piracy are attested to in documents such as one dated May 18, 1486, which calls for the immediate apprehension of Juan Martico and Juan de Zarauz, residents of Zumaia, the two men having been accused of attacking Breton ships during peacetime. See *Colección de cédulas*, cited in Tomás González, vol. 3 (Madrid 1829), 92–94 (no. 29). Also to be found in the same volume of *Colección* (no. 31) is a provision prohibiting the Gipuzkoan armorers from taking part in pirateering without having first provided security. As regards seizures of ships, in volume 1 (Madrid 1829), 162–63 (no. 40), a royal letter from Málaga dated August 23, 1487 mentions vessels weighing more than "thirty tons" (large ships, caravels, and fustas). Regarding the law of 1501, see Francisco López de Gomara, *Crónica de los Barbarrojas*, which can be found in *Memorial histórico español*, vol. 6 (Madrid 1853), 357–60 (especially 359).

As regards the activities of Hernán Suárez de Toledo and Esteban de Garibay, see "Memorias" in *Memorial histórico español*, VII (Madrid, 1851), pp. 290–93 (book 3, title 12), 293–95 (book 3, title 13). *Los vascos y la Historia a través de Garibay* (Donostia-San Sebastián 1972), 90. A number of lists are presented for the purpose of determining the number of vessels that existed is provided by Fernández Duro, in *A la mar madera. Disquisiciones náuticas*, V (Madrid 1880), pp. 357 (1533), 362 (1558). The pragmatic considerations that spurred the construction of higher capacity ships are presented in *Novísima recopilación*, Book 9, title 8, laws 4, 8, etc. The entire title deals with large ships, as well as the goods that were shipped: Volume 3, 200–7 of the edition of *Los códigos españoles concordados y anotados*, volume 9 (Madrid 1850). The previously cited 1501 law is 9 (203 ff.).

Regarding the tradition that it was a Basque sailor who Columbus listened to, the most important text is that of Francisco López de Gomara, "Primera parte de la Historia General de las Indias" in *Historiadores primitivos de Indias* (B.A.E., XXII), 165 ff., which presents the opinion that Columbus was a Bizkaian "who had dealings with England and France." Other legends depicted Columbus as Andalusian or Portuguese. Gonzalo Fernández de Oviedo makes reference to this and refers to such ideas as "novel" (*Historia general y natural de las Indias*, [B.A.E., CXVIII], 16 b (book 1, chapter 2). As indicated above, what is interesting in this respect is that such speculation was later repeated by Basque historians.

The bibliography regarding this subject is immense. See the apologetic work of Don Segundo de Ispizua, *Historia de los vascos en el descubrimiento, conquista y civilización de América*, 2 volumes (Bilbao 1914–1915).

One work that is indispensable for any researcher is that of Don Martín Fernández de Navarrete, *Colección de los viajes y descubrimientos que hicieron por mar los españoles desde fines del siglo XV*, 5 volumes (Madrid 1825–1837). A more recent edition of this same work exists (Madrid 1880), also comprising five volumes. Portions of this work have been reprinted in the *Boletín de la Real Academia Española* (BAE; these reprints were used by the present writer). For documents regarding the voyage of Magellan, see vol. 2 (LXXVI), pp. 415-418, 421–27, and especially 501–17 (in no. 17).The entire fourth part is devoted to Magellan's voyage. The fifth part

(III, LXXVII), page 1,250 is devoted to Loaisa, and includes writings by Urdaneta and others.

The Cod Revolution

Arte para fabricar, fortificar y aparejar naos de Guerra y merchant... was printed in Seville in 1611. See fol. 5 r. A recent edition of this work has been prepared by Enrique Marcos Dorta (La Laguna 1964), 47. The text of *Viaje a España del magnífico señor Andrés Navajero, embajador de la República de Venecia ante el emperador Carlos V (1524–1526)*, translated by J. M. Alonso Gamo (Valencia, 1951), pp. 102–3 served as an inspiration for my "*La tradición técnica del pueblo vasco, o una interpretación ecológica de su Historia*" which was published in *Vasconiana* (Madrid 1957), 105, and I continue to consult that classic sixteenth-century work as a reference.

As regards "cod fever" the information collected by Fernández de Navarrete in his work on Basque voyages to Newfoundland is illuminating. See *Colección de los viajes*... (previously cited), vol. (LXXVI), 115–18. Information on Cristóbal Barros may be found on page 117. Regarding the words "*bacalao*," "*laberdano*," etc., see J. Corominas, *Diccionario crítico etiomológico de la lengua castellana*, (Madrid 1954), 358–59. For Pierre de Lancre's description, see his *Tableau de l'inconstance des mauvais anges et demons* (Paris 1612), 30–47 (book 1, discourse 2).

Eminent Persons

There is a vast literature on the colonization of the Philippines. One notable work is, once again, authored by Don Martín Fernández de Navarrete, *Biblioteca marítima española*, I (Madrid 1851), 99–106, where he provided a biographical sketch of Urdaneta, emphasizing the importance of his work. Some of Urdaneta's letters are published and discussed in Miguel López de Legazpi, 492–94. The history of piracy in the Philippines is a topic of great interest. Information gathered from contemporary sources was compiled by W. G. [sic] Retana in his edition of Dr. Antonio de Morga's *Sucesos de las islas Filipinas* (Madrid 1910).

See the "account of the exploits of Pedrarías Dávila in the provinces of Terra Firme or Castillo de Oro, and of the discovery of the Southern Sea and the coasts of Peru and Nicaragua, written by adelantado Pascual de Andagoya," in Fernández de Navarrete, *Colección de los viajes*, (LXXVI), 233–65, followed by a biographical note on 266–77. Other writings are cited in the *Biblioteca maritime*..., vol. 2, 519–20. Lope Martínez de Isasti, *Compendio historial* (previously cited), 646-650 (book 6, chapter 1) provides accounts of both sea captains and generals of the Armada (431–34, book 3, chapter 25); admirals (434–39, book 3, chapter 26) and captains of galleons and large ships (439–42, book 3, chapter 27). See Marqués de Seoane, *Navegantes guipuzcoanos* (Madrid 1908), 81–94, which provides a different list that includes the nineteenth century. Regarding Juan de la Cosa, see Fernández de Navarrete, *Biblioteca maritime*..., vol. 2, 208–15. With respect to his being thought of as Bizkaian and even being referred to as "Bizkaian," the most relevant document is one that was sent to the Casa de Contratación, and which is reprinted in *Colección de los viajes*..., vol. 2 (LXXVI), 75–76 (no. 21, 1503). See also, in this respect, Fray Bartolomé de las Casas, *Historia de las Indias*... (book 2, chapter 2), *Obras*, vol. 2 (B.A.E., XCVI, 8): "... Juan de la Cosa, a Biscayan, who at that time was the most minor [sic] pilot of those seas, because he had accompanied the Admiral on all of his voyages . . ."

Cosmographers, Naval Architects, and Warriors.

As regards Andrés de Poza and his book 5, see Nicolás Antonio, Bibliotheca Hispana Nova I (Madrid 1783), 83 and Fernández de Navarrete, *Biblioteca maritime* . . . , vol. 1, 96–97. The article in the latter is titled as follows: *The most spectacular mapping of the seas ever . . . Composed by Andrés de Poca, a native of the city of Urduña (Orduña), an emissary of the Noblest and Most Loyal Seignioryof Bizkaia* (Bilbao: Matías Mares, 1587). See also the reprinted facsimile of the *Instrucción nautical para navegar*, by Dr. Diego García de Palacio (Madrid 1944). See folios 82 r.–108 r. (book 4, chapters 1–14).

On Don Antonio de Urquiola (Urkiola), see *Biblioteca maritime* . . . , vol. 1, 201. On later events, see C. Fernández Duro, *A la mar Madera. Libro quinto de las Disquisiciones náuticas* (Madrid 1880), 7–266 (construction of ships), with a list of shipbuilders, etc. (267–352) that includes Urkiola. Personal data of Juan del Puerto and Juan Echeverri appear on pages 53–55. The 1617 list of conditions appears on pages 62–69.

More recently, a particular document has been reprinted that shows how certain individuals benefited illegally from traffic in materials that were the property of the Crown, and that were used to construct ships. "*Información judicial sobre la construcción de un navío en los astilleros de Lezo*," 1615, in *Colección de documentos inéditos para la Historia de Guipúzcoa*, vol. 2 (Donostia-San Sebastián 1958), 107–20.

In *La tradición técnica del pueblo vasco* . . . (121–26) I have conducted a brief analysis of the life and ideas of Tomé Cano. That same work also discusses the life and ideas of General Zubiaur (1556–1605) (Madrid 1946), 69, 81, 83. See a discussion of pages 162–164 of Bacon's text in note 63 ("*Considerations politiques pour entreprendre la guerre contre l'Espagne*," Cramoisay, 1634: Oeuvres philosophiques, morales et politiques de Francis Bacon . . ." (Paris 1836), 635–51.

Regarding quarter-decks, see "*Diálogo anónimo entre un vizcaíno y un montañes sobre construcción de naves*," in Fernández Duro, *Arca de Noé. Libro sexto de las náuticas* (Madrid 1881), 142. Duro was of the opinion that the Dutch were the best shipbuilders (108). The lavish book written by Don Gervasio de Artiñano y Galdacano, *La arquitectura naval española (en Madera), bosquejo de sus condiciones y rasgos de su evolución* (Madrid 1924), includes a very large number of drawings reproduced from original material.

In *Biblioteca maritime* . . . , vol. 2 (264–65) Fernández de Navarrete cites and discusses a number of the writings of Juan Martínez de Recalde (who died in 1588).

Regarding the Spanish Armada, see Garret Mattingly, *The defeat of the Spanish Armada* (London 1961). Apologetic works include Esteban Calle Iturrino, *Hombres de mar de Vizcaya* (Bilbao 1949), 27–31. José María Donosty, *Marinos guipuzcoanos* (Madrid 1968). Zubiaur's collected letters have already been mentioned. Regarding other figures, it is important to note that, at times, letters have been published that provide a narration of their activities in the form of stories. Such is the case for Don Tomás de Larraspuru with respect to his voyage to the dam of Mamora. This work has been reprinted by Ignacio Bauer, *Relaciones de África*, vol. 2 (Madrid), 289–91 (1628).

Other accounts that survive are of anonymous authorship. See the letters of Don Carlos de Ibarra, *Biblioteca maritime*, vol. 1, 258–259; of Don Antonio de Oquendo idem, vol. 1, 175 (biography on pages 165–175). See also the biography of Oquendo written by his son Don Miguel, *El Héroe Cántabro. Vida del Sr. D. Antonio de Oquendo* ... (Toledo 1666). Regarding Don Miguel, see idem vol. 2, 495–496. There are also modern biographies of Antonio, such as Rafael Estrada's *El Almirante Don Antonio de Oquendo* (Madrid 1943).

Commercial Activity

For an overview of the history of commerce, see the article "*Comercio*" in the *Diccionario enciclopédico vasco*, vol. 7 (Donostia-San Sebastián 1976), 373b–403a, with a modern bibliography. Local histories, including those written centuries ago, are also sources of valuable information. For the commission of 1483, see Tomás González's *Colección de cédulas*, vol. 1, 86–88 (no. 21). Many documents provide information regarding the merchandise carried to the Indies. Two such works are *A la Madera. Disquisiciones náuticas*, vol. 6, 359; and Navajero, *Viaje* ... (previously cited, 103). As regards fishing, there are published collections of documents, such as that compiled by José Manuel Imaz, *La industria pesquera en Guipúzcoa al final del siglo XVI (Documentos de la época)* (Donostia-San Sebastián 1944). This work, along with the works already cited, sheds a great deal of light on the subject. One document that describes the activities of Basque sailors in the Italian Mediterranean as transporters, and which was written circa 1517, has been reprinted in *Colección de documentos inéditos para la Historia de Guipúzcoa*, vol. 2 (Donostia-San Sebastián 1958), pp. 9–48. This work is confusing, yet at the same time dramatic.

There are also collections of documents that include very blunt statements regarding relations with Flanders, such as the work compiled by Don Carmelo de Echegaray, *Índice de documentos referents a la Historia vasca que se contienen en los archives de Brujas* (Donostia-San Sebastián 1929). These documents cover the period 1350–1765, yet with a strong emphasis on the sixteenth century.

For a bibliography of works on Donostia-San Sebastián, see H. Ch. Lea, *A History of the Inquisition of Spain,* vol. 3 (New York 1907), 517.

CHAPTER 14. **The Basques Yesterday and Today**

1. *The Royal Congregation of San Fermín de los Navarros* (1683–1961) (Madrid 1963), 27–44. This work was an indispensable resource for the writing of the present chapter.

2. Sagües, op. cit., 92.

3. The signatures of a number of the founders of the congregation appeared in a document dated August 18, 1683, under the phrase, "By the Assembly of the Nation."

4. Sagües, op. cit., 303–13.

5. Sagües, op. cit., 95–96.

6. The authorization granting this permission can be found in the Historical Archive of the Madrid Registry, file 13, 155.

7. The list of those who were commissioned to collect funds can be found in Sagües, op. cit., 96–98.

8. Brief treatise of a dispute and difference of opinion between two friends, one a Castilian from Burgos and another from the Basque Country, in the town of Potosí, in the domain of Peru in *Castellanos y vascongados* (Madrid 1876), 23 (chapter 1).

9. *Castellanos y vascongados*, 7 (prologue by Z^a, or Justo Zaragoza).

10. Martín de Vizcay, Residents rights that the natives of the *merindad* of San Ivan del Pie del Puerto have in the Kingdoms of the Castillian Crown (Zaragoza, 1621), 10–174. The *merindad* of Ultrapuertos is another name for Lower Navarre.

11. "Native of the *Villa* of Donibane Garazi" is how he is characterized in the royal decree granting privileges, written in Valladolid on July 6, 1592, and extending favor to his son Luis, who appears among those listed in the *Examen de ingenios para las sciencias* (Baeza, 1594) in folio 3 r. of the first section. One can also find Spanish inscriptions in that zone. Some of these can be seen in the famous study of Louis Colas, *La tombe basque, Recueil d'inscriptions funéraires et domestiques du Pays Basque Français* (Bayonne-Paris 1923), especially the atlas. The longest inscription reprinted there is from the house of Ospitalia in Irisarri (Irissarry), written by Don Martín de Larrea in 1607 (109, no. 382). The author sometimes had doubts about how to decipher these inscriptions. This was the case for a 1601 inscription referring to "Pelenaut Basaguiz, Lord of Olloki (Olloqui)" in Méharin (150, no. 522). Sometimes, these inscriptions contained a combination of Spanish and Basque, such as that of Iholdi (Iholdy), referring to "Don Pedro de Perostegui (e)guin(a)" (83, no. 275).

During the time of Philip IV, the polemics among persons of different regions and domains of the peninsula began to grow more heated. There was one broadside directed especially against the "Bizkaians," which circulated in both printed and—more frequently—handwritten from, which was called *El buho gallego* ("The Galician Owl"). This pamphlet contained a virulent defense of Galicia. In the second part of this work (the printed version consists of nine folios), in folio 7 r., there is also a harangue against the Navarrese, who are represented in the assembly of birds by a kestrel. The attack is rather foolish, and yet interesting in the way that such foolishness often is: ". . . and for this reason, we turn to the kestrel of Navarre, which in Old Spanish is the same as 'hovering' and 'callus,' which so well epitomize this nation from the North to the South, for it hovers over France and Spain, having a presence in both of these nations, and the name of their homeland shows this, since Navarre means either "having no soil" or "novice"—in other words, not being part of either Old France or Old Spain. In fact, it is said that, if one dissects the heart of each one of these birds, one will find a distinctive imprint of a fleur-de-lys. And for this reason—as I've already told you—there is no place for this bird in this assembly . . . ." A work was composed in response to this allegory, called *El tordo vizcaíno* (The Bizkaian Thrush) (90 rr., undated). It is said to have been written by Garibay. But on page 88, there is a reference to the siege of Hondarribia (Fuenterrabia) in 1638, and therefore would have to have been written well after the death of that chronicler. For this reason, I also believe that *El buho gallego* would have to have been written some time after 1620, which is the approximate date ascribed to the work in Miguel Herrero García, *Ideas de los españoles del siglo XVII*, 2nd edition (Madrid 1966).

12. Jean de Jaurgain, *Troisville, d'Artagnan e les tois mousquetaires. Études biographiques et héraldiques* (Paris 1910). There is a prior undated edition that has much less information, 100 copies of which were printed, in Paris (H. Champion).

13. *Mémoires de Charles de Batz-Castelmore Comte d'Aragnan rédigés par Gatien Courtilz de Sandras, Prefacés et annotés par Gérard-Gailly* (Paris 1928), 177–205 (at 8).

14. *Executoria de la nobleza, antiguedad y blasones del valle de Baztán, que dedica a sus hijos y originarios Juan de Goyeneche* (Madrid 1685), pages unnumbered.

15. Goyeneche, op. cit., at 14.

16. Goyeneche, op. cit., at 2.

17. In the Zuberoa code of laws, see rubric 24, article 11 (P. Haristoy, Recherches historiques sur le Pays Basque, 2 (Baiona-Paris 1884), 420. Etienne Ritou, De la condition des personnes chez les basques français jusqu'en 1789 (Baiona 1890), 68.

18. *Relation du voyage fait en 1679 au devant et a la suite de la reine, Marie-Louise d'Orléans, wife of Charles II* (Paris 1902), 32.

19. P. Boissonnade, *Histoire de la reunion de la Navarre a la Castille*" (Paris 1893), 403–7.

20. Emiliano Jos, *La expedición de Ursúa al Dorado, la rebellion de Lope de Aguirre y el itinerario de los marañones* (Huesca 1927), 37–42 (data regarding Ursúa).

21. My land borders France, and I was there for four years—the best years of my life. I am not French, but rather *beamontés*.

22. Goyeneche, op. cit., at 4. In reality, the title of the Count of Gerena, in favor of Don Pedro de Ursúa, dates back to 1650: *Catálogo alfabético de los documentos referentes a títulos del reino y grandezas de España conservados en la sección de consejos suprimidos (del Archivo Histórico Nacional)*, 2 (Madrid 1952), 39, file 9,046, no. 1; 5240, 3 bis.

23. *Nobiliario del valle de la Valdorba con los escudos de sus palacios y casas nobles y relación de la conquista de Itza en la nueva España por el conde Lizarraga por el Doctor Don Francisco de Elorza y Rada, Abad de Barasoain*. It has recently been published by the *Sociedad de Bibliófilos Españoles* (Madrid 1958), 199.

24. Sagües, op. cit., 96. A detailed account of the conquest of Itza (or Ytza) may be found on 201–50 of the *Nobiliario* of Elorza and Rada. The granting of the title of Count of Lizarraga to Martín de Ursúa y Arizmendi occurred on April 14, 1705. *Catálogo*, cit. 2 (Madrid 1952), 245; file 4474, no. 68; 5240, no. 3 bis.

25. The proverb went as follows: *Iglesia, o mar, o casa real, quien quiera medrar* ("Church, or sea, or the royal house—for all who stand ready to seek their fortune.").

26. The fact that a humble friar could accumulate significant wealth in order to finance costly construction projects and create charitable foundations was surprising to people in the seventeenth century. One possible explanation for this was that—at

least in Navarre—a friar was sometimes the brother of a wealthy captain. This was the case of the once-famous Carmelite Friar Raimundo De Lumbiar (born 1616), who was a native of Zangoza (Sangüesa) and who came from a poor family, but who with his brother's money established two public granaries in his hometown, as well as another in Zaragoza in 1683 (this apart from the construction of factories, which he also financed). See *Vida del Rm.P.M. Fr. Raymundo de Lumbier*. Thanks to Doctor Joseph Boneta, I have this book (without a cover) in my possession. It indicates a publication date of August 8, 1687 (25–36; chapter 6 of the first part). Regarding architectural projects, etc, see 105–19 (chapters 5-7 of the second part).

27. He wrote this in the first chapter of his novel, *Peter Simple*, which was published in 1834. In contrast, the French of the eighteenth century believed that the prosperity in question was due to the sons of the nobles of the most distinguished families venturing off to seek their fortunes through naval careers (i.e., to become admirals). These men began their apprenticeship in merchant ships. In the *Eloge de René Duguay-Trouin*, which is part of the *Ouvre diverse de M. Thomas*, part 1 (Amsterdam 1772), and which was actually written in 1761, see 85–87 for a number of interesting observations regarding this matter.

28. Julio Caro Baroja, *La tradición técnica del pueblo vasco o una interpretación ecológica de su historia* in *Vasconiana* (Madrid 1957), 103–77.

29. An example would be *El desdén del Alameda*, written by Gonzalo de Céspedes y Meneses (in *Historias peregrinas y ejemplares*, Volume II of *Selected Classic Spanish Novels* (Madrid 1906), 90. In this work, a character appears by the name of Claudio *Irunza*. This personage is represented as living in Seville some fifty years before the work was published (Zaragoza, 1623). He is a "*noble* man, and a possessor of one of the greatest fortunes in all of Europe, for his estate his worth one million, and his credit and confidence have an even greater value. After he had reached the age of forty, he married a woman from an upstanding family, the daughter of a powerful Bizkaian merchant . . . ."

30. Lope de Vega, *El premio del bien hablar*, act 1, scene 2, lines 121–30, 160–64, and 237–40.

31. Manuel de Larramendi, *Corografía o descripción general de la muy noble y muy leal provincia de Guipúzcoa* (Barcelona 1882), 121–33.

32. For the history of these rivalries, see *Castellanos y vascongados*, 64–151 (which refer to the life of Bartolomé Arranz de Ursúa y Vela).

33. Given that Navarre contains such a strong element of healthy and energetic youth, a certain proportion of them cross the ocean to seek their fortunes in Mexico or Peru. From these lands, they later send or bring back abundant riches. In the meantime, those who have stayed behind in the mother country have sought riches—with at least as much vigor—in the exercise of commerce or agriculture in their native lands. J.A. Zaratiegui, *Vida y hechos de Don Tomás de Zumalacárregui*. (Madrid 1845), 2.

34. "At that time (1673) I made good friends with an elegant young man, a merchant from Donostia-San Sebastián named Juan de Echeverría. I could tell by his name and from the distinctive Basque manner of his speech, that he was from Bizkaia." *Memorias de Raimundo de Lantery mercader en Indias 1673–1700, publícalas Álvaro*

Picardo y Gómez (Cádiz 1949), 11. On 12, there is a mention of a widow who is the only child of a very rich man from Bizkaia.

35. Lantery, op. cit., 292, 293, 298–99, 311, 331, 333–35, 342, 354, 356.

36. Lantery, op. cit., 248 (it says there that he was a bookkeeper from Andalucía de México), 293: And so, my son, I proceeded to write to your father-in-law, Juan Francisco de Sabalza. I was quite annoyed at having found out that he was displeased with the marriage of his daughter with my son—something I had found out from a number of friends who wrote to me. He apparently looked into who I was and who my wife was. This, as you know, annoyed me. Don't both sides of the family have the right to be concerned about one another? I thus wrote some harsh words in the letter. After all, he is no better than I am, since he was nothing more than a provincial Navarrese, who had gone off to Mexico as a protégé of a Viceroy. And that's why he was putting on airs in that letter."

37. Lantery, op. cit., 333. There are a considerable number of Basque and Navarrese surnames that appear in these memoirs. Mentioned among the important merchants of Cádiz in 1673 are Juan de Manurga, a captain who is frequently the object of lavish praise (6, 56, 148, 198, 228, 229, 276 and 278) and Matías de Jaúregui. Among the French Basques, there is Juan de Artiaga (p. 7). And among the Basque Navarrese, there are the following: Miguel de Vergara, Juan y Pedro de Bordas (Borda), Bernardo de la Peña (95), Don Diego de Egües y Beaumont (278, 292, 306, 309, 310), Agustín de Arizcum (Arizkun) (302) and others.

38. Francisco de Elorza y Rada, *Nobiliario del valle de la Valdorba*, ed. Cit., 47.

39. Elorza, *Nobiliario . . . cit., ed. cit.* 60–61. This work mentions some twenty-four natives of the Orba Valley Orbaibar (Valdorba) who achieved distinction in the Americas.

40. *Memorias del general Don Francisco Espoz y Mina, escritas por* él mismo, vol. 1 (Madrid 1851), 109. Zaratiegui, who was on the opposite side, expressed similar sentiments in his previously cited work, *Vida y hechos de Don Tomás de Zumalacárregui . . .* ", 2.

41. Sagües, op. cit., 165 (note 51). Re Fernández de Mendivil, see 136 (note 4). Don Francisco Fernández de Mendivil acted as a lawyer for the Royal Councils, and also was a collector of general and provincial revenues for the domain of Madrid, where he and his wife granted power of attorney to draft a will on January 12, 1759. According to this power of attorney, he was a native of Iruñea-Pamplona, son of Don Joseph (who had been born in Yabar ("Arachil Valley") and of Doña María Antonia de Arbeiza, of Estella. Don Francisco's wife, Doña Ana María Lacarra, was born in Valtierra, and was the daughter of Don Félix de Lacarra and Doña Cristina de Larraga, also of Valtierra. *Archivo Histórico de Protocolos, protocol no. 17, 262, folio 332–34, vto*. On July 15, 1759, he was elected prefect of the Congregation of San Fermín. He was re-elected prefect on July 20, 1770. Sagües, op. cit., 316.

List of Sources

Chapter 1. Neighboring Peoples and the Historical-Cultural Context. Published in the *Revista de Dialectología y Tradiciones Populares*, volume 29 (1973), nos. 1 and 2, 23–47.

Chapter 2. The Basque Country, 1500-1800. *Introducción a la historia social y económica del pueblo Vasco*. Donostia-San Sebastián: Txertoa, 1974.

Chapter 3. Cultural Cycles and Basque Identity. "Homenaje a J. Ignacio Tellechea Idígoras." *Boletín de Estudios Históricos sobre San Sebastián*, no. 16–17 (1982–1983): 1087–1103.

Chapter 4. Origins: Basque-Iberianism. Originally published in the journal *Emerita* 10, no. 2 (1942): 236–286; XI, no. 1 (1943): 1–59.

Chapter 5. Historical Cultural Problems of the Basque Language. *Los pueblos de españa* (Madrid: Istmo, 1976), 63–75. Originally published in 1946.

Chapter 6. On the Basque Lexicon. "Sobre Historia y Etnografía Vasca." *Estudios Vascos* 11 (1982): 265–282.

Chapter 7. The Basque Country and Dialectology. The material in this chapter originally was published in the *Revista de dialectología y tradiciones populares* 14 (1958): 425–440.

Chapter 8. The Historical Bases of a "Traditional" Economy. *Cuadernos de Etnología y Etnografía de Navarra* 1, no. 2 (1969): 7–33.

Chapter 9. The Structure and Function of the House. *Cuadernos de Etnología y Etnografía de Navarra* 21, no. 1 (1969): 35–66.

Chapter 10. Agriculture and Cattle Raising. *Introducción a la historia social y económica del pueblo Vasco*. Donostia-San Sebastián: Txertoa, 1974.

Chapter 11. The Shipbuilding and Iron Industries. *Introducción a la historia social y económica del pueblo Vasco*. Donostia-San Sebastián: Txertoa, 1974.

Chapter 12. The Basques and the Sea. *Los Vascos y el mar*. Second edition. Donostia-San Sebastián: Txertoa, 1985. Originally published in 1981.

Chapter 13. The Feeling of Belonging in the Basque Diaspora. *La hora Navarra del XVIII: Personas, familias, Negocios e ideas*. Iruñea-Pamplona: Diputación Foral de Navarra/Institución Príncipe de Viana, 1969.

Chapter 14. The Basques: Yesterday and Today. In *Pueblos de la tierra* (Donostia-San Sebastián: Burulan, 1976) and *Los vascos y el mar*, 2nd ed. (Donostia-San Sebastián: Txertoa, 1985), 133–159.

Suggestions for Further Readings

This short list of suggested reading is intended to orient the nonspecialist reader toward Caro Baroja's major works and influences. An original mind as voracious and deeply delving as Caro Baroja's cannot be fully comprehended even in a full bibliography; and this list is intended more as a general introduction than as an exhaustive list of all of the author's influences. It consists of three sections: Caro Baroja's own major works, some selected general bibliography on Caro Baroja, and an introductory list of mostly contemporary works on Basque history and culture that relates to the broad themes discussed in the present work and is weighted toward English-language studies.

Selected Bibliography of Julio Caro Baroja

Algunos mitos españoles. Madrid: Ediciones del Centro, 1974.

Análisis de la cultura (etnología, historia, folklore). Barcelona, 1949.

Los Baroja: Memorias familiares. Madrid, 1972.

Las brujas y su mundo. Madrid, 1961. Translated as *The World of the Witches*. Chicago, 1964.

Escritos combativos. Madrid, 1985.

Estudios saharianos. Madrid, 2008. First published 1955.

Los judíos en la España moderna y contemporánea. 3 vols. Madrid, 1961–1962.

El laberinto vasco. San Sebastián, 1984.

Los pueblos de España. Madrid, 2003. First published 1946.

Los pueblos del norte de la península Ibérica: Análisis histórico-cultural. Burgos, 1943.

Terror y terrorismo. Barcelona, 1989.

Vasconiana. San Sebastián, 1974.

Los vascos. 1st ed. San Sebastián, 1949. 2nd ed. Madrid, 1958. 3rd ed. Madrid, 1971. The present translation is of the 3rd edition.

La vida rural en Vera de Bidasoa. Madrid, 1944.

Vidas mágicas e Inquisición. 2 vols. Madrid: Taurus, 1967.

Selected Bibliography on Julio Caro Baroja

Azaola, José Miguel de et al. *Barojatarrak eta itsasoa/Los Baroja y el mar.* Donostia: Gipuzkoako Foru Aldundia, 1995.

Batllori, Miguel. *Las moradas de Julio Caro Baroja.* Madrid: Delegación en Corte, Real Sociedad Bascongada de los Amigos del País/Gorteko Ordezkaritza, Euskalerriaren Adiskideen Elkartea, 1997.

Caro Baroja, Julio. *Una amistad andaluza: Correspondencia entre Julio Caro Baroja y Gerald Brenan.* Translated, introduction and notes by Carmen Caro. Madrid: Caro Raggio, 2005.

———. *Conversaciones en Itzea*, edited by Francisco J. Flores Arroyuelo. Madrid: Alianza, 1991.

Carreira, Antonio et al. *Bibliografía de Julio Caro Baroja.* Madrid: Sociedad Estatal de Conmemoraciones Culturales, 2007.

———. *Julio Caro Baroja, etnógrafo.* Santander: Universidad de Cantabria, Aula de Etnografía, 1995.

Castilla Urbano, Francisco. *El análisis social de Julio Caro Baroja: Empirismo y subjetividad.* Madrid: Consejo Superior de Investigaciones Científicas, Departamento de Antropología de España y América, 2002.

Garrido Morraza, Antonio et al. *Homenaje a Julio Caro Baroja (1914–1995).* Málaga: Ayuntamiento de Málaga, 1996.

Maraña, Félix. *Julio Caro Baroja. El hombre necesario (1914–1995).* San Sebastián: Bermingham, 1995.

Marrodán, Mario Ángel. *Historial artístico de Julio Caro Baroja.* Madrid: Loret, 1993.

Molina Campuzano, Miguel. *Con Julio Caro Baroja, en mi adicción de siempre.* Madrid: Caro Raggio, 2000.

Morales Lezcano, Víctor. *Recordando a Salvador de Madariaga y Julio Caro Baroja.* Las Palmas de Gran Canaria: Anroart, 2006.

Paniagua, Juan Antonio. *Etnohistoria y religión en la antropología de Julio Caro Baroja.* Foreword by Pío Caro Baroja. Fuenlabrada: Diedycul, 2003.

Porcel, Baltasar. *Retrato de Julio Caro Baroja*. Barcelona: Círculo de Lectores, 1987.

Rodríguez Becerra, Salvador, ed. *El diablo, las brujas y su mundo. Homenaje andaluz a Julio Caro Baroja*. Sevilla: Signatura Ediciones de Andalucía, 2000.

Rubio, Rogelio et al. *Homenaje a Julio Caro Baroja*. Madrid: Centro de Investigaciones Sociológicas, 1978.

Rubio de Urquía, Guadalupe et al. *La tradición técnica del pueblo vasco: El hombre y su medio: Homenaje a Julio Caro Baroja: Actas IV Semana Delegación en Corte de la Real Sociedad Bascongada de los Amigos del País*. Madrid: Delegación en Corte/Gorteko Ordezkaritza, 1997.

Select Bibliography on Basque History and Culture

Allard, William Albert. *A Time We Knew. Images of Yesterday in the Basque Homeland*. Photographs by William Albert Allard. Text by Robert Laxalt. Reno: University of Nevada Press, 1990.

Aulestia, Gorka. *The Basque Poetic Tradition*. Reno: University of Nevada Press, 2000.

Barandiarán, José Miguel de. *Selected Writings of José Miguel de Barandiarán: Basque Prehistory and Ethnography*. Translated by Fredrick H. Fornoff, Linda White, and Carys Evans-Corales. Compiled and with an introduction by Jesús Altuna. Reno: Center for Basque Studies, University of Nevada, Reno, 2007.

Collins, Roger. *The Basques*. Oxford: Basil Blackwell, 1986.

Douglass, William A., ed. *Essays in Basque Social Anthropology and History*. Reno: Basque Studies Program, University of Nevada, Reno, 1989.

Douglass, William A. and Joseba Zulaika. *Basque Culture: Anthropological Perspectives*. Reno: Center for Basque Studies, University of Nevada, Reno, 2007.

Gallop, Rodney. *A Book of the Basques*. 1930. Reprint, Reno: University of Nevada Press, 1970.

Henningsen, Gustav. *The Witches' Advocate: Basque Witchcraft and the Spanish Inquisition*. Reno: University of Nevada Press, 1980.

Lagarde, Anne-Marie. *Les basques. Société traditionnelle et symétrie des sexes. Expression sociale et linguistique*. Preface by Txomin Peillen. Paris: L'Harmattan, 2003.

Madariaga Orbea, Juan, ed. *Anthology of Apologists and Detractors of the Basque Language*. Translated by Frederick H. Fornoff, María Critina Saavedra, Amaia Gabantxo, and Cameron J. Watson. Reno: Center for Basque Studies, University of Nevada, Reno, 2006.

Mitxelena, Koldo. *Koldo Mitxelena: Selected Writings of a Basque Scholar*. Translated by Linda White and M. Dean Johnson. Compiled and with an introduction by Pello Sallaburu. Reno: Center for Basque Studies, University of Nevada, Reno, 2008.

Monreal Zia, Gregorio. *The Old Law of Bizkaia (1452): Introductory Study and Critical Edition*. Translated by William A. Douglass and Linda White. Preface by William A. Douglass. Reno: Center for Basque Studies, University of Nevada, Reno, 2005.

Ott, Sandra. *The Circle of the Mountains: A Basque Shepherding Community*. 1981. Reprint, Reno: University of Nevada Press, 1993.

Xamar [pseudonym, Juan Carlos Etxegoien]. *Orhipean: The Country of Basque*. Translated by Margaret L. Bullen. Pamplona: Pamiela, 2006.

Zulaika, Joseba. *Del cromañon al carnival. Los vascos como museo antropológico*. Donostia: Erein, 1996.

Index

affairs of the quill, 67
Age of Discovery, 224, 247
ager, 48, 83
agramonteses, 260, 272
agriculture, 45, 83, 93–94, 127, 166, 202, 208–9, 214, 303 n2, 322 n33
agricultural implements, 207, 229, 250
Álava, *see* Araba, 67
Alfonso X, 223
Alquegui, Martín de, 187–88, 190, 192, 193–94, 199, 311 n20, 312
Americas, 68, 73–74, 77, 88–89, 116, 125, 184, 227, 237, 240–41, 250, 255–56, 264, 271, 276, 303 n1, n3, 315 n35, 323 n39; discovery of, 88, 240
Aquitania, 50, 107, 150, 181, 268
Aquitainian language, 151, 300 n24
Araba, 22, 59–60, 67, 73–74, 84, 87–89, 111–12, 135, 147, 150–51, 153, 156, 209–11, 214, 229–30, 237, 259, 264, 270–71, 274, 278, 280, 282–83, 293 n37, 294 n45
Arana Goiri, Sabino, 105, 281
Aranzadi, Telesforo de, 81, 214, 268, 298 n50
arrantzale, *see* fisherman, 227
Artiñano, Gervasio de, 247, 318
Astarloa, Pedro Pablo de, 104–5, 107, 158
Asturian people, 101, 112, 152–53, 294 n44, 301 n31,
Autrigon, 47, 83, 112, 150, 294 n46
Axular, *see also* Guero, 147, 294 n38
Azkue, Resurrección María de, 132–42, 148, 228, 269

Baiona, 7, 85, 87, 167–68, 221, 270, 302 n40
bands, 60, 66, 88, 260
Barandiarán, Jose Miguel de, 12–13, 30, 81, 127, 208, 214, 269, 298 n50
Baroja, Pío, 11, 24, 33, 282
baserri, 186, 204, 211, 216
Basque armaments industry, 235–36

Basque declension, 114, 117–18, 125
Basque dialectology, see also Basque dialects, 145–47, 149, 151, 156
Basque dialects, 145–51, 155–57; dialectical boundaries, 150; dialectical fragmentation, 155; dialectical variation, 134, 146–47, 156
Basque Economic Society, 215, 275
Basque-Iberianism, 99, 101–2, 105–9, 113
Basque-Iberianist, 99–103, 105, 268, 293 n29
Basque Royal Economic Society of Friends of the Country, 280
Basque shipyards, 222, see also shipbuilding industry
Basque verbs, 115, 123–25, 136, 140
Basse Navarre, see Lower Navarre, 270
Bay of Biscay, 83–84
Bayonne, see Baiona, 7
Baztan Valley, 146, 173, 211, 257–58, 260, 302 n40, 307 n36
beamonteses, 260, 272
Bera, 9, 11, 19–20, 166–77, 181–83, 194–99, 302 n40, 303 n8, 305 n10, n13, n15–16, 306 n29, 308 n40, 309 n3, 311 n19–20, 314 n31
Berber, 50, 118–20
Bergara Accord, 278
Beterri variant, see also dialectical variations of Basque, 148
Bilbao, uprising of 1634, 71

biology, 45, 56
Bizkaia, 22, 67, 71–74, 87–89, 91, 111–12, 134–35, 137, 147–48, 150–51, 210–12, 221, 224, 229–30, 232–33, 235–37, 239–42, 246–50, 259, 262, 264, 270–71, 273–75, 280, 282–83, 290, 316–18, 320, 322 n34, 323 n34
Bizkaitarrak, 282
Bonaparte, Louis Lucien, 145, 148, 155, 295 n7, 308 n41
borda, 140, 142, 175, 176–77, 184
Bortziriak, 167, 182, 230, 302 n32
Brown, Radcliffe, 179–80, 204, 310 n6, 310 n7
buho gallego, El, 72, 274, 320

caballerito, 76
cabilas, 64
cabildo, 196, 312 n20
calligraphy, 67–68
Campión, Arturo, 148, 150
Cano, Tomé, 242, 248, 318,
Cánovas del Castillo, Antonio, 279
Cantabrian language, 101, 152; people, 152
Caristii, 46–47, 83, 112, 150–51
Carlism, 277–80, 283
Carlist War, First, 90, 169, 278, 283, 314 n31; Second, 77, 90, 279, 283
Carlists, 90–91, 276–83, 314 n31
Carthaginians, 48–49, 106, 292 n25

Castile, 52, 67, 87–88, 163, 168, 210, 213, 256, 259–260, 262, 271–72, 277, 307 n32,
Catalan language, 91, 127, 239, 279–81, 298 n50
Catalonia, 48, 50, 52, 92, 104, 127, 273, 280
Celtic invasions, 106
cattle trails, 212–13
Celtiberian language, 104; people 128
Celtic language, 110, 113–14, 292 n27
Celts, 50, 104, 106–07, 112, 128–29, 289 n13, 292 n25, 293 n37, 294 n45
Charles I, 74, 89, 272
Charles II, 73–74, 76, 89, 164, 226, 248, 255–56, 309 n44, 321 n18
Charles III, 76, 89, 177, 227, 230
Charles IV, 69, 76, 177, 227, 275, 309 n44
Cinca River, 47
Cisiberian, 47
Charles V, 223, 235, 242, 272
Civil War, Spanish, 11, 90, 92, 94, 282–83
coastal shipping, 84, 87, 224
cod, 242–44, 317
collective nobility, Basque notion of, 172, 178, 212
Compendio historial de Guipúzcoa, 68
corregidor, 88, 298 n7
Count Duke of Olivares, 71, 75, 273
county of Álava, 58, 270, 290 n24

Covarrubias, 131
craftsmen, 167–68, 171, 175
crops, introduction of in the Basque Country, 215
crossbow, 235, 241
cultural cycles, 12–3, 15, 23, 25–26, 82–86, 88, 90–95; related to biological, 55-56

deep-sea fishing, 87–88
Diccionario de Autoridades, 131, 298 n1
Diodorus, 128
Dixon, Roland, 113, 121
donatio propter nuptias, 173, 188, 190, 199, 203–4, 258
Donibane Garazi, 256, 307 n32, 320 n11
Donostia-San Sebastian, 7, 87, 137, 148, 222, 280, 282–83, 319, 322 n34
Don Quixote, 68
dowry, 188–91, 193, 203, 312 n20
Durkheim, Emile, 88, 95, 180

Ebro River, 46–48, 83, 87
egalitarianism, Basque, 75, 273
Elcano, Juan Sebastián, 241–42
Enlightenment, 75–76, 276, 280
erdeldun, 80, 267
Erro y Azpiroz, Juan Bautista, 105
Erronkari, 56, 147, 149, 154–55, 212–13
España sagrada, 105, 146
Espartero, Baldomero, 278–79
Etcheberri, Joannes d', 147, 157
etxekoandre, 200, 258
Euskaldun, 80, 267–68

Euzkadi, 131, 280–81
Euzkadi (newspaper), 282

famine, 76
Ferdinand I, 86
Ferdinand III, 223
Ferdinand VII, 76–77
Fernández of Navarrete, Martín, 241
Festo, 57
First Carlist War, *see* Carlist War, First
fisherman, 227, 243–44, 271
fishing, 22, 87–88, 223–24, 243, 249, 319
Flórez, Enrique, 101, 103, 105, 146
folklore, 9, 11, 13–15, 132, 139, 234, 269
fortifications, 61, 165. See also fortified houses
foundational name of Basque houses, 174
foundry, 58, 77, 231–34. *See also* ironworks
Franco, Francisco, 11.
Franks, 51, 85–86, 270
French Revolution, 276
Fuero de Vizcaya, 66
fueros, 69, 86–87, 223, 282, 308 n37
funerary stelae, 201

Gárate, Justo, 156–57, 302 n43
Garibay, Esteban de, 9, 14–15, 67–69, 72, 100–1, 105, 169, 224, 231, 236, 240–41, 269, 272, 289 n18, 292 n27, 316, 320 n11

Gaul, 50, 84, 149, 153, 221–22, 229, 268, 305 n12
Gaztañeta, Antonio de, 227
Germanic peoples, 50, 84, 114
Gipuzkoa, 22, 45–46, 58, 68–69, 74, 87–89, 103, 111–12, 137, 146–47, 150, 173, 181, 208, 211–12, 230, 232–33, 235–37, 263, 268, 270–71, 273–74, 280, 283, 290 n22, 294 n45, 309 n45
Gipuzkoan Company, 275
Goierri variant, *see also* dialectical variations of Basque, 148, 208
Goyeneche, Juan de, 74–75, 174, 258–60, 307 n32, 308 n39, 321 n22
Guero, *see also* Axular, 147, 294 n38
Graebner, Fritz, 82, 180, 310 n4
Guipúzcoa, *see* Gipuzcoa, 22

Habsburgs, 70, 227, 249
Hervás y Panduro, Lorenzo, 105, 290 n2
highlands, 28, 46–47, 208, 212, 215, 268–69
Hübner, Emilio, 108, 293 n31
human habitation, history of, 58, 115
Humboldt, Wilhelm von, 99–100, 104–8, 121, 136, 268, 292 n19, 293 n29

Iberian language, 107–9, 114, 128, 151–52, 293 n31
Iberian Peninsula, 41, 43, 49–50, 80, 83, 99, 117, 146, 149, 239, 267, 273

Iberians, 29, 50, 100, 104, 106–7, 114, 128, 268, 289 n13, 292 n25, 293 n29; similarity to Iberians of the Caucasus, 113–14
identity, dynamic, 79–80, 82, 93–94; static, 79–81, 93
Ilergete, 47, 48, 50, 289 n12
Indo-European languages, 115–16, 121, 123, 152
infanzon, 141, 230
inheritance, Basque system of, 173, 189–90, 192–94, 197, 202, 256, 258
iron, 22, 120, 217, 221, 229, 234, 237, 243, 250, 262, 314 n31; cycle of transformation of, 229; exploitation methods of, 229, 231–33; weapons, 250
iron industry, 87, 171, 207, 229–30, 236–37, 250, 276
ironmonger, 171, 233–34, 274
ironworking, 45
ironworks, 59, 170–71, 230–31, *see also* foundry
Iruñea-Pamplona, 7, 76, 79, 84–85, 87, 111, 135, 149, 195, 198, 201–2, 264, 280, 300 n14, 306 n29, 308–9 n43, 313 n28, 323 n41
Isabel II, 277, 279–80
Islam, 50, 56, 63–64

Jaungoikoa ta lagi zára, *see also* "God and the Old Laws," 281
Jesuits, 74–75, 89

kingdom of Navarre, 47, 87–88, 101–2, 154, 181, 212–13, 253, 256, 270–71, 301 n251-94, 305 n15

Labourd, *see also* Lapurdi, 151, 171, 221
Lapurdi, 151, 171–72, 186, 221, 244, 270
Lapurdum, 85, 151, 221
Larramendi Garragori, Manuel de, 75, 102–5, 107–9, 132–44, 147–49, 158, 228, 234, 245, 262, 273–74, 281, 290 n2, 291 n11, 292 n27, 299 n10, n12, 300 n14, 302 n46, 309 n45
Latin language, 54, 111
law of free choice of heirs, 173
laya, 25, 208, 214
Legazpi, Miguel López de, 245, 317
Lesaca, *see* Lesaka
Lesaka, 167–68, 170, 172, 176–77, 182, 302 n32, 303 n5, 303 n8, 305 n10, 307 n37, 308 n40, 309 n3
letters patent of nobility, 172, 307 n32
Lévi-Strauss, Claude, 179, 310 n2
Liberals, Basque, 90
Libros de fuegos, 167
lineages, 58–59, 63, 66, 71, 88–89, 149, 153, 166–67, 171, 187, 211, 215, 233, 270–73, 301 n27, 303 n7, 309 n43
locative suffix, 156
López Mendizábal, Isaac, 157
lowlands, 46–47, 59, 153, 212, 268

machinada, 234
Magellan, Ferdinand, 241, 316
magister pagi, 153–54
Malinowski, Bruno, 179–80
manor house, 55, 181, 201, 204, 311 n4, 313 n26, 314 n30, 314 n32
mariñel, see sailor, 227
Martínez de Isasti, Lope, 68, 246, 299 n4, 317
Martínez de Recalde, Juan, 249, 318
Masdeu, Juan Francisco de, 103–4, 292 n21, n22
material culture, 20–21, 25, 64, 201
material decline of peoples, 165
medium, 41–42, 44, 47, 55, 60, 62, 147, 288 n3
Mendoza, Antonio de, 71, 75
modern era, 65, 73, 171, 223, 230, 233
Moors, 56, 60, 274, 290 n22
Morales, Ambrosio de, 53, 100–1, 105, 290 n22, 297 n27
Moret, José de, 101–2, 104–5, 107, 154, 289 n18, 292 n27
municipal justice, 86, 134, 166, 170–71, 173, 187, 196, 198, 231, 307 n37
Muslim, 54, 270–71

Napoleonic invasions, 76
Napoleonic Wars, 90, 276
nationalism, Basque, 92, 94, 279, 281–83
nationalists, Basque, 92, 281–83
naufragios, 222
naval industry, 87, 90, 229, 235

Navarre, 7, 13, 22, 47, 50, 53, 55, 60, 73–74, 76–77, 84–89, 111–12, 127, 146–51, 153–55, 157–58, 164, 166–68, 170–73, 175–78, 180–83, 186, 197, 201–2, 204, 209–13, 215, 225, 229–30, 232–33, 237, 241, 253–64, 270–72, 274–80, 283, 290 n25, 293 n37, 294 n45, 299 n4, 300 n14, 302 n40, 303 n8, 304 n9, 305 n13, n15, n17, 306 n26, 307 n36, 308 n37, n43, 320 n10, n11, 321 n26, 322 n33, 323 n36, n37
Noguera Ribagorzana, 48
Normans, 221, 222, 224, 270

ocean fishing, 223
Oiartzun, 84, 221, 229
Oihenart, Arnaud, 101–2, 107, 150
olaguizon, 233–34, *see* ironmonger
Old Law (fuero) of Bizkaia, 233
Oquendo, Miguel de, 225, 249, 319
Orrega, 84
Oyarzun, *see* Oiartzun, 84

pagus, 151, 154
pasotismo, 94
patronage, 73, 85, 171–73
Peninsular War, 77, 165, 227, 276
Philip II, 69–70, 74, 89, 223, 226, 243–44, 247–48, 262, 272
Philip III, 70, 89, 226, 247, 262

Philip IV, 71, 89, 226, 228, 248, 254–55, 260, 262, 273–74, 320 n11,
Philip V, 74–75, 80, 89–90, 164, 172, 177, 272, 274
Pliny, 106, 181, 221, 229, 310 n10
Posidonius, 128
Poniente Islands, 245
premio del bien hablar, El, 262
Pre-Pyrenees Mountains, 53
Ptolemaic tablets, 84, 103, 152
Ptolemy, 50, 152
Pyrenees Mountains, 47, 49–50, 53, 56, 77, 85–86, 107, 110, 112, 114–15, 126–27, 175, 182, 212–13, 256, 268, 270, 283, 289 n13, 305 n12

Real Sociedad Bascongada, 76
Reconquista, 47, 52, 55, 88, 154, 213, 307 n33
reja de San Millán, La, 150
requeté, 283
Reparaz, Juan de, 201–3, 312 n26, 313 n28, 313 n29
Romanization, 48, 84, 111–112, 152, 154, 158, 270, 294 n45, 301 n31 n39
Romans, 48–49, 51, 57, 84, 103, 107, 153, 221, 292 n25, 294 n45
Roncal, *see also* Erronkari, 56, 147, 154, 212
Roncesvalles, *see* Orrega, 84–85
rural society, change in, 165
Royal Congregation of San Fermín de los Navarros, 254–55, 261, 264, 319 n3, 232 n41

sailors, Basque, 22, 45, 51, 67, 138, 222–27, 240–42, 244–47, 259, 271–72, 274, 319
Saint-Jean-Pied-de-Port, *see* Donibane Garazi, 256
Salic Law, 277
saltus, 48, 83
Sancho the Wise, 87
Schuchardt, Hugo, 108–9, 113–15, 117–24, 156, 268, 293 n33, 302 n42
scientific discourse, 44
seafaring, 22, 66–67, 222–25, 240, 242, 248, 261, 299 n9
Second Carlist War, *see* Carlist War, Second
Second Republic, Spanish, 10, 282
Seignoir, 69
seignoiry, 133, 171, 230, 232, 233, 318
Seneca, 50
Señorio, see seignior, 133, 230,
Seven Years' War, 77
shepherding, Basque system of, 26, 207, 209, 212–13
shipbuilding industry, 221, 250, 276
shipping industry, collapse of, 76–77, 88, 223
Sociedad Económica Bascongada, 215
Society of Jesus, *see also* Jesuits, 74, 89
Soule, *see also* Zuberoa, 7, 147, 151, 154
Spanish Armada, 248–49, 318, *see also* Invincible Armada
Spanish empire, 263, 276

spoils, 56
St. James' Way, 51, 271
Stieler Handatlas, 41
Strabo, 12, 48–50, 80, 101, 110, 112–14, 122, 208, 289 n13
structural models, 179
Suárez de Toledo, Hernán, 240, 316

technical pessimism, of the Basques, 247
Traggia de Santo Domingo, Joaquín, 103
trainera, 224
Trebiñu, 151
Treviño, *see* Trebiñu
toponymy, 63, 84, 104, 106, 156–57, 210, 231, 233

Uhlenbeck, C.C., 113–17, 122–23, 126, 295 n52, 297 n46
Unamuno, Miguel de, 282
Urdaneta, Andrés de, 242, 245, 317

vallis Subola, 154, 300 n22
Varduli, 46–47, 83, 85, 101, 112, 150–51, 294 n42
Vascon, 46–48, 50, 52–53, 57, 68, 83, 85, 101, 111–12, 150–53, 231, 270, 273, 291 n8, 294 n45, 297 n42, 299 n5, 300 n14, 300 n16, 303 n7, 317, 320 n8, 320 n9, 322 n28, 322 n32, 327

vascongado, 68, 320 n8, 320 n9, 322 n32
Vasconia, 83, 111, 150, 152, 231
Vera de Bidasoa, *see* Bera, 9
Vinson, Julien, 124, 148, 290 n2, 300 n14
Visigoths, 51, 85, 270
Vitoria-Gasteiz, 7, 87, 250, 259, 280
vizcaíno, 68, 242, 246, 262, 274, 318, 320
Vizcaya, *see* Bizkaia, 22; seigniory of, 133
Völkerwanderung, 51
von Üexküll, Jakob, 13, 31–32, 44, 288 n5, 289 n16

War of the Hundred Thousand Sons of St. Louis, 77
War of the Pyrenees, 77
War of Spanish Succession, 76, 303 n2
Way of St. James, 51

Zabaleta lineage, 167
Zuberoa, 7, 133, 147–48, 151, 202, 213, 256, 258, 270–71, 321 n17
Zubiaur, Pedro de, 70, 225–26, 248, 318
Zuloaga, Ignacio, 282
Zumalacárregui, Tomás de, 277, 279
Zyhlars, Ernst, 118–20